Classical Subjects Creatively Taught™

GOD'S GREAT covenant

A Bible Course for Children

Old Testament 2

1 Samuel to Malachi

Claire A. Larsen

God's Great Covenant, Old Testament 2:
Teacher's Edition

Version 2.0

Classical Academic Press
515 S. 32nd St.
Camp Hill, PA 17011

www.ClassicalAcademicPress.com

ISBN: 978-1-60051-050-2

Book cover and illustrations by:
Rob Baddorf

Book design by:
David Gustafson

PGP.02.19

Table of Contents

Maps

Introduction

"The king is coming! The king is coming!" All around you men, women, and children are shouting loudly. You are pushed and shoved, first this way and then that. Each person wants to be the first one to see the king's procession. The city is crowded, and everyone's excited. You are an Israelite child, and King David has come to your city!

God's people, the Israelites, didn't always have a king. Many centuries before King David ruled, God had made a covenant with a man named Abraham. "You will be the father of a great nation," the LORD promised. "I will be your God, and you will be My people." 1

The LORD kept his promise to Abraham. Abraham had a son named Isaac, who had a son named Jacob who had a very large family. Jacob's family moved to Egypt, and 400 years later there were so many descendents of Jacob living in Egypt that the pharaoh was afraid of them. He made Jacob's descendents, called Hebrews or Israelites, slaves so they wouldn't be a danger to his kingdom. The Israelites weren't a nation yet, and they certainly didn't have a king.

The LORD sent Moses to free the Israelites from Egypt. They spent forty years in the great and terrible wilderness, and then arrived at the Promised Land. The LORD appointed Joshua as Israel's commander. The people fought many battles, some mighty victories because they trusted the LORD and some terrible defeats because they disobeyed Him. Finally, they possessed the land that the LORD had promised to Abraham. Now the Israelites were a nation with their own land, but they didn't have a king.

The Israelites lived in the land and enjoyed all the good things that the LORD provided. Sometimes they obeyed the LORD and worshipped only Him. Many times, however, they disobeyed the LORD and worshipped Baal, Asherah, and the other Canaanite gods. The Israelites did what they wanted to do, not what God had commanded them to do.

Because of their idolatry, the LORD sent other nations to bring trouble to the Israelites. When the Israelites became miserable enough, they cried out to the LORD for help. Then the LORD sent men called judges to deliver them from their enemies. The judges ruled the land and saved the people from suffering and oppression. But the people continued to turn away from the LORD, and they didn't have a king.

9

Notes to Teachers and Parents:

1 The LORD made a covenant in Genesis 12 to be Abraham's God and the God of Abraham's children. He promised to give Abraham a son who would become the father of many nations. He promised to give Abraham's descendents a land of their own. Finally, He promised to make Abraham a blessing to many nations. Later, in Genesis 15 and Genesis 17 God confirmed this covenant and reminded Abraham that He would keep His promise. *God's Great Covenant, Old Testament 1: A Bible Course for Children* tells the story of God's faithful keeping of the covenant as it unfolds from Genesis through Ruth. God's promise to Abraham is the same as His promise to His people today: "I will be your God, and you shall be My people" (Jeremiah 7:23).

Notes:

2 God's kingdom is a spiritual, eternal kingdom, and Jesus Christ is the King. All the events in the Old Testament point to Jesus, the King who will come and establish His Kingdom on earth. Even though it appears at times that wicked men have thwarted God's plan, His plan never fails. As King of kings and Lord of lords, God preserves His kingdom and accomplishes His purposes despite the actions and intentions of sinful men. In Romans 9:6, the Apostle Paul writes, "For they are not all Israel who are of Israel." In other words, even though the nation of Israel was God's covenant people, not every Israelite was a member of God's spiritual kingdom. The nation of Israel was a kingdom located in Canaan, but within that physical kingdom was a spiritual kingdom of men and women who, by faith, worshipped and obeyed Jehovah. All through Old Testament history, the Lord preserved a remnant of people who trusted Him and looked forward to the Savior who would someday come to redeem His people spiritually. After the resurrection of Jesus Christ, God's spiritual kingdom spread from Jerusalem outward to the ends of the earth. Today, God's kingdom consists of all those throughout the world who trust in the saving grace of the Lord Jesus. All through history God has preserved His kingdom so that we may truly say that God is the Keeper of His Kingdom.

Notes:

Yet from the beginning the Israelites did have a king! God, creator of the world and King of all kings, was Israel's King. Because the LORD was Israel's King, they didn't need a human king.

God's Great Covenant, Old Testament 2: A Bible Course for Children continues the story that *God's Great Covenant, Old Testament 1* began. In the book of 1 Samuel, the Israelites asked God for a king. "We want a king like other nations," they demanded. So the LORD gave them a king. Over the next 500 years the people had many kings. A few of the kings were godly men who worshipped the LORD and ruled the nation well. However, most of the kings were wicked men who rejected the LORD and worshipped foreign gods. The kings' actions and the disobedience of the people eventually brought about the destruction of the nation.

God's Old Testament story would be a tragedy except for one thing: God's kingdom is greater than the nation of Israel. Israel's earthly kingdom was a picture of God's spiritual, eternal kingdom. Behind the scenes, God reigned supreme. He used
2 even the disobedience of wicked kings to bring about His plan. He guided all of history toward its most important event—the coming of the Messiah.

Prophets prophesied about the Messiah, and their words became God's Scriptures. God's people prayed that the Messiah would come soon. Through the centuries, even when times were bleak and sin darkened men's hearts, the LORD's plan was right on schedule.

God's people had times of obedience and prosperity as well as times of disobedience and judgment. Through it all, God's kingdom remained secure because the LORD God was the Keeper of His Kingdom.

"Behold, He who keeps Israel Shall neither slumber nor sleep. The LORD is your keeper." (Psalm 121:4–5a)

What is the Old Testament?

The Old Testament, God's holy Scripture, has thirty-nine books written over 1,200 years by more than 30 authors. It tells you how God created man, how sin entered the world, and how God made a covenant to be the God of His people. Beginning in Genesis 3:15, God hints that a Savior would come. This Savior, or Messiah, would die for His people's sin and then set up an eternal kingdom where He would rule forever. Everything in the Old Testament points to Jesus Christ—the Savior, the Messiah, the King of kings, and the Lord of lords.

Books of the Old Testament

Type	Old Testament Books	
Pentateuch: The Law (5 books) *History before entering the Promised Land*	Five books of the Law: Genesis Leviticus Deuteronomy	 Exodus Numbers
History (12 books) *History after entering the Promised Land*	Nine books of history before the Exile: Joshua Ruth 1 and 2 Kings Three books of history after the Exile: Ezra Esther	 Judges 1 and 2 Samuel 1 and 2 Chronicles Nehemiah
Poetry (5 books)	Five poetry books: Job Proverbs Song of Solomon	 Psalms Ecclesiastes
Major Prophets (5 books)	Five books of the Major Prophets: Isaiah Lamentations Daniel	 Jeremiah Ezekiel
Minor Prophets: The Twelve (12 books)	Nine books of the Minor Prophets before the Exile: Hosea Amos Jonah Nahum Zephaniah Three books of the Minor Prophets after the Exile: Haggai Malachi	 Joel Obadiah Micah Habakkuk Zechariah

17 Historical Books + 5 Poetry Books + 17 Prophets = 39 Books in the Old Testament

UNIT I

The Early Kingdom...The God Who Anoints

Theme: The Keeper of the Kingdom anoints those who lead His people.

Shalom. Let me introduce myself. I am Tobias, the royal chronicler, and I work in the king's palace. It's my job to record with utmost accuracy all the royal comings and goings. So with my expertise and wide experience (oh my, oh my, how humble I am!), I'm here, my friends, to retell this amazing story of how God faithfully keeps the promises of His great covenant. He is the keeper of His kingdom. **1**

When the story begins, Israel is at the brink of historic changes. In only 100 years, the scattered tribes of Israel would become a mighty kingdom with a powerful army, a magnificent palace, and a world-renowned king. God made this happen through three men: Samuel, Saul, and David. **2**

Until now, Israel's only King was God. When the Israelites demanded a king like other nations, they were rebelling against God. **3** In the covenant, Israel had agreed that God would be their King and have authority over them. Samuel, the last judge and the first prophet, directed the people back to the LORD. It was because of Samuel that Israel's kingdom started out well. Samuel was godly and pleased the LORD.

Israel's first king, Saul, was tall, handsome, and strong. The people thought that he was the perfect king. Too soon, though, Saul's heart became proud. He disregarded the LORD's words and did things his own way.

Although Saul ruled Israel for more than twenty years, the LORD rejected him early in his reign. His sons would never rule after him. He was not a godly ruler. To everyone's surprise, the LORD chose David, a simple shepherd boy, to be the next king. Even though David was young and small, he was brave and mighty, and, most of all, his heart trusted in the LORD his God.

Each of these men—Samuel, Saul, and David—was specially chosen and anointed by God to serve Him. (Being anointed means being chosen by God and equipped by His Spirit to serve God in a particular job.) **4** Now that I have introduced the main characters, let's go back in time to learn exactly how the early kingdom came about.

13

Notes to Teachers and Parents:

1 In this book, the fictional character of Tobias is used as a literary device to capture the attention of the children. However, his job of royal chronicler has an historical connection. Both King David and King Solomon had within their royal cabinets a position of recorder and a position of scribe. The specific tasks of the recorder are not certain, but scholars think that the recorder was a man of high rank similar to a secretary of state, royal record keeper, or royal herald. The scribe, also called a secretary, was responsible for writing royal correspondence and keeping the written annals of events during a king's reign. Jehoshaphat, son of Ahilud, was the recorder for both King David and King Solomon (see 2 Samuel 8:15-18; 1 Chronicles 18:14-17; 2 Samuel 20:23-26; and 1 Kings 4:3). Both kings also had secretaries or scribes. Three men are mentioned as secretaries for David: Seraiah (see 2 Samuel 8:15-18), Shavsha (see 1 Chronicles 18:14-17), and Sheva (see 2 Samuel 20:23-26). Elihoreph and Ahijah, sons of Shisha, are mentioned in 1 Kings 4:3 as secretaries of King Solomon. During King Hezekiah's reign, Joah, the son of Asaph, was the recorder, and Shebna, was the secretary. These two men represented Hezekiah on royal business (see 2 Kings 18:18, 37). These verses also mention Eliakim, who had the position of palace administrator. King Josiah's recorder, Joah, son of Joahaz, helped supervise the repairs to the temple (see 2 Chronicles 34:8). (See *Illustratated Manners and Customs of the Bible*, pp. 319-329 for additional information on the structure of civil government during Israel's monarchy.)

2 First Samuel can be divided into three main sections based on the person who is primary in the narrative: a) chapters 1–8: Samuel, Israel's last judge; b) chapters 9–15: Saul, Israel's first king, and c) chapters 16–31: David, the anointed fugitive. In other words, even though Samuel is mentioned in 1 Samuel 1–15, he is only the primary character in chapters 1–8. The same applies to Saul and David. Chronologically, most biblical scholars believe that the events of 1 Samuel 1-8 occurred concurrently with Judges 10-16 so that Eli was priest at the tabernacle in Shiloh at approximately the same time that Jephthah was fighting the Ammonites, and Samson, as a one-man army, was subduing the Philistines. Throughout his life, Samuel had the roles of judge, prophet, and priest, and as the last of the judges, he ushered in the monarchy in Israel. During Samuel's lifetime, Israel went from being a nation of loosely allied individual tribes to being a united kingdom. Because of Samuel's godly character and his dependence upon the LORD, the change from a nation of tribes to a united kingdom had a God-directed emphasis. Saul was the first king anointed by the Lord, but he quickly turned away from serving the LORD to serving his own selfish interests. David, Israel's second king, was a godly man who ruled Israel as a theocratic king, recognizing the supreme Kingship of the LORD.

3 Because they had no central ruler to unite them against their enemies, the Israelites felt vulnerable to the nations around them. They had forgotten that they had the Supreme Ruler providing for them. They were rejecting God as their ultimate King. Other nations' kings did not acknowledge God's authority as ruler over all mankind, and even claimed to be gods themselves. But, Israel was supposed to be different, for God had called them to be a theocratic nation. (A theocracy is a nation that considers itself to be ruled directly by God through divinely given laws and God-ordained leaders.) As part of God's covenant with Israel, the Lord God was to be Israel's supreme King, and any person who ruled Israel reigned under His authority. The Lord knew that the time would come when Israel would want and need to be united under the central rule of a king and He did not view that desire as evil or harmful in and of itself. In fact, a centralized government for the twelve tribes could have unified them and made them a stronger force against their enemies. For this reason, God provided guidelines in the Mosaic Law regarding how Israel's king should rule (see Deuteronomy 17:14-20). At the same time, God made it clear that all Israelites, even the king, were to recognize Him as their supreme authority. Therefore, Israel's sin in requesting a king was not in the act of wanting a king, but rather that they essentially wanted to reject God's rule over them and to be like the heathen nations around them.

4 The theme of Unit I is "the God who anoints." Each of the three main characters in 1 Samuel—Samuel, Saul, and David—was chosen by God in a unique way and for a definite role in His kingdom. Not only did God choose them, but He also equipped them by His Holy Spirit to accomplish the role that He had planned for them. He also protected them as they executed their roles until He determined that their jobs were done. Samuel and David, even though they were sinners who needed the grace of God's forgiveness, were faithful in the role to which God had appointed them. By contrast, the empowering and equipping Spirit of God left Saul because of his disobedience (see 1 Samuel 16:14).

5 Psalm 23 is the suggested memory passage for Unit I. In addition, each chapter will have a memory verse that pertains directly to the story content. As the teacher or parent using this text, you may choose to have your students memorize both the unit passage and the chapter verses or you may choose to memorize only the chapter verses. The footnotes in each chapter give a brief explanation of each chapter verse.

6 In the book *A Shepherd Looks at Psalm 23*, Phillip Keller describes in great detail the relationship between a shepherd and his sheep. Keller, who spent years tending sheep on his own sheep farm, brilliantly explains and brings deeper meaning to this psalm so beloved by God's people through the ages.

PSALM 23 A Psalm of David

1. The Lord is my shepherd;
   I shall not want.
2. He makes me to lie down in green pastures;
   He leads me beside the still waters.
3. He restores my soul;
   He leads me in the paths of righteousness
   For His name's sake.
4. Yea, though I walk through the valley of the shadow of death,
   I will fear no evil;
   For You are with me;
   Your rod and Your staff, they comfort me.
5. You prepare a table before me in the presence of my enemies;
   You anoint my head with oil;
   My cup runs over.
6. Surely goodness and mercy shall follow me
   All the days of my life;
   And I will dwell in the house of the Lord
   Forever. **5**

David, the shepherd boy, wrote Psalm 23, which is commonly called the "Shepherd's Psalm." In this psalm, the Lord is the Shepherd, and His people are the sheep.

Sheep do not naturally know what they need. They will not lie down and rest if they are tired, bothered by nasty little insects, or frightened by other animals. When they are thirsty, they do not always choose the refreshing, cool water of the meadow streams. They will drink whatever water they find, even if the water is dirty or unsafe to drink.

A good shepherd takes care of his sheep, even if he must lead them through dark and dangerous valleys to reach the lush mountain pastures where good food and clear water are plentiful. With his rod, a symbol of his strength, and his staff, a symbol of his care, the shepherd protects and comforts his sheep.

In John 10, Jesus Christ is called the Good Shepherd. As the Shepherd, the Lord loves His people, protects them from all evil, and leads them carefully through all the circumstances of life. The Lord does only good things for His people, and His mercy goes with them all the
6 days of their lives until they go to live in His house with Him forever.

14

Notes:

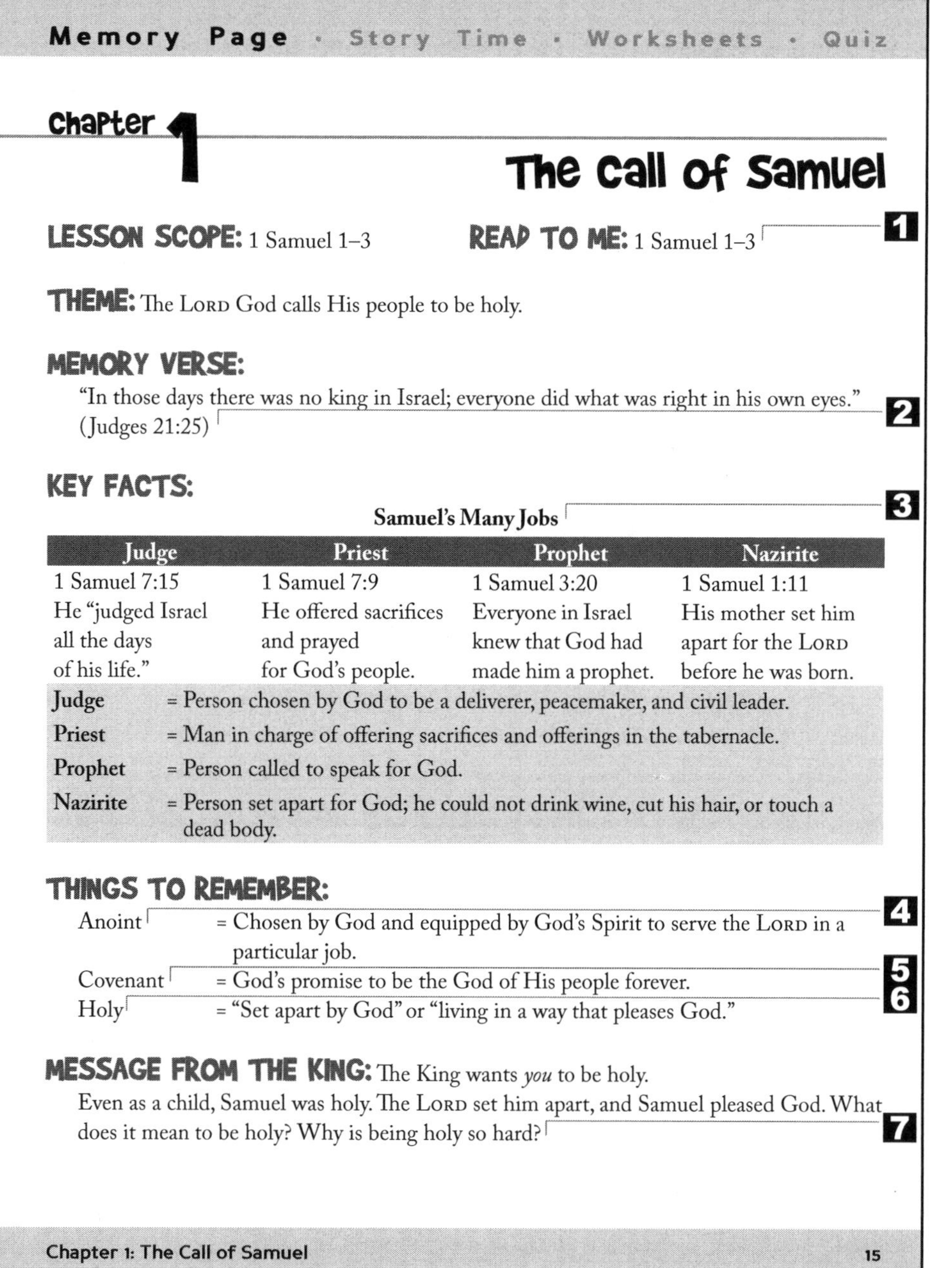

Memory Page · Story Time · Worksheets · Quiz

Chapter 1

The Call of Samuel

LESSON SCOPE: 1 Samuel 1–3 **READ TO ME:** 1 Samuel 1–3 1

THEME: The LORD God calls His people to be holy.

MEMORY VERSE:

"In those days there was no king in Israel; everyone did what was right in his own eyes." (Judges 21:25) 2

KEY FACTS:

Samuel's Many Jobs 3

Judge	Priest	Prophet	Nazirite
1 Samuel 7:15 He "judged Israel all the days of his life."	1 Samuel 7:9 He offered sacrifices and prayed for God's people.	1 Samuel 3:20 Everyone in Israel knew that God had made him a prophet.	1 Samuel 1:11 His mother set him apart for the LORD before he was born.

Judge	= Person chosen by God to be a deliverer, peacemaker, and civil leader.
Priest	= Man in charge of offering sacrifices and offerings in the tabernacle.
Prophet	= Person called to speak for God.
Nazirite	= Person set apart for God; he could not drink wine, cut his hair, or touch a dead body.

THINGS TO REMEMBER:

Anoint = Chosen by God and equipped by God's Spirit to serve the LORD in a particular job. 4

Covenant = God's promise to be the God of His people forever. 5

Holy = "Set apart by God" or "living in a way that pleases God." 6

MESSAGE FROM THE KING: The King wants *you* to be holy.

Even as a child, Samuel was holy. The LORD set him apart, and Samuel pleased God. What does it mean to be holy? Why is being holy so hard? 7

Chapter 1: The Call of Samuel 15

Notes to Teachers and Parents:

1 On the memory page of each chapter of *God's Great Covenant, Old Testament 2*, you will find a Lesson Scope and a Read to Me passage. The Lesson Scope passage identifies the entire portion of Scripture that is encompassed in the lesson, even though every event in this passage may not be mentioned in the chapter narrative. The Read to Me passage is the portion of Scripture that applies most directly to the chapter narrative and is best suited to reading aloud to the students. Reading the Scripture narrative out loud helps to emphasize to the students that the Bible stories are true events that occurred in history and that God communicates His truth to us through stories.

2 When the Old Testament story continues in 1 Samuel, there is no king in Israel. Eli was priest in Shiloh, serving in the tabernacle during the days of the judges (Jephthah and Samson), and Israel was a loosely knit nation of twelve individual tribes. Most of the Israelites had forgotten the LORD God who had miraculously delivered them from Egypt and had made a covenant with them at Mt. Sinai. They had forgotten the Law given to Moses on the mountain, and every person was a law unto himself. The Lord's command in Leviticus 11:44, "Be holy; for I am holy," had no meaning for them. The people's actions and the intentions of their hearts were not to please God, but to please themselves.

3 Samuel was unique in that he was the only man to hold all three positions of judge, prophet, and priest. In contrast to the other judges, who each ruled locally in one of the tribes, Samuel was recognized by all Israel as judge. However, he primarily ruled in the southern tribes of Judah, Benjamin, and Simeon. As priest, Samuel offered sacrifices at the tabernacle and faithfully prayed for the people. Like Moses before him, Samuel loved the Israelites and continually called the people back to worshipping God in the proper manner. Samuel was the defining example for the prophets who succeeded him. Although the role of prophet existed before Samuel, most scholars agree that he was the first of the great Old Testament prophets. The prophet's role was to speak for God to the people, and particularly, to bring God's word to the kings. Since the kings were to be theocratic kings and rule under the authority of God, they needed to know God's will. Most of the Old Testament prophets appeared after the kingdom was divided in two (Unit III–V) and were closely associated with a king. If the king recognized God's right to rule over Israel, the prophet was able to be a counselor and guide to the king. If not, the prophet became the king's adversary. Samuel was also a Nazirite, dedicated to God before his birth by his mother, Hannah. In comparison to Samson, who did not take his position of Nazirite seriously, Samuel lived a godly life and kept the rules required of a Nazirite.

4 Being anointed by God included three things: a) being chosen by God for a specific role (priest, prophet, or king); b) being equipped by God's Spirit to fulfill the responsibilities associated with that job; and c) being protected by God while in that role. Thus, being anointed by God was something to be taken seriously. For example, after David was anointed king, he refused to kill Saul or do anything to depose him prematurely from the throne. David respected Saul's anointing, and refused to harm the LORD's anointed king, even though Saul was purposefully trying to kill David. David chose to wait for the LORD's timing to assume his kingly role. (See chapters 3-5 for the stories of Saul and David.)

5 What is God's covenant? It is the arrangement whereby God promises His people, "I will be your God, and you will be My people." (see Exodus 6:7). God made a covenant with Adam in the Garden of Eden (see Genesis 3:15) to send the Savior (the Seed that would crush the head of the serpent) so sinful people could be reconciled once again to a holy God. God reaffirmed the covenant with Noah after the Flood, promising never to destroy the whole earth again with a flood and giving the rainbow as a sign of that promise (see Genesis 8-9). It was with Abraham, however, that the LORD renewed the covenant in a more personal way. He promised that Abraham would have a son, inherit the land of Canaan, and bless many nations (see Genesis 12, 15, and 17). God chose Abraham's decendants to be the recipients of His special blessing. Abraham's family increased, and centuries later left Egypt as a nation under the leadership of Moses. In the wilderness, the LORD once again renewed His covenant with His people, and His people agreed to obey Him and worship Him as their God. Despite Israel's repeated idolatry, the LORD kept His promise to be their God, because the covenant does not depend upon the faithfulness of God's people, but upon the faithfulness of God. Once in the Promised Land, God's people forgot Him and each did "what was right in his own eyes" (Judges 21:25). Israel's demand for a human king, thereby rejecting God as their supreme Ruler, was one indication that the people did not respect and honor God's covenant with them. At the same time, the LORD had not forgotten His covenant with His people. Each of the three main characters in 1 Samuel was chosen and anointed by God to the role of leading Israel. In Unit I, the narrative focuses on how Israel became a kingdom. Then in Unit II, the LORD renews His covenant with His people through King David. As we follow the progress of God's covenant with His people, we are constantly reminded that though His people forget Him, the LORD is always faithful. The covenant rests on the unchanging nature and faithfulness of God.

The Call of Samuel

Every year it was the same. The whole family walked through the hill country of
8 Ephraim to the tabernacle at Shiloh to worship the LORD. Hannah dreaded these
pilgrimages. Hannah loved the LORD, and she loved her husband, Elkanah. He was a
good man, and she knew he loved her. But these trips always made her sad because Hannah had no children.

Elkanah's other wife, Peninnah, had many children. With gleeful pleasure, Peninnah would tease Hannah mercilessly about having no children until Hannah
9 would weep in agony and could not enjoy the ceremonial
meal.

> **Jesus in the OT**
> A prophet is a person called to speak God's words. How is Samuel, the prophet, like Jesus Christ, the Prophet?

This year Hannah stood before the LORD with a bitter soul and prayed in tears, "O
LORD Almighty, see my misery and remember me. If you give me a son, I will give him
10 back to you, and he will serve You his whole life. He will be a Nazirite, and he will never
cut his hair."

Eli, the priest, saw Hannah's lips moving, but couldn't hear her words. He thought she was drunk, and rebuked her harshly. Quickly Hannah responded, "Oh, I am not drunk, my LORD, but I am deeply troubled. I was pouring out my heart to the LORD, hoping He would hear my plea." Eli comforted her, saying, "Go in peace. May God grant you your request."

11 The LORD did answer Hannah's prayer and gave her a son. "I will
name him Samuel," she said, "because I asked the LORD for him."

For the next three years, Hannah stayed home when
the family went to Shiloh to worship, and she nursed
Samuel. Then came that special day when Hannah would
dedicate her son to the LORD. Holding Samuel's small hand, she
12 walked to the tabernacle with him. She took offerings of a young
bull, a basket of flour, and a flask of wine along with her.

After the sacrifice, Hannah brought Samuel to Eli. "Remember me?" she asked. "In tears I prayed for this child, and the LORD answered my prayer. Now I give him to the LORD for his whole life." Hannah then sang a song of thanksgiving to the LORD, and when she left the tabernacle, Samuel stayed with Eli.

6 The word "holy" has two meanings. First, holy means being set apart by God for use in His kingdom. God's people are holy because God sets them apart from those who do not trust and worship Him. He loves His people in a special way, and they have a special place of ministry in His kingdom. Objects can also be holy. The furniture in the tabernacle was holy because the pieces were set apart for the sole purpose of being used in the of worship of God. Second, holy means morally perfect. Only God is absolutely holy because only God never sins. God's people are to reflect God's holiness and by God's grace to live in ways that are morally good. They are to please God from the heart.

7 Holiness is fundamentally an attitude of the heart, not simply a way to behave. Being holy means that worshipping and pleasing God is the primary motivation for anything we do. A holy person reflects the nature and character of God, and even though we will never be perfectly holy until we are with the LORD, by His grace we can make good moral choices for good reasons. Being holy is difficult because even as Christians we have stubborn hearts that resist God's transforming work of grace in us. And, even when, by His grace, we exhibit holy motives and actions, our holiness is not always welcomed by those around us.

Although Eli was a godly man, his sons, Hophni and Phinehas, were wicked. The LORD was very angry with them because they treated His offerings with contempt. **13** Samuel, on the other hand, grew up in the LORD's presence and served the LORD well. Every year, his mother would bring him a little robe; The LORD blessed Hannah with other children.

One day a man of God brought bad news to Eli, saying, "The LORD is angry because you honor your sons more than you honor Him. You didn't stop them when they sinned against Him. Both your sons will die on the same day, and the LORD will choose a faithful priest from a different family." **14**

Years went by. Eli became old and blind. Samuel served the LORD under Eli's care. Unlike in the days of Moses and Joshua, the LORD did not often speak directly to people, but things were about to change.

One night, when Samuel was in bed, the LORD called him. Thinking it was Eli who had called, Samuel immediately ran to him. "You called me, Eli? Here I am," Samuel said. Eli was puzzled, and said, "Go back to bed, Samuel. I didn't call you." Samuel obeyed.

The LORD called Samuel a second time, and a second time Eli told Samuel to go back to bed. Samuel didn't know it was God who was calling him. When Samuel heard the voice a third time, Eli realized the LORD was calling Samuel. He told Samuel, "It's the LORD who is calling you. If He calls again say, 'Speak, for Your servant hears.'" The LORD did call again, and Samuel replied as Eli had instructed him.

The LORD's message to Samuel was frightening. The LORD said that He was going to judge Eli's family for their great sin against Him. No sacrifice would ever atone for their sin. **15**

In the morning, Eli asked Samuel to tell him what the LORD had said. Samuel was afraid. How could he speak of God's judgment to Eli? After much urging, Samuel told Eli the sad news, and Eli accepted what God had spoken. "He is the LORD. Let Him do what He thinks is best," Eli said. **16**

The LORD was with Samuel, and he grew up to be a godly man. The LORD revealed Himself to Samuel, and all Israel from the north to the south knew that Samuel was the LORD's prophet. **17**

8 When the events of 1 Samuel occurred, the tabernacle was located in the city of Shiloh. In 1 Samuel 3:3, the word "temple" (NIV) is translated "tabernacle" in the New King James version. The temple was not built until Solomon's time, so during Eli's priesthood the Israelites were still worshipping at the tabernacle. It was at the tabernacle that Samuel served the LORD as a child and later as a priest. At this time, the tabernacle was a more permanent, tent-like structure than the easily movable tent of the days of the wilderness journey, but it was still the same type of building that the Israelites had erected during the time of the book of Exodus.

9 The theme of barrenness is common in Scripture. There were many other women in Scripture who were grieved because they could not have children. A story similar to Hannah's is that of Jacob's two wives, Leah and Rachel. Jacob loved Rachel more than he loved Leah, but Leah had children and Rachel was barren. There was jealousy and strife between these two sisters, and Rachel suffered greatly because of her inability to have a child. Finally, Rachel gave birth to Joseph, the most loved son of Jacob, and to Benjamin, Jacob's youngest son.

10 A Nazirite was a man or woman who was set apart for service to the Lord as a result of a vow made to God. This voluntary vow was usually made for a specific period of time. During the time of the vow, the Nazirite could not drink wine, cut his hair, or touch a dead body. In the cases of Samson and Samuel, the vow was made by the parents and extended for the entire lifetime of the child. Unlike Samson, who took the vow lightly, Samuel kept the conditions of the vow and served the LORD well. Numbers 6:1-21 describes the requirements for a Nazirite in detail.

11 The name Samuel has several meanings, including "heard of God," "he who is from God," or "promised of God."

12 Although Scripture does not specify how old Samuel was when Hannah took him to the tabernacle, we can make a reasonable guess that he was about three years old based on the following: 1) At that time, women nursed their children up to about the age of three; and 2) Scripture says that Samuel was weaned. Therefore, if Hannah took Samuel to the tabernacle shortly after he was weaned, he would have been approximately three years old.

13 Eli's sons were not following the rules set forth in the ceremonial law regarding animal sacrifices. In Leviticus 3:16-17, the law says that "all the fat is the LORD's" and that the priest is not to eat any fat or blood from the animal sacrifices. The burning fat of the sacrifice was a pleasing aroma to the LORD, and thus it was reserved for Him. Eli's sons were taking meat from the sacrifice to eat before the fat was burned up. By their blatant disregard of God's requirements for the sacrifices, Eli's sons were showing contempt for the LORD. In addition, Eli's sons practiced sexual immorality with the women who served in the tabernacle.

14 Eli was not responsible for the sins of his adult sons. He was, however, responsible for not taking action when his sons disregarded his reproof and continued to sin against God. Eli did not discipline his sons or remove them from the office of priest when they continued to desecrate the sacrifices. The LORD interpreted this negligence as Eli honoring his sons more than he honored the LORD. Because of this, the LORD said that all Eli's descendents would die young ("in your family line there will never be an old man" [1 Samuel 2:32, NIV]) and that the priesthood would one day be transferred to a different family.

15 There was no remedy for Hophni and Phinehas's sins for two reasons. First, their sins were intentional and committed in defiance of the LORD's specific commands. Their hearts were not repentant. Second, bringing a sacrifice was the way for a repentant person to atone for his sin, and Eli's sons were doing sacrifices in a contemptuous manner. Since they were despising the only remedy that God had provided for the forgiveness of sin, there was no atonement for them.

16 Despite his shortcomings and sins, Eli was a godly man. His response to the LORD's judgment upon him and his family was an acceptance of God's judgment and an acknowledgment of God's goodness.

17 The ministry of Samuel ushered in a new era in Israel's history. Samuel united the tribes by judging all Israel from the northern city of Dan to the city of Beersheba in the south. The LORD who had seemed to be silent during the dark days of the judges was now revealing Himself to Samuel, and Samuel was drawing the people back to the Lord. Samuel was recognized by all of Israel as a prophet and a spiritual leader.

Review Worksheets

A. MEMORY VERSE:

"In those days there was no ___king___ in Israel; everyone did what was ___right___ in his own ___eyes___." (Judges 21:25)

B. KEY FACTS: Put the answers to the questions in the boxes below.

1. Judge: How long did Samuel judge Israel?
2. Priest: What two things did Samuel do as a priest in the tabernacle?
3. Prophet: Who made Samuel a prophet over everyone in Israel?
4. Nazirite: Before Samuel was born, what did his mother do?

Samuel's Many Jobs

Judge	Priest	Prophet	Nazirite
1. All the days of his life	2a. offered sacrifices b. prayed for God's people	3. God	4. Set him apart for the LORD

C. STORY FACTS: Fill in the blanks below.

1. Elkanah's family worshipped at the tabernacle at ___Shiloh___.
2. Hannah prayed that the LORD would give her a ___son___.
3. The LORD said Eli honored ___his___ ___sons___ more than he honored God.
4. Hannah sang a song of ___thanksgiving___ because God gave her a son.
5. Anoint means ___chosen___ by God and ___equipped___ by God's Spirit to ___serve___ the LORD in a particular job.
6. God's promise to be the God of His people forever is His ___covenant___.

Notes:

D. WHAT'S THE RIGHT ANSWER?

Circle the word that completes the sentence correctly.

1. When Eli saw Hannah praying, he thought that she was ___________.

   angry   (drunk)   depressed

2. One night the LORD called Samuel ___________ times.

   two   three   (four)

3. Hannah named her son Samuel because she ___________ God for him.

   (asked)   yelled at   cursed

4. The LORD's message to Samuel was about ___________ for Eli's family.

   blessing   prosperity   (judgment)

E. WHAT DOES THIS PERSON DO? Match the job with the description of the job.

__4__ Judge — 1. Person called to speak for God

__3__ Priest — 2. Person set apart to serve God

__1__ Prophet — 3. Man who offered sacrifices

__2__ Nazirite — 4. Deliverer, peacemaker, and civil leader

F. HOW DID SAMUEL ANSWER THE LORD?

Circle every other letter and put the letters in the spaces below.

ASEPCETAUKIFYOKR
QYROTUFRDSRECRBVEATNLTJHMENATRES

S P E A K, F O R Y O U R
S E R V A N T H E A R S

G. FIND OUT...

Who else did God call to serve Him? Look up the verses below to find out.

__Moses__ Exodus 3:4,10   __Jeremiah__ Jeremiah 1:1-5

__Matthew__ Matthew 9:9   __Paul__ Romans 1:1

What did the LORD call these men to do? __His work__

Notes to Teachers and Parents:

1 The ark of the covenant was kept in the Holy of Holies in the tabernacle. It was a rectangular, gold-covered box made of acacia wood. It "contained the gold jar of manna, Aaron's staff that had budded, and the stone tablets of the covenant" (Hebrews 9:4). On top of the ark were two golden cherubim that guarded the mercy seat. Once a year, on the Day of Atonement, the high priest, after making a sacrifice for the people, entered the Holy of Holies and sprinkled blood on the mercy seat. Poles were permanently attached to the sides of the ark for use in transporting it. Everyone was forbidden to look inside the ark or even touch it, and if they did, they died instantly. The ark was not supposed to be worshipped as an idol or to be looked upon as a magic box that guaranteed good fortune, but the Israelites at times used the ark in this way. The purpose of the ark was to remind Israel of the LORD's presence with them, to remind them of the necessity of a blood sacrifice to atone for sin, and to point the people to the Savior who would someday die for the sins of His people.

2 Samuel set up the Ebenezer stone to remind Israel that the Lord had protected them by confusing and subduing the Philistines. This stone was designed to be a memorial, or reminder, not an object of worship. When we set up visible reminders of God's goodness to us, we must never think of that object as a good luck piece or a magic stone. It is God, not any created thing that protects, cares for, and guides us. On the other hand, because we are people who forget quickly, visible reminders of God's care can be helpful. God used many things to help His people remember His goodness. In the New Testament, Jesus instituted the Lord's Supper as a way for the church to remember what He did for us on the cross. Today we have many visible reminders of God's love and mercy, including stained glass windows and cross symbols. Prayer notebooks are another way to remember what God has done. Keeping a journal of prayer requests and God's answers to those prayers encourages us when we have doubts that the LORD hears us.

Chapter 2

Samuel—The Last Judge

LESSON SCOPE: 1 Samuel 4–7 **READ TO ME:** 1 Samuel 4–7

THEME: The LORD God shows His power over idols.

MEMORY VERSE:

"Remember the former things of old, For I am God, and there is no other; I am God, and there is none like Me." (Isaiah 46:9)

KEY FACTS:

The Ark of the Covenant's Journey

From Shiloh	Where it sat in the tabernacle.
To the battlefield	Because Israel wanted victory over the Philistines.
To Ashdod	Where God destroyed Dagon in his temple, struck the Philistines with tumors, and sent rats to ravage the land.
To Gath and Ekron	Where God sent more tumors and rats to the Ekron and Gath Philistines.
To Israel	Where it stayed at Abinadab's house for twenty years.

THINGS TO REMEMBER:

1 Ark of the covenant = Box that contained the Ten Commandments and reminded Israel that God was with them.

Ichabod = Means "the glory [of the LORD] has departed from Israel."

Ebenezer = Means "thus far has the LORD helped us."

MESSAGE FROM THE KING: Do you have an Ebenezer stone?

2 Samuel set up an Ebenezer stone to remember what the LORD had done for Israel. How can you set up an Ebenezer stone to remind you of what God has done for you?

Notes:

Memory Page · **Story Time** · Worksheets · Quiz

Samuel—The Last Judge

The battle was over, and 4,000 Israelites were dead! How could the LORD let this happen? The elders of Israel shook their heads in disbelief, and said, "Maybe if we bring the ark from Shiloh, the LORD will protect us from the Philistines. If the ark is with us, the LORD will be with us, too." **3**

So they sent for the ark of the covenant, which was in the tabernacle at Shiloh. When the ark entered Israel's camp, the Israelites shouted so loudly that the ground trembled. Hearing the deafening shouts, the Philistines exclaimed, "A god has come into the Israelites' camp. We're in trouble now. But don't give up. We must be strong and fight!" The Philistines attacked again and won another mighty victory over Israel.

Meanwhile, old Eli was sitting along the road near Shiloh, anxiously awaiting news. A messenger with ragged clothes and dust covering his head ran into town. "I've come from the battlefield and have dreadful news," he shouted. "Thirty thousand Israelites are dead, Hophni and Phinehas have been killed, and the Philistines have captured the ark!"

> **Jesus in the OT**
> What does a priest do? A priest makes sacrifices for sin. Samuel, as priest, offered a sacrifice for the people's sin, and the LORD forgave them. What does Jesus' sacrifice on the cross do for you?

Eli's grief over his sons' deaths was great, but to Eli the capture of the ark was the worst thing that could ever happen to Israel because it may have meant that the
4 LORD's presence was gone from Israel. Unable to bear this, Eli fell backwards from his chair and died. Phinehas's wife was expecting a child. When she heard the news, she went into labor and had a son. In the last moments before she died, she named the baby Ichabod, meaning "the glory [of the LORD] has departed from Israel," because her husband and father-in-law were dead and the ark was captured by the Philistines. **5**

What was happening? Israel wasn't supposed to lose battles. Wasn't the LORD stronger than the gods of the Philistines? The problem was that the Israelites thought the ark was a magic box that would always bring them good fortune. They had forgotten that God was holy and desired holiness from His people. They thought that they could do

3 This reaction of the elders of Israel indicates how far the people had wandered away from the LORD. First, they were surprised that they had lost the battle with the Philistines. They didn't realize how much their idolatry and sinful actions as a people affected their relationship with the LORD. They had forgotten the connection between obedience and God's blessing. Second, they were using the ark in an irreverent manner. The ark was supposed to remain in the Holy of Holies and be seen only by the high priest once a year on the Day of Atonement. It was not a magic box to be carted wherever they wanted victory in battle. Third, they erroneously believed that the ark had to be in their presence in order for the LORD to be present with them. Rather, the LORD would be with them anytime they were obedient and trusted in Him.

4 Although Eli had dishonored the LORD by allowing his sons to continue to defile the temple and the sacrifices, Eli still had a reverence for the LORD. In 1 Samuel 3:18, Eli expressed his belief in God's goodness and humbly accepted God's judgment upon him and his family. In 1 Samuel 4:12-18 Eli was waiting to hear news of the battle. He knew that taking the ark to the battlefield was not appropriate. He had a serious concern over the safety of the ark, and when he heard it was captured, he understood the spiritual significance of losing it. It was the news of the ark's capture, not his sons' deaths, that distressed him so greatly that he fell backwards off his chair and died.

5 This is the only mention of Phinehas's wife, but it is a significant one. Like her father-in-law, Eli, she understood the dire spiritual consequences of losing the ark to a pagan nation. To her, the ark represented the glory of the LORD, and its absence meant that the LORD had also departed from Israel. This thought was too great for her to bear, and she died in sorrow and despair.

Notes:

6 Israel's defeat didn't mean that the

gods of the Philistines were stronger than the LORD. Instead, the LORD was using Israel's defeat in battle as a means to get their attention and point out their sin. The Israelites had forgotten that God desired holiness from His people. Even the priests were dishonoring God through their sexual immorality and irreverence in the tabernacle. A holy God could not turn away and ignore such sin; He had to bring judgment on His disobedient people.

7 Dagon was a prominent god, not only in Philistia, but in surrounding nations. It was in the temple of Dagon that Samson had pushed down the temple pillars, causing the deaths of thousands of Philistines as well as his own. The word "Dagon" is associated with grain, and as such he was a fertility god. Putting the ark in Dagon's temple was a way of trying to make Israel's "god" subservient to the Philistines' god. Even though the ark was not an idol to the Israelites, the Philistines understood the ark to be Israel's god. The LORD showed His power over Dagon by causing the statue to fall down before the ark and eventually be destroyed.

8 These events took place over the period of seven months (see 1 Samuel 6:1). The Philistines finally realized that the ark would bring disaster to whatever city it entered.

9 The Philistine leaders asked counsel of their own priests and men associated with witchcraft and sorcery. Even at this point, the Philistines were not totally certain that it was Israel's God who had brought the plagues upon them, but they no longer desired to have the ark with them. They sent a guilt offering back with the ark in order to pay honor to Israel's God. The five gold tumors and five gold rats represented the five primary cities in Philistia (Ashdod, Ekron, Gath, Gaza, and Ashkelon). The priests and sorcerers were wise enough to see a connection between their experience with the ark and the plagues in Egypt (see 1 Samuel 6:6). They were reluctant to harden their hearts as the Egyptians and Pharaoh did.

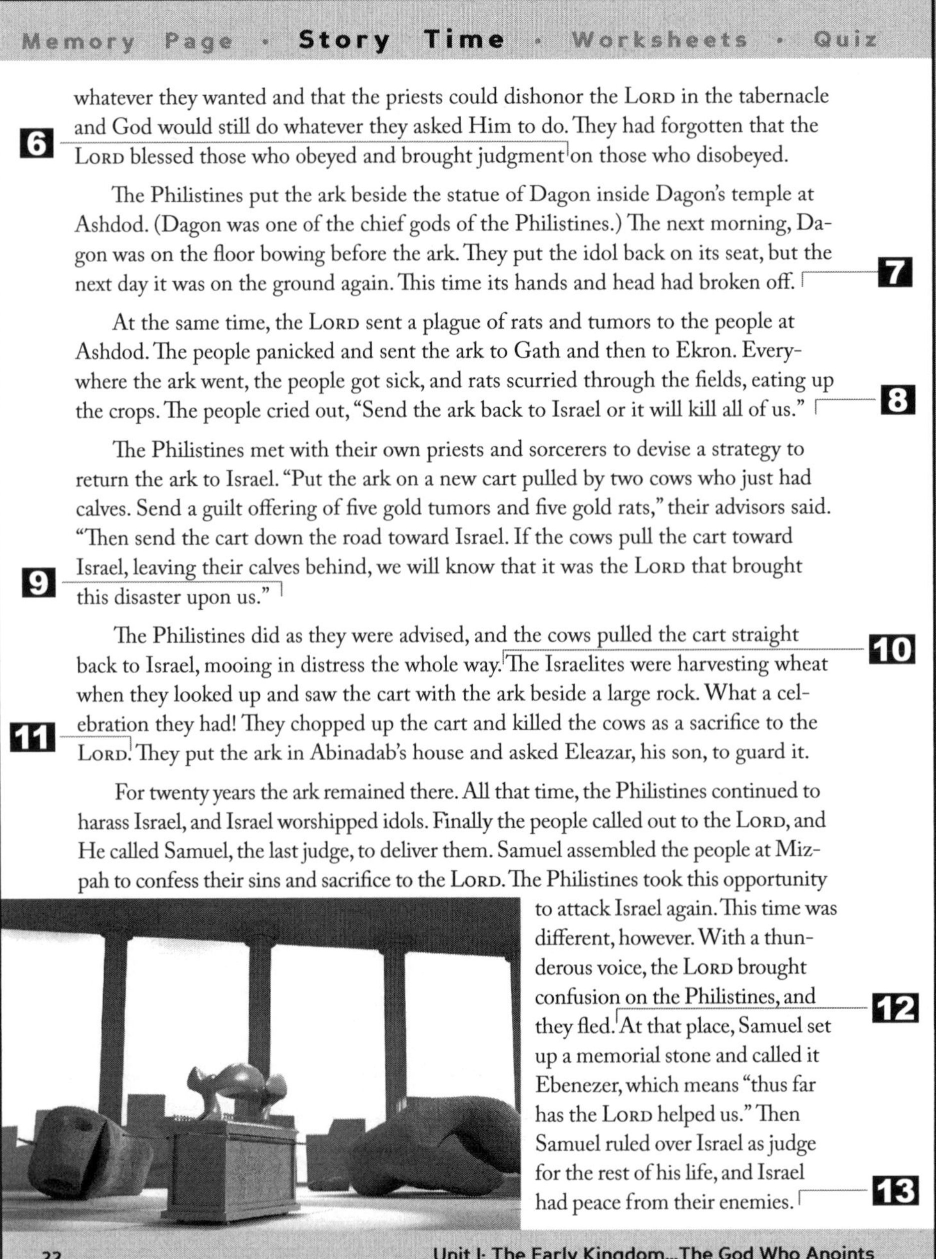

Memory Page • **Story Time** • Worksheets • Quiz

whatever they wanted and that the priests could dishonor the LORD in the tabernacle
6 and God would still do whatever they asked Him to do. They had forgotten that the LORD blessed those who obeyed and brought judgment on those who disobeyed.

The Philistines put the ark beside the statue of Dagon inside Dagon's temple at Ashdod. (Dagon was one of the chief gods of the Philistines.) The next morning, Dagon was on the floor bowing before the ark. They put the idol back on its seat, but the next day it was on the ground again. This time its hands and head had broken off. 7

At the same time, the LORD sent a plague of rats and tumors to the people at Ashdod. The people panicked and sent the ark to Gath and then to Ekron. Everywhere the ark went, the people got sick, and rats scurried through the fields, eating up the crops. The people cried out, "Send the ark back to Israel or it will kill all of us." 8

The Philistines met with their own priests and sorcerers to devise a strategy to return the ark to Israel. "Put the ark on a new cart pulled by two cows who just had calves. Send a guilt offering of five gold tumors and five gold rats," their advisors said. "Then send the cart down the road toward Israel. If the cows pull the cart toward
9 Israel, leaving their calves behind, we will know that it was the LORD that brought this disaster upon us."

The Philistines did as they were advised, and the cows pulled the cart straight 10
back to Israel, mooing in distress the whole way. The Israelites were harvesting wheat when they looked up and saw the cart with the ark beside a large rock. What a cel-
11 ebration they had! They chopped up the cart and killed the cows as a sacrifice to the LORD. They put the ark in Abinadab's house and asked Eleazar, his son, to guard it.

For twenty years the ark remained there. All that time, the Philistines continued to harass Israel, and Israel worshipped idols. Finally the people called out to the LORD, and He called Samuel, the last judge, to deliver them. Samuel assembled the people at Mizpah to confess their sins and sacrifice to the LORD. The Philistines took this opportunity to attack Israel again. This time was different, however. With a thunderous voice, the LORD brought
confusion on the Philistines, and 12
they fled. At that place, Samuel set up a memorial stone and called it Ebenezer, which means "thus far has the LORD helped us." Then Samuel ruled over Israel as judge for the rest of his life, and Israel had peace from their enemies. 13

22 Unit I: The Early Kingdom...The God Who Anoints

10 This was a miracle from the LORD. Mother cows would not normally walk in a direction away from their calves. Also, these cows had never been yoked and would not easily subject themselves to a yoke the first time. The Philistines designed this plan so that there would be no doubt in their minds that the plagues upon them had been sent from Israel's "god." Throughout the entire journey back to Israel, the cows lowed mournfully because they wanted their calves, but the animals were driven by a power stronger than their own instincts–that of the LORD God of Israel.

11 When the Israelites saw the ark in the cart, they celebrated with a sacrifice. Some men showed irreverence to the ark and looked inside. God immediately killed them in response to their dishonor and disobedience (see 1 Samuel 6:19).

12 The ark remained at Abinadab's house. The Israelites did not immediately turn from their idolatry and worship the LORD. Twenty years passed, and the Philistines continued to be a problem for Israel. Finally, Israel called to the LORD for help. Samuel exhorted the people to turn from their idolatry and confess their sin. He assembled the people at Mizpah, and there the people fasted, confessed their sins, and sacrificed to the LORD. Now the people were sincerely repentant. The Philistines decided to take advantage of this gathering of Israelites, but when they tried to attack, the LORD brought confusion upon them

Memory Page · Story Time · **Worksheets** · Quiz

Review Worksheets

A. MEMORY VERSE: "Remember the former things of old, For I am God, and there is no other; I am God, and there is none like Me." (Isaiah 46:9)

B. KEY FACTS: Use the words below to answer the questions. (Hint: One word is used twice.)

Shiloh Battlefield Dagon's temple Ashdod Gath Ekron Abinadab's house

1. Where was Dagon's temple located? Ashdod
2. Where did the ark stay for twenty years? Abinadab's house
3. Where was the tabernacle located? Shiloh
4. Where did the Philistines put the ark after they captured it? Dagon's temple
5. In what cities did the Philistines get tumors? Ashdod, Gath, and Ekron
6. Where did the Israelites take the ark to give them good fortune? battlefield

Can you find Ashdod, Gath, Ekron, and Shiloh on Map 1?

C. STORY FACTS: Cross out the answer that is NOT correct.

1. When the Philistines heard the Israelites' loud shouts, they said, "____________."
   Don't give up Be strong ~~Let's make a treaty~~
2. Eli was sad when he heard the news of ____________.
   his sons' death the ark's capture ~~the plague of rats~~
3. The Israelites forgot that God was holy and ____________.
   judged sin desired holiness ~~changed the rules~~
4. The Philistines' plan to send the ark back to Israel included ____________.
   a new cart a guilt offering ~~two mother donkeys~~
5. When Samuel assembled the Israelites at Mizpah, the people ____________.
   ~~sang songs~~ confessed sin sacrificed to the Lord

Chapter 2: Samuel—The Last Judge 23

and they fled. This time, the Lord delivered them from the Philistines because the people were crying out to Him with trusting, humble hearts.

13 The Ebenezer stone was a reminder to Israel of God's protection and care. For the next several years, the Israelites had few problems with the Philistines. Samuel continued to judge Israel until the time of his death many years later.

Notes:

14 Other answers include:
- Made of silver and gold
- Have ears but do not hear
- Have noses but do not smell
- Have hands but "do not handle"
- Have feet but do not walk
- Do not "mutter through their throat"

Notes:

D. DO YOU KNOW THE REASON? Circle the statement that completes each sentence.

1. The Israelites moved the ark from Shiloh to the battlefield because ______.
   a. they thought the ark would be safer there than at the tabernacle
   (b.) they thought the ark would protect them from the Philistines
   c. God commanded them to move the ark
2. The Philistines defeated the Israelites in battle because ______.
   a. the Philistines had a bigger and stronger army
   b. the Philistines' god Dagon was mightier than Israel's God
   (c.) the LORD was bringing judgment on Israel for their sin
3. The Philistines sent the ark back to Israel because ______.
   a. Israel threatened to burn up their wheat fields if they didn't
   (b.) they thought the ark would kill all of them if they kept it
   c. they wanted to make peace with the Israelites

E. IMPORTANT NAMES TO REMEMBER...

1. I C H A B O D Means "the glory [of the LORD] has departed."
2. E B E N E Z E R Means "thus far has the LORD helped us."

F. FIND OUT...

Psalm 115 compares God, who is in heaven, with idols. Write down three things that Psalm 115 says about idols.

1. Made by the hands of man **14**
2. Have mouths but cannot speak
3. Have eyes but cannot see

How is our God greater than idols?

God is all-powerful, and all of creation must submit to His will. Idols—manmade creations—have no power and cannot give true satisfaction or comfort.

Chapter 3

Saul—The First King

LESSON SCOPE: 1 Samuel 8–15 **READ TO ME:** 1 Samuel 8–12, 15

THEME: The LORD God anoints and removes the rulers of His people.

MEMORY VERSE:

1 "Behold, to obey is better than sacrifice,
And to heed than the fat of rams." (1 Samuel 15:22b)

2 **KEY FACTS:**

Israel's Neighbors

Nation	Founder of Nation	Famous Events	Israelite Defenders
Amalek	Amalek: grandson of Esau	Israel defeated Amalek at Rephidim in the wilderness. King Saul defeated King Agag.	Moses Saul
Ammon	Ben-Ammi: son of Lot and his second daughter	Jephthah defeated Ammon. Saul defeated Ammon and was accepted as king by Israel.	Jephthah Saul
Edom	Esau: son of Isaac	Israel could not pass through their land on the way to Canaan.	
Moab	Moab: son of Lot and his first daughter	King Balak of Moab asked Balaam to curse Israel. Ehud defeated King Eglon.	Moses Ehud
Philistia	Sea People from Aegean Sea	The Philistines captured Samson. They captured the ark, but returned it after they got sick. They threatened Saul with chariots.	Samson Samuel Saul

Can you find these nations on map 1?

MESSAGE FROM THE KING: The King wants you to obey from your heart.

The LORD your King wants you to do the right thing for the right reason. What are some wrong reasons for doing the right thing? Why is obeying the LORD from the heart so important? 3

Notes to Teachers and Parents:

1 Through Samuel, the Lord was telling Saul that He preferred an inward attitude of love and obedience over outward acts of worship. Saul's sacrifice was an act of disobedience because he usurped the authority that God had given to Samuel as priest. He offered a sacrifice that he had no right to offer and thought that he was pleasing God by being religious. In a similar way, God is not pleased with us when we do religious acts (going to church, praying, reading the Bible, etc.) but have hearts that do not desire Him. The LORD wants us to heed His Word and obey Him.

2 Of the five nations described in the table on the **Memory Page**, four of them had some direct relationship to Abraham. Isaac, Abraham's son, had two sons, Jacob and Esau. The Edomites were the descendents of Esau (Edom was another name for Esau). Amalek, the founder of the Amalekites, was the grandson of Esau. The Moabites and the Ammonites were related to Abraham through Lot, Abraham's nephew. Lot had two daughters who escaped from Sodom and Gomorrah with him. The older daughter had a son named Moab, who fathered the Moabites, and the younger daughter's son, Ben-Ammi, was the founder of the Ammonites. The only nation listed on this table that did not directly descend from Abraham was the Philistines. These people were part of the Sea People who came from the island of Crete (called Caphtor in Scripture [see Amos 9:7]) in the Aegean Sea. As a result of a great disaster that devastated their homeland, the Sea People (or Philistines) traveled across the Mediterranean Sea to live in the coastal areas of Canaan prior to the time of Samuel and King Saul (approximately 1250 BC).

3 Obedience to the LORD requires doing the right thing for the right reason. If our motive is sinful, then our behavior does not glorify God, even though our action may be morally right. Godly motives come from a heart that wants to please God. Anytime we choose to act from a heart of self-centeredness or fear, we are not glorifying God (examples: sharing a toy to avoid a parent's displeasure, giving a gift so the person will like you, saying "I'm sorry" simply to avoid a more severe punishment). Obeying God from the heart is important because obeying God for any other reason is not God-honoring.

Notes:

4 Samuel's sons were dishonest and they perverted justice. The elders of Israel used the wickedness of Samuel's sons as a legitimate reason to demand a king. Also, the elders were weary of not having a central ruler over Israel to protect them from their enemies and to lead the nation. Having a king was not wrong, because the LORD had made provision for a king in the Mosaic law, but the elders wanted a king "like other nations." They did not want to be a theocracy in which God was their supreme Ruler and the king ruled under His authority.

5 The LORD was making it very clear to Samuel that the people were rejecting Him, not Samuel and his leadership over the past twenty years. Israel's problem was a spiritual one because the elders were refusing to accept God's authority over them.

6 Samuel's warning came true. David had armies and fought against Israel's enemies (see 2 Samuel 8). Solomon amassed an army of chariots (see 1 Kings 4:26; 1 Kings 10:26-29). The number of people required to manage the royal household increased as Israel's kings became wealthier and more prominent.

7 Even though Saul quickly turned away from the LORD, he was God's choice for Israel's first king. The LORD directly led Samuel to Saul so that there was no doubt as to whom the LORD had chosen.

8 If God chooses a person and equips him with His Spirit, the person is able to fulfill his role no matter what weaknesses or limitations the person might have. Saul came from the smallest clan in the smallest tribe, yet he was the one who the LORD had chosen. Samuel assured Saul that the Lord God would go with him.

Notes:

Saul—The First King

Samuel was old, tired, and discouraged. He had judged Israel well over the years,
but his sons were wicked men, and the elders of Israel were now demanding that
4 a king rule over them.

Samuel cried out to the LORD, and the LORD
answered, "It's not you that the people are rejecting.
They're rejecting Me as their King. They are again
forsaking Me and the covenant. Let them have a
king, but warn them what a king will do when he
5 rules over them."

> **Jesus in the OT**
>
> Saul thought that because he was king he could do whatever he wanted. He forgot that God is the great King above all kings. In the New Testament, we learn that Jesus is the King of kings.

Samuel spoke frankly to the people, "A king will take your sons and make them
go to war in chariots. Some will be commanders over thousands, and others will
harvest the king's fields. A king will take your daughters to be bakers and cooks in his
palace. He'll take the best of your fields and olive groves, your faithful servants, and
your flocks and livestock. You will have to pay high taxes, and you will be his slaves. Is
6 this what you want?" No matter what Samuel said, the people kept demanding, "We
want a king like other nations to lead us and fight our battles."

One day a tall, handsome young Benjamite named Saul and his servant were out looking for his father's lost donkeys. After many unsuccessful days, Saul was ready to give up and go home. "No, don't stop now," said his servant. "A prophet named Samuel lives in this town. He's highly respected and what he says comes true. Let's ask him."

The day before, the LORD had spoken to Samuel, "Tomorrow a man will come to
7 visit you. Anoint him to be king in Israel." Samuel met Saul, told him where the donkeys were, but more importantly, anointed Saul to be Israel's first king. Saul said he was
from the smallest tribe, Benjamin, and the smallest family in the tribe. He thought he
was not important enough to be the king. But Samuel assured him, "The LORD has
8 chosen you to be king, and God will go with you."

Actually, Saul was anointed king three times. The first anointing happened privately at Samuel's house. Sometime later, Samuel gathered the people

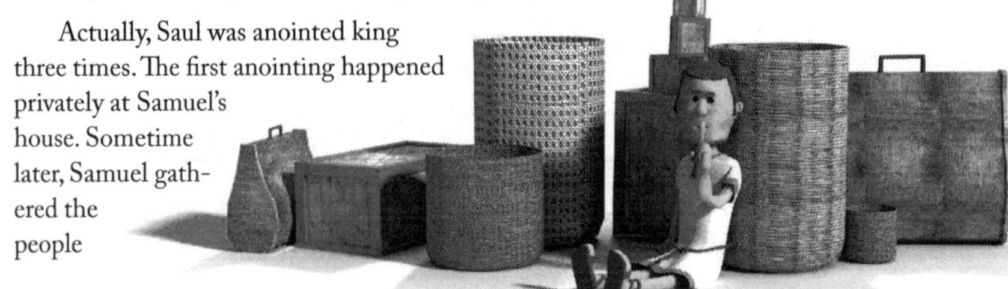

together at Mizpah to anoint Saul publicly, but Saul was shy. He was hiding behind some baggage. The people found him, and Samuel anointed him in front of everyone. Then they shouted, "Long live the king!"

Some Israelites doubted that Saul was the right man to be king, but soon all doubts were gone. The Ammonites besieged Jabesh Gilead in Israel. When Saul heard the cruel terms of the Ammonites' treaty, he was furious. God's Spirit came upon him, and he led Israel in an attack upon the Ammonites, killing most of them and scattering the few who had survived. Now all the Israelites gladly accepted Saul as their king, and he was anointed the third time.

After Saul's third anointing, Samuel made a farewell speech to the people, begging them to follow the LORD as their supreme King. The people repented of their sin in asking for a king and worshipping idols. They asked Samuel to pray for them. **9**

Saul was king about two years when he committed his first big sin against the LORD. The Philistines were threatening Israel with thousands of chariots and soldiers. Saul's soldiers were hiding in caves and among the rocks, and Samuel had not arrived to offer the sacrifice asking for God's help in battle. Instead of waiting for Samuel, Saul offered the sacrifice himself. Out of fear, Saul had acted foolishly. He was not a priest and had no right to offer sacrifices to the LORD. The consequence for Saul's
10 disobedience was severe: God decided to take the kingdom away from Saul and give it to a man with a godly heart!

Sometime later the LORD told Saul to attack the Amalekites because they had attacked Israel in the Sinai wilderness many years earlier. Saul ambushed the Amalekites and crushed their army, destroying everyone and everything just as God had commanded, except he took the best of the cattle and flocks to sacrifice to the LORD,
11 and he didn't kill Agag, the Amalekite king, as God had instructed! When Samuel heard the bleating of the sheep, he confronted Saul, "Why did you disobey God? Don't you know that obedience is better than sacrifice? Because of your sin, the LORD has rejected you as king."

Saul was not repentant of his disobedience. By his actions, Saul had shown that he
12 didn't want God to be the supreme King of Israel. The LORD was grieved that He had
13 made Saul king, but there was no going back. Sadly, Samuel left Saul and that's the last time Samuel ever saw Saul.

9 After Saul was confirmed as king, Samuel gave his farewell speech to the people. He reminded them that he had not oppressed or cheated them in any way, and the people agreed with him. He summarized Israel's history of disobedience and fickleness, and called them to commit themselves to serving the LORD. Finally, he rebuked them for their sinful motives in demanding a king and rejecting God as their King. When God responded to Samuel's speech with thunder and lightning, the people stood in awe of God and of Samuel, His prophet. The people begged Samuel to pray that they remain faithful to the LORD, and Samuel responded with the well-known words, "Far be it from me that I should sin against the LORD by failing to pray for you" (1 Samuel 12:23, NIV).

10 We don't know why Samuel was late in arriving at the battlefield, but his delay caused Saul anxiety. Saul decided to presumptuously take the situation into his own hands instead of trusting the LORD. Saul allowed circumstances, not trust in the LORD, to dictate his actions. If Saul had been ruling as a theocratic king under God's authority, he would have obeyed God and waited, even when his army appeared to be scattering and the situation seemed out of control. When we trust God, the situation is never really out of control, even though it may appear so to us. Saul's sin in 1 Samuel 13 ended any hope that Saul would be the first of a dynasty of kings. The consequence of Saul's sin was that the kingship would leave his family. Saul's son, Jonathan, a man who pleased the LORD, would never be king because of his father's sin. In 1 Samuel 16, God chose another man, David, to be the next king. From David would come a long line of kings, and eventually the Messiah would be born from his lineage.

11 Once again, Saul did not carry out God's instructions. God had told Saul to destroy everything and everyone. Saul said he spared the animals to offer them as a sacrifice to the Lord. Saul did not give a reason why he spared Agag's life. Clearly, Samuel was not fooled by Saul's excuses and responded, "To obey is better than sacrifice" (1 Samuel 15:22b.) After being confronted by Samuel, Saul did admit to disobeying God, but he blamed the people for his sin. In disobeying God in this situation, Saul showed once again that he did not want to be a theocratic king who submitted himself to the supreme authority of God. Not only did he disobey God, but he also made excuses for his sin when found out, and evidenced no sign of a repentant heart. God's consequence to Saul was severe, but just. By Saul's disobedience in 1 Samuel 15, he lost the right to personally be king. Though he would sit on the throne for many more years until his untimely death, he had been rejected as king. In 1 Samuel 16, God anoints David to be the next king, even though he would not actually rule until nearly twenty years later.

12 Twice Saul said, "I have sinned," but the genuineness of his repentance is questionable. In 1 Samuel 15:24 Saul admitted his sin, but immediately blamed the people for his actions. In 1 Samuel 15:30 Saul said he was sorry, but he seemed more interested in having the good opinion of the elders than in having God's forgiveness.

13 God is omniscient and was not surprised by Saul's disobedience. Saul was God's choice to be Israel's first king, and his disobedience did not thwart God's plan. Rather, the disobedience that led to God's rejection of Saul as king was part of God's plan. Yet, at the same time, the Lord was sincerely grieved by Saul's disobedience.

Notes:

Review Worksheets

A. MEMORY VERSE: "Behold, to obey is better than sacrifice,
And to heed than the fat of rams." (1 Samuel 15:22b)

B. KEY FACTS: Use the table on the **Memory Page** to answer the questions. The words can be used more than once.

Amalekites Ammonites Moabites Philistines

1. The nation that Israel defeated in the wilderness: Amalekites
2. The nation that captured Samson and took away his strength: Philistines
3. The nation that Jephthah fought and defeated: Ammonites
4. The nation that captured the ark in battle: Philistines
5. The nation ruled by King Eglon: Moabites
6. The nation that came to Canaan from across the sea: Philistines

C. STORY FACTS: Fill in the blanks.

1. The elders of Israel were demanding that God give them a king.
2. Saul was looking for his father's donkeys when Samuel anointed him to be Israel's king.
3. Saul was anointed as king three times by Samuel.
4. After the battle with the Amalekites, Saul refused to destroy two things: King Agag and best of cattle and flocks.
5. Saul was not allowed to make sacrifices because he was not a priest.
6. Agag was the king of the Amalekites.

D. WHAT'S TRUE AND WHAT'S NOT?

Circle "T" if the sentence is true. Circle "F" if the sentence is false.

1. The people were rejecting Samuel when they demanded a king. T (F)
2. Saul disobeyed God when he offered a sacrifice. (T) F
3. The LORD was grieved that He made Saul the king. (T) F
4. Saul thought he was not important enough to be a king. (T) F

E. WHAT WOULD A KING BE LIKE?

Write three things that God said a king would do if he ruled over Israel.

1. Take sons to go to war
2. Take daughters to cook and bake in his palace
3. Take the best of their fields, servants, and flocks

F. DO YOU KNOW THE ANSWER?

Put the answers in the spaces on the left. Then use the boxed letters to find the answer to the question below.

M [O] A [B] Eglon was king of ________.

[E] [D] O M Esau was founder of ________.

K [I] N G The people demanded to have a ________.

W I C K [E] D Eli's sons were ________.

D O [N] K E Y S Saul was looking for ________.

[C] H A R I O T S The Philistines had thousands of ____.

T H R E [E] Saul was anointed ________ times.

What does the LORD say is better than sacrifice?

O B E D I E N C E

G. FIND OUT...

You can obey God with good motives or with selfish ones. In John 14:15, Jesus gives you a good motive for obeying him. What does He say?

If you love Me, you will keep My commandments.

Notes to Teachers and Parents:

1 When choosing people to serve Him, the LORD looks at a person's inward thoughts and the motivations of his heart, not his outward appearance. What's important to the LORD is not how handsome, tall, or strong a person is, but whether the person is godly. God wants someone who will trust Him and depend upon His wisdom, not his own wisdom, in difficult circumstances. (Of course, it is only by God's grace, which He generously gives us, that any one of us can obey Him and trust in Him.) In 1 Corinthians 1:18-31, the Apostle Paul writes that God chooses the weak, lowly, and despised things of the world so that no one can boast in his own strength, wisdom, or abilities. God chooses those that no man would reasonably choose, and then, as that person trusts Him, God does mighty things through him. Then we see the fulfillment of the verse that says, "Let him who boasts, boast in the Lord" (1 Corinthians 1:31; Jeremiah 9:24 NIV).

2 Hebrew poetry does not contain the rhyme or meter that English poetry has. Rather, Hebrew poetry uses the mechanism of thought parallelism. There are three types of parallelism in Hebrew poetry: a) synonymous: the second line of the poetic thought repeats an idea similar to that of the first line (called "repeated" on the Memory Page); b) antithetical: the second line of the poetic thought gives an opposite idea to the first line (called "contrasted" on the Memory Page); and c) synthetic: the second line of the poetic thought completes the first line by giving additional information (called "continuing" on the Memory Page). Take time with the students to examine other psalms to find examples of these three types of parallelism.

3 There are many types of psalms in Scripture—not all of them are discussed in this chapter. The following are brief descriptions of each type of poetry mentioned on the Memory Page. **Hallelujah psalms** (Psalms 146–150): these five

Chapter 4

David Anointed as King

LESSON SCOPE: 1 Samuel 16, Psalms **READ TO ME:** 1 Samuel 16

THEME: The LORD God looks at man's heart, not his outside appearance.

MEMORY VERSE:

1 "For the LORD does not see as man sees; for man looks at the outward appearance, but the LORD looks at the heart." (1 Samuel 16:7b)

2 **KEY FACTS:**

Types of Hebrew Poetry

Category	Definition	Example
Repeated	Second line has a similar meaning to the first line.	"The heavens declare the glory of God; And the firmament shows His handiwork." (Psalm 19:1)
Contrasted	Second line has an opposite meaning to the first line.	"He regards the lowly; But the proud He knows from afar." (Psalm 138:6)
Continuing	Second line adds meaning to or continues the thought of the first line.	"You who laid the foundations of the earth, So that it should not be moved forever." (Psalm 104:5)

3 Types of Psalms

Category	Definition	Examples
Hallelujah Psalms	Giving praise to God.	Psalms 146–150
Historical Psalms	Reminding Israel of who God is and what He has done.	Psalms 105–106
Judgment Psalms	Asking God to judge the wicked.	Psalms 35, 52, 55, 109
Messianic Psalms	Talking about the Messiah.	Psalms 2, 22, 45, 72
Passover Psalms	Sung during Passover meal.	Psalms 113–118
Pilgrim Psalms	Sung during journeys to Jerusalem.	Psalms 120–134
Repentance Psalms	Feeling sorry for one's sin.	Psalms 6, 32, 51, 130
Thanksgiving Psalms	Thanking God for His mercy and answers to prayer.	Psalms 18, 66, 107, 138
Wisdom Psalms	Giving wise counsel to the godly.	Psalms 1, 37, 49

4 **MESSAGE FROM THE KING:** The King says, "I have given you the psalms so that you can know how to pray and praise Me from the heart."

psalms form a group that focuses on praising the Lord, creating a doxology that concludes the book of Psalms. **Historical Psalms** (Psalms 105–106): these psalms remind Israel of God's might and His care for them (manifested through the keeping of His covenants with them) by briefly summarizing the key events of Old Testament history. The two psalms listed on the table are two examples of historical psalms. **Judgment psalms** (Psalms 35, 52, 55, 109): these psalms, also called "imprecatory psalms" ask God to bring judgment upon the wicked. Because they have a harsh tone, one might think that the psalmist (usually David) was acting sinfully in praying these prayers. Aren't we supposed to love our enemies? Understanding these psalms requires an understanding of the context in which they were written. When David prayed for judgment on the enemies who were seeking his life, he was praying for judgment on people who were God's enemies as well. These enemies were trying to destroy David, God's anointed king, and thus were attempting to thwart the purposes of God Almighty. David was not praying out of a bitter and unforgiving spirit. Rather, he was praying out of a love and concern that God's kingdom be preserved and advanced. **Messianic psalms** (Psalms 2, 22, 45, 72): these psalms describe a real historical occurrence while at the same time point in very specific ways to Jesus, the Messiah, who would come many years later. The psalms listed on the Memory Page are only a few of the Messianic psalms. **Passover psalms** (Psalms 113–118): these six psalms were sung as part of the annual Pass-

David Anointed as King

Upside down and backwards! Sometimes it seems that's the way God does things.
In Isaiah 55:8, the LORD says, "For My thoughts are not your thoughts, nor are
5 your ways My ways." Even when you don't understand what God is doing, He always
has a plan, and it's always good.

Saul was tall, handsome, and courageous, but he refused to obey God, the real King of Israel. Who would the LORD choose to be Israel's next king? God's choice surprised everyone.

The LORD asked Samuel, "How long will you be sad that I have rejected Saul?
6 Go to the family of Jesse, who lives in Bethlehem, and anoint one of his sons to be
the next king."

"What if Saul hears about this and tries to kill me?" asked Samuel, who was afraid of what Saul would do when he learned that Samuel had anointed a new king. The LORD responded, "Take a calf for a sacrifice. Invite Jesse to the sacrifice, and I will show you what to do next."

Jesse came to the sacrifice with seven sons. Samuel saw the oldest son, Eliab, and thought, "Look how tall he is. Certainly he must be the LORD's choice to be king." But the LORD said to Samuel, "He's not the man I've chosen. Don't look at his outward appearance. Look at his heart as I do."

One by one all of Jesse's sons stood before Samuel, and one by one the LORD said, "He's not the one." Finally, Samuel asked Jesse, "Are these all your sons?" Jesse replied, "My youngest son is in the fields, watching the sheep." Samuel said, "Go, get him right away."

In the hills surrounding Bethlehem, Jesse's youngest son, David, spent many days by himself caring for his father's sheep. His days were long, and often lonely, but he amused himself with two things: a sling and a lyre.

Watching sheep in the deserted hills could be dangerous. Wild animals roamed the hills looking for their next meal. David

over meal. They praise God by remembering Israel's exodus from Egypt. **Pilgrim psalms** (Psalms 120–134): these fifteen psalms, also called "songs of Ascents," were sung by Jewish families making their annual pilgrimage to Jerusalem to worship. Common themes in these psalms include worshipping God in the tabernacle and God's deliverance of His people from captivity or from their enemies. **Repentance psalms** (Psalms 6, 32, 52, 130): these psalms focus on the confession of sin and thankfulness for God's forgiveness. The two best-known repentance psalms are Psalm 32 and Psalm 51, songs composed by David after repenting of his sin with Bathsheba. The psalms on the Memory Page are only a few examples of this type of psalm. **Thanksgiving psalms** (Psalms 18, 66, 107, 138): these psalms are joyful expressions of gratitude to the LORD for all His blessings and mercies. A common theme in these psalms is the joy of answered prayer. **Wisdom psalms** (Psalms 1, 37, 49): these psalms provide counsel to the godly and warning to the ungodly. One well-known wisdom psalm is Psalm 1, which compares the godly man who is like a tree planted by the river to the ungodly man who is blown away like chaff by the wind. There are many other examples of wisdom psalms in Scripture. (*The Kingdom of God* by Francis Breisch, Jr., has three chapters describing the psalms in a simple, yet comprehensive way.)

4 Sometimes we don't have the right words to pray. The psalms can be an aid to our devotional life by aiding us in our prayers and our worship. Have you ever prayed through a psalm? Praying the psalms means using the actual words of the psalm to pray and, after each verse or two, applying the words to your own life. Also, you can encourage students to write their own psalm of praise, repentance, or thanksgiving.

5 God works in a mysterious way in our lives. Often it seems upsidedown and backwards, and we can't make any sense out of what we experience. The confidence we have from Scripture is that God does have a plan, and nothing is really out of control. Not only is God sovereign, but He is also good. He does only good things in our lives (see Romans 8:28-29).

6 God directed Samuel to go to Bethlehem to find the next king. Micah 5:2 predicted that the Savior, born from the line of David, would be born in Bethlehem. The decree from Caesar Augustus to take a census was the historical event orchestrated by God to move Mary and Joseph to Bethlehem so that this important prophecy could be fulfilled just as God decreed it to be. God told Samuel to anoint one of Jesse's sons to be the next king. Jesse was the son of Obed, who was the son of Boaz and Ruth, the Moabitess. (See *God's Great Covenant, Old Testament 1*, "The Story of Ruth," pp. 193-194, for more information.)

Notes:

7 The instrument that David played was a lyre (called a harp in the NKJV), a small rectangular or trapezoidal stringed instrument played with a pick similar to the way a guitar is played. David may not have used a pick, but may have plucked the strings instead. The lyre had a sweet, pleasing sound and was played in secular as well as sacred settings (Brand, p. 1161). During the lonely days in the fields, David practiced two things: shooting his slingshot and playing his lyre. Both of these would later play an important part in his life. With his slingshot, he would kill Goliath and become known to the Israelites as a brave warrior, and with his lyre he would soothe Saul's troubled spirit and thus gain access to Saul's palace and the important men in the kingdom. Time spent alone in the fields was not wasted as he practiced these two activities, which would later be used to bring God's purposes to pass in his own life and in God's kingdom.

8 People in Saul's court recognized that God's Spirit was present with David. This presence of God, more than any other of David's characteristics, was what prepared David for his role as king and opened the way for him to assume the throne at Saul's death.

9 Armorbearers went with military leaders into battle. Their job was to carry extra weapons, position shields for the commanders, and sometimes kill wounded enemy soldiers left behind on the battlefield (Brand, p. 116).

10 David's preparation to be king of Israel took about twenty years. During that time, he was a fugitive, fleeing the wrath of Saul and living as a hunted man. Even though he had opportunities to kill Saul and take over the throne that was rightfully his, he never did. He respected Saul as God's anointed king and trusted that in God's time, and in God's way, he would some day take his place as rightful king of Israel.

Brand, Chad and Trent C. Butler, Charles Draper, and Archie England, eds. *Holman Illustrated Bible Dictionary*. Nashville: Holman Bible Publishing, 2003.

spent hours practicing with his sling, ready to protect his sheep from preying animals.
Once he killed a bear, shooting it with his sling and then wrestling it until it died.
Another time he killed a lion the same way. During the
quiet hours he played his lyre, a small stringed musical
7 instrument, and sang praise songs that he wrote himself.
These songs are called psalms.

Jesus in the OT
How is David, the shepherd, like the Lord Jesus? How is Jesus, the Good Shepherd, greater than David?

When David, handsome and ruddy from his days in the sun, stood before Samuel, the LORD said, "He's the one. Anoint him." That day, the Spirit of the LORD came upon David to equip him with power for his role as king.

Meanwhile, God's Spirit had left Saul, and a distressing spirit from the LORD
troubled him. Saul's servants were concerned about him and suggested that Saul find
someone to play music to calm his spirit. One servant suggested that
Saul send for David. "This man is skilled at playing music, and
8 he's brave and handsome as well. Not only that,
but the LORD is with him." So Saul sent for
David to come to his palace.

9 Immediately, Saul liked David very much, and David
became one of Saul's armorbearers. From that time on,
whenever Saul became distressed, David would play soothing
music, and Saul would be refreshed.

David had been anointed to be the next king, but it wasn't time
for him to take over the throne yet. David had many things to learn
about trusting the LORD, and the LORD would bring much suffering into his
10 life. Yet in God's time, David would rule over Israel as a king who served the
LORD God as his King.

THE BOOK OF PSALMS

Right in the middle of the Bible is God's poetry book. Containing 150 chapters, Psalms is the biggest book of the Bible. The Hebrew title for Psalms is "Book of Praises." The hallelujah and thanksgiving psalms praise God for His greatness, His salvation, His Word, and His many blessings.

Even though Psalms is called the "Book of Praises," not all the chapters are songs of joy. The writers of Psalms expressed many different feelings and thoughts. Sometimes a writer was mournful because of his sin and begged for God's mercy and

Notes:

forgiveness. Other times a writer would be angry because of the wickedness he saw around him, and he would ask God to send judgment on those who hurt people and sinned against Him.

Some psalms were written for a specific purpose. The Israelites sang the pilgrim psalms as they walked to Jerusalem to worship. The Passover psalms were part of the annual Passover meal. Reading the historical psalms reminded Israel of all that their Lord had done for them in the past and that he had kept the covenants He made with them, His people. In the wisdom psalms, the psalmists gave wise counsel to those who were suffering or experiencing temptation. The Messianic psalms described present situations while at the same time pointed to Jesus, the Messiah.

Although David wrote more psalms than anyone else (seventy-three), other people (Moses, Asaph, Solomon, and the sons of Korah) also wrote some of the psalms. Many of the psalms do not tell you who wrote them.

Psalm 117, the shortest psalm, reminds us of God's faithfulness to the covenants He has made with His people. Psalm 119, the longest psalm, is a song of praise for God's Word. All but four verses (vs. 84, 121, 122, and 132) mention God's Word.

PSALMS WORD FIND

Find the words listed in the right column in this word find.

P	H	A	L	L	E	L	U	J	A	H
O	M	I	R	G	L	I	P	U	S	I
M	O	D	S	I	W	P	I	D	A	S
C	N	A	O	P	I	A	L	G	P	T
N	O	D	L	S	S	S	E	M	H	O
O	C	I	N	A	I	S	S	E	M	R
M	P	V	D	L	L	O	K	N	E	I
O	E	A	U	M	B	V	O	T	S	C
L	N	D	J	P	O	E	T	R	Y	A
O	V	E	R	K	O	R	A	H	A	L
S	R	E	P	E	N	T	A	N	C	E

Asaph
David
Hallelujah
Historical
Judgment
Korah
Messianic
Passover
Pilgrim
Poetry
Psalm
Repentance
Solomon
Wisdom

Jesus in the OT

David was anointed king, but it wasn't time for him to rule yet. How is this like the Lord Jesus' life?

Notes:

Review Worksheets

A. MEMORY VERSE: "For the Lord does not see as man sees; for man looks at the outward appearance, but the Lord looks at the heart." (1 Samuel 16:7b)

B. KEY FACTS:

What type of poetry are the verses below (repeated, contrasted, or continuing)?

"The young lions lack and suffer hunger; But those who seek the Lord shall not lack any good thing." (Psalm 34:10) — contrasted

"The Lord is high above all nations, His glory above the heavens." (Psalm 113:4) — repeated

"The Lord is my shepherd; I shall not want." (Psalm 23:1) — continuing

Match the type of psalm with its definition.

6	Psalm sung during the Passover meal	1. Hallelujah
4	Psalm asking God to judge the wicked	2. Wisdom
9	Psalm expressing sorrow over sin	3. Historical
1	Psalm giving praise to God	4. Judgment
8	Psalm sung on journeys to Jerusalem	5. Thanksgiving
7	Psalm talking about the Messiah	6. Passover
3	Psalm reminding Israel of what God did	7. Messianic
2	Psalm giving wise counsel	8. Pilgrim
5	Psalm thanking God for His mercy	9. Repentance

The Hebrew title for Psalms is …

B O O K   O F   P R A I S E S

C. STORY FACTS: Fill in the blanks.

1. With his sling David killed a lion and a bear.
2. God looks at the heart, not the outward appearance.
3. Samuel anointed David, Jesse's youngest son.
4. Psalm 119 is the longest psalm. It is a psalm of praise about God's Word.
5. When a distressing spirit troubled Saul, David played music to calm him.
6. In addition to David, these men wrote Psalms: Asaph, Moses, Solomon, and sons of Korah.
7. David and his family came from the town of Bethlehem.
8. The book of Psalms has a total of 150 psalms.

D. WHO AM I? Unscramble the names and then draw a line from the name to the description on the right.

SEJES	JESSE	I anointed David to be Israel's king.
VADDI	DAVID	I was Jesse's oldest son.
BEALI	ELIAB	I was the father of David.
MELUSA	SAMUEL	I was a shepherd who wrote psalms.

E. WHAT'S THE REASON? In God's time, how would David rule Israel? Write the answer below.

David would rule as a king who served the LORD as his king.

F. FIND OUT...

Psalm 119 gives nine words that mean God's Word. Can you find all nine?

Law, Statutes, Ways, Precepts

Decrees, Commands, Word, Promises, Judgments

Notes to Teachers and Parents:

1 There is a direct relationship between our trust in the LORD and God's faithfulness to us. God's faithfulness is not dependent upon our faith, because faithfulness is part of God's character. Yet, when we choose to trust Him, He gives us good success, as He did for David. It is by faith that we are able to trust the LORD. By His grace, He shows us our weakness and gives us the ability to respond in faith to Him. At the same time, trust is a response we make. At any point in time, we can choose to be afraid and not do what God calls us to do, or we can choose to believe that He will be with us and will give us success if we have faith in Him.

2 Being afraid, particularly being afraid of people who can hurt us in some way, is a common human response. We can be afraid for our physical safety. In today's world, the fear of physical harm is a reality that too many children face. We can also be afraid emotionally. Bullying, peer pressure, rejection, ridicule from friends or family, harshness from parents or other authority figures—these situations are a normal part of a child's life. The LORD's promise to us is that our physical and emotional safety is in His hands. Ultimately, our lives and our confidence rest in the LORD, who keeps His covenants with us, who loves us as His own children, and who delights in us (see Zephaniah 3:17, NIV) When our confidence is in the LORD, we can say, "What can man do to me?" As written in Proverbs 29:25, "The fear of man brings a snare, But whoever trusts in the LORD will be safe."

Notes:

Chapter 5

David in Saul's Court

LESSON SCOPE: 1 Samuel 17–20 **READ TO ME:** 1 Samuel 17–20

THEME: The LORD God is faithful to those who trust in Him.

MEMORY VERSE:
"In God I trust; I will not be afraid. What can mortal man do to me?" (Psalm 56:4b, NIV)

KEY FACTS:

The LORD's Faithfulness to David **1**

By faith, David trusted the LORD...	The LORD was faithful to David.
He stood up to the giant in the LORD's name.	David killed Goliath with one stone, and the women sang about David.
He did whatever Saul told him to do.	The LORD gave him success.
He obeyed Saul and went to battle against the Philistines.	The LORD gave him victory over his enemy. All Israel loved David.
He played music to soothe Saul.	The LORD protected him from Saul's jealousy.
He made a covenant of friendship with Jonathan.	Jonathan helped David escape Saul's anger.

MESSAGE FROM THE KING: The King says, "Do not be afraid."

Who are the giants in your life? The King reminds you that you don't have to be afraid because He is more powerful than those who are against you, and He is always with you. **2**

David in Saul's Court

The nine-foot giant was so tall that a man had to bend his head back and look up, up, up to see to the top of Goliath's bronze helmet. His threatening voice boomed out across the Valley of Elah, "I defy the army of Israel. Send out a man, and we will fight each other!"

By the time David arrived at the battlefield, bringing food supplies to his brothers, the giant had been making blasphemous threats against Israel and the LORD, day and night, for forty days. All of King Saul's army was terrified. When David heard Goliath's threats, he said, "Don't lose heart. I'll fight him. I killed a lion, and I killed a bear. This pagan Philistine will be like them because he has defied the armies of the living God."

King Saul dressed David in his armor and gave him his sword. But the armor was so heavy that David couldn't take a step. Instead, David chose five smooth stones from the stream and walked across the valley toward Goliath. David knew the LORD went with him. The giant scoffed when he saw this young lad accepting his challenge. Confidently, David said, "You come against me with sword and spear, but I come to you in the name of the LORD Almighty, whom you have defied." **3**

Step by step, Goliath thundered toward David. David picked a stone from his pouch and, placing the stone in his sling, he flung it at the giant.

Z-i-n-n-g! The stone zipped through the air and hit Goliath in the middle of his forehead, the only spot on his body not covered by armor. Seeing their hero lying dead on the ground, the Philistines fled in terror. With a victorious shout, the Israelite army pursued them. Meanwhile, David cut off Goliath's head and held it up for all to see.

After this, David stayed with Saul, and whatever Saul told him to do, he did successfully. Women all over Israel sang, "Saul has slain thousands, but David, tens of thousands." Their praise of David made Saul jealous. One day, the troubling spirit came upon Saul while David was playing his lyre for him. Saul lifted up his spear and, whoosh, he hurled

3 Saul's armor was much too large and heavy for David, but David's confidence was not in armor anyway. His confidence was not in his skill with the slingshot either, though he was very proficient with it. Rather, David's confidence was in the name of the LORD. Goliath had defied Israel's God and blasphemed His name. David was accepting Goliath's challenge to show both the Philistines and the Israelites the mighty power of Elohim, Israel's God.

Notes:

4 No matter what Saul did, God protected David. Saul tried to kill David by throwing a spear at him and by sending him into battle. In every situation, the LORD was with David and gave him success. Saul recognized that David had supernatural protection, his fear grew, and he became more and more determined to kill David.

5 Jonathan, as Saul's son, was the man who would naturally succeed Saul as king. Yet Jonathan accepted David's anointing to be the next king as God's will for his life as well as for David's. He and David made a covenant to be loyal friends, and God used Jonathan as a means to protect David from the capriciousness of Saul's wrath.

Notes:

it at David. Twice Saul threw the spear, and twice David dodged it. Now Saul was afraid of David, because he knew that the LORD was with him.

Saul appointed David to be an army commander and sent him out to battle the Philistines, hoping David would be killed. To Saul's dismay, David had more military successes than any other commander, and his name was well-spoken of throughout the land. Because Saul knew that the LORD was with David, he became more and
4 more afraid of him.

Saul had a son named Jonathan. He was a righteous man, and even though he knew David would someday take his place as king, he made a covenant
5 with David to be loyal friends. Jonathan warned David, "My father is trying to kill you. Go into hiding and be on guard."

Jonathan rebuked his father about his hatred of David, and Saul replied, "As the LORD lives, David will not be put to death." But Saul's promise didn't last long. A short time later after returning from another battle, David was once again playing music for Saul. Saul was fingering his spear when, in a fit of intense jealousy, Saul tried to pin David to the wall with his spear. David jumped sideways, and the spear sunk deep into the wall. David fled.

David's wife, Michal (she was Saul's daughter), said, "If you don't run for your life today, my father will kill you." Michal helped David escape. She put an idol in David's bed and covered it, making it appear that David was asleep. By the time Saul's soldiers realized that David was not at his house, David had safely run away.

David and Jonathan devised a plan. David would not attend the New Moon festival and would hide out in the field behind a large stone. If Saul got angry about David's absence from the festival, Jonathan would shoot three arrows beyond David's hiding place. If not, he would shoot the arrows to the side. The next day at the festival, Saul flared up in anger, and shouted, "David must die!" Jonathan followed through with the plan and warned David of Saul's intention to kill him. Then the two friends sadly parted.

David's troubles with Saul were not over yet, but through each difficulty and danger, the LORD would be faithful to David, who had put his trust in Him.

Review Worksheets

A. MEMORY VERSE: "In God I trust; I will not be afraid. What can mortal man do to me?" (Psalm 56:4b, NIV)

B. KEY FACTS: Answer the questions below.

What are two ways that David trusted in the LORD?

1. He stood up to the giant Goliath in the LORD's name.
2. He played music for Saul even after Saul had thrown a spear at him.

What are two ways that the LORD was faithful to David?

1. He gave David victory over the enemies of Israel.
2. He protected David from Saul's jealousy.

C. STORY FACTS: Circle "T" if the sentence is true and "F" if the sentence is false.

1. David went to the battlefield to take food to his brothers. (T) F
2. David was angry because Goliath insulted King Saul. T (F)
3. Goliath threatened the Israelite army for twenty days and nights. T (F)
4. David was confident because he had great skill with a sling. T (F)
5. Whatever Saul told him to do, David did successfully. (T) F
6. Saul sent David into battle so that David would be killed. (T) F
7. Saul threw a spear at David because David married his daughter. T (F)
8. David chose ten stones from the stream for his sling. T (F)
9. Women sang, "David has slain tens of thousands." (T) F

The LORD was faithful to David, who had put his T R U S T I N G O D.

Notes:

D. DO YOU KNOW THE ANSWERS? Complete the crossword puzzle.

Across:

1. The Philistine giant was named ________. **GOLIATH**
6. David's wife was named ________. **MICHAL**
7. The Philistine giant was ________ feet tall. **NINE**
11. Saul was afraid because the ________ was with David. **LORD**

Down:

2. Saul's son was named ________. **JONATHAN**
3. Jonathan knew he would never be ________. **KING**
4. David put his ________ in the LORD. **TRUST**
5. David killed a bear and a ________. **LION**
8. Michal put an ________ in David's bed. **IDOL**
9. David met Goliath in the Valley of ________. **ELAH**
10. Jonathan shot three ________ to tell David that Saul wanted to kill him. **ARROWS**

E. WHO SAID IT? Draw a line from the quote to the person who said it.

Saul David Goliath Jonathan

- I come in the name of the LORD. — David
- As the LORD lives, David will not be put to death. — Saul
- My father is trying to kill you. — Jonathan
- Send out a man and we will fight each other. — Goliath

F. FIND OUT...

In Proverbs 3:5-6, King Solomon wrote about trusting in the LORD. What did he say about how you should trust in the LORD?

Trust in the LORD with all your heart.

What will happen when you trust the LORD?

He will direct your paths.

Chapter 6

David—The Fugitive

LESSON SCOPE: 1 Samuel 21–31
1 Chronicles 10

READ TO ME: 1 Samuel 24, 26, 30

THEME: The Lord God's plan for His kingdom is right, just, and good.

MEMORY VERSE:

"For the word of the Lord is right, And all His work is done in truth. He loves righteousness and justice; The earth is full of the goodness of the Lord." (Psalm 33:4-5)

KEY FACTS:

David's Pictures of God 1

These are some of the word pictures that David used to describe God.

Picture	Verse	Description
Fortress	Psalm 62:2	He is a strong, safe place in trouble.
King	Psalm 5:2	He has power and controls everything that happens in the world.
Light	Psalm 27:1	He shows His people the right thing to do.
Rock	Psalm 28:1	He is unchangeable and unmovable.
Shepherd	Psalm 23:1	He perfectly cares for all His people.
Shield	Psalm 3:3	He protects His people from their enemies.
Strength	Psalm 18:2	He strengthens His people when they are weak.

THINGS TO REMEMBER:

Medium = Person who talks to the spirits of people who have died.

MESSAGE FROM THE KING: The King's plan is always right and good.

Sometimes God's plan doesn't make sense to us. Sometimes people ask, "What is God doing?" Remember, even if God's plan seems confusing,
2 everything He does is good, because He is good.

Notes to Teachers and Parents:

1 David and the other psalmists used many metaphors or pictures to describe what God was like. The word pictures in the Key Facts table are just some of the metaphors used throughout the book of Psalms. Take some time to think through these pictures with your students. One way to do this is with a three-step process: 1) Choose a word picture and describe all the characteristics of it. Example: a large rock is hard to move, doesn't change from day to day, is something to lean against for support, can be seen from a distance, and can act as a landmark for directions, etc. 2) Meditate on the nature of God and how His spiritual nature is similar to the physical characteristics of the picture. Example: God never changes, what He says remains steady and firm forever, He is a support for us in trouble, and His Word provides direction for our lives. 3) Use a picture of the object as an aid to make the metaphor more understandable. Example: find a picture of a large rock in the western deserts or plains of the United States and talk about how this rock that we can see and visit today is the same rock that pioneers saw 200 years ago when traveling west. As you read through Psalms, look for additional metaphors for God. The Find Out… section in this chapter gives an opportunity for your students to discover additional metaphors (see p. 45).

2 The goodness of God is one of the most important truths in Scripture. Being convinced of God's goodness helps us trust God when life is confusing and God's will is unclear. We don't always know why the Lord is doing what He's doing, but we can always be certain that God is good and that He does only good things in our lives. When faced with difficult circumstances that cause us to doubt God's love, we must believe what the written Scripture says, not what our feelings tell us. The Lord does not always tell us why things happen to us, but He does want us to turn to Him and trust Him even when we don't have all the answers.

Notes:

David—The Fugitive

This wasn't the way a king was supposed to live—running for his life, living in caves, scrounging for enough food to feed himself and his small band of men. David had been anointed king, but his life was more like that of a common bandit than a king. What was the LORD doing?

David left Saul's court and fled to Nob, the town of priests. (The tabernacle had
3 been at Nob ever since the Philistines stole the ark many years earlier.) David begged
Ahimelech, the priest, to give him some food. The only food Ahimelech had was the
bread from the tabernacle, so he gave five loaves of consecrated bread to David and
4 his men. Ahimelech also gave David Goliath's sword, which had been safely kept
in Nob since David had killed the giant. As David left, he saw Doeg the Edomite,
Saul's head shepherd, watching him. That could mean only trouble!

David went to Gath in Philistia, but, fearing for his safety, he pretended to be
5 insane and escaped from the city to the hillside caves of Adullam. All who were
distressed, in debt, or discontented went to David, and he became the leader of a
little army of 400 men.

Meanwhile, Doeg was ready to cause trouble. He told Saul that Ahimelech
and the priests at Nob had helped David. Saul sent for Ahimelech, and said to
him, "How dare you give David food and a sword! Because you have aided this
rebel, you and your family will die!" Saul ordered his guards and Doeg to kill all
6 eighty-five priests in Nob along with all their women, children, and animals. Only
Abiathar, son of Ahimelech, escaped. He fled to David's camp and became one of
his men. David was grieved because he felt responsible for the massacre at Nob.

David continued to move from place to place. He protected the city of Keilah from the Philistines, but soon after, that city became unsafe. David and his band of men, which had grown in number to 600, hid in rocky strongholds in the desert and in the hills in the Desert of Ziph. Saul pursued David relentlessly, but God prevented Saul from discovering David's hiding places. In the Wilderness of Maon, Saul abruptly called off his search to fight the Philistines who were raiding Israel's countryside.

Once, David and his men were hiding deep within a cave when Saul and his soldiers entered the cave. David crept stealthily to the front of the cave and cut off a corner of Saul's robe. As Saul left the cave, David came out, and said to him, "Why do you listen to the men who say I want to kill you?" David showed Saul the piece of robe, and continued, "Look! I could have killed you, but I spared your life."

3 In 1 Samuel 1:24-28, Hannah brought Samuel to the tabernacle at Shiloh to be dedicated to the LORD. In 1 Samuel 4, the priests took the ark from Shiloh to the battlefield, and it was captured by the Philistines. Either at this time or sometime soon after, the Philistines destroyed Shiloh (see Jeremiah 7:12-14). When the ark returned to Israel on the new cart pulled by two mother cows (see 1 Samuel 6:7-13), the ark stayed at Kirjath Jearim in the house of Abinadab. In 1 Samuel 21, we learn that Nob was the town of priests where the tabernacle was located. Sometime between the events recorded in 1 Samuel 4 and those recorded in 1 Samuel 21, the center of worship moved from Shiloh to Nob.

4 The consecrated bread was the bread from the table of showbread in the holy place of the tabernacle. This bread was also called the "bread of the Presence" (Exodus 25:30, NIV). Jesus mentioned this event in Matthew 12:1-14 when discussing the Sabbath with the Pharisees. Jesus' point in this discussion was that we must not have an inflexible, legalistic interpretation of the Sabbath, but rather understand the intention of the Lawgiver behind the Sabbath rules. The purpose of the Sabbath was for mankind to worship God and develop a closer relationship with Him, not simply to exercise arbitrary worship practices. Giving David and his men bread from the tabernacle was an act of mercy by Ahimelech. There is no indication in Scripture that the LORD was displeased with Ahimelech's action, and Jesus' discussion with the Pharisees in Matthew 12 seems to confirm this.

5 David thought he could escape to Gath in Philistia with the sword of Goliath and be safe. He was wrong. He was recognized as the "king of the land" and as the one who had killed "his tens of thousands" (1 Samuel 21:11 NIV). (Isn't it interesting that the Philistines were identifying David as king when he would not be recognized and established as king of Israel by the Israelites until after the death of Saul many years later?) When David realized that Achish, king of Gath, knew who he was, he knew he was in danger. He feigned insanity in order to escape and then found refuge in the cave of Adullam.

6 Killing all the priests at Nob, including all their family members, shows the extent of Saul's fear and jealousy of David and the extremes to which he would go to kill David and preserve his throne. Murdering the anointed priests of the LORD shows the depth of Saul's spiritual darkness. Compare Saul's actions to David's actions. David refused to kill Saul, the LORD's anointed king, even when Saul was actively trying to destroy David.

Notes: ____________________

Memory Page · **Story Time** · Worksheets · Quiz

Another time, David and Abishai crept into Saul's camp at night. While Saul slept, David stole his spear and water jug, but he refused to kill Saul, even though Abishai told him to do so. David sneaked back to his own camp, and then yelled to Saul, "Why are you still pursuing me? What have I done wrong? Once again I could have killed you, but I didn't."

Both times, Saul admitted his sin of chasing after David, but Saul's sorrow was not from the heart. He continued his evil plan to kill David. **7** Why didn't David kill Saul when he had the opportunity? David's response was the same each time: "God forbid that I should kill the Lord's anointed." David knew that the Lord had a plan, and even though the plan wasn't clear to David, he wasn't going to rush God's timing by killing Saul. He knew that God's plan was right and good. He just had to wait patiently. **8**

While Saul was still pursuing David, Samuel the prophet died, and all Israel mourned for him. Around that time, the Philistines gathered together to make war on Israel once again. Saul was terrified, and when the Lord didn't answer his cries for help, he became even more terrified. Saul then did something strictly forbidden by God. He disguised himself and went to the medium at Endor. **9**

> **Jesus in the OT**
> Rejected, homeless, hated by authorities—there are so many ways in which David's life as a fugitive was like Jesus' life.

At Saul's request, the medium called up the spirit of Samuel to talk with Saul. Samuel gave Saul the worst possible prophecy: God would give the kingdom to David, Saul's enemy, and Saul and his sons would die in the battle with the Philistines. **10** The next day, the battle was fierce. The Philistines killed three of Saul's sons, including Jonathan. Then an archer shot an arrow and critically wounded Saul. In fear and despair, Saul asked his armorbearer to kill him, but the man refused. So Saul took his own sword, fell on it, and died. **11**

Thus ended the reign of Saul, and thus began the reign of David, who had waited patiently for the LORD's will to happen.

Chapter 6: David—The Fugitive 43

7 Saul's momentary regret was not true repentance from the heart. If he had been repentant, he would not have continued his pursuit of David. David knew that Saul's words of sorrow were not genuine. When Saul invited David to come back and promised not to harm him again in 1 Samuel 26:21, David refused and went a different way.

8 David was committed to honoring Saul as the LORD's anointed king. He was even conscience stricken about cutting off a piece of Saul's robe. He refused to harm Saul in any way, and required that his band of men also respect Saul's position.

9 At this time of impending battle, Saul was in a predicament. The LORD was not hearing and answering his prayers. He had ordered the killing of all the priests at Nob who could have been spiritual advisors to him. Samuel was dead. Saul had no one to whom he could turn. He decided to get spiritual advice from Samuel through the help of a medium, even though he had earlier expelled all the mediums (witches) from the land.

10 There are several views of what happened. Some say Saul simply saw a vision. Some say the woman deceived Saul. A third view is that Samuel actually appeared. Because the woman was afraid, the view that Samuel appeared in person is a reasonable interpretation. Even though God, in the Mosaic Law, had forbidden the practice of talking to the dead (see Leviticus 19:31; Deuteronomy 18:9-13), this third view holds that, for some reason, the LORD apparently allowed Samuel to appear and give this important prophecy to Saul. After hearing Samuel's dire prophecy, Saul was so filled with fear that he had no strength left and refused to eat or drink anything until urged by the medium and his men to do so.

11 Once again, Saul refused to trust in the LORD's providence. Being wounded, he was afraid of being captured by the enemy and tortured. When his armorbearer refused to kill him, Saul took his own life. Even in death he was determined to do things his own way.

Notes:

Notes:

Review Worksheets

A. MEMORY VERSES: "For the word of the LORD is __right__, And all His work is done in __truth__. He loves __righteousness__ and __justice__; The earth is full of the __goodness__ of the LORD." (Psalm 33:4-5)

B. KEY FACTS: Using the information on the **Memory Page**, draw a line from the phrase on the left to the matching description of God.

David's Names for God

1. When you feel weak and helpless…	God is your Shield.
2. When you're confused and don't know what to do…	God is your King.
3. When you need a safe place from danger…	God is your Fortress.
4. When everything around you is changing…	God is your Shepherd.
5. When you need tender care and comfort…	God is your Light.
6. When enemies are attacking you…	God is your Rock.
7. When you need to know that someone is in charge of the world…	God is your Strength.

C. STORY FACTS: Fill in the blanks.

1. Ahimelech gave David consecrated bread from the __tabernacle__.
2. __Doeg__ told Saul that Ahimelech had helped David.
3. David stole Saul's __spear__ and __water__ __jug__ while he slept.
4. David knew that the LORD's plan was __right__ and __good__.
5. Saul sinned by going to a __medium__ in Endor for advice.
6. Saul's armorbearer refused to __kill__ Saul.

D. WHAT HAPPENED HERE? Unscramble the words on the left and then draw a line from the word to its description.

BON	NOB	A dangerous city for David and his men
PHIZ	ZIPH	Where David pretended to be insane
THAG	GATH	City where eighty-five priests were killed
HAKLIE	KEILAH	Hills where David and his men hid

E. WHAT HAPPENED NEXT? Put the story boxes in order.

6	Saul was killed in battle with the Philistines.	2	David hid in caves, and Saul pursued him.	4	Samuel died, and all Israel mourned.
1	David fled to Nob and got bread from the tabernacle.	3	David had a chance to kill Saul, but he didn't.	5	Saul visited a medium to get advice.

F. WHY DIDN'T DAVID KILL SAUL?

Circle every other letter below to find the answer. (Start with the second letter.)

A S T A C U S L A W M A T S Y G B O R D V S Z A S N K O N I Y N O T D E F D

S A U L W A S G O D'S A N O I N T E D.

G. FIND OUT...

The Bible gives you many pictures of what the Lord is like. Find some other pictures of God in the verses below. Using the **key facts** table as an example, write your own description of one of the word pictures you find in these verses.

Psalm 18:1-2 Rock, Fortress, Deliverer, Shield, Horn, Stronghold

Psalm 46:1 Refuge Strength

Description:

Deliverer: One who rescues a person from an enemy 12

12 Other answers include:

Strength: The energy or force within us that enables us to do what formerly seemed much too hard to do
Rock: Something solid, immovable, and stable
Refuge: A safe place to which we flee for protection
Fortress: A safe place in which we can hide and be safe from attack
Stronghold: A natural fortification to which we can run when we need protection
Shield: A strong defensive weapon used to protect
Horn: Animal sacrifices were tied to the horns of the altar to secure them. God is the horn of our salvation.

Notes:

Notes:

Chapter 7 Looking Backwards...Looking Ahead

LESSON SCOPE: 1 Samuel 1-31 **READ TO ME:** Psalm 21
Psalms, 1 Chronicles 10

"Who's in charge here? Who's the boss?"

Were you ever in a situation in which everyone was running around doing his own thing, and the result was that nothing got done and everyone was unhappy? That's what was happening in Israel when God's story opened in 1 Samuel. There was no king in Israel, and everyone was doing what he or she thought was right. Actually, God was the King, but nobody was listening to Him!

In Unit I you learned that the Israelites had forgotten who they were—God's people! The LORD had made a covenant with them at Mt. Sinai and had promised to be their God. They, in turn, had promised to worship Him.

The Israelites hadn't totally forgotten about the LORD, but they didn't love Him from their hearts. They thought the ark was a magic box that would give them success in battle. They only prayed to Him when they were in trouble or were afraid. But the LORD wanted more from His people than outward worship; He wanted them to worship and obey Him out of love.

Because they asked, Israel got their king, but Saul wouldn't let the LORD be his King. Saul died in disgrace on the battlefield. In Unit II, you will learn how the next king, David, took his rightful place on the throne. The LORD renewed the covenant with David and promised to bless David if he loved and honored Him. During the reign of David and of David's son, Solomon, the LORD did bless the kingdom of Israel, and it became a kingdom of power and wealth.

IMPORTANT THINGS TO KNOW:

Word	Meaning of the Word
Anoint	Chosen by God and equipped by God's Spirit to serve the LORD in a particular job.
Priest	Man in charge of offering sacrifices and offerings in the tabernacle.
Holy	Means "set apart by God" or "living in a way that pleases God."
Covenant	God's promise to be the God of His people forever.
Medium	Person who talks to the spirits of people who have died.
Prophet	Person called to speak for God.
Psalms	"Book of Praises."

The BOSS

Review Worksheets

A. MEMORY VERSE REVIEW—VERSE SCRAMBLE: Put the words in the boxes in the right order and then write the memory verse phrase on the line beside the boxes.

1. Behold, to obey is better than sacrifice, And to heed than the fat of rams.
(1 Samuel 15:22b)

obey Behold fat
than sacrifice better
to to than rams
heed of is And the

2. In God I trust; I will not be afraid. What can mortal man do to me?
(Psalm 56:4b, NIV)

afraid God I be
man trust What
me In to will I
not can do mortal

3. In those days there was no king in Israel; everyone did what was right in his own eyes.
(Judges 21:25)

everyone days what
in Israel king no
In his eyes right
own those in was
was there did

B. MEMORY VERSE REVIEW—FILL IN THE BLANK: Answer the questions below using your memory verses.

1. What are two things that God says about Himself in Isaiah 46:9?

I am God, and there is no other. I am God, and there is none like me.

2. The Lord does not see as man sees. How does He see differently?

"Man looks at the outward appearance, but the Lord looks at the heart." (1 Samuel 16:7b)

3. According to Psalm 33:4-5, what does the Lord love?

righteousness and justice

Notes:

C. WHAT WAS THE THEME OF UNIT I? Answer the questions in the blanks beside them. Then take the first letter of each answer to complete the phrase below.

A G A G Who was the king that Saul didn't kill?

N I N E How many feet tall was the giant Goliath?

O B E D I E N C E What is better than sacrifice?

I C H A B O D What name means "the glory [of the Lord] has departed from Israel"?

N O B In what town were eighty-five priests killed?

T U M O R S What plague did God send on the Philistines?

S H I L O H In what town did Eli serve in the tabernacle?

The theme for Unit I

The God who A N O I N T S.

D. WHERE DID THE ARK GO ON ITS JOURNEY? Follow the ark of the covenant from the tabernacle at Shiloh back to Israel.

Shiloh
Tabernacle
Ekron Plagues
Gath Plagues
Battle with Philistines
Cart with Cows
Temple of Dagon
Abinadab's house
Israel

E. WHAT DO YOU REMEMBER ABOUT THE TYPES OF PSALMS?

Match the type of psalm to its definition.

5 Hallelujah	1. Psalm sung during the Passover
6 Historical	2. Psalm thanking God for His mercy and answers to prayer
9 Judgment	3. Psalm sung on journeys to Jerusalem
7 Messianic	4. Psalm giving good counsel
1 Passover	5. Psalm praising God
3 Pilgrim	6. Psalm reminding Israel of who God is
8 Repentance	7. Psalm talking about the Messiah
2 Thanksgiving	8. Psalm expressing sorrow over sin
4 Wisdom	9. Psalm asking God to judge the wicked

What are the three types of Hebrew poetry?

Repeated Contrasted Continuing

F. WHAT'S THE REASON? Circle the **correct** answer.

1. Samuel set up the Ebenezer stone so that Israel would ___________.
   (remember that God had helped them) have victory in battle
2. The LORD rejected Saul as king because Saul didn't ___________.
   pray for the people (obey God as supreme King)
3. The Israelites wanted a king so that they could ___________.
   (be like other nations) worship the LORD better
4. David refused to kill Saul when he found him in the cave because ___________.
   Saul was his friend (Saul was God's anointed)
5. The LORD gave David protection and good success because ___________.
   (by faith David trusted God) David was a kind person
6. David killed the Philistine giant because Goliath had ___________.
   killed many Israelites (defied the LORD)

Notes:

G. WHAT THINGS GO TOGETHER?

Draw a line from the word on the left to the word on the right that describe it.

Covenant	Man who offered sacrifices
Prophet	Loyal friend of David
Ebenezer	Weapon used to kill a giant
Psalms	Priest at the tabernacle in Shiloh
Spear	God's promise to His people
Gath	Means "Book of Praises"
Sling	Weapon stolen from King Saul
Samuel	Person called to speak for God
Jonathan	Means "thus far has the LORD helped us"
Eli	Town where God sent a plague
Priest	Last judge in Israel

UNIT II

The Glorious Kingdom...The God Who Blesses

Theme: The Keeper of the Kingdom brings blessing to His people.

Shalom. It's I, Tobias, again. Oh, what a busy man I've been, trying to record with utmost accuracy all of David's many adventures in and out of caves. Isn't the LORD amazing, keeping David safe from King Saul's wicked schemes? Now Saul is dead, and David will take his place as king over all of Israel.

But wait, it isn't quite that simple, my friends. For years David had trusted the LORD by faith, believing in God's promises and waiting patiently as the LORD worked out His plan. David's waiting wasn't done yet. But although it didn't happen all at once, and it didn't happen quickly, eventually David did indeed become the king of Israel. **1**

The years of David's reign and, later, the reign of Solomon, were good years. In so many ways the LORD blessed Israel. David's military successes over the Moabites, Edomites, and other neighboring nations expanded Israel's territory in every direction. Israel became prosperous, and Solomon's palace and temple became known far and wide for its glorious splendor. The LORD blessed David with mercy and forgiveness when he sinned greatly, and He gave Solomon the wisdom that made him the wisest man who ever lived.

Yet greater than all these things was the blessing of the covenant. Through the prophet Nathan the LORD renewed the covenant with David. The covenantal blessings—a son, a land, and a great name—had a familiar sound. This is what the LORD had promised to Abraham. The covenant to David, however, had one big difference: the
2 LORD promised to establish David's kingship forever!

David knew that there was a King greater than he was, a King who demanded to be worshipped exclusively and obeyed completely. This greater King promised David, "I will be your God. I will be with you, bless you, and make your kingdom
3 great."

Covenant and kingship linked together—this was the LORD's plan for His people. Now let's see what the glorious kingdom looked like.

51

Notes to Teachers and Parents:

1 David did not automatically become the king of all Israel at the death of Saul. For seven-and a-half years, Ishbosheth, Saul's son, ruled the northern tribes. The LORD required that David be patient and submit to His timing. Over the course of his short reign, Ishbosheth's influence among the northern tribes had decreased so much that after his assassination, the northern tribes welcomed David as their king. (Ishbosheth was murdered by two men from the tribe of Benjamin, Baanah and Rechab. They sneaked into Ishbosheth's house in the middle of the day while he was sleeping, stabbed him in the stomach, beheaded him, and slipped away. They took his head to David, thinking that David would reward them for eliminating his rival. David was furious that these men had killed an innocent man. Their "reward" for killing Ishbosheth was execution.)

2 The Davidic covenant was not a new covenant; it was a renewal and expansion of the covenant given to Abraham and later to Moses. The LORD promised David the same blessings that He had promised to Abraham: a son, a land, and a great name that blessed many nations. The covenant to David expanded upon the Abrahamic covenant to include the promise of an eternal kingdom coming from David's line. The king of this eternal kingdom was, of course, the Messiah, Jesus Christ, son of David, and Savior of the world. Chapter 8 will explain the nature of the Davidic covenant in greater detail.

3 Unlike Saul, David was a theocratic king. David recognized that his power and authority as king came to him from God and that he was ruling God's people as God's servant. As mentioned in Unit I, it was not the fact that Israel desired a king that displeased the LORD. Rather, it was having a king in Israel who refused to acknowledge the Kingship of the LORD and who had no respect for the covenantal relationship between God and His people. Through David, the covenant promise ("I will be your God, and you will be My people") was linked together with the establishment of the earthly kingdom. The kingdom became the structure through which the LORD could fulfill His covenant promise.

Notes:

4 The story of David's sin with Bathsheba is presented in chapter 9.

5 All sin comes from allowing our desires or fears to rule our hearts. Our desires and fears become the idols of our hearts, replacing our worship of the LORD. The result is sinful behavior. That's why all sin is primarily and ultimately sin against God.

6 Scripture is clear that every person is born with a sinful nature and that this sinful nature causes us to sin. We never have to be taught to lie, hate, or act selfishly. All sin arises from a heart that is naturally inclined to resist God and seek its own way.

7 The only hope we have is that, by God's grace, He will forgive us in His lovingkindness and tender mercy when we confess our sin with a repentant heart. It is this hope that moves us from despair to joy because the LORD will never despise "a broken and a contrite heart" (Psalm 51:17).

Notes:

PSALM 51:1–6 A Psalm of David

1. Have mercy upon me, O God,
According to Your lovingkindness;
According to the multitude of Your tender mercies,
Blot out my transgressions.
2. Wash me thoroughly from my iniquity,
And cleanse me from my sin.
3. For I acknowledge my transgressions,
And my sin is always before me.
4. Against You, You only, have I sinned,
And done this evil in Your sight—
That You may be found just when You speak,
And blameless when You judge.
5. Behold, I was brought forth in iniquity,
And in sin my mother conceived me.
6. Behold, You desire truth in the inward parts,
And in the hidden part You will make me to know wisdom.

"Have mercy on me!" That was the cry from David's heart.

David had sinned greatly. A man was dead, and many people were suffering because of David's selfishness and greed. Not until Nathan, the prophet, confronted David with God's
4 truth did David take responsibility for his sin and repent from his heart. Psalm 51 is what David said to the LORD in repentance.

Psalm 51 teaches you two truths about sin. The first truth is that all sin is against the LORD. When you steal candy from a drugstore or tell lies about your friend, you are sinning against a person. At the same time, you are also sinning against God. Whenever you sin, you
5 are actually saying, "What I want to do is more important to me than doing what God wants me to do."

The second truth taught in Psalm 51 about sin is that sinning is as natural as breathing. We sin against God because we were born with a sinful nature. It's only by God's grace that
6 anyone can be holy and please Him.

7 Just like David, you can ask for God's mercy when you sin. And, because of the tender mercies of the LORD, you, too, can be forgiven.

Memory Page · Story Time · Worksheets · Quiz

Chapter 8
The Covenant with David

LESSON SCOPE: 2 Samuel 1–7
1 Chronicles 11–17

READ TO ME: 2 Samuel 2, 5–7

THEME: The LORD God remembers His promises and renews His covenant.

MEMORY VERSE:

"I have made a covenant with My chosen, I have sworn to My servant David: 'Your seed I will establish forever, And build up your throne to all generations.'" (Psalm 89:3-4)

KEY FACTS:

God's Covenant with David: 2 Samuel 7 **1**

David's covenant was like the covenant with Abraham because…	
God Promised:	A son to succeed David on the throne of Israel (7:12).
	A land that was peaceful (7:10-11).
	A great name among the men of the earth (7:9).
	The blessing of God's love and presence (7:9,15).
David's covenant was greater than the covenant with Abraham because…	
God Promised:	That David would be the first in a line of kings (7:12).
	That David's son would build God a temple (7:13).
	That David's son would rule after him (7:12b).
	That David's kingdom would endure forever (7:16).
	That the Messiah would be born from David's line (7:16).
The everlasting kingdom is the kingdom of Jesus Christ.	

MESSAGE FROM THE KING:

The King says, "I will never stop loving you."

2 Just as He promised to love David, the LORD promises to always love you. Every day this week, write down one way that the LORD shows His love to you. You'll be surprised by what you learn.

Chapter 8: The Covenant with David 53

Notes to Teachers and Parents:

1 The covenant made with David was not a new covenant. The Davidic covenant was a continuation of the covenant with Abraham and with Moses. It was initiated by God and contained promises that the LORD committed Himself to fulfill. The LORD promised David a son to sit on the throne, a land that had peace with its enemies, a name that would be great among the nations, and the blessing of God's presence and love. Not only was the Davidic covenant like the Abrahamic covenant, but it also showed the fulfillment of the promises that the LORD had made to Abraham. Abraham had a son, Isaac, who had a son, Jacob, whose twelve sons had become the nation of Israel. Israel now had its own land with a unified government under a godly king. Abraham's name was revered by the Israelites, and the blessing of God's love had continued with Israel through the centuries. With the Davidic covenant, the LORD established the kingdom in Israel through David's line, a dynasty from which the Messiah would come. The Messiah would establish the everlasting kingdom that would eventually include people from every tribe and nation in the world. The LORD called David to faithfulness, but only the LORD was completely faithful. Everything the LORD had promised happened just as He said it would.

2 If we pay attention, we can see manifestations of God's love for us every day. Examples may be dramatic answers to prayer or simple revelations of God's tender care. Discuss with the students specific ways in which God has shown love to them. If we look for examples every day, we will become more attuned to how God continues to love us as our Heavenly Father.

Notes:

3 Once again, we see that David waited on the LORD. David did not demand that he become king immediately. After some time had passed, David asked for the LORD's direction, and the Lord told him to go to Hebron. For seven-and-a-half years, David was king only in Judah, and he didn't attempt any self-motivated action that would gain him the rest of the kingdom ahead of God's timing.

4 Ishbosheth was king over the eleven tribes for two years (see 2 Samuel 2:10). That means that David was king in Judah for about five-and-a-half years before Ishbosheth became king over the other tribes.

5 Ishbosheth accused Abner of sleeping with one of his father's concubines (see 2 Samuel 3:7). This false accusation so enraged Abner that he turned against Ishbosheth and began negotiations with David. Abner's own words tell us that he knew all along that David was God's choice to be king of Israel and that he had acted against God's will in helping Ishbosheth to become king over the eleven tribes.

6 Ishbosheth knew that Abner had great influence and power. Ishbosheth knew that if Abner made a threat against him, Abner was able to carry it through. That's why Ishbosheth was afraid of Abner.

7 Once again, David demonstrated his unwillingness to condone human actions that violated the moral law of God. Even though Ishbosheth's death made it possible for David to be king over all of Israel, David disapproved of this murder. David responded by ordering the execution of the men who murdered Ishbosheth.

8 David was king for a total of forty years.

Notes:

The Covenant with David

How does an anointed king become the ruling king? Do you say, "Here I am! I'm your new king!"? Do you wait until the people ask you to be king? This was David's dilemma. He was the anointed king, but he wasn't sitting on the throne
3 yet. David waited for the LORD's time, and then the LORD said, "Go to Hebron." So David did, and the men anointed him king over Judah.

4 Meanwhile, Abner, commander of Saul's army, made Ishbosheth, Saul's son, the king over all Israel except Judah. Soon a civil war broke out. The Israelites in Judah, led by Joab, fought against all the other Israelites led by Abner. God's people were fighting against each other. How sad it was!

One day, at the end of the day's fierce fighting, Asahel, Joab's brother, took off after Abner, determined to chase him down and kill him. Abner repeatedly asked Asahel to stop chasing him. Asahel, swift as a wild gazelle, wouldn't give up. Finally, Abner stopped running and speared Asahel right through the stomach. Asahel died in the hills of Gibeon.

Then Abner had a quarrel with Ishbosheth and turned against him. "May God
5 deal with me severely," Abner threatened, "if I don't try to make David king over all Israel." Ishbosheth was now afraid of Abner. **6**

Joab, still angry because Abner had killed his brother Asahel, didn't trust Abner. Joab pretended to talk with Abner, but then killed him because Abner had killed Asahel. David rebuked Joab for killing Abner, and David and his people mourned Abner's death. Not long after, two men crept into Ishbosheth's house while he was sleeping, killed him, and brought his head to David. Although these murders made it possible for David to be king over all Israel, David was angry about the deaths. He didn't want
7 other men murdered so that he could be king. David executed the men who killed Ishbosheth. David was thirty years old when he was crowned king. He reigned for seven- **8**
and-a-half years in Hebron and for thirty-three years over all Israel.

Now that he was king, David did three important things. First, he established a capital city. Hebron was too far south to unite the nation as one people, so he moved the capital to Jerusalem. Jerusalem was the perfect choice because it was a

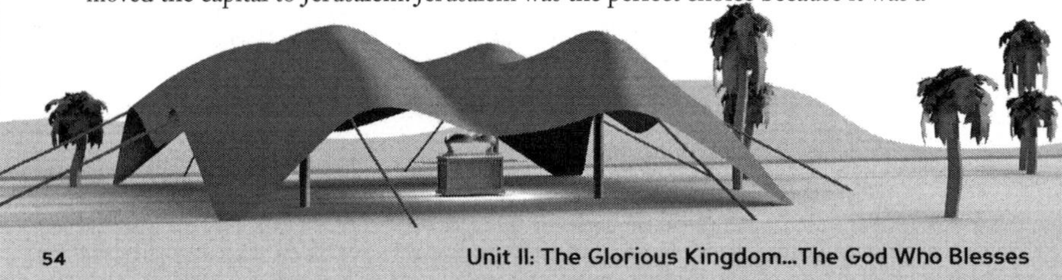

Notes:

well-fortified city built on a hill more centrally located in Israel. The only problem was that the Jebusites still lived there. But, David conquered this seemingly unconquerable city easily because the LORD God Almighty was with him.

Jesus in the OT
Jesus Christ is the fulfillment of God's covenant promises to David. He is the Son of David who rules forever and whose kingdom will never fail.

Second, David conquered the Philistines who had been continually attacking Israel for many years. Third, David sent for the ark of the covenant to be
9 brought from Abinadab's house, where it had sat for twenty years. The men put the ark on a new cart with Abinadab's sons, Uzzah and Ahio, to guide it. The people danced in front of it, singing songs and playing lyres, tambourines, and cymbals. Along the way, the oxen stumbled, and Uzzah reached out to steady the ark. Instantly, the LORD struck him down, and he died. All celebration stopped, and David put the ark in Obed-Edom's house.

Why did God kill Uzzah? The ark was holy to the LORD, and David had not followed the LORD's instructions on moving the ark. Three months later, David tried again, this time following God's rules. The Levites carried the ark between two poles all the way to Jerusalem. David and the people danced before the LORD with loud singing and blasts of trumpets. The ark then rested in the tent in Jerusalem that
10 David had pitched for it.

Sitting in his palace, contented after subduing all his enemies, David said to Nathan the prophet, "It's not right that I have this beautiful palace while the ark of God remains in a tent. I want to build a temple for the ark."

That night the LORD spoke to Nathan, "Go and tell My servant David: you are not the one to build Me a house." David wasn't to build the LORD's temple, but the LORD had wonderful promises for David. The
11 LORD was renewing His established covenant with David.

The covenant with David was like the one with Abraham. Through the prophet Nathan, the LORD told David that David's son would rule after him and build a temple for the LORD, the land would have peace with its enemies, and David's name would be great among the nations. The covenant was also greater. The LORD said David's throne would endure forever; the Messiah would someday be born from David's line. No matter what happened, the
12 LORD would be his God and never take away His love.

When David heard the words of God's covenant, he humbly thanked the LORD for His mercy and grace.

9 The ark had remained at Abinadab's house ever since the Philistines had captured it and then returned it seven months later to Israel. Abinadab's son, Eleazar, had been the caretaker of the ark during these twenty years (see 2 Samuel 6:1-7:1).

10 David's intention of moving the ark to Jerusalem and putting it in a tent prepared for it was good, but he didn't research the proper procedures for transporting this sacred object before he moved it. The LORD had given detailed instructions (see Exodus 25:12-14; Deuteronomy 10:8) on how to move the ark from place to place. The ark was holy. By striking Uzzah dead, the LORD was emphasizing the importance of showing reverence for the ark and, by association, reverence for the LORD. (At this time, the tabernacle constructed in the wilderness and the bronze altar of sacrifice were located at the high place in Gibeon [see 1 Chronicles 21:29]).

11 The covenant with David was not a new covenant, but a continuation and renewal of the one covenant that began in Genesis 3:15 and continued through Noah, Abraham, and Moses.

12 The basic essence of God's covenant with His people is this: "I will be your God, and you will be My people."

Notes:

Review Worksheets

A. MEMORY VERSE: "I have made a covenant with My chosen, I have sworn to My servant David: 'Your seed I will establish forever, And build up your throne to all generations.'" (Psalm 89:3-4)

B. KEY FACTS: Answer the questions below.

1. What four things about the covenant with David were like the covenant with Abraham? son land name blessing
2. What are some of the ways in which the LORD's covenant with David was greater than His covenant with Abraham?
   a. David's son would build God a temple.
   b. David's kingdom would endure forever.
   c. The Messiah would be born from David's line.

What is the everlasting kingdom? The kingdom of Jesus Christ

C. STORY FACTS: Unscramble the words. Then fill in the blanks.

David was first anointed king in Hebron (HONBER). He was thirty (HIRTTY) years old when he became king in Judah. After Abner (BREAN) and Ishbosheth were murdered, David became king over all Israel (LARESI).

David conquered the Jebusites and made Jerusalem his capital (PILATAC).

He conquered the Philistines who had attacked Israel for many years (ARESY).

When David brought the ark to Jerusalem, Uzzah (HAZUZ) touched it and died.

The LORD made a covenant (TOVENCAN) to make David's kingdom eternal.

D. WHAT DO YOU KNOW? Circle the names in the word find. Then match the names with the descriptions below.

1. Abner 5. Hebron 9. Nathan
2. Ahio 6. Ishbosheth 10. Obed-Edom
3. Asahel 7. Joab 11. Temple
4. David 8. Judah 12. Uzzah

A	H	A	O	T	T	D
J	O	A	B	E	E	A
I	N	L	E	M	U	V
S	H	E	D	P	Z	I
H	E	H	E	L	Z	D
B	B	A	D	E	A	L
O	R	S	O	I	H	A
S	O	A	M	W	E	B
H	N	A	H	T	A	N
E	D	O	J	H	T	E
T	J	U	D	A	H	R
H	U	O	N	V	A	D

1 Saul's commander

7 David's commander

3 Killed by Abner

9 Prophet

6 King in Israel for a short time

12 Touched the ark and died

5 City in Judah

10 Kept the ark in his house

11 What David wanted to build

2 Brother of Uzzah

4 Crowned king in Hebron

8 David was first anointed king of this part of Israel

E. WHAT HAPPENED TO UZZAH? Answer the question below.

The Lord struck down Uzzah when he touched the ark because the ark was...

H O L Y T O T H E L O R D

F. FIND OUT...

The Lord promised that the Messiah would come from David's line. What do the verses below tell you about the Messiah?

Isaiah 7:14 The virgin shall be with child and give birth to a son.

Isaiah 53:3, 5 He was despised and rejected; he was pierced.

Micah 5:2 He will be born in Bethlehem.

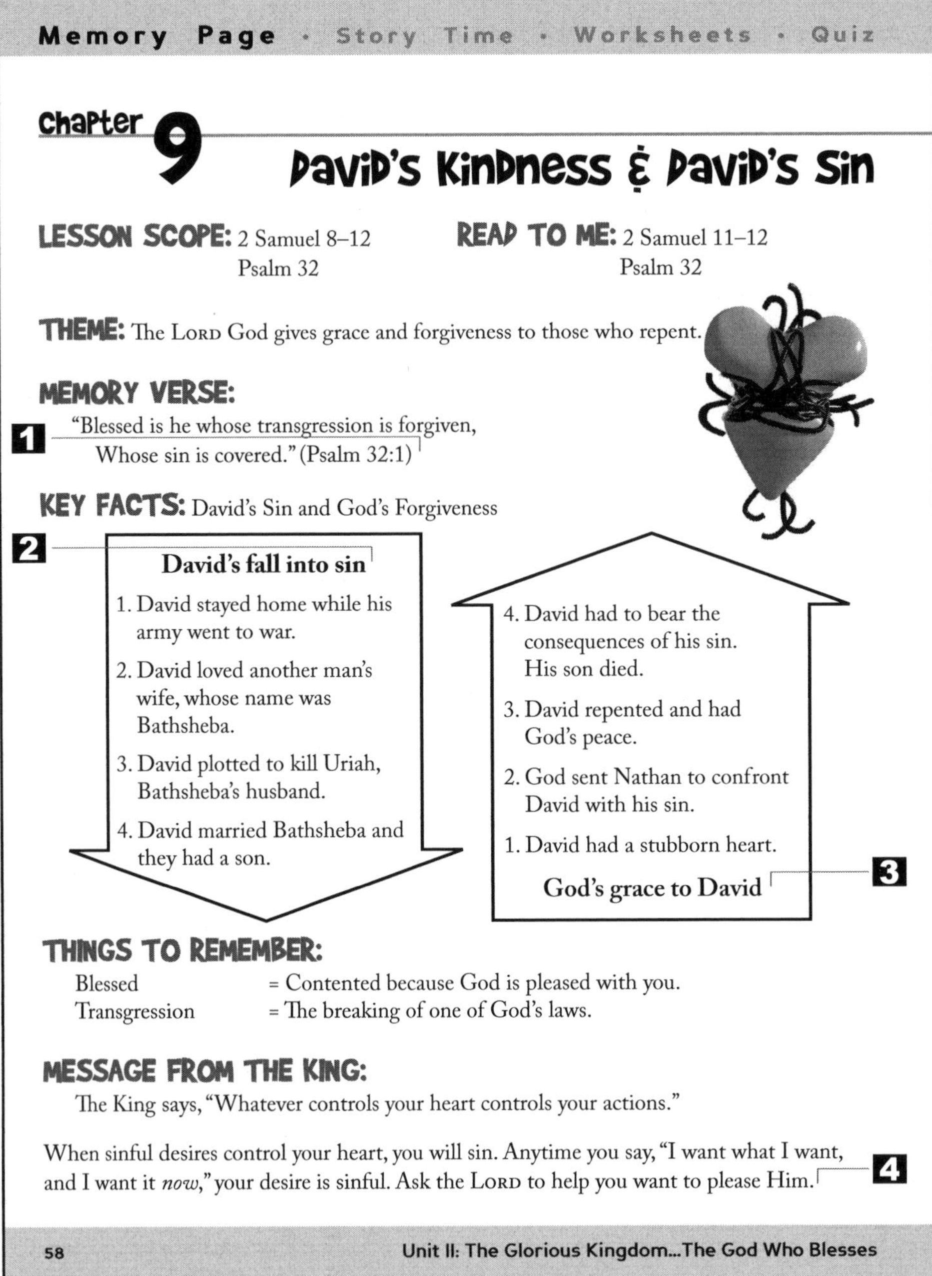

Memory Page · Story Time · Worksheets · Quiz

Chapter 9 David's Kindness & David's Sin

LESSON SCOPE: 2 Samuel 8–12
Psalm 32

READ TO ME: 2 Samuel 11–12
Psalm 32

THEME: The Lord God gives grace and forgiveness to those who repent.

MEMORY VERSE:

1 "Blessed is he whose transgression is forgiven,
Whose sin is covered." (Psalm 32:1)

KEY FACTS: David's Sin and God's Forgiveness

2 **David's fall into sin**

1. David stayed home while his army went to war.
2. David loved another man's wife, whose name was Bathsheba.
3. David plotted to kill Uriah, Bathsheba's husband.
4. David married Bathsheba and they had a son.

4. David had to bear the consequences of his sin. His son died.
3. David repented and had God's peace.
2. God sent Nathan to confront David with his sin.
1. David had a stubborn heart.

God's grace to David 3

THINGS TO REMEMBER:

Blessed = Contented because God is pleased with you.
Transgression = The breaking of one of God's laws.

MESSAGE FROM THE KING:

The King says, "Whatever controls your heart controls your actions."

When sinful desires control your heart, you will sin. Anytime you say, "I want what I want, and I want it *now*," your desire is sinful. Ask the Lord to help you want to please Him. 4

58 Unit II: The Glorious Kingdom...The God Who Blesses

Notes to Teachers and Parents:

1 Psalm 32 is one of the repentance, or penitential, psalms that we discussed in chapter 4. David described the pain of an unrepentant heart in verses 3-4: "my bones grew old…for day and night Your hand was heavy upon me; My vitality was turned into the drought of summer," and the joy of forgiveness in verse 1: "blessed is he whose transgression is forgiven." The word "blessed" has the connotation of joy or contentment, particularly the contentment experienced by someone who has confidence that God is pleased with him because his heart is right with Him. Blessedness is a state of being that is deeper than happiness because it comes from one's soul and is not dependent upon one's outside circumstances.

2 David's fall into sin has a progression that begins with David's neglecting his kingly responsibility of leading his army into battle and giving it to Joab, his commander. If he had been on the battlefield where he was supposed to be, he would not have been tempted to fill his leisure time with immoral activity. David's experience shows how one sin leads to another in an attempt to cover up the first sin. His momentary negligence led to adultery, deceit, murder, and the death of a child. It also led to a time in David's life when he refused to acknowledge his sin, and his blessed relationship with God was broken. The Lord never abandoned David, and actually arranged the circumstances through which David repented, but during the time of David's stubborn sin, David did not have the peace and contentment that resides in a forgiven heart.

3 For a period of time—we don't know specifically how long—David stubbornly refused to repent from his sin. In His mercy, the Lord sent Nathan, the prophet, to confront David with his sin and his refusal to repent. Instead of a direct declaration of guilt, Nathan used a story to break through David's self-deceit so that, in his own words, David condemned himself. The Lord opened David's eyes to his sin, and David finally repented. Only as the Lord opens our spiritual eyes will any one of us see our sin and be willing to repent of it. Psalms 32 and 51 give us glimpses into David's soul after he repented. God restored David's joy and renewed the closeness he had felt to the Lord. Forgiveness, however, does not stop the consequences of sin. As a result of David's sin, David's and Bathsheba's son died. Other consequences followed: for the remaining years of David's reign as king, strife and trouble plagued David's family and kingdom. The rippling effect of David's sin trickled down to every person in the nation of Israel. Sin has drastic consequences and, though we can be truly forgiven by God and cleansed from the condemnation of our sin, we cannot escape the ugliness that sin brings into our world.

4 Sin originates in the heart when we desire, fear, or trust in something other than God. The desire may be an evil desire, or it may be a good and proper desire that becomes an idol when we are willing to disobey God to satisfy that desire.

Memory Page · **Story Time** · Worksheets · Quiz

David's Kindness & David's Sin

Unusual kindness one day and dreadful sin another day—that was the life of King David. When he lived by faith, trusting the Lord, David acted in kindness when other people would have taken revenge. When sinful desires controlled his
heart, however, David loved another man's wife and plotted the man's murder. 5

David had peace from his enemies. The Edomites, Moabites, Philistines, and Amalekites were defeated by David's army. David's kingdom expanded from the bor-
6 der of Egypt to the middle of Syria, from the Mediterranean Sea to the edge of the Eastern Desert.

One day, David asked, "Is there anyone alive from Saul's family to whom I can show kindness?" Ziba, a servant of Saul's household, answered, "Yes, Mephibosheth, a son of Jonathan. He is crippled in both feet." (Mephibosheth was injured as a child
7 when he and his nurse were fleeing after the death of Saul and Jonathan.)

David sent for Mephibosheth. "Don't be afraid," he said. "I want to show kindness to you because of my covenant of friendship with your father, Jonathan. I will give you back the land that belonged to your grandfather, Saul, and you can live in my palace and eat at my table always." As king, David had the power of life and death. Just a word from him and a person would be executed. Yet David was
8 a man after God's heart. He chose to show kindness to the grandson of his enemy, King Saul.

9

In the spring, when kings go off to war, David ordered Joab, his chief commander, to go to battle against the Ammonites. David should have led the army himself, but he stayed at home in his palace in Jerusalem.

Restless and bored one evening, David climbed to the roof of the palace and leisurely walked around. Looking down from the rooftop, he saw in the distance a woman taking her evening bath. She was very beautiful, and David wanted to love her as only

Jesus in the OT
What did Mephibosheth do to merit kindness from King David? Absolutely nothing. What do you do to merit salvation from Jesus? Absolutely nothing. It's all by grace.

Chapter 9: David's Kindness & David's Sin 59

5 We are no different than David. By the grace of God we, too, can be kind and show love in situations that would normally result in hatred and bitterness. At the same time, we are all capable of the most heinous actions when sin controls our hearts. We cannot take pride in our goodness, because it's only by God's grace that we can act righteously. We cannot take pride in not doing evil, because it's only by God's grace that we do not commit the worst of sins.

6 Through his victories in battle, David more than doubled the size of the kingdom of Israel. All the territory from the Mediterranean Sea to the Eastern Desert and from Egypt into Syria, except Philistia and Phoenicia, was under David's rule. The Philistines kept their own territory, a small area that stretched along the sea, and during the period of David's reign, they made no attempts to expand into Israel's territory. The Phoenicians were friendly to Israel. Their territory hugged the coast of the Mediterranean Sea next to the northern part of Israel. Ammon, Edom, Moab, Amalek, and certain Aramean kingdoms sent tribute to David.

7 Mephibosheth first appears in 2 Samuel 4:4. The kindness David showed Mephibosheth was uncharacteristic of kings at that time. David's kindness was the result of God's grace in his life.

8 First Samuel 13:14 says that David was a man after God's own heart. David's actions in 2 Samuel 11–12 do not negate that statement. David was a sinner, sometimes sinning in great and dramatic ways, but the direction of David's heart was to serve God as his King. Even David's refusal to repent for a period of time did not negate this fact. David's heart was stubborn for a long time, but the Lord opened David's eyes and David responded with a contrite heart. David's actions must be a grave warning to us: any Christian who loves the Lord can be tempted and can fall into serious sin.

9 Kings went off to war in the spring because the winter rains had stopped and the summer harvest had not yet begun.

Notes:

10 In 1 Chronicles 11:41 Uriah the Hittite is listed as one of David's mighty men.

11 Joab was a loyal supporter of David. Yet Joab had a quick temper and an independent spirit. He murdered Abner because Abner had killed his brother, Asahel (see 2 Samuel 3), and though David was angry at Joab's actions, he did not execute him like he did the men who murdered Ishbosheth. Joab was willing to obey David's command to have Uriah killed and offered no resistance to this deceptive, evil plan. Joab will appear again in chapter 10.

12 Psalms 32 and 51 are repentance (penitential) psalms and are generally thought to be written by David after his repentance over his sin with Bathsheba. In Psalm 32:3-5, David says, "When I kept silent, my bones wasted away through my groaning all day long. For day and night your hand was heavy upon me; my strength was sapped as in the heat of summer. Selah Then I acknowledged my sin to you and did not cover up my iniquity" (NIV). Hiding his sin greatly affected both David's relationship with God and his physical health. We see that after David admitted his sin and repented of it, God blessed him. He expressed this in these words in Psalm 32: "You are my hiding place…the LORD's unfailing love surrounds the man who trusts in him…be glad, you righteous; sing, all you who are upright in heart!" (Psalm 32:7a, 10b, 11, NIV).

13 Refusal to repent of known sin has an effect on our physical bodies as well as our spirits. Because David was a man after God's own heart, he could not live with unconfessed sin without his body and spirit being affected.

14 The LORD took the first step in David's repentance by sending Nathan to David. Conviction of sin is a gift from God. Recognizing sin and being willing to repent comes only as the LORD opens our eyes and softens our hearts. This is God's grace.

a husband should. At this time, David had several wives, and this woman, Bath-
10 sheba, was married to Uriah, one of David's mighty soldiers. What David wanted was
against God's law, but he didn't turn away from his own desires. The temptation was
strong, and David sinned.

A short time later, Bathsheba sent a message to David, saying, "I'm going to have a baby." Since Uriah was still fighting the Ammonites with Joab, David knew that he was the father of Bathsheba's baby. He panicked and immediately sent for Uriah. He ordered Uriah to go home and spend time with his wife. Uriah, a loyal soldier, refused to enjoy the pleasures of his home while his fellow soldiers were fighting and dying on the battlefield.

David's plan had failed. He sent a letter to Joab, who was still at the battlefield, and plotted a wicked plan. "Put Uriah at the front of the army where the fighting is the fiercest. Then withdraw the rest of the men. I want Uriah to die in battle," David told Joab in his note.

11 Joab obeyed David, and Uriah died. Bathsheha mourned
for her husband, and after the time of mourning was over, David
brought her to his palace to be his wife. In time, she had a son.
But all was not well, because the LORD was not pleased with David.

David knew he had sinned against the LORD. His body became sick
12 and his soul was in distress, but he still refused to repent of his sin. The LORD had **13**
mercy on David and sent Nathan, the prophet, to visit David. "Listen to this sad **14**
story," Nathan said. "There were two men, a rich man with many flocks, and a poor
man who had but one sheep, which was kept as a family pet. One day a traveler came
to the rich man's house. The rich man took the poor man's one sheep and served it as
dinner for his guest."

David was enraged when he heard the story. "This is wrong!" he shouted. "Bring this rich man to me at once. He deserves to die." Nathan, looking straight at David, said, "You are the man."

By his own words, David had condemned himself. The LORD opened David's
eyes, and David realized he was the rich man in the story. He who had many wives
had taken the one wife of his loyal soldier, Uriah. In great sorrow, David repented,
and the LORD forgave him. However, a great consequence of David's sin would soon
follow: the son born to Bathsheba would get sick and die. From that time forward,
David experienced many troubles in his kingdom. **15**

15 David's sin had great consequences. From this time forward until the end of David's reign, there was trouble, strife, immorality, murder, and sadness in David's family and in the kingdom. Although David was truly forgiven by God, the impact of David's sin had devastating effects on many people. This event in David's life should teach us that the temptation to sin must be firmly resisted through God's grace and that the ugliness of sin cannot be denied.

Notes:

Review Worksheets

A. MEMORY VERSE: "Blessed is he whose transgression is forgiven, Whose sin is covered." (Psalm 32:1)

B. KEY FACTS: Circle "T" if the answer is true and "F" if the answer is false.

1. The LORD told David to stay home from war. T (F)
2. David loved Bathsheba in a way that pleased the LORD. T (F)
3. David had a stubborn heart and refused to repent for a long time. (T) F
4. David's sin was too great for the LORD to forgive. T (F)
5. David repented after he heard Nathan's story about the rich man. (T) F
6. Because David repented, there were no bad consequences for him. T (F)

C. STORY FACTS: Circle the **correct** answer.

1. David showed kindness to Mephibosheth because ___________.
   (of his friendship with Jonathan) — of his great respect for Saul
2. In the spring, when the kings went off to war, David ___________.
   led his army to battle — (stayed home in his palace)
3. When David was tempted to love Bathsheba in the wrong way, he ___________.
   resisted and obeyed God — (sinned and displeased God)
4. When Uriah refused to go home to be with his wife, David ___________.
   praised him for his loyalty — (plotted to have him killed)
5. When David refused to repent of his great sin, ___________.
   (his soul was in distress) — God stopped loving him
6. After David heard Nathan's story, he ___________.
   sent Nathan away in anger — (repented of his sin)

Notes:

D. WHAT WAS IN DAVID'S HEART?

Sometimes David pleased God and sometimes David sinned. What controlled his heart when he did right and when he did wrong?

Faith ______ — When David showed kindness

Sinful Desires — When David plotted murder

E. WHAT HAPPENED WHEN NATHAN TALKED TO DAVID?

Nathan's Story

There was a rich man with many sheep. There was a poor man with one sheep. A traveler visited the rich man. The rich man took the poor man's one sheep and served it as dinner for his guest.

When David got angry about the rich man's actions, what did Nathan say?

You are the man.

How did David condemn himself? By his own words

Who opened David's eyes to see his sin? The LORD

F. FIND OUT...

Read 1 John 1:9. What happens when you confess your sin?

The LORD forgives our sin and cleanses us from all unrighteousness.

Why does God forgive you when you confess your sin?

He is faithful and just.

Chapter 10 Troubles in the Kingdom

LESSON SCOPE: 2 Samuel 12–24
1 Chronicles 18–27
Psalm 3

READ TO ME: 2 Samuel 15–18, 22
Psalm 3

1 **THEME:** The LORD God is present with His people even when they suffer the consequences of their sin.

MEMORY VERSE:

"But You, O LORD, are a shield for me, My glory and the One who lifts up my head.... I lay down and slept; I awoke, for the LORD sustained me." (Psalm 3:3, 5) 2

KEY FACTS: David's Troubles

These **events** resulted in these **reactions**.

When...	Then...
Amnon sinned against his sister.	David was angry, but didn't punish him.
Absalom killed Amnon.	David was sad, but did nothing.
Absalom plotted against David.	David was rejected as king and fled from Jerusalem.
Joab killed Absalom in battle.	David mourned Absalom's death and returned to Jerusalem to be king.
Sheba revolted against David, and eleven tribes rejected David as king.	David made Amasa commander in order to win back the people's loyalty.
Joab killed Amasa, and the people in Aram killed Sheba.	David made Joab commander again, and David was once again accepted as king.
David ordered a census.	The LORD punished David and sent sickness to Israel.

MESSAGE FROM THE KING:

The King wants you to know the truth about consequences.

Even when the Lord forgives you, you may still suffer natural consequences. Continue trusting God even when consequences are difficult, because the Lord still loves you.

Notes to Teachers and Parents:

1 God's presence is always with His people. He promises never to leave or forsake us (see Hebrews 13:5). God also always forgives us when we confess sin with a repentant heart (see 1 John 1:9). At the same time, we must remember that we will suffer consequences as a result of sin. Suffering consequences does not mean that we are not forgiven. When we suffer because of our sin or because of someone else's sin against us, the LORD wants us to come to Him for comfort, strength, and grace. Though we may not feel His presence, He never takes His presence from His children.

2 David wrote Psalm 3 when he fled from his son, Absalom. Take time to read this entire psalm to the students and place it in the context of David fleeing from Jerusalem. He had many enemies—his own son, Absalom, as well as his countrymen, who had rejected him to follow Absalom. A man named Shimei pelted David and his procession with stones and curses as they fled Jerusalem. David's many sorrows caused him to weep. Yet David expressed confidence that the LORD was his shield. The LORD gave him strength and relief from his feelings of overwhelming sadness. David cried out to the LORD and was confident that the LORD heard him. Understanding the circumstances in which Psalm 3 was written gives added meaning to the hope expressed at the end of the psalm.

Notes:

Troubles in the Kingdom

Troubles, troubles, there were troubles in the kingdom. Ever since David had sinned with Bathsheba, all kinds of troubles happened in David's family and in
3 the kingdom. The LORD had forgiven David, but David was God's anointed king, so the ripples of his sin reached far and wide.

4 It began with the death of David and Bathsheba's son. After Nathan's visit to David, the child became ill. For seven days David fasted and prayed, pleading for the child to live. When the child died, David went to the LORD's house to worship. "Can I bring him back?" he asked. He knew this was impossible. "I will go to him, but he will not return to me." David accepted his child's death as from the LORD. Soon after, David and Bathsheba had a second son. They named him Solomon, meaning "peace."

Time passed. Amnon, one of David's sons, fell in love with his own half-sister, Tamar. Instead of loving her properly, Amnon sinned against her and hurt her badly. David was furious at Amnon, but didn't punish him. Tamar's brother, Absalom, hated Amnon for what he did to Tamar.

5 Two years later, David had still not punished Amnon. Absalom decided to take action. Absalom invited Amnon to a feast, and after Amnon got drunk, Absalom's men killed him. Then Absalom fled to the country of Geshur. David was sad that Amnon was dead and that Absalom had fled, because he loved both Amnon and Absalom, but he did nothing. Though David yearned to see his son, he didn't tell Absalom to come home. After three years, David told Joab to bring Absalom back to Jerusalem, but David refused to talk to Absalom for two more years.

Absalom was handsome and charming. He sat at the city gate and talked with people as they entered Jerusalem. He listened to all their problems, and said, "If I were judge in the land, I would hear your complaints, and everyone would get justice." So the people all loved him.

Meanwhile, Absalom was plotting how to steal the kingdom from his father David. More and more people turned away from David to follow Absalom. Soon David realized that Jerusalem was not safe for him. As David, his men, and his

3 Sin always brings consequences. Therefore, when a leader of God's people sins, the rippling effect of that sin flows in many directions. David was the anointed king of Israel and the representative head of the covenant. His sin had a devastating impact upon his family and the entire nation as well. James warns that those who presume to be teachers will be judged more strictly (see James 3:1). Why? Teachers, pastors, counselors, and spiritual leaders will be judged more strictly because their sin has such a great impact on those under their care. Although leaders are not held culpable for the sin of those they lead, they *are* responsible if their actions cause those who look up to them to stumble. A position of authority should always be undertaken with great humility and a sense of seriousness about how one's actions will inevitably affect others.

4 Although the prophet, Nathan, had prophesied that the child would die, David had hope that, as long as the child lived, there was a possibility that God would spare the child's life. For seven days David fasted and pleaded with the Lord to let his child live. But when the child died, David accepted the judgment of the LORD. His first actions after the child died were to wash himself, put on clean clothing, and go to the house of the LORD to worship. He showed his acceptance of God's will when he responded to his servants, "While the child was still alive, I fasted and wept.... But now that he is dead, why should I fast? Can I bring him back again? I will go to him, but he will not return to me" (2 Samuel 12:22-23 NIV).

5 When David failed to enact justice and punishment as his position of father and king required him to do, Absalom became frustrated. In his frustration, Absalom resented David for his inaction and hated Amnon for his sin against his sister. These feelings brought on a tragic series of events that led to the death of Amnon, the rebellion of Absalom, civil war, and eventually Absalom's own death. Although David's inaction did not cause Absalom to sin (every person sins out of his own heart), David's negligence provided a circumstantial context in which Absalom allowed his resentment to grow and breed hatred and violence. This story emphasizes the importance of discipline in the family and in the Church. Disciplining sinners is a loving action because discipline may bring about repentance in the sinner and may prevent further sin from occurring.

6 In the past, David had prayed for the LORD's guidance before making decisions. He recognized that the LORD was his King and didn't move ahead of God's plans. In this situation, David's desire to please the people and win back the eleven tribes who had rejected him as king governed his decision-making process. He believed that if he removed Joab as commander and replaced him with Amasa, commander of Absalom's army, all Israel would once again follow him as king. Instead of trusting the LORD, David made a decision out of his fear that resulted in tragedy—the death of Amasa.

7 David appointed Amasa to be his chief commander and told him to prepare the men of Judah for battle in three days. David wanted to squelch Sheba's rebellion. For some reason, Amasa was not able to accomplish this in the time given. Whether the men of Judah were reluctant to follow Amasa or whether Amasa was reluctant to follow David's command, we can't be sure. However, Amasa's failure proved deadly for him. When Amasa

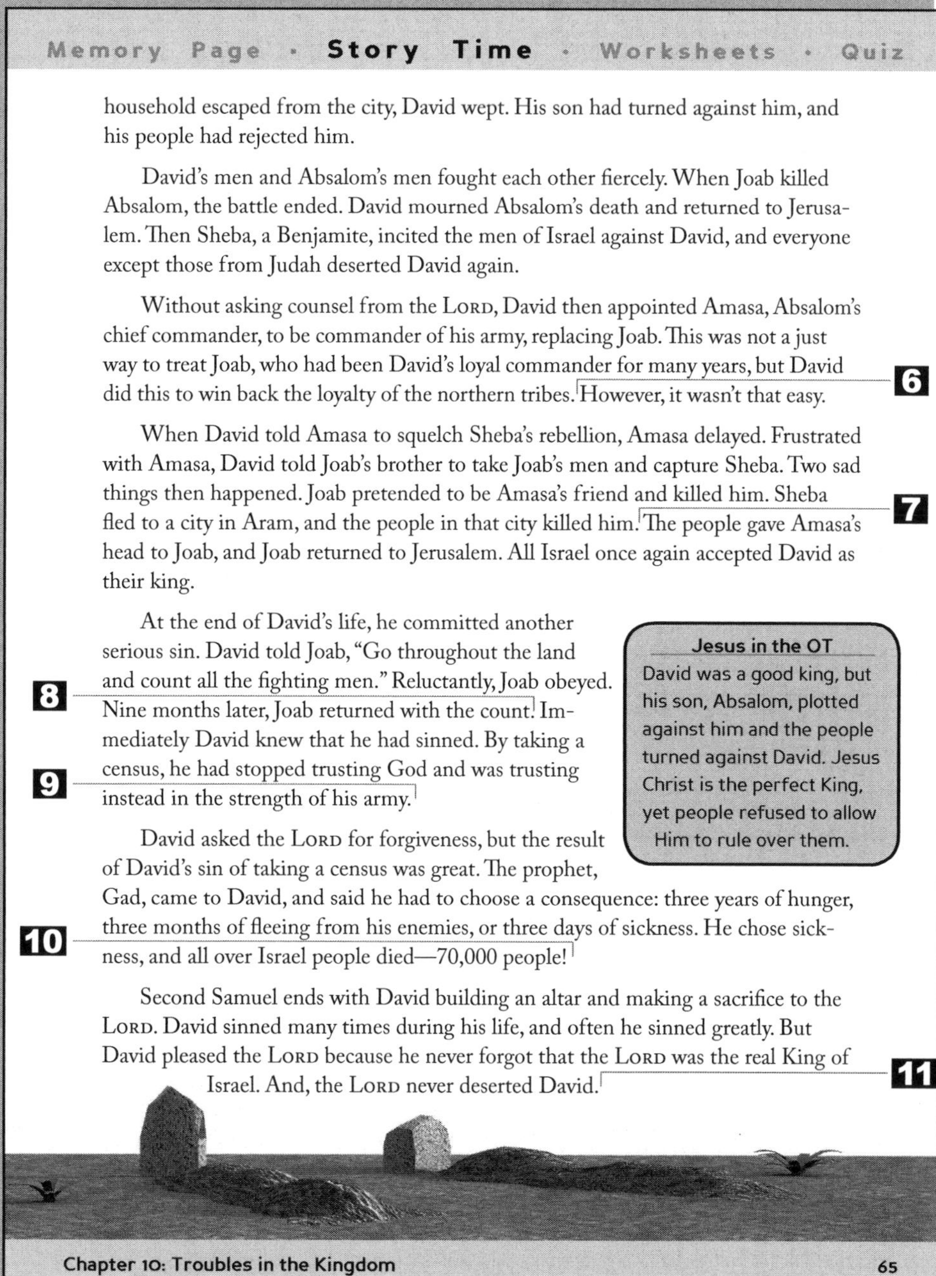

household escaped from the city, David wept. His son had turned against him, and his people had rejected him.

David's men and Absalom's men fought each other fiercely. When Joab killed Absalom, the battle ended. David mourned Absalom's death and returned to Jerusalem. Then Sheba, a Benjamite, incited the men of Israel against David, and everyone except those from Judah deserted David again.

Without asking counsel from the LORD, David then appointed Amasa, Absalom's
chief commander, to be commander of his army, replacing Joab. This was not a just
way to treat Joab, who had been David's loyal commander for many years, but David **6**
did this to win back the loyalty of the northern tribes. However, it wasn't that easy.

When David told Amasa to squelch Sheba's rebellion, Amasa delayed. Frustrated
with Amasa, David told Joab's brother to take Joab's men and capture Sheba. Two sad
things then happened. Joab pretended to be Amasa's friend and killed him. Sheba **7**
fled to a city in Aram, and the people in that city killed him. The people gave Amasa's
head to Joab, and Joab returned to Jerusalem. All Israel once again accepted David as
their king.

At the end of David's life, he committed another
serious sin. David told Joab, "Go throughout the land
8 and count all the fighting men." Reluctantly, Joab obeyed.
Nine months later, Joab returned with the count. Immediately David knew that he had sinned. By taking a
9 census, he had stopped trusting God and was trusting
instead in the strength of his army.

Jesus in the OT

David was a good king, but his son, Absalom, plotted against him and the people turned against David. Jesus Christ is the perfect King, yet people refused to allow Him to rule over them.

David asked the LORD for forgiveness, but the result
of David's sin of taking a census was great. The prophet,
Gad, came to David, and said he had to choose a consequence: three years of hunger,
10 three months of fleeing from his enemies, or three days of sickness. He chose sickness, and all over Israel people died—70,000 people!

Second Samuel ends with David building an altar and making a sacrifice to the
LORD. David sinned many times during his life, and often he sinned greatly. But
David pleased the LORD because he never forgot that the LORD was the real King of **11**
Israel. And, the LORD never deserted David.

tarried, David asked Abishai, Joab's brother, to pursue Sheba with Joab's men. The end result was that Joab pretended to be Amasa's friend, but instead killed him with his dagger. As Amasa lay dying alongside the road, Joab rallied Judah's army to follow him, and then Joab and the army pursued Sheba to the city of Abel in Bethel Maacah in Aram.

8 First Chronicles 21:6 says that Joab didn't include the tribes of Levi and Benjamin in the count. He stopped counting before he finished all the tribes because taking the census was "repulsive" to him.

9 David's sin was not in the action of taking a census, but in his motive for taking a census. Maybe David was taking pride in his large fighting army. Maybe he was trusting in his army for protection and security instead of trusting the LORD. Whatever David's motive was, he was turning from the LORD.

10 Once again, because of his position as king and covenant head, David's sin had a drastic effect on the entire nation. David showed his faith in the LORD by choosing the third option and deciding to "fall into the hands of the LORD" (2 Samuel 24:14) instead of the hands of men. His statement about God's great mercy in that same verse indicates that he recognized his sin but knew that God had forgiven him of that sin. The plague was deadly—70,000 people throughout Israel died. When the angel stretched forth his hand to destroy Jerusalem, the LORD was grieved because so many people had died. "Enough," the LORD spoke out, and He stopped the hand of the angel. The sight of the angel of the LORD at the threshing floor of Araunah the Jebusite brought David to repentance. He said, "I am the one who has sinned and done wrong. These are but sheep. What have they done? Let your hand fall upon me and my family" (2 Samuel 24:17, NIV). David recognized that he was the one who had sinned in this situation, not his people, and he was asking the LORD to show mercy to his people.

11 Unlike Saul, David always came back to the recognition that the LORD was the King of Israel, and he, as ruler, had to submit to God's ultimate authority. Even when Absalom plotted against David and David almost lost his kingdom, when David's beloved son was killed in battle, and when sickness nearly decimated his kingdom, David continued to believe that his God was sovereign. David held firmly to the promise of God's faithfulness. He knew that God was guiding the events of Israel's history and that God's plan was never at risk or His kingdom purposes jeopardized. The book of 2 Samuel ends with David offering a sacrifice and worshipping the Lord.

Notes:

Notes:

Review Worksheets

A. MEMORY VERSE: "But You, O Lord, are a shield for me, My glory and the One who lifts up my head.... I lay down and slept; I awoke, for the Lord sustained me." (Psalm 3:3, 5)

B. KEY FACTS: Match the **event** with the **reaction**.

When...	Then...
Amnon sinned against Tamar	The Lord sent sickness
Joab killed Amasa	David made Joab commander again
Absalom killed Amnon	David mourned Absalom's death
Eleven tribes followed Sheba	David had to flee from Jerusalem
David ordered a census	David was sad, but did nothing
Absalom plotted against David	David didn't punish Amnon
Joab killed Absalom in battle	David told Amasa to squelch Sheba

C. STORY FACTS: Unscramble the names & match the name to the person's description.

BOJA	JOAB	David and Bathsheba's son
DAG	GAD	Commander who replaced Joab
NAMON	AMNON	Man who killed Absalom
LASBAMO	ABSALOM	Man killed by Absalom
ONMOLSO	SOLOMON	David's son who plotted against him
SMAAA	AMASA	Prophet who spoke to David

When David sinned and ordered the census, Gad, the prophet gave David the choice of three consequences. What were they?

1. Three years of hunger
2. Three months of fleeing from enemies
3. Three days of sickness

D. WHAT WAS THE REASON? Circle the **correct** answer.

1. David had many troubles in his family and in his kingdom because _____.
   a. the LORD was angry with David
   (b.) the effect of his sin brought many consequences
   c. David refused to repent of his sin after Nathan confronted him
2. David sinned when he decided to count his fighting men because _____.
   (a.) he was trusting in the strength of his army, not in the LORD
   b. he lied to Joab about the reason for the census
   c. commanding that a census be taken was against God's law
3. Despite his sin, David was a king that pleased God because _____.
   a. he helped many people and all the people loved him
   (b.) he remembered that the LORD was the real King of Israel
   c. he prayed and offered sacrifices to the LORD

E. HOW DID DAVID WORSHIP GOD? Unscramble the words to find the answer.

David did two things to worship the LORD...

TILUB NA TARAL

B U I L T A N A L T A R

FREDOFE A CAFRICIES

O F F E R E D A S A C R I F I C E

F. FIND OUT...

Psalm 139:7-10 says that the LORD is always present with you. Write down some times when you especially feel God's presence with you.

God is present with me when I I feel sick, am afraid, feel lonely, take a test, etc.

Memory Page • Story Time • Worksheets • Quiz

Chapter 11

The Wisdom of Solomon

LESSON SCOPE: 1 Kings 1–4, Proverbs 1–31 **READ TO ME:** 1 Kings 2–4
Ecclesiastes 1–12, Song of Songs 1–8

THEME: The Lord God gives holy wisdom to those who ask.

MEMORY VERSE:

1 "The fear of the Lord is the beginning of wisdom, And the knowledge of the Holy One is understanding." (Proverbs 9:10)

KEY FACTS: Old Testament Poetry Books

Book	Primary Author(s)	Theme
Job	Unknown Israelite	Trusting God during suffering. 2
Psalms	David, Asaph, sons of Korah, other unknown authors	Praising and worshipping the Lord in all circumstances.
Proverbs	Solomon, Agur, Lemuel	Being wise through the fear of God and by making godly choices. 3
5 Ecclesiastes	"The Preacher" (maybe Solomon)	Finding purpose in the fear of God, not earthly pleasures. 4
Song of Songs	Solomon	Celebrating God's gift of love. 6

THINGS TO REMEMBER:

Fear God = Be in awe of God so that you respect and obey Him.

MESSAGE FROM THE KING:

The King says, "To be wise, fear God and obey His commands."

What makes a person wise? Old age and gray hair? Years of going to school? Absolutely not! Long life and years of schooling simply make a person old and educated, not wise. You will be wise if you fear the Lord and obey what He says. Are you becoming a wise person?

68 Unit II: The Glorious Kingdom...The God Who Blesses

Notes to Teachers and Parents:

1 To fear the Lord means to be in awe of Him and to respect His holiness so that loving and obeying Him becomes the goal of our lives. It means submitting to God's holy will as found in Scripture. Obtaining wisdom is different from obtaining knowledge. To obtain knowledge, we gather information. To obtain wisdom, we use the information we have received from Scripture and the work of the Holy Spirit in our lives to live in a way that glorifies God. Until we understand the holiness of God and are in awe of His perfection, we will never understand holy wisdom. Being wise begins with a desire to know God deeper and to please Him more fully.

2 The theme of the book of Job is not to understand why suffering happens to righteous people. God never really answers that question. Rather, the theme of Job is that God is always good and trustworthy when we are called to suffer. Nothing happens to us without the sovereign permission of God. Therefore, we can confidently come to Him for comfort and strength in both good times and bad times.

3 Wisdom does not come through pursuing more knowledge. Wisdom comes when we put the knowledge we have into the context of living life before the face of the Lord. Proverbs emphasizes the concept that knowledge begins with the fear of God, and this understanding is the basis from which we make practical, godly choices.

4 After showing the meaninglessness of finding purpose in pleasure, wisdom, possessions, and work, The Preacher concludes the book by saying, "Fear God and keep his commandments, for this is the whole duty of man" (Ecclesiastes 12:13, NIV). Any attempt to center our lives on anything other than the fear of God results in meaninglessness.

5 There are two views about who "The Preacher" is. Traditionally, the Church has said that Solomon was the author of Ecclesiastes because he describes himself as son of David and king in Jerusalem. Others, including Martin Luther, have just as emphatically claimed that Solomon could not be the author. They say that "son of David" could mean descendant of David and that using the past tense in Ecclesiastes 1:12 ("I...was king over Israel") means that the writer was no longer king. Since Solomon was king until his death, this description does not fit. For these and other textual reasons, biblical commentators today are divided on this subject. However, whether Solomon or someone else wrote this book, the author drew heavily from Solomon's wisdom.

6 Some Bible scholars say that Song of Songs is a description of the physical love between a man and a woman. They say that God included this book in Scripture to emphasize that God gave sexual love to mankind as His gift. Some scholars say that Song of Songs is an allegory of God's love for His children (God is the husband and His people are the bride) or of Christ's love for His church.

7 First Kings 4:29-34 describes the great wisdom of Solomon. News of his great wisdom spread throughout the known world at that time.

8 Adonijah was the full brother of Absalom, and like Absalom, he was very handsome and charming. He was also conniving and tried to usurp the throne from Solomon. (Although Adonijah was older than Solomon, the right of succession to the throne

Memory Page • **Story Time** • Worksheets • Quiz

The Wisdom of Solomon

"Mirror, mirror, on the wall. Who's the wisest of them all?"

In 970 BC, the answer to that question would have been, "Solomon, King of Israel." He was wiser than all the sages in the East. The greatest wisdom in Egypt couldn't compare to his, and his fame spread throughout the known world. He spoke 3,000 proverbs and composed over 1,000 songs. He wrote about plants,
7 animals, and creatures of all kinds. Men from all over the world came to sit at his feet and listened to him speak. But how did Solomon become king of Israel?

In his old age, David was feeble in mind and body, and his son Adonijah decided to take advantage of his father's weakness. He invited important men in the kingdom, including Joab and Abiathar, the priest, to a sacrificial meal. His intention was that at the end of the meal, these men would proclaim him to be the new king of Israel. 8

Nathan, the prophet, heard of the plot and told Bathsheba. She went to David, and asked, "Isn't my son, Solomon, to be the next king? Why is Adonijah scheming to be king?" While she was speaking, Nathan approached David, and asked, "Have you heard that Adonijah plans to be king by the end of the day?" Then David told Nathan and Zadok, the priest, to anoint Solomon as king immediately. They obeyed quickly,
9 and soon all the people were playing flutes, and shouting, "Long live King Solomon!" so loudly that the ground shook.

David had learned that justice must be done if there was to be peace in the land.
10 He told Solomon to remove Abiathar from his office as priest and banish him. Adonijah, Joab, and others who revolted were executed.

At that time there was no central place to worship. The tabernacle and altar of burnt offerings were at Gibeon, and the ark was in Jerusalem in the tent that David had prepared for it. People offered sacrifices to the Lord in many high places throughout the land. King Solomon went to Gibeon to make an enormous sacrifice. He desired to begin his reign by seeking the Lord.

Jesus in the OT
Was Solomon really the wisest man of all? In Colossians 2:2-3, the Apostle Paul said that all the treasures of wisdom and knowledge are found in Jesus Christ.

Chapter 11: The Wisdom of Solomon 69

depended not on birth order, but upon the king's decision. David had promised Bathsheba that her son, Solomon, would succeed him as king.) Joab and the priest, Abiathar, supported Adonijah while Nathan, the prophet, and Zadok, the other priest, refused to join in this conspiracy. Without David's knowledge, Adonijah arranged a large ceremonial meal after which he would be crowned king. In God's providence, Nathan learned about Adonijah's scheme and preempted the plot when he and Bathsheba told David about Adonijah's plans (see 1 Kings 1).

9 Adonijah's actions necessitated that David take immediate action. The only thing that could prevent Adonijah from becoming king at this point was a declaration by David that Solomon was king. Because both Bathsheba and Nathan approached David about the situation, David recognized the urgency and acted quickly (see 1 Kings 1:28-40).

10 David had learned that ignoring sin only brought more problems. Ignoring Amnon's sin with Tamar and Absalom's sin against David resulted in revenge, conspiracy, and death. David's advice to act firmly against those involved in Adonijah's rebellion was wise, and Solomon acted upon that advice. When Abiathar was removed from the office of priest and banished, the prophecy given to Eli was completely fulfilled (see 1 Samuel 2:27-36). The man of God had told Eli that eventually the priesthood would be taken away from his line. The immediate fulfillment of this prophecy came through the death of his two sons, Hophni and Phineas. The next part of the prophecy fulfillment occurred when the priests of Nob were massacred. Abiathar was the only priest who escaped. With the removal of Abiathar from his priestly office, the priestly line of Eli finally ended. From this time forward, all priests came from Zadok's line.

Notes:

11 Solomon's wisdom penetrated below the surface of man's behavior to the intentions of the heart. This was evident in his settling of the case of the two women disputing over the child. This penetrating wisdom frightened those whose motives were to oppress others and profit selfishly, but made the righteous feel safe.

12 Even though the person of Job is somewhat of a mystery to us, we can determine several facts based upon the information given to us in Scripture. First, the land of Uz was located on the eastern side of the Jordan River, stretching north to south from the Aramean lands in the north to Edom in the south (see Genesis 10:23, 22:21, 36:28; see also the notes on Job 1:1 from *The NIV Study Bible*). Second, because there is no mention throughout the book of Job of Moses, the Law, or the Exodus, and because Job offered sacrifices for himself and his children (see Job 1:5), it appears that he lived before the time of Moses and the giving of the Law. After the Law was given on Mt. Sinai, only priests could offer sacrifices to the LORD for the sins of the people. Once the Law had been given, if an ordinary person offered a sacrifice, the LORD became angry. For instance, when King Saul decided to offer sacrifices because Samuel had delayed his coming to Gilgal (see 1 Samuel 13:1-15), Samuel rebuked him severely and told Saul that his actions had cost him the kingdom. Since Job received no rebuke from God for offering sacrifices, he must have lived before the sacrificial system was implemented. Third, Job's friend, Eliphaz, had Edomite connections. Eliphaz is an Edomite name (see Genesis 36:11; see also the notes on Job 2:11 from *The NIV Study Bible*). From this information, we can conclude with some certainty that Job lived between 2000-1000 BC in the area east of the Jordan River, probably in the southern portion known as Edom.

13 The book of Job is discussed more fully in *God's Great Covenant, Old Testament 1*, chapter 31.

While in Gibeon, the LORD appeared to Solomon in a dream. "Ask for whatever you want, and I'll give it to you," the LORD said. Solomon replied, "Give me a discerning heart to rule my people well and to make right choices." The LORD was pleased with Solomon's request for wisdom and fulfilled it.

Soon all Israel knew about Solomon's great wisdom and respected him. One day two women came to him, bringing a young baby with them. The women shouted at each other, "This is my son. My son is alive and your son is dead." How would Solomon know which woman was telling the truth? Solomon said, "Bring me a sword. We'll cut the child in half and give half to one and half to the other." One woman cried out, "Please, no! Don't hurt the baby! Give the baby to her." Solomon then knew that the woman who was willing to give up the child to save its life was the real mother. By God's grace, Solomon could discern the motives of men's hearts and give sound judgments. The
11 wicked were afraid of such wisdom, and the righteous felt safe under the care of a king who feared God.

OLD TESTAMENT POETRY BOOKS

In the middle of the Old Testament, there are five books of poetry: Job, Psalms, Proverbs, Ecclesiastes, and Song of Songs. Written by many different people, some unknown by name, these books show you how to trust God when you are suffering, how to praise and worship the LORD at all times and in all circumstances, and how to be a wise person.

The book of Job tells the story of Job, an Edomite who lived during the days 12
of Isaac and Jacob. (Genesis 21-50 gives the stories of the lives of Isaac and Jacob.) He was a righteous man who trusted God and prayed faithfully for his children. God allowed Satan to bring trouble into Job's life, taking his children, his riches, and finally his health away from him. Satan was certain that when Job had nothing left, he would curse God.

Job never cursed God, but he didn't understand why he was suffering so much. His friends said it was because he had sinned. When Job asked God, "Why am I suffering?" the LORD turned the conversation around and asked Job question upon question until Job was overwhelmed by God's greatness. The LORD never answered Job's
13 "why" question, but instead taught Job to trust in His goodness and love in the midst of suffering.

Notes:

The book of Psalms is God's "Book of Praises." David wrote about half of the 150 psalms. Most of the psalms were written during one of three times in Israel's history: 1) during Moses's life; 2) during the time of David and Solomon; or 3) after God's people returned from exile. The book of Psalms is like a hymnbook, giving you songs to sing no matter what circumstances you might be experiencing. In the Psalms we learn about who God is and how He wants us to trust and put our hope in Him. (Chapter 4 describes the different types of psalms.)

The book of Proverbs gives practical advice about how to be a wise and godly person. Wisdom begins with fearing God. (To fear God means to be in awe of God in such a way that you respect Him and obey His commands.) God's children don't have to be terrified of God, but they should take their sin seriously and confess it quickly.

In Proverbs 1–8 Solomon used the words "my son" many times as he wrote about the beauty and value of wisdom. Later he compared the "wise man" to the "foolish man," explaining the blessings that happen when a person listens to instruction and the hardship that happens when wise words are rejected or ignored. Proverbs gives general principles of life, not absolute promises. In other words, if a person chooses to act in a particular way (either wisely or foolishly), generally speaking, a particular result will occur. Proverbs does not guarantee happiness to those who do the right things (because bad things often happen to righteous people), but it does promise God's blessing to those who fear Him. Even though the wicked may prosper for a time, in the end they will die and stand before God their Judge.

Proverbs has the same types of Hebrew poetry that are found in Psalms (repeated, contrasted, and continuing). One of the most well-known chapters is Proverbs 31, a description of the virtuous wife. This woman of noble character cares for her family, has the respect of her husband, is a successful businesswoman, and is industrious and wise. Most important, the virtuous woman is beautiful and should be praised because she fears the LORD.

Ecclesiastes, written by "The Preacher," tells you to find purpose in fearing God and obeying His commands, not in earthly pleasure, fame, and possessions. Over and over, The Preacher said, "Vanity of vanities," exclaiming over the hopelessness of looking for joy in anything but God.

Song of Songs, also referred to as the Song of Solomon, celebrates God's gift of love. Some people think the book describes the love that a man and a woman have for each other. Other people think this book is a beautiful picture of God's love for His people.

Notes:

Review Worksheets

A. MEMORY VERSE: "The fear of the LORD is the beginning of wisdom, And the knowledge of the Holy One is understanding." (Proverbs 9:10)

B. KEY FACTS: Match the theme with the Old Testament book.

3 Job	1. Celebrating God's gift of love.
5 Psalms	2. Being wise and making good choices.
2 Proverbs	3. Trusting God during suffering.
1 Song of Songs	4. Finding purpose in the fear of God.
4 Ecclesiastes	5. Praising and worshipping the LORD.

1. Who wrote Psalms? Give three names:
   Asaph, David and Sons of Korah
2. Who wrote Proverbs? Give three names:
   Solomon, Agur and Lemuel
3. What book did The Preacher write? Ecclesiastes
4. During what three times in Israel's history were most of the Psalms written?
   Moses' life, days of David and Solomon and after God's people returned from exile

C. STORY FACTS: Cross out the **wrong** word.

1. David's son (~~Amnon~~/Adonijah) tried to make himself king in Israel.
2. Solomon asked the LORD for (wisdom/~~strength~~) when he became king.
3. Job's friends said he was suffering because he was (~~righteous~~/sinful).
4. Proverbs 31 describes the (~~wise man~~/virtuous woman).
5. Proverbs 1–8 describe the (beauty of wisdom/~~goodness of God~~).
6. Wisdom begins with (~~seeking knowledge~~/fearing God).
7. Proverbs gives (~~absolute promises~~/general principles) about daily living.

D. WHAT ARE THE ANSWERS? Complete the crossword puzzle.

Across:

1. The ______ wrote Ecclesiastes. **PREACHER**
3. Solomon was a king who feared _____. **GOD**
5. Solomon asked God for_____. **WISDOM**
6. Song of Songs celebrates God's gift of ____. **LOVE**
7. Zadok, the _____, anointed Solomon as king. **PRIEST**
9. Psalms is the "Book of ____." **PRAISES**
10. _____ wrote some of the Psalms, but not as many as David. **ASAPH**
11. The Old Testament has _____ books of poetry. **FIVE**
12. Solomon was the _____ man. **WISEST**

Down:

1. _____ is a book about wisdom. **PROVERBS**
2. Satan said that Job would _____ God. **CURSE**
4. ____ learned to trust God when he suffered. **JOB**
7. _____ has 150 chapters. **PSALMS**
8. The Preacher said, "____ of vanities." **VANITY**

E. WHAT DOES IT MEAN TO FEAR GOD? Write the definition.

To be in awe of God in such a way that you respect God and obey His commands.

F. FIND OUT...

James 1:5 tells you what to do if you want wisdom. What should you do?

Ask God for wisdom and He will give you wisdom generously.

Notes to Teachers and Parents:

1 Although it's true that the LORD blesses those who obey Him, His blessing is not totally dependent upon our behavior. The LORD may bless us even when we are not faithful to Him. Even though Solomon turned from God and worshipped idols, he had wealth, prosperity, and fame. Ultimately, the LORD did bring judgment on Solomon's family and the nation of Israel because of Solomon's sin, but this judgment was not immediate.

2 The LORD renewed the covenant given to Abraham, Jacob, Moses, and David with David's son, Solomon. Once again, this is not a new covenant, but the same covenant renewed with the same conditions as in the past. The LORD promised that Solomon's sons would never fail to rule on Israel's throne if Solomon obeyed the LORD and refused to worship idols. Of course, God's people can be faithful only as they rely on God's grace to help them. Like the men before him, Solomon did not keep the covenant all the days of his life. As a result, the consequences for Solomon's sins were severe.

3 Idols of the heart are desires that we want so much that we choose to sin in order to get them. The idol may be a desire for an object or for a relationship. The idol may also be a desire for such things as love, power, respect, approval, or pleasure. The LORD wants to capture our hearts and turn them to worship and trust in Him (see Ezekiel 14:1-5).

Notes:

Chapter 12 The Reign of Solomon

LESSON SCOPE: 1 Kings 5–11, 1 Chronicles 28, 2 Chronicles 1–9 **READ TO ME:** 1 Kings 8–10

THEME: The LORD God brings blessing even when His people are unfaithful. **1**

MEMORY VERSE:

"Praise be to the LORD, who has given rest to his people Israel just as he promised. Not one word has failed of all the good promises he gave through his servant Moses." (1 Kings 8:56, NIV)

KEY FACTS:

God's Covenant with Solomon **2**

If...	Then ...
Your heart is upright before Me AND you obey all I command...	I will establish your throne over Israel forever as I promised.
If...	**Then ...**
You or your sons turn away from Me AND you disobey My command and worship idols...	I will cut Israel off from this land AND I will reject this consecrated temple AND other nations will laugh at Israel.

MESSAGE FROM THE KING:

When the King says, "Worship only Me," He means what He says.

Idols can be made of gold or silver. Idols can also be desires of the heart that cause you to disobey God. Every time you sin, you are worshipping an idol. What idols do you worship? **3**

The Reign of Solomon

Peace and prosperity settled over the land of Israel. King Solomon was wise and just, and the people felt safe and secure under his rule.

Solomon remembered the words of the LORD's covenant with his father David: "Your son will build a house for my Name." Because David had been a warrior, the LORD wanted Solomon, whose name means "peace," not David, to build His temple. Before he died, David made preparations for the building of the temple. He gathered together gold, silver, bronze, wood, and precious stones. He wrote down all the detailed plans for the temple building and furnishings that God's Spirit had given to him and gave them to Solomon. Then David charged Solomon, "Be strong and courageous. Don't be afraid to build this temple because the LORD will not fail you." **4**

Solomon sent a message to Hiram, king of Tyre, **5** saying, "Give me cedars of Lebanon to build the LORD's temple, and in exchange I'll give you wheat and olive oil." Solomon raised up a force of Israelites to transport timber from Tyre and large stones from quarries in Israel. Skilled craftsmen fashioned elaborate, carved cherubim and covered the cherubim and the inner walls of the temple with gold.

Solomon hired Huram, a highly skilled craftsman from Tyre, to create two decorated bronze pillars for the portico of the temple. The pillar to the south he called Jachin (meaning, "He establishes"), and the northern pillar he called Boaz (meaning, "in Him is strength").

For seven years, hundreds of thousands of stonecutters, craftsmen, and laborers worked to build the magnificent temple. When it was completed, Solomon called the leaders of Israel together. The priests and Levites carried the ark and all the furnishings to the temple and arranged them inside. As the priests withdrew from the Holy Place, the cloud of God's presence filled the temple. Then Solomon stood before the people and dedicated the temple. His prayer, the longest prayer in Scripture, blended

4 First Chronicles 22:6-10 explains that the LORD did not want David to build the temple because he had been a warrior and had fought many battles. The LORD wanted Solomon, a man of peace, to be the king who built His dwelling place. Because David had a great desire that a temple be built and because he believed that his son Solomon was young and inexperienced, David made extensive preparations for the temple before he died. He provided architectural drawings, work plans, and materials (dressed stone, iron made into nails, cedar logs, gold, silver, and bronze). First Chronicles 22 describes David's preparations.

5 The city of Tyre was located on the Mediterranean Sea at the southern part of the country of Phoenicia. Hiram, king of Tyre, had been on friendly terms with David during his reign, and now he continued this friendly relationship with Solomon. Hiram was pleased when Solomon requested help and materials from him. His response was praise to the LORD that He had given Israel a wise king to follow in the footsteps of King David.

Notes:

together in a perfect way the greatness of Elohim, God the Creator, and the closeness of Yahweh, God of the covenant.

> **Jesus in the OT**
> "I will establish your throne forever." These were God's words to Solomon. Who would be on Solomon's throne forever? Jesus Christ!

The LORD appeared to Solomon and renewed the covenant. The LORD promised that if Solomon and his sons worshipped and obeyed the LORD, his kingdom would stand firm. But serious consequences would follow if they forgot the LORD and worshipped idols.

After Solomon finished the temple, he built his own palace. It took thirteen years
to build it. His throne was inlaid with ivory and overlaid with gold, with six steps leading up to it. Lions stood on either side of the throne, and lions sat on either side of the
six steps. He built ships that sailed far and wide, bringing gold and treasures, as well
as apes and baboons to the kingdom. In Solomon's kingdom, silver was as common as
stone and cedar wood as plentiful as sycamore. He imported horses from Egypt and
6 had thousands of chariots. His wealth, as well as his wisdom, was known throughout
the world, and kings and wise men came to sit at his feet and hear him speak.

One day, the queen of Sheba, having heard of his fame and his God, visited Solomon. In her caravans she brought spices, gold, and precious stones as a gift. She talked about everything on her mind, and Solomon answered all her questions. Then she said, "In my country I heard about your achievements and wisdom, and I didn't believe that what I heard could be true. Now I have seen with my eyes and what I see far exceeds the report. Praise to the LORD who put you on the throne of Israel." Solomon gave the queen all that she asked for and more.

Yet all was not right in the kingdom. Solomon married women from many foreign nations. These women brought with them their foreign gods—Chemosh of the
Moabites, Molech of the Ammonites, Ashtoreth of the Sidonians—yet Solomon continued to love these wives. As he grew older, his wives turned his heart from the LORD.
He built altars on the high places so they could worship their gods. The LORD was angry
with Solomon. Twice He had appeared to Solomon, yet Solomon forgot the covenant. 7

In the kingdom was a hard-working man named Jeroboam. Solomon put him in
charge of the laborers from Ephraim and Manasseh. One day, Ahijah, the prophet,
met Jeroboam in the countryside. Ahijah took his new robe and tore it into twelve
pieces. He gave ten pieces to Jeroboam, and said, "Take these pieces. Because of Solomon's disobedience, the LORD will give you ten tribes to rule after Solomon's death. 8
His son will rule over only the people of Judah and Benjamin." Solomon, the wisest
9 man, became foolish. He worshipped idols, and at his death the nation of Israel, the
glorious kingdom, split in two.

6 In Deuteronomy 17:14-17, the LORD forbade future kings of Israel from accumulating large amounts of gold and silver, having many wives, and acquiring many horses. In his pursuit of wealth, pleasure, and power, Solomon did all these things.

7 Many times the LORD spoke against marrying women from foreign nations (see Deuteronomy 17:17; Exodus 34:16; Joshua 23:12-13). The LORD knew that the idolatrous practices of these women would pull the hearts of Israelite men from worshipping Him. This was what happened to Solomon. His wives brought their religious practices to Israel and Solomon built altars on the "high places" so they could sacrifice to their gods. Once the high places were built, many Israelites, not just their foreign wives, worshipped idols there. Solomon's sin and the idolatry of his wives turned the hearts of many Israelites away from worship of the true God, Yahweh.

8 The nation of Israel consisted of twelve tribes, each of which possessed its own territories. The tribes originated from ten of Jacob's sons and two of Joseph's sons. The descendents from Jacob's son, Levi, did not own their own property, but were scattered throughout the nation, serving priestly functions within the other tribes. Joseph, another of Jacob's sons, was given a double portion in that two of his sons, Ephraim and Manasseh, were given sections of the land. That means that the nation's twelve tribes were made up of ten sons from Jacob (excluding Levi and Joseph) and two sons from Joseph. When the nation split and became two kingdoms, ten tribes banded together and became the northern kingdom of Israel. Jeroboam was the first king of the northern kingdom. The remaining two tribes, Judah and Benjamin, became the southern kingdom of Judah. In 1 Kings 12:20-24 there are two confusing statements: 1) "only the tribe of Judah remained loyal to the house of David"; and 2) Rehoboam "mustered the whole house of Judah and the tribe of Benjamin…to regain the kingdom for Rehoboam son of Solomon" (NIV). There are two possible explanations for the seemingly conflicting statements in 1 Kings 12 and for the words in 1 Kings 11:13 that say that Solomon's son received only one tribe. One explanation could be that Solomon's son already had one tribe (Judah), and the giving of one tribe could be the addition of *one more* tribe—the tribe of Benjamin. A second explanation could be that at this time Benjamin was such a small tribe, and was so closely tied to Judah, that the two tribes were almost considered as one. Reigning over the large tribe of Judah and the very small tribe of Benjamin could be thought to be ruling over one tribe. Whatever the explanation, we know these things: 1) there were twelve tribes of Israel at the time of Solomon; 2) Jeroboam became ruler over ten tribes, just as Ahijah the prophet predicted; 3) the people of Benjamin allied with Judah when the kingdom split; and 4) Rehoboam, Solomon's son, ruled over the territories inhabited by the people of Judah and the people of Benjamin.

9 Through the prophet, Ahijah, the LORD predicted the split of the kingdom. Jeroboam was to be God's instrument to bring divine judgment upon Solomon for his idolatry and the breaking of God's covenant. Somehow, Solomon learned of Ahijah's prophecy and tried to kill Jeroboam, but Jeroboam fled to Egypt until Solomon's death. Because of God's promise to David that the kingship would remain in David's family, Jeroboam would only rule ten tribes, and Solomon's son would rule two tribes.

Review Worksheets

A. MEMORY VERSE: "Praise be to the LORD, who has given rest to his people Israel just as he promised. Not one word has failed of all the good promises he gave through his servant Moses." (1 Kings 8:56, NIV)

B. KEY FACTS:

God's Covenant with Solomon

IF...Solomon had an... Upright Heart

AND obeyed God...

THEN...God said, "I will establish your throne over Israel as I promised."

BUT IF Solomon turned from God and worshipped idols THEN...

1. God would cut off Israel from the land.
2. God would reject the consecrated temple.
3. Other nations would laugh at Israel.

C. STORY FACTS: Fill in the blanks.

1. David couldn't build the temple because he had been a warrior.
2. Hiram of Tyre gave Solomon cedars of Lebanon for the temple.
3. The names of the two temple pillars were Boaz and Jachin.
4. It took 7 years to build the temple and 13 years to build the palace.
5. The Queen of Sheba heard of Solomon's fame and visited him.
6. The prophet Ahijah told Jeroboam he would rule ten tribes.
7. The LORD was angry with Solomon because he forgot the covenant.

Notes:

Notes:

D. WHAT DOES NOT BELONG?

Cross out the word(s) that do(es) **not** belong with the other words.

1. Names of idols:

   Chemosh ~~Sheba~~ Molech Ashteroth

2. Materials for the temple:

   gold ~~sycamore wood~~ precious stones bronze

3. Animals that Solomon brought to Israel:

   baboons apes Egyptian horses ~~elephants~~

4. Ways that Solomon sinned against the LORD:

   married foreign wives built altars on high places

   ~~built a large palace~~ forgot the covenant

5. Wealth that Solomon possessed:

   many sailing ships ~~robes trimmed with diamonds~~

   thousands of chariots lions standing beside his throne

E. SOLOMON'S PRAYER:

Solomon used two names for God in his prayer. Write a description of each one.

Elohim: The Creator who is mighty, strong, and majestic.

Yahweh: God promises to be the God of His people and keeps His promises.

When the priests withdrew from the Holy Place, what happened?

The cloud of God's presence filled the temple.

F. FIND OUT...

What promises did the LORD give to Moses? Be prepared to discuss with the teacher how the LORD fulfilled them.

Exodus 6:7a I will take you as My people and I will be your God.

Exodus 6:8 I will bring you to the land I promised to Abraham.

Deuteronomy 28:7 He will defeat enemies who rise up against them.

Deuteronomy 28:8-9 He will bless everything they do and will make them His holy people.

Chapter 13 Looking Backwards...Looking Ahead

LESSON SCOPE: 2 Samuel 1–24, 1 Kings 1–11, 1 Chronicles 1–28, 2 Chronicles 1–9, Proverbs 1–31, Ecclesiastes 1–12, Song of Songs 1–8

READ TO ME: 2 Chronicles 6–7, Psalm 72

So many blessings from God! The LORD blessed the Israelites with an upright man, David, to be their king. The LORD gave them peace from their enemies and forgiveness for their sins. He promised to be present with His people, even after they had sinned greatly. Most importantly, the LORD remembered His promise to be Israel's God.

The LORD blessed Solomon with great wisdom and wealth, and Solomon became renowned for the decisions he made and the magnificent palace he inhabited. After years of hard work and skilled craftsmanship, Solomon's temple was finished. The LORD's presence filled the temple just as it had filled the tabernacle in the wilderness. Israel's territory had expanded. No longer was Israel a small nation of loosely allied tribes. As we learned in Unit II, Israel had become the glorious kingdom that attracted royalty and sages from faraway countries to see its wealth and learn from its wisdom.

In Unit II, you learned how the LORD blessed His people. Israel reached the height of its glory as a nation. But the hearts of Israel turned from the worship of Yahweh to the pagan gods of the nations surrounding them, and tragedy was soon to come.

In Unit III, you will learn about the split of Israel into two kingdoms. Solomon's son, Rehoboam, would rule one tribe because the LORD had promised that David's line would endure. The ten other tribes would rebel against Rehoboam and set up Jeroboam as their king. How sad, how tragic, that the glorious kingdom would be divided in two because of Israel's unfaithfulness to the LORD. Yet, despite Israel's sin, the Almighty King reigned supreme in Israel. His will could not be thwarted! He was the Keeper of His Kingdom.

IMPORTANT THINGS TO KNOW:

Word	Meaning of the Word
Blessed	Contented because God is pleased with you.
Covenant	God's promise to be the God of His people forever.
Fear God	Be in awe of God so that you respect and obey Him.
Prophet	Person called to speak for God.
Psalms	"Book of Praises."
Transgression	The breaking of one of God's laws.

Notes:

Review Worksheets

A. MEMORY VERSE REVIEW: Cross out the **wrong** word(s) in the memory verse phrases. You will find one wrong word in each line. Write the **correct** word in the blank.

1. "Blessed is he whose ~~wickedness~~ is forgiven…" transgression
2. "But you, O LORD, are a ~~protection~~ for me, shield
   My glory and the One who lifts up my ~~heart~~." head
3. "I have made a covenant with My ~~people~~… chosen
   'Your ~~family~~ I will establish forever, seed
   And build up your ~~kingdom~~ to all generations." throne
4. "The ~~love~~ of the LORD is the beginning of wisdom, fear
   And the knowledge of the Holy One is ~~truth~~." understanding
5. "Praise be to the LORD, who has given ~~hope~~ to his people… rest
   Not one word has failed of all the ~~just~~ promises he gave…" good
6. "I lay down and ~~cried~~; slept
   I awoke, for the LORD ~~helped~~ me." sustained

What are three things David asked the LORD to do in Psalm 51:1-6?

1. "Have mercy upon me, O God."
2. "Wash me thoroughly from my iniquity."
3. "Cleanse me from my sin."

B. RHYMING STORY FACTS: Write the rhyming story facts in the blanks below.

Curse	Health	Fame	Lyre	Name	Nurse
One	Sacrifices	Son	Spices	Tyre	Wealth

1. **What Solomon gained** — **what Job lost**
   wealth rhymes with health
2. **What God promised to make great** — **what spread abroad**
   David's name rhymes with Solomon's fame
3. **What instrument David played** — **where cedar wood came from**
   lyre rhymes with Tyre
4. **Who fled with Mephibosheth** — **what Satan said Job would do**
   nurse rhymes with curse
5. **What the Queen of Sheba brought** — **what were made on high places**
   spices rhymes with sacrifices
6. **Number of sheep the poor man had** — **relation of Absalom to David**
   one rhymes with son

C. WHAT WAS THE THEME OF UNIT II? What is God's blessing like? Fill in the blanks below to find out.

R E M E M B E R S — God _____ His promises.
L O V E — God never takes His _____ away.
G R A C E — God gives mercy and _____.
P R E S E N T — God promised to be ____ with us.
M E S S I A H — The _____ will be born.
W I S D O M — God gives _____ to those who ask.
C O V E N A N T — God renews His _____.
F O R G I V E N E S S — God gives _____ for sins.

Notes:

D. WHAT DO YOU KNOW ABOUT THESE PEOPLE? Match the person to the words that describe him.

11 Absalom	1. Man who wrote several Psalms
7 Uzzah	2. King who built the temple
12 Ishbosheth	3. God of the Ammonites
10 Nathan	4. Commander of Saul's army
4 Abner	5. Son of Jonathan who couldn't walk
9 Joab	6. King of Tyre
5 Mephibosheth	7. Man who touched the ark and died
2 Solomon	8. Husband of Bathsheba killed in battle
3 Molech	9. Commander of David's army
8 Uriah	10. Prophet who spoke to David
1 Asaph	11. David's son killed by Joab
6 Hiram	12. Saul's son who was king for a brief time

E. THE RENEWED COVENANT: Unscramble the words and use them to fill in the blanks in the paragraph below.

God renewed the covenant (VOCENTAN) with David. He said that David's son would build the temple (MELTEP) and David's kingdom would endure (ERENUD) forever. He said He would never take away His love (VELO). When David heard these words, he thanked the LORD for His mercy (CYMER) and grace (ACREG). God renewed the covenant with Solomon, but Solomon turned away from the LORD (HET ROLD) and worshipped idols (SLOID).

F. WHAT'S THE REASON? Circle the **correct** answer.

1. Uzzah died when he touched the ark because the ark ___________.

   was holy to the LORD fell on top of him

2. David sinned by loving Bathsheba because ___________.

   she was an idol worshipper she was another man's wife

3. The LORD forgave David of his sin because ___________.

   David was a good king David repented in sorrow

4. The LORD was pleased with David because David never ___________.

   forgot that God was King was frightened in battle

5. Solomon was the wisest of all men because ___________.

   he asked God for wisdom he had wise teachers

6. Solomon sinned when he married many foreign wives because ___________.

   he made many enemies he started worshipping idols

G. WHAT DO YOU KNOW ABOUT THE BOOKS OF POETRY?

Cross out the **wrong** word in the sentences below.

1. The Old Testament has (five/six) books of poetry.
2. Job's friends said he was suffering because he was (righteous/sinful).
3. After God asked Job question upon question, Job was overwhelmed by God's (anger/greatness).
4. Psalms is the Old Testament ("Book of Praises"/"Book of God's Law").
5. Proverbs says that wisdom begins with (fearing God/making good decisions).
6. Proverbs gives (absolute promises/general principles) about life.
7. The Preacher wrote the words ("my son"/"vanity of vanities") many times.
8. Song of Songs celebrates God's gift of (love/wisdom).

Notes to Teachers and Parents:

1 Many of the consequences of Solomon's sins occurred after his death. He condoned idolatry and led his people astray from worship of the LORD. His sin brought about the destruction of a united Israel. It was only because the LORD was faithful to His covenant promise to David—"Your kingdom will endure forever" (2 Samuel 7:16, NIV)—that two tribes, Judah and Benjamin, remained under the rule of Solomon's son, Rehoboam.

2 Because the "fear of the LORD is the beginning of wisdom" (Psalm 111:10) Solomon became a foolish man when he encouraged idolatry instead of worshipping the LORD.

3 From this point on in the Old Testament story, the northern ten tribes are called Israel and the southern two tribes are called Judah.

4 Jeroboam set up two worship centers: one at Dan in the northern part of his kingdom and one in Bethel at the southern portion. He knew that if the people continued to go to Jerusalem to worship, his influence over the northern kingdom would be weakened. At each of these worship centers, Jeroboam put a golden calf. These calves were not to represent a god other than Jehovah, but were to be symbolic images of Jehovah, to help the people worship Him. Images like these, however, were forbidden in the Ten Commandments because no image or representation of the LORD was permissible. Instead of pointing the people to the one true God, the images turned the people's hearts away from the LORD to the worship of idols. The end result of Jeroboam's actions was that he instituted a new system of worship in Israel, and, in doing so, effectively solidified the division, religiously as well as politically, between Israel and Judah. In the years that followed, some of Judah's kings would worship the LORD faithfully, but Israel would never again have a ruler who did right in the eyes of the LORD.

UNIT III

The Divided Kingdom...The God Who Reigns

Theme: The Keeper of the Kingdom rules over the kingdom of men.

Oh my, oh my, I can't believe this is happening! It is I, Tobias, the royal chronicler, and things are looking bad. How can I record with utmost accuracy the events of the kingdom when my heart is so heavy with sadness? Yet, I promise to record the story with confident faith, because the LORD is King, and He is keeping His kingdom safe.

What a glorious kingdom Israel was in the days of King Solomon! Wealth, fame,
wisdom, and many blessings came from the LORD, the King of kings. The tragedy was
that Solomon forgot that the LORD blesses those who fear His name and punishes 1
those who sin. God's people cannot sin without enduring the consequences. Turning from the worship of the one true God to pagan idols made the wisest man in the
2 world become a foolish man, and after his death, the glorious kingdom split in two.

Solomon's son, Rehoboam, also was a foolish man. He threatened the people
with higher taxes. His harshness caused the ten northern tribes that King Jeroboam 3
ruled to split apart from Judah and Benjamin and form their own country. Rehoboam
was not wise enough, powerful enough, or godly enough to win back the allegiance of
these tribes, and the nation was permanently divided in half.

Jeroboam, king of the northern tribes, set up his capital at
Shechem. He built worship centers at Dan and Bethel because
he didn't want people going to Jerusalem to worship. His actions
made the split between the two kingdoms politically and religiously unsettled. In years to come, he would be known as "the
4 son of Nebat, who had made Israel sin" (1 Kings 22:52).

In the next eighty years, the northern kingdom of Israel
would have eight kings, none of whom served the LORD, and the
southern kingdom of Judah would have four kings, two of whom wor-
5 shipped the LORD. The story of the divided kingdom started out sad
and became even sadder as years went by. But in the darkness, some
6 light shone. Prophets spoke God's truth, and the LORD, the Keeper
of His Kingdom, directed all events by His sovereign hand. Even in
the divided kingdom, the LORD reigned supreme.

84

5 In the first eighty years of the divided kingdom, Israel had eight kings, some who reigned only a year or less. This constant turnover of leadership made Israel politically unstable. By contrast, Judah had only four kings during the first eighty years. The two kings with the longest reigns, Asa and Jehoshaphat, were kings who strove to serve the LORD.

6 From the time of Samuel, prophets played an important role in Israel's history. (Remember Nathan and Gad who talked with David and Ahijah who prophesied that Jeroboam would rule ten tribes.) From this time forward, the prophets played an even greater role. The prophets brought God's word to the people, and particularly to the kings, warning of judgment for disobedience and promising blessing for faithfulness. Appendix E provides a timeline of the kings and prophets of Israel and Judah.

Notes:

PSALM 121 A Song of Ascents

1. I will lift up my eyes to the hills—
   From whence comes my help?
2. My help comes from the LORD,
   Who made heaven and earth.
3. He will not allow your foot to be moved;
   He who keeps you will not slumber.
4. Behold, He who keeps Israel
   Shall neither slumber nor sleep.
5. The LORD is your keeper;
   The LORD is your shade at your right hand.
6. The sun shall not strike you by day,
   Nor the moon by night.
7. The LORD shall preserve you from all evil;
   He shall preserve your soul.
8. The LORD shall preserve your going out and your coming in
   From this time forth, and even forevermore.

Isn't it comforting to know that the LORD, Creator of heaven and earth, the Maker of the majestic mountains that reach high and sturdy into the skies, is the One who keeps you safe? Who can move a mountain, even an inch? No one. Just think, the LORD's protection is as secure as the highest, unshakable mountain.

In the darkness, when the lights are out and you are alone, sometimes you can feel afraid. But remember, the LORD never goes to bed at night. All night long He stays awake, never sleeping even for a minute, keeping you safe and secure.

When the burning heat of the sun or the chill of the moonlit night surrounds you, the LORD stays by your side. He keeps you safe from evil and safeguards your soul from enemies. Each day and in everything you do, the LORD's protection never fails.

The LORD is Keeper of His Kingdom, but He is also the Keeper of you, His precious child and heir to the eternal Kingdom of Almighty God.

Notes to Teachers and Parents:

1 Any time that something or someone that God has created becomes more important to us than God, that person or thing has become an idol. When we worship an idol, we believe the lie that God's gifts, not God, will make us content. Eve "worshipped" the fruit from the tree of the knowledge of good and evil and thought she would be happier if she ate it. Ever since Eve's sin in the garden, people have been seeking happiness from the creation, not the Creator.

2 There are many different and appropriate ways to worship the Lord, but several important principles should apply to any worship style: 1) worship must not violate any direct commands of God (e.g., "you shall not make for yourself a carved image" [Exodus 20:4] and "everything should be done in a fitting and orderly way" [1 Corinthians 14:40, NIV]); 2) worship must not be contradictory to the character of God; 3) worship should be God-focused rather than self-focused (in other words, focused on praising and glorifying God rather than on feeling good); and 4) worship should include all the elements that Scripture commands (e.g., prayer, praise, confession, and preaching of God's truth).

Notes:

Chapter 14

A Nation Divided

LESSON SCOPE: 1 Kings 12–16
2 Chronicles 10–16

READ TO ME: 1 Kings 12
2 Chronicles 15–16

THEME: The Lord God rules even when kings are wicked and turn against Him.

MEMORY VERSE:

"[They] exchanged the truth of God for the lie, and worshiped and served the creature rather than the Creator, who is blessed forever. Amen." (Romans 1:25) **1**

KEY FACTS: The Divided Kingdom—The First Eighty Years

	Judah	Israel
Kings	Four kings: Evil—Rehoboam, Abijah Godly—Asa, Jehoshaphat	Eight kings: All eight kings did evil in God's eyes—Jeroboam, Nadab, Baasha, Elah, Zimri, Tibni, Omri, Ahab
Capitals	Jerusalem	First: Shechem, Second: Samaria
Tribes	Two tribes: Judah and Benjamin	Ten tribes: Reuben, Simeon, Dan, Naphtali, Gad, Asher, Issachar, Zebulun, Ephraim, Manasseh
Religion	Worship at temple in Jerusalem; priests were Levites	Worship at high places in Dan and Bethel; priests were not Levites; use of images of golden calves
Prophets	Azariah, Hanani	Ahijah, Jehu, Elijah

MESSAGE FROM THE KING: The King says, "Worship Me in a holy way."

2 Psalm 96:9 says, "Worship the Lord in the splendor of his holiness!" (NIV). God wants you to be joyful but respectful in your worship. What are some right and wrong ways to worship the Lord?

A Nation Divided

What makes a man a wise king? A wise king desires to bring well-being and prosperity to his people and heeds the advice of wise, godly men. Rehoboam, Solomon's son, did neither of these things.

Jesus in the OT
Rehoboam promised to put heavy burdens on the people. In contrast, King Jesus' "burdens" are not hard to carry. In fact, Jesus said, "My yoke is easy, and My burden is light."

The people cried out to Rehoboam, "Your father, Solomon, made us pay high taxes and do harsh labor. Lighten our burdens, and we will serve you." The older men who had served Solomon urged Rehoboam to listen to the people, but Rehoboam was stubborn. He listened to the young men, who said, "Make the burden on the people even heavier!" The people rebelled, and all the tribes but Judah and Benjamin proclaimed Jeroboam to
3 be their king. This was the fulfillment of Ahijah's prophecy to Jeroboam several years earlier. Now there were two nations: Israel and Judah.

In Israel, Jeroboam set up his capital in Tirzah. Because he wanted his people to be loyal to him, he created his own way of worshipping God. He built high places
4 in Dan and Bethel as worship centers and made golden calves to help the people worship. This was wrong because the LORD had commanded that everyone worship at the temple in Jerusalem and had strictly forbidden the use of images for worship. Jeroboam also let men who were not Levites become priests, even though God had said that only Levites were to be priests. All of these things angered the LORD.
5 Even after a prophet warned Jeroboam of his sin and the altar at Bethel split apart, Jeroboam continued in his wicked ways.

When Jeroboam's son became ill, Jeroboam sent his wife in disguise to Ahijah, the prophet, to ask for healing. Ahijah, though blind, was not fooled by the disguise, and the LORD told him to say, "Because Jeroboam has done more evil in Israel than
6 anyone who lived before him, the LORD will bring disaster to his family. One day a king in Israel will kill everyone in Jeroboam's family." Jeroboam's wife returned home, and the young boy died.

Jeroboam's son, Nadab, ruled after Jeroboam's death and was just as evil as Jeroboam, his father. After two years, a man named Baasha plotted against Nadab and killed him and all the rest of Jeroboam's family. This was the fulfillment of the LORD's prophecy against Jeroboam by the prophet Ahijah.

3 In 1 Kings 11:26-40, Ahijah prophesied that Jeroboam would be king of ten tribes. Ahijah met Jeroboam in the countryside, tore his new robe into twelve pieces, and gave Jeroboam ten of the pieces to signify that Jeroboam would rule ten tribes after Solomon's death. When Solomon heard about this prophecy, he tried to kill Jeroboam. Jeroboam escaped to Egypt and stayed there until he heard that Solomon had died. When the people discovered that Rehoboam would be more oppressive as a king than his father had been, they rallied around Jeroboam, and ten tribes crowned him as their king. Only Judah and Benjamin remained with Rehoboam. This action split the kingdom in two parts, and never again would the nation be united as one.

4 These golden calves were not supposed to be images of gods other than Jehovah, but rather were constructed to facilitate worship of the LORD. However, making these images was wrong for two reasons. First, God had forbidden the use of images in worship. Second, these images became a means by which Canaanite religious practices were brought into Israel. Under Jeroboam's rule, polytheism was reintroduced into Israel.

5 God sent a prophet from Judah to Jeroboam to warn him of the danger of his "new" religion. Even when the altar at Bethel split apart and ashes poured out from it after the prophet rebuked Jeroboam, Jeroboam refused to reject his idolatrous religion and turn back to the LORD.

6 This prophecy was fulfilled when Baasha, Israel's third king, killed Nadab (Jeroboam's son, Israel's second king) and everyone else in Jeroboam's family.

Notes:

Notes:

Baasha ruled for twenty-four years. Like Nadab and Jeroboam before him, Baasha displeased the Lord with his constant sin. The word of the Lord came to Baasha through the prophet Jehu, saying, "I made you leader of my people Israel, but you walked in the ways of Jeroboam and caused My people to sin. So I am about to consume you and all your house. (This prophecy would be fulfilled after Baasha's death, during the rule of his son, Elah.)

Baasha remained king until he died of natural causes. After Baasha died, his son, Elah, became king. But after only two years, Zimri, one of Elah's officials who had command of half of Elah's chariots, plotted against Elah, killed him, and became king. After murdering Elah, Zimri immediately killed all of Baasha's family, every single male, in accordance with the Lord's words spoken by Jehu the prophet to Baasha. The Lord used Zimri, wicked as he was, to bring about the fulfillment of His justice.

Jesus in the OT

The king was the representative of the covenant between God and the people. Isn't it sad that most of the kings forgot the covenant and led their people far from the Lord? Jesus, the King, is the representative of the covenant with you. Following Him brings you closer to your heavenly Father.

When the Israelite soldiers encamped near the Philistine town of Gibbethon heard how Zimri had murdered Elah and set himself up as king, they revolted against Zimri, and that very day they proclaimed Omri, commander of Israel's army, to be king of Israel.

With Omri in charge, the army then marched to Tirzah, and laid siege to the city. When Zimri saw that Omri's army had taken the city, he lost hope. He went to the citadel of the palace, set the palace on fire all around himself, and died. Zimri had been king in Israel for only seven days.

The northern kingdom of Israel was now in turmoil. Two men, Omri and Tibni, fought to gain control of the kingdom. The people of Israel were split: Half of them supported Omri and half of them supported Tibni. It was a confusing, uncertain, and violent time, but in the end, Omri's army was stronger than Tibni's army. No one knows exactly how, but Tibni died during the struggle between the two groups of Israelites, and Omri was crowned king in Israel.

While he was king, Omri stabilized the government and moved Israel's capital to Samaria. Within Israel and among neighboring nations, Omri was respected as an impressive ruler. In God's eyes, Omri was an idolater who hurried his nation closer to the day of judgment. After Omri's death, Ahab, Omri's son, became Israel's eighth king.

who no longer knows how to take warning" (NIV).

Notes:

In Judah, when Rehoboam died, his son, Abijah, became king in Judah. Abijah's
7 heart wasn't devoted to the Lord, and he did evil in God's eyes. He ruled only three
years. When he died, his son, Asa, became king in Judah.

Asa commanded that the people of Judah seek the Lord
8 and obey His commands. He smashed the foreign altars and
cut down the Asherah poles. He was fully committed to the
Lord, and the kingdom was at peace because the Lord gave
rest to the land.

The Spirit of God came upon the prophet Azariah, and he said to Asa, "The Lord is with you. Be strong. Don't give up. You will be rewarded." So Asa took courage and removed all the detestable idols from Judah. He even removed his grandmother from her position as queen because she had an Asherah pole. Asa's heart was committed to the Lord all his life.

Off and on throughout these years, Israel and
9 Judah fought against each other. Late in Asa's life, he
made a treaty with Ben-Hadad, king of Aram, to ally with him against Baasha, king
of Israel. Hanani, the seer, warned Asa, "You were foolish because you trusted Ben-
Hadad instead of the Lord. You will be at war from now on." Asa was so angry at
10 Hanani that he put him in prison and brutally oppressed some people who agreed
with Hanani. Then Asa got a severe foot disease and sought help from doctors, not
from the Lord. Because of this disease, his son Jehoshaphat ruled alongside him for
his last few years.

How sad that the first eight kings of Israel and two of Judah's first four kings (Rehoboam and Abijah) refused to acknowledge the Lord as King. When the kings and the people forgot God's covenant, they were ignorant of the blessing that worshipping God could bring to them.

7 First Kings 15:4 says, "...for David's sake the Lord his God gave him a lamp in Jerusalem by raising up a son to succeed him and by making Jerusalem strong" (NIV). Abijah was just as wicked as his father, Rehoboam, had been. Because of God's promise to David to always have a king on the throne, Abijah was able to be king for three years. Abijah's son, Asa, followed him as king and reigned for forty-one years as one of Judah's godly kings.

8 Asherah was a Canaanite goddess. Asherah poles were carved wooden poles that represented this goddess.

9 This was Ben-Hadad I who ruled in Damascus (Aram) around 900–860 BC. His grandson, Ben-Hadad II, was the Aramean king who lived during the days of Elisha.

10 After Hanani rebuked Asa, Asa was so angry with the seer that he put him in prison as a punishment and then brutally treated some of the men who agreed with Hanani. This event shows that in his last years, Asa's heart was not open to godly rebuke, and it emphasizes the importance of perseverance in one's relationship with God. We must never become neglectful of heeding God's Word or resentful when a godly person confronts us with our sin. Life is a marathon that often is more difficult as we near the end of the race. We need God's grace to finish well as much as we needed God's grace to begin the race. Ecclesiastes 4:13 says, "Better a poor but wise youth than an old but foolish king

Notes:

Review Worksheets

A. MEMORY VERSE: "[They] exchanged the truth of God for the lie, and worshiped and served the creature rather than the Creator, who is blessed forever. Amen." (Romans 1:25)

B. KEY FACTS: If the word(s) below describe(s) Judah, write "Judah" in the blank. If the word(s) describe(s) Israel, write "Israel" in the blank.

Eight evil kings	Israel	Prophet Ahijah	Israel
Temple at Jerusalem	Judah	Golden calves	Israel
Two godly kings	Judah	Capital at Samaria	Israel
Ten tribes	Israel	King Jeroboam	Israel
Levites as priests	Judah	Two tribes	Judah
King Rehoboam	Judah	King Asa	Judah
Prophet Azariah	Judah	King Omri	Israel

C. STORY FACTS: Circle **all** the **correct** answers.

1. When Rehoboam became king, the people got upset about the ________.
   (high taxes) bad roads (harsh labor)
2. Rehoboam took the advice of the ______________.
   (young men) older wise men priests
3. Jeroboam built worship centers in the cities of ___________.
   (Dan) Shechem (Bethel)
4. Because Asa was committed to the LORD, he ______________.
   built a new temple (smashed foreign altars) (removed idols)
5. Tribes that made up the kingdom of Judah were ____________.
   Ephraim (Benjamin) (Judah)

D. HOW WELL DO YOU KNOW THE KINGS? Find the kings' names in the Word Find. Then in the blank beside each name put a "J" if he was king in Judah and an "I" if he was king in Israel.

Ahab I
Elah I
Asa J
Abijah J
Jeroboam I
Rehoboam J
Jehoshaphat J
Nadab I

Tibni I
Omri I
Zimri I
Baasha I

T	I	B	R	I	M	O	A	H
A	R	B	E	H	A	H	T	O
H	T	A	H	A	B	A	I	P
P	Z	D	O	J	A	J	B	H
A	I	A	B	A	A	I	N	A
H	M	N	O	H	S	B	I	T
S	A	S	A	S	H	A	L	E
O	I	R	M	O	A	A	T	L
H	A	J	I	T	U	S	E	A
E	I	R	M	I	Z	H	N	P
J	E	R	O	B	O	A	M	O

One king is found twice in the Word Find.

Who is it? Baasha

E. GODLY AND EVIL KINGS:

1. What are two things that King Jeroboam did to change worship in Israel?

See note **11**

2. What are two godly things that King Asa of Judah did?

He smashed the foreign altars and cut down the Asherah poles. He removed all the detestable idols from Judah.

3. What is one thing that King Asa did that displeased the LORD?

He made a treaty with Ben-Hadad, king of Aram.

F. FIND OUT... Jeroboam disobeyed God in his worship. What did the LORD say about correct worship in the Scripture passages below?

Images (Exodus 20:4-6) You should not make an idol and worship it.

Priests (Numbers 3:5-12) Priests should only be from the tribe of Levi.

Place of sacrifices (Exodus 29:42-43) Offerings are to be made at the tabernacle.

11 These are the things that Jeroboam did to change worship in Israel (see 1 Kings 12:23-33): a) he built worship centers in Dan and Bethel with a golden calf at each one so the people wouldn't have to travel to the temple in Jerusalem; b) he built shrines in high places; c) he appointed non-Levite men as priests; d) he instituted worship festivals so the people could offer sacrifices to the golden calves; and e) he installed priests at the high places he had made.

Notes:

Notes to Teachers and Parents:

1 As Christians, sometimes we "fall down," but because the LORD is our covenant God, we will never be utterly "cast down." No matter what happens to us or how we feel, we can be confident that the LORD will continue to uphold us. How do we know that? We know that because He said it through His Word.

2 Throughout Elijah's life, God showed His power in every area of life, often times in miraculous ways. Whether through the provision of daily life, resurrection from death, victory over enemies and foreign gods, the powers of nature, or relief from strong emotions, God showed His sovereignty over everything. Nothing escaped the attention and governing of an Almighty God.

3 One of the times we become the most prone to discouragement is immediately after a great spiritual experience. Like Elijah, we must get apart from the distractions of life and listen for the gentle whisper of God's encouragement. God's promise to us as His covenant people is that He will never leave or forsake us (see Deuteronomy 31:6). So, when we feel discouraged, we must listen to God's words of truth, not our strong emotions.

Notes:

Chapter 15 Elijah—God's Voice of Judgment to a Wicked King

LESSON SCOPE: 1 Kings 16:29–19:18 **READ TO ME:** 1 Kings 16–19

THEME: The LORD God proves He is God over nature, kings, and foreign gods.

MEMORY VERSE:

"The steps of a good man are ordered by the LORD, And He delights in his way. Though he fall, he shall not be utterly cast down; For the LORD upholds him with His hand." (Psalm 37:23-24) **1**

2 **KEY FACTS:** God Shows His Sovereign Power

During Elijah's life, the LORD showed...

His power over...	When He...
Weather	...stopped the rain and dew in Israel for several years.
Daily Food	...provided flour and oil for the widow and her son.
Death	...brought the widow's son back to life.
Pagan Idols	...showed that He was God, not Baal.
Enemies	...helped Elijah escape from wicked Queen Jezebel.
Discouragement	...took away Elijah's discouragement and helped him serve faithfully.

MESSAGE FROM THE KING:

The King says, "Listen to my gentle whisper of encouragement."

Isn't it strange that Elijah became so discouraged after his big victory on Mt. Carmel? Discouragement often happens after great spiritual triumphs. But God hasn't changed. If you listen to His gentle voice, He'll remind you of how much He loves and cares for you. **3**

Elijah—God's Voice of Judgment to a Wicked King

A large black bird hovered overhead and then glided down, landing on the flat rock beside the brook. A few seconds passed before the bird dropped the chunk of meat in its beak onto the rock and flew off. Elijah, God's prophet, thanked the LORD for the food and ate his evening meal.

The ravens had provided food for Elijah—bread and meat in the morning and evening—ever since the drought began. Elijah had warned Ahab, Israel's wicked king, saying, "As the LORD lives, no rain or dew will fall in the next few years except at my word." There at the Kerith Ravine, the LORD provided food and water for Elijah while famine stalked the rest of Israel.

Ahab, son of Omri, did more evil in God's eyes than any king before him, even Jeroboam. He married Jezebel, a worshipper of Baal, and rejected the LORD to serve Baal. He built a temple to Baal in Samaria and told the people to worship Baal. Because of his sin, there was no rain in Israel for several years. **4**

When the brook dried up, the LORD sent Elijah to Zarephath. "I have commanded a widow to take care of you," the LORD said. Elijah met the widow at the city gate and asked for bread. "I have no bread," she replied. "I have only a little flour and oil to make my last meal. After we eat that, my son and I will die."

Elijah encouraged her not to be afraid, saying, "Feed me from what you have, and the LORD promises that your flour will not be used up nor your oil run dry until the LORD sends rain." She did as Elijah said, and from that day, she cared for Elijah and always had plenty of flour and oil.

One day, the widow's son got sick and died. "What do you have against me? What sin have I done that my son must die?" she cried out. Elijah took the son in his arms and carried him to his bed. Three times he stretched himself out on top of the boy, and prayed, "O LORD God, let this boy's life return to him!" The LORD answered Elijah's prayer, and the boy came back to life. The widow exclaimed, "Now I know that you are a man of God and that God's words from your mouth are truth."

Some time later, King Ahab set out to meet Elijah, and asked him, "Is that you, troublemaker?" Elijah answered, "By worshipping Baal, you have brought trouble to Israel." Elijah challenged Ahab to a contest: the 450 prophets of Baal against Elijah, the prophet of the LORD.

4 Ahab married Jezebel, daughter of Ethbaal, king of Sidon, as a result of an alliance made between Ahab's father, Omri, and Ethbaal. Jezebel was an ardent worshipper of Baal and brought her religion with her to Israel. After his marriage with Jezebel, Ahab forsook worship of Yahweh and became a Baal worshipper, actually building a temple for Baal in the city of Samaria. This idolatry was a more serious breaking of God's covenant than any of the idolatrous actions of Israel's former leaders (see 1 Kings 16:33). It was because of Ahab's sin that God stopped the rain and brought famine to Israel.

Notes:

5 Despite all their actions, the prophets of Baal could not get their god to answer them. Elijah's words showed the contrast between Baal and Yahweh. Baal might be sleeping or on a trip, but Yahweh is the God who "neither slumbers nor sleeps" (Psalm 121:4) and is the constant keeper of Israel.

6 Elijah wanted there to be no doubt that the fire that would light the sacrifice came directly from the LORD. Only an omnipotent God could light a water-drenched sacrifice.

7 The LORD's response to Elijah's prayer was immediate. Dramatically, fire fell from heaven and consumed not just the sacrifice, but the altar and all the water lying in the trench.

8 The LORD's response to the people's declaration, "The LORD, He is God," was to send rain. Because of Ahab's idolatry, the LORD had stopped the rain, and, subsequently, because the people began to worship Him again, He allowed rain to fall on Israel once again.

9 Mt. Horeb is another name for Mt. Sinai. Elijah sought refuge on the mountain where God gave the Law to Moses and showed Himself through fire and thunder to the Israelites (see Exodus 19:16-19). Mt. Sinai is also where the LORD made the covenant with His people, promising to be their God and be present with them. Elijah's experience was very different than Moses's experience. On Mt. Horeb (Mt. Sinai), the LORD spoke to Elijah in a gentle whisper instead of booming thunder (see 1 Kings 19:11-13).

Notes:

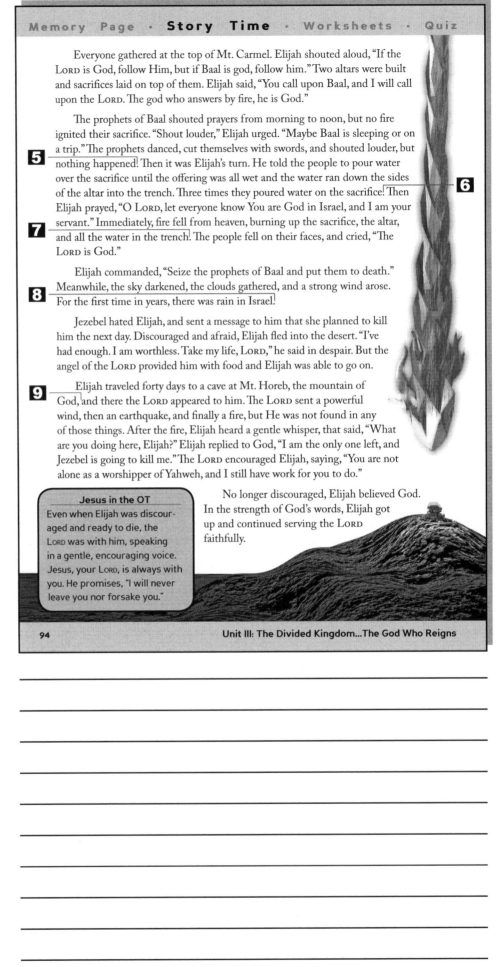

Everyone gathered at the top of Mt. Carmel. Elijah shouted aloud, "If the LORD is God, follow Him, but if Baal is god, follow him." Two altars were built and sacrifices laid on top of them. Elijah said, "You call upon Baal, and I will call upon the LORD. The god who answers by fire, he is God."

The prophets of Baal shouted prayers from morning to noon, but no fire ignited their sacrifice. "Shout louder," Elijah urged. "Maybe Baal is sleeping or on a trip." The prophets danced, cut themselves with swords, and shouted louder, but
5 nothing happened! Then it was Elijah's turn. He told the people to pour water over the sacrifice until the offering was all wet and the water ran down the sides of the altar into the trench. Three times they poured water on the sacrifice! **6** Then Elijah prayed, "O LORD, let everyone know You are God in Israel, and I am your servant." Immediately, fire fell from heaven, burning up the sacrifice, the altar,
7 and all the water in the trench! The people fell on their faces, and cried, "The LORD is God."

Elijah commanded, "Seize the prophets of Baal and put them to death." Meanwhile, the sky darkened, the clouds gathered, and a strong wind arose.
8 For the first time in years, there was rain in Israel!

Jezebel hated Elijah, and sent a message to him that she planned to kill him the next day. Discouraged and afraid, Elijah fled into the desert. "I've had enough. I am worthless. Take my life, LORD," he said in despair. But the angel of the LORD provided him with food and Elijah was able to go on.

9 Elijah traveled forty days to a cave at Mt. Horeb, the mountain of God, and there the LORD appeared to him. The LORD sent a powerful wind, then an earthquake, and finally a fire, but He was not found in any of those things. After the fire, Elijah heard a gentle whisper, that said, "What are you doing here, Elijah?" Elijah replied to God, "I am the only one left, and Jezebel is going to kill me." The LORD encouraged Elijah, saying, "You are not alone as a worshipper of Yahweh, and I still have work for you to do."

Jesus in the OT
Even when Elijah was discouraged and ready to die, the LORD was with him, speaking in a gentle, encouraging voice. Jesus, your LORD, is always with you. He promises, "I will never leave you nor forsake you."

No longer discouraged, Elijah believed God. In the strength of God's words, Elijah got up and continued serving the LORD faithfully.

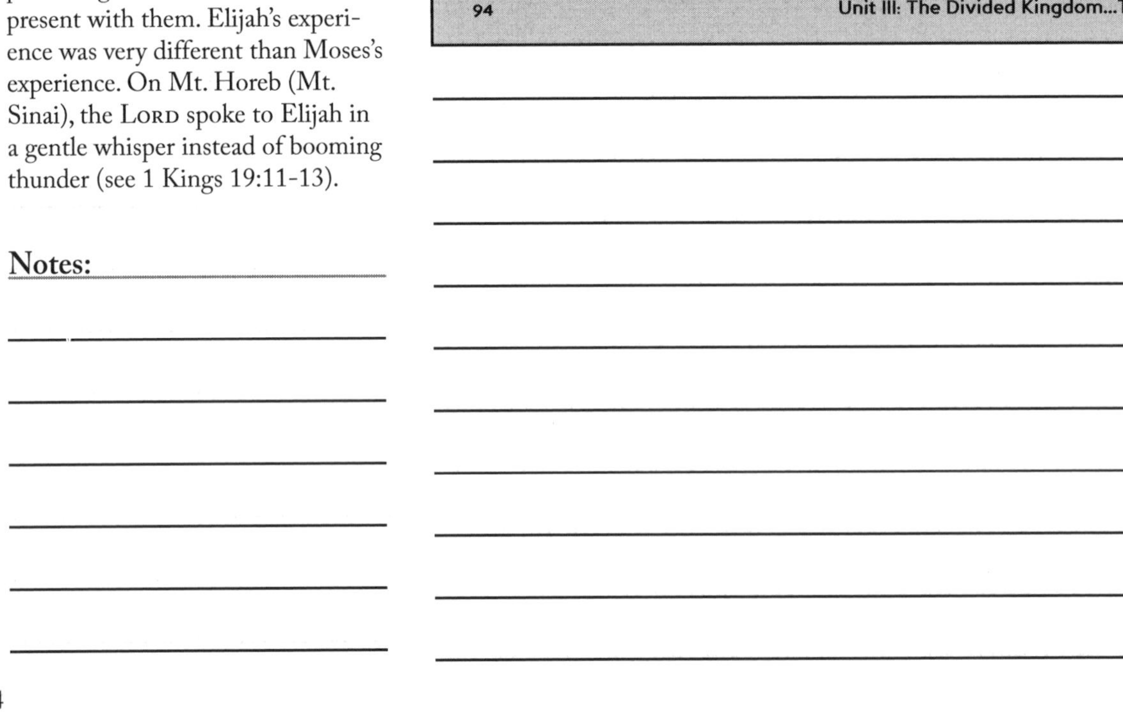

Review Worksheets

A. MEMORY VERSE: "The steps of a good man are ordered by the LORD, And He delights in his way. Though he fall, he shall not be utterly cast down; For the LORD upholds him with His hand." (Psalm 37:23-24)

B. KEY FACTS: Fill in the blanks.

The Life of Elijah

BY GOD'S POWER… Elijah spoke the words from God and the rain and dew stopped for several years. He promised the widow she would always have flour and oil to make bread, and he brought her son back to life. Elijah showed the people that the LORD, not Baal, was God. He escaped from wicked Queen Jezebel. God spoke to him in a whisper, and Elijah was no longer discouraged. He continued to serve God faithfully all his life.

C. STORY FACTS: Circle the **correct** answer.

1. The LORD sent ________ to bring food to Elijah.
   eagles — (ravens) — pigeons
2. Ahab was more wicked than Jeroboam because he ______.
   (built a temple for Baal) — killed prophets — fought many wars
3. There were ________ prophets of Baal on the top of Mt. Carmel.
   40 — (450) — 7,000
4. When Elijah was discouraged, God spoke to him ________.
   by a strong wind — by an earthquake — (in a gentle whisper)
5. After the LORD spoke to Elijah in the cave at Mt. Horeb, Elijah ____.
   (served God faithfully) — built an altar to God — went to the desert

Notes:

D. WHO SAID THIS? Draw a line from each quote to the person who said it. Some of them said more than one thing.

Ahab Elijah Widow God's People The Lord

- I am worthless. Take my life, Lord.
- I know the words from your mouth are God's truth.
- Is that you, troublemaker?
- I have no bread.
- The Lord is God.
- O Lord, let everyone know you are God in Israel.
- I have commanded a widow to take care of you.
- No rain or dew will fall except at My word.
- You are not the only one who worships the Lord.

E. WHAT HAPPENED ON MT. CARMEL? Put the story boxes in order.

5 Fire burned up Elijah's sacrifice.

2 Elijah said, "Shout louder. Maybe your god is sleeping."

4 Elijah had water poured on his sacrifice three times.

3 The prophets of Baal danced, shouted louder, and cut themselves.

6 The people shouted, "The Lord is God."

1 The prophets of Baal prayed until noon, but nothing happened.

F. FIND OUT... Read Psalm 42. Then circle every other letter and put the letters in the blanks to find out what to do when you are discouraged. (Start with the second letter.)

A P O U S T E Y R O T U M R I H E O S P O E N I K N W G L O S D

P U T Y O U R H O P E I N G O D

Chapter 16

Ahab & Jehoshaphat—Two Very Different Kings

LESSON SCOPE: 1 Kings 20–22
2 Kings 1–2
2 Chronicles 17–21

READ TO ME: 1 Kings 20–22

THEME: The LORD God controls the course of history.

MEMORY VERSE:

1 "Many are the plans in a man's heart, but it is the LORD's purpose that prevails." (Proverbs 19:21, NIV)

KEY FACTS: Two Very Different Kings

King Jehoshaphat: Judah	King Ahab: Israel
Turned people back to the LORD.	Turned people away from the LORD.
Worshipped at Jerusalem's temple and instructed people in the fear of God.	Built a temple to Baal and encouraged idol worship.
Walked in the ways of godly King David.	Walked in the ways of wicked King Jeroboam.
Jehu prophesied God's blessing on him.	Micaiah prophesied his death.
Neighboring nations were at peace.	Aram attacked Israel several times.
Prayed before battle.	Ignored a prophet's advice and put that prophet in prison.

MESSAGE FROM THE KING:

The King says, "Nothing happens by accident. I am sovereign!"

How often do you say, "That was an accident! It wasn't supposed to happen that way!"? Since the whole world is under God's sovereign control,
2 there can't really be accidents. Isn't it comforting to know that the world isn't spinning out of control?

Notes to Teachers and Parents:

1 In its arrogance, the human heart actually believes that God's plan can be subverted by human actions. For example, Ahab thought that disguising himself would protect him from Micaiah's prophecy. (Micaiah said Ahab would die on the battlefield.) It is the LORD's purpose that always prevails.

2 No one can give a completely satisfactory explanation of the sovereignty of God. However, we know from Scripture that two things are true: 1) God is totally sovereign in all circumstances; and 2) people make real choices and are responsible for the choices they make. Though we can't explain how both are completely true, we must rest in the knowledge that they are true and find comfort in knowing that we have a God who is big enough to take perfect care of us no matter what our circumstances may be.

Notes:

Ahab & Jehoshaphat—Two Very Different Kings

Arising from the shambles of Solomon's glorious kingdom were two very different kingdoms with two very different kings. What made these kingdoms so different? Each king's reaction to the covenant, that's what!

3 King Ahab of Israel rejected God's covenant, and disobeyed the LORD's com- 4
mands. While Ahab was king, Ben-Hadad, king of Aram, along with thirty-two
other kings, besieged the city of Samaria. "Give me your silver, gold, and the best of
your wives and children," Ben-Hadad demanded.

At first, Ahab agreed to give Ben-Hadad what he wanted, but when Ben-Hadad demanded more, the elders of the people told Ahab, "Don't listen to him or agree with his demands."

Then a prophet came to Ahab, and said, "Start the battle against Ben-Hadad. God will give you victory, and then you will know that He is the LORD."

Ahab attacked Ben-Hadad, and a drunken, defeated Ben-Hadad escaped with
5 his army. Undaunted, Ben-Hadad returned the next spring to fight Israel. With
God's help, Israel again conquered the Arameans. When Ben-Hadad begged for his
life, Ahab disobeyed the LORD and let him live. He made a treaty with Ben-Hadad.
6 A prophet then confronted Ahab, saying, "Because you set free a man that the LORD
had determined should die, you will die." (Ben-Hadad was to die because he had
dishonored the name of the LORD and had attacked God's people.)

Near Ahab's palace was a well-groomed, fruitful
vineyard belonging to Naboth. Ahab wanted this vineyard, and when Naboth refused to sell it to him, Ahab
pouted like a little child. Seeing her husband so sullen,
Jezebel rebuked Ahab, "Is this how a king acts? If you
want something, you should have it because you are
the king! I'll get it for you." Jezebel plotted a wicked
scheme. She hired two men to lie about Naboth, saying
he had blasphemed God. When the elders of Naboth's
town heard that Naboth had blasphemed, they dragged
7 him outside the city and stoned him to death. (This
was the penalty for anyone who blasphemed God.)

Jesus in the OT

When Ahab refused to kill Ben-Hadad, he was not a faithful king. He wasn't defending the honor of the LORD and wasn't protecting his people from enemies who wanted to destroy them. Jesus, as King, always honors God the Father and protects His people from those who would destroy them.

The LORD sent Elijah to Ahab. "Because you have
murdered a man, you and your sons will die, every last one, and the dogs will lick up
8 your blood." Hearing this, Ahab humbled himself, and the LORD delayed the destruction of Ahab's whole household until the days of his son.

3 Ahab was a worshipper of Baal.

4 This Ben-Hadad was probably the grandson of Ben-Hadad I, who fought with Asa in 1 Kings 15.

5 Ben-Hadad did not understand that Israel's God was Elohim, the one and only God of the universe. He believed that Israel's God was the god of the hills and that if he provoked a battle on the plain, Israel's God would not be able to help them. (Maybe Ben-Hadad thought this because both Samaria, the capital of Israel, and Jerusalem, the capital of Judah, were built upon hills.) In those days, people believed that battles were not fought simply between opposing nations, but between opposing gods as well. Ben-Hadad thought that his best chance of defeating Israel was to fight on the plain where Israel's "god of the hills" could not help them. Ben-Hadad did not honor and respect the name of God Almighty. God delivered the Arameans into Israel's hands so that Ben-Hadad and his army would know that Israel's God was the LORD. The LORD gave Israel an astonishing victory over Ben-Hadad, and by this victory demonstrated His sovereign power.

6 Undaunted by his defeat, Ben-Hadad attacks Israel again the next spring. Scripture describes the scene like this: "The Israelites camped opposite them like two small flocks of goats, while the Arameans covered the countryside" (1 Kings 20:27, NIV). Israel was able to defeat Ben-Hadad's powerful army, killing 100,000 soldiers in one day. The rest of Ben-Hadad's army fled to the city of Aphek. There, a wall collapsed, killing 27,000 more soldiers. Then, Ben-Hadad hid deep inside the city. All this happened because the LORD wanted to show Ben-Hadad that He was not just a "god of the hills." Unfortunately, Ahab didn't understand this himself. He didn't regard the LORD as King. Ahab thought that he could disregard the LORD's instructions and do as he pleased. When Ben-Hadad asked to be spared from death, Ahab called him a "brother," instead of recognizing him as an enemy of the LORD. Ahab made a treaty with Ben-Hadad and set him free. Ahab's decision was wrong for two reasons. First, Ahab made a treaty with a foreign king. This action was in direct disobedience to God's command in Deuteronomy 7:1-6, which forbids Israel from making treaties with foreign nations. Second, Ahab allowed a man to live that "I [the LORD] had determined should die" (1 Kings 20:42, NIV). The LORD had determined that Ben-Hadad should die because he had dishonored the name of the LORD. Instead of obeying the LORD, Ahab decided to overrule God and make his own kingly decision. Ahab's response to the prophet's rebuke was not repentance for his disobedience, but anger and sullenness. In summary, Ahab experienced the mighty deliverance of the LORD, but nonetheless immediately took matters into his own hands; he disobeyed a direct command from God and then was unrepentant for his sin.

7 Blasphemers were punished by being taken outside the camp of Israel and then stoned to death (Leviticus 24:13-16). Second Kings 9:26 indicates that all Naboth's sons were killed along with him

8 In His mercy, God delayed the fulfillment of this prophecy until after Ahab's death.

9 After the victory over Ben-Hadad in 1 Kings 20, there were three years of peace between Israel and Aram (Syria). According to the *Spirit of the Reformation Study Bible:*

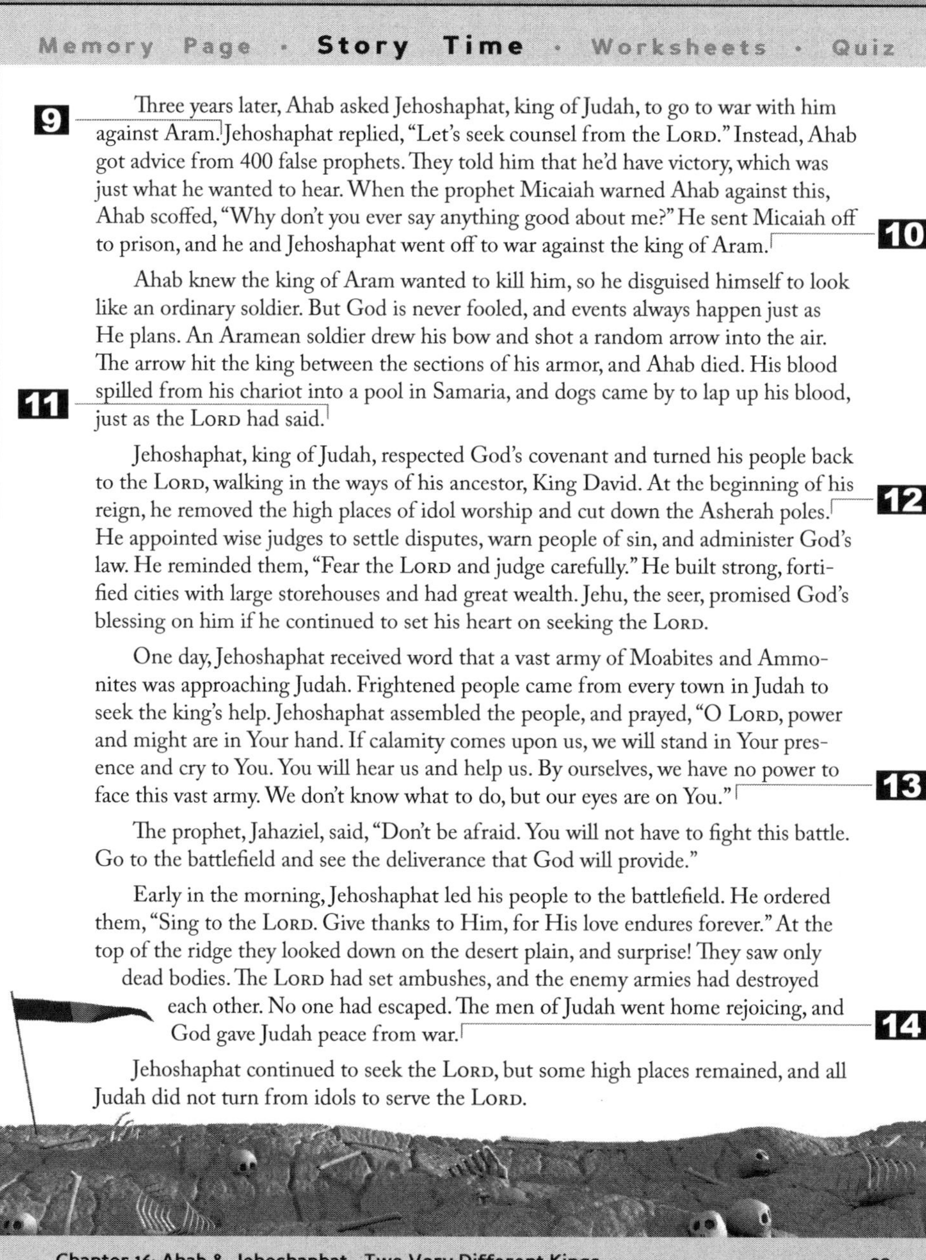

9 Three years later, Ahab asked Jehoshaphat, king of Judah, to go to war with him against Aram. Jehoshaphat replied, "Let's seek counsel from the LORD." Instead, Ahab got advice from 400 false prophets. They told him that he'd have victory, which was just what he wanted to hear. When the prophet Micaiah warned Ahab against this, Ahab scoffed, "Why don't you ever say anything good about me?" He sent Micaiah off to prison, and he and Jehoshaphat went off to war against the king of Aram. **10**

Ahab knew the king of Aram wanted to kill him, so he disguised himself to look like an ordinary soldier. But God is never fooled, and events always happen just as He plans. An Aramean soldier drew his bow and shot a random arrow into the air. The arrow hit the king between the sections of his armor, and Ahab died. His blood
11 spilled from his chariot into a pool in Samaria, and dogs came by to lap up his blood, just as the LORD had said.

Jehoshaphat, king of Judah, respected God's covenant and turned his people back to the LORD, walking in the ways of his ancestor, King David. At the beginning of his reign, he removed the high places of idol worship and cut down the Asherah poles. **12** He appointed wise judges to settle disputes, warn people of sin, and administer God's law. He reminded them, "Fear the LORD and judge carefully." He built strong, fortified cities with large storehouses and had great wealth. Jehu, the seer, promised God's blessing on him if he continued to set his heart on seeking the LORD.

One day, Jehoshaphat received word that a vast army of Moabites and Ammonites was approaching Judah. Frightened people came from every town in Judah to seek the king's help. Jehoshaphat assembled the people, and prayed, "O LORD, power and might are in Your hand. If calamity comes upon us, we will stand in Your presence and cry to You. You will hear us and help us. By ourselves, we have no power to face this vast army. We don't know what to do, but our eyes are on You." **13**

The prophet, Jahaziel, said, "Don't be afraid. You will not have to fight this battle. Go to the battlefield and see the deliverance that God will provide."

Early in the morning, Jehoshaphat led his people to the battlefield. He ordered them, "Sing to the LORD. Give thanks to Him, for His love endures forever." At the top of the ridge they looked down on the desert plain, and surprise! They saw only dead bodies. The LORD had set ambushes, and the enemy armies had destroyed each other. No one had escaped. The men of Judah went home rejoicing, and God gave Judah peace from war. **14**

Jehoshaphat continued to seek the LORD, but some high places remained, and all Judah did not turn from idols to serve the LORD.

New International Version, the two nations actually made a coalition, and along with ten other kings, they allied together to fight off an invasion from Assyria (Zondervan, 544). When Jehoshaphat of Judah went to visit Ahab (see 1 King 22), Ahab suggested that the two of them ally against Aram. The Syrians were occupying the territory of Ramoth Gilead, a territory formerly part of Israel, and Ahab thought it was time to capture it back. He wanted to break his alliance with Aram and create this alliance with Judah in order to accomplish the recapturing of this land.

10 This event shows the difference between godly Jehoshaphat and wicked Ahab. Jehoshaphat's first thought was to seek counsel from the LORD. Ahab's plan of action was to seek counsel from 400 false prophets who would tell him what he wanted to hear. When Micaiah spoke the truth, Ahab threw him in prison and continued doing what he wanted to do.

11 Despite all Ahab's conniving and trickery, his death occurred exactly as the prophets Elijah and Micaiah had prophesied. Micaiah had prophesied that Ahab would die in the battle, and Elijah had prophesied years before that dogs would lick up Ahab's blood. ("In the place where dogs licked up Naboth's blood, dogs will lick up your blood—yes, yours!" [1 Kings 21:19, NIV]). God's word through the prophets was fulfilled just as they had said. The king of Aram was almost fooled by Ahab's scheme (see 1 Kings 22:29-30), but two events ordained by God showed God's perfect execution of His will. First, when the king of Aram's chariot commanders heard Jehoshaphat's voice, they knew that the man dressed in kingly robes was not Ahab, but Jehoshaphat. The king of Aram had commanded his men, "Do not fight with anyone, small or great, except the king of Israel" (1 Kings 22:31, NIV), so chariot commanders heard Jehoshaphat's voice and stopped pursuing him. Second, a "random" arrow by an unknown bowman found its mark in the tiny gap between the sections of Ahab's armor. Because God is sovereign, His purpose always prevails, and there are no true accidents or random events. We will prevail only as we bow down before the almighty King of the universe.

12 Comparing 2 Chronicles 17:6 with 1 Kings 22:43, we understand that Jehoshaphat removed the high places and Asherah poles at the beginning of his reign, but at the end of his reign there were still high places. Either he had not removed all of the high places or he had become lax and had allowed new high places to be built and to remain.

13 Jehoshaphat's first response to danger was to pray. He recognized his own powerlessness and knew that his nation's only hope lay in deliverance from God.

14 Jehoshaphat marched to the battlefield, singing praise to the LORD. The LORD gave Judah victory without their shooting one arrow. The result was total destruction of the enemy armies and peace with their neighboring nations during Jehoshaphat's reign as king (see 2 Chronicles 20).

Notes:

Notes:

Review Worksheets

A. MEMORY VERSE: "Many are the plans in a man's heart, but it is the LORD's purpose that prevails." (Proverbs 19:21, NIV)

B. KEY FACTS:

Two Very Different Kings

Jehoshaphat served the LORD. Ahab served Baal and other idols. The god they served made a difference in what their kingdoms looked like. Using the **key facts** table, describe these two different kingdoms in the blanks.

Kingdom of Jehoshaphat	Kingdom of Ahab
Turned people back to the LORD	Turned people away from the LORD
Worshipped at Jerusalem	Built a temple to Baal
Walked in ways of godly David	Walked in ways of wicked Jeroboam
At peace with neighbors	Aram attacked Israel several times
Prayed	Ignored God's prophet

C. STORY FACTS: Fill in the blanks.

1. When Ahab worshipped Baal, he was rejecting God's covenant.
2. Ahab disobeyed God when he refused to kill Ben-Hadad.
3. Ahab wanted to buy Naboth's vineyard, but Naboth wouldn't sell it.
4. Two men lied, and said that Naboth had blasphemed God.
5. Jehoshaphat wanted to seek advice from the LORD.
6. Ahab was killed by a random arrow shot into the air.
7. Jehoshaphat walked in the ways of his ancestor King David.
8. The prophet Jahaziel told Jehoshaphat not to be afraid.
9. When Judah arrived at the battlefield, they saw only dead bodies.

D. JEHOSHAPHAT'S WISE JUDGES: Cross out all the I's, P's, and S's to discover what Jehoshaphat told his wise judges.

FIESPARISTIHSPELIOSIRID
JISUPSIDGSECISPARSESPFIULILSPY

F e a r t h e L O R D AND

j u d g e c a r e f u l l y.

What three tasks were Jehoshaphat's judges told to do?

1. Settle disputes 2. Warn people of sin

3. Administer God's law

E. JEHOSHAPHAT'S PRAYER: Unscramble the words and then use them to complete Jehoshaphat's prayer.

"O Lord, power (ROPEW) and might (THIMG) are in Your hand. If calamity (TAILAMCY) comes upon us,... hear (REAH) and help (LEPH) us.... We have no power to face this vast army (MYRA).... Our eyes (YESE) are on You."

F. FIND OUT... What is a prophet?

A prophet is a person who speaks for God. The three different Hebrew words for a prophet are translated into English as "prophet" or "seer." **15**

1. How does a person become a prophet? (Jeremiah 14:14, NIV)

The Lord sends, appoints, and speaks to them.

2. How did the people know whether a prophet spoke God's words or lied?

(Deuteronomy 13:1-3) If he says to worship idols, he is not from God.

(Deuteronomy 18:22) If what he says does not happen, he is not from God.

Notes to Teachers and Parents:

15 In Scripture, a prophet is a person who speaks for God. Most prophets were men, but a few prophetesses are mentioned (Miriam in Exodus 15:20; Deborah in Judges 4:4; Huldah in 2 Kings 22:14; Noadiah, a false prophetess, in Nehemiah 6:14; and Anna in Luke 2:36). The Hebrew word for prophet means "one who speaks." Two other Hebrew words have a similar meaning and are translated into English as "seer." One of these Hebrew words for "seer" means "one who sees," and the other means "one who sees a vision." Although some Old Testament prophets predicted future events ("foretold"), more often a prophet was one who spoke forth ("forth told") God's words. A person became a prophet because the Lord chose the person and then sent him or her forth to speak for Him (see Jeremiah 1:4-5, 14:14-15). There were self-appointed prophets, but the Lord spoke out against them. The test of a prophet was twofold: 1) the prophet's words could not contradict God's written commands; and 2) the prophet's words must come true. If a prophet's words did not meet both of these qualifications, the person was a false prophet. Prophets were considered false for two reasons: 1) the prophet worshipped a god other than Yahweh; or 2) the prophet claimed to worship Yahweh but did not meet the tests of a true prophet. The prophet was also supposed to be the "watchman" over God's people, pointing out the people's sin, warning of God's judgment to come, and leading the people in the way of God's truth. Most of the time, the people did not appreciate the prophets' words, and many prophets were persecuted. Not all the godly prophets wrote books. Some of the non-writing godly prophets mentioned in Scripture are Nathan, Gad, Ahijah, Micaiah, Azariah, Hanani, Jehu, Jahaziel, Elijah, and Elisha.

Notes:

Notes to Teachers and Parents:

1 Nebuchadnezzar spoke these words after his sanity was restored to him. In Daniel 4:28-30, Nebuchadnezzar bragged about what he had accomplished as king of Babylon by his mighty power and for his own glory. The LORD judged Nebuchadnezzar for these arrogant words, and immediately this prideful king became like a beast of the field, eating grass and living like an animal. By God's grace, Nebuchadnezzar's sanity was restored, and his response to God's mercy was a hymn of praise to the LORD. Mighty Nebuchadnezzar recognized that the Lord God was the one who ruled the dominions of the world and that human rulers reigned only by God's divine permission. This passage from Daniel is one of the most powerful passages describing God's sovereign control over the nations of the world.

2 Elisha did many amazing miracles, but every one of them was accomplished by God's power and for God's glory.

3 Why do we fret and worry so much? It's because we don't really believe that God has everything under His control. When life is going well, we can easily believe that we have life under control. That control, however, is simply an illusion, because in a moment everything about our lives could dramatically change. When life is going badly, we can easily believe that life is out of control. This is just as erroneous a belief, because our sovereign God has control of all life's circumstances, and life is never out of control, even though it may feel like it is. Our comfort in life is in knowing that a sovereign God, who is also our loving heavenly Father, is orchestrating all events for His glory and our good.

Notes:

Chapter 17

Elisha—God's Voice to Rulers & Ordinary People

LESSON SCOPE: 1 Kings 19:19–21
2 Kings 1–8

READ TO ME: 2 Kings 2, 5–7

THEME: The LORD God controls the destiny of rulers and ordinary people.

MEMORY VERSE:

"[The Most High] does according to His will in the army of heaven And among the inhabitants of the earth. No one can restrain His hand Or say to Him, 'What have you done?'" (Daniel 4:35b) 1

KEY FACTS: **God's Sovereignty and Elisha's Ministry** 2

God is sovereign over…	By God's power Elisha was able to…
Nature	Divide the Jordan River and heal the bad waters.
Ordinary People's Lives	Make the widow's oil fill up many jars.
Life and Death	Bring the Shunammite woman's son back to life.
Disease	Heal Naaman from leprosy.
Enemies and Nations	Know the battle plans of the king of Aram.
Disaster and Good Fortune	Prophesy the end of the Aramean siege.
Rulers	Prophesy the future actions of Hazael of Aram.
How big is God?	
God is **sovereign.**	God controls all things.
God is **omnipotent.**	God is all-powerful.
God is **omniscient.**	God knows all things.

MESSAGE FROM THE KING: The King says, "Don't fret and worry. I've got everything under control."

What do you worry about? Most of the things you worry about probably won't ever happen. Psalm 37:8 says, "Do not fret—it only causes harm." You can trust God because today, tomorrow, and forever are under His control. 3

Notes:

Elisha—God's Voice to Rulers & Ordinary People

One minute the two prophets were walking side by side, chatting together. The next minute, a fiery chariot pulled by flaming horses swooped down from heaven and parted the men, just before a twirling, swirling whirlwind wrapped around one of them and swooshed him into the clouds. **4**

Elisha stared heavenward at the spot where his teacher had vanished from sight. Elijah, the prophet of judgment, was gone, and Elisha, the prophet of mercy, received
5 a double portion of Elijah's spirit. Elisha was now God's messenger to Israel and the neighboring nations. Picking up Elijah's discarded cloak, Elisha struck the Jordan River with it and passed through the divided water to the other side. This was the first of many miracles that Elisha would do to show God's mercy or to proclaim His absolute control over heaven and earth.

As God's prophet, Elisha walked from town to town. In Jericho, the men of the city said, "The water here is bad, and the crops won't grow. Can you help us?" Elisha asked for a new bowl filled with salt. He sprinkled the salt into the spring water, saying, "This is what the LORD says, 'I have healed this water.'" Instantly, the water was pure and healthy.

In another town, a poor widow begged him, "My husband is dead, and I have nothing but a little oil. If I don't pay my creditor, he will make my two sons his slaves." Elisha had compassion on her, and said, "Find as many jars as you can. Pour the oil into the jars, and keep pouring until all the jars are filled." She did as Elisha said, and one by one she filled jar after jar after jar. When all the jars were filled from her tiny supply of oil, she sold the oil and had plenty of money to provide for her sons.

A rich woman from Shunem showed hospitality to Elisha whenever he **6**
passed through her town. The woman grieved because she had no son. In gratitude for her kindness and to show God's power, Elisha promised that in a year

4 Contrary to many artists' conceptions of this event, Elijah was not taken to heaven in a chariot of fire, but in a whirlwind. The chariot of fire separated Elijah and Elisha so that the whirlwind could sweep Elijah swiftly up to heaven.

5 Francis Breisch, Jr., in his book *The Kingdom of God*, makes this helpful distinction between Elijah and Elisha (Breisch, 127-128). Elijah spoke words of judgment to King Ahab, Queen Jezebel, and the prophets of Baal. In doing so, he was speaking to the people of Israel as well, warning them of the grave danger of the sin of idolatry. Elisha, on the other hand, worked many miracles of mercy (healing the waters, feeding the people, healing Naaman, etc.). Elisha had an impact on ordinary people and mighty rulers, and everywhere he went he proclaimed God's righteousness as well as His mercy.

6 This rich woman's husband was old. She was concerned what would happen to her after his death because she had no son to care for her in her old age. Elisha recognized the kindness of this woman in providing food, drink, and lodging for him and his servant. He desired to reward her for her hospitality. Though she asked for a son, she doubted that Elisha was able to make this desire happen for her. ("Don't mislead your servant, O man of God" 2 Kings 4:16b, NIV)

7 The woman's response to her son's death was to seek out Elisha immediately. Once she found him, she persisted, even though Elisha's servant tried to push her away, until Elisha came with her to her house. Her faith was rewarded; her son was brought back to life.

8 Most likely, this was Ben-Hadad II, grandson of Ben-Hadad I who fought against Asa (see 1 Kings 15).

9 The disease of leprosy was a death sentence at this time. Leprosy had no cure, and its victim lived a tragic life of isolation (because the disease was so contagious) and gradual physical deterioration. In Israel, a leper was ceremonially unclean (Leviticus 13:3) and could not worship at the tabernacle/temple. Anyone who came in contact with a leper was considered unclean, so lepers were forced to live apart from family and friends.

10 Israel's king knew it was impossible for him to cure the dreaded disease of leprosy. When he heard Ben-Hadad's request, Israel's king panicked, thinking that this was an attempt by Ben-Hadad to start a war.

11 Naaman, an important man and a valiant commander, was insulted by being met by Elisha's servant instead of Elisha himself. Naaman had traveled from Aram, whose capital was Damascus, and arrived in style in military dress and with a contingent of horses and chariots, and the humble prophet would not even take the time to speak with him personally. In addition, Elisha's instructions for Naaman to wash in the dirty and uninviting waters of the Jordan seemed ridiculous and insulting to Naaman. He said, "Are not Abana and Pharpar, the rivers of Damascus, better than any of the waters of Israel? Couldn't I wash in them and be cleansed?" (2 Kings 5:12, NIV). His response to Elisha's instructions was to turn away in an arrogant rage.

God would give her a son, and He did. Several years later, this son died. The woman
7 immediately sent for Elisha. Arriving at her house, Elisha lay on top of the son once, and then again. The boy sneezed seven times and opened his eyes. The Lord had brought him back to life.

8
Naaman, a valiant commander in Ben-Hadad's army, had the dreadful disease
9 of leprosy. A young Israelite slave girl in his household said, "God's servant, Elisha, could cure you." When Naaman told Ben-Hadad what the girl said, Ben-Hadad sent Naaman to the king of Israel. In panic, Israel's king tore his robe. "How can I cure
10 leprosy?" he exclaimed. Hearing this, Elisha told the king to send Naaman to him.

When Naaman arrived at Elisha's house, Elisha sent a messenger to Naaman with the strangest instructions: He said, "Go wash seven times in the dirty Jordan River." Naaman was furious. He was an important man! Why couldn't Elisha talk
11 to him in person? Aren't the rivers of Aram better than the Jordan River? What a ridiculous thing to ask him to do! Naaman left in a rage, but his servants gave him
12 good advice. "If the prophet had given you some great thing to do, wouldn't you have done it? Why not do this simple thing?" So Naaman bathed seven times in the Jordan River, and immediately upon rising up the seventh time, his skin became perfectly
13 healthy. Naaman praised God, saying, "Now I know that there is no God in the world except Israel's God."

Once again, Ben-Hadad, the king of Aram, fought against Israel. Yet each time he moved his army, Israel's king was aware of his plans and evaded his attack. Ben-Hadad called his officers together, and demanded, "There is a spy among us. Which one of you is telling Israel's king what our battle plans are?" One of the officers replied, "It's not us! It's the prophet Elisha!" for through the Lord's revelation, Elisha knew all about Ben-Hadad's military strategy.

In response, Ben-Hadad and his army marched to Dothan where Elisha was staying. In the morning, Elisha and his servant saw a mighty army of horses and chariots surrounding the city. "What shall we do?" the frightened servant exclaimed. "Don't be afraid," Elisha replied. "Those that are with us are more than those that are with them." Then he prayed, "Lord, open my servant's eyes so he can see." The Lord opened the servant's eyes, and in the hills he saw horses and chariots of fire—God's heavenly host—protecting the city.

As the Aramean army advanced toward the city, Elisha prayed, "Strike the army with blindness." Then Elisha led the blinded soldiers into the city of Samaria. When the Lord opened their eyes again, the enemy soldiers were standing in the middle of

12 Isn't this a good picture of many people's response to the salvation that is available through Jesus Christ? God's way of salvation seems ridiculous and too simple to them. Just like Naaman, they want to do something dramatic to be cleansed. Naaman had to accept this humble bathing in a dirty river as a means of receiving cleansing from the disease that would bring certain death if not cured.

13 Naaman's response after being cured of leprosy was to acknowledge who God was. Israel's God was not just greater than the gods of Aram, but was the only God. Naaman accepted the God of Israel as his own God.

Notes:

Israel's capital city. Israel's king fed them and sent them back to their own country. **14**
For a time, no Arameans invaded Israel's territory.

The threat from the Arameans wasn't over, however. Ben-Hadad strengthened his army and planned for a grand siege of Samaria. Weeks and weeks passed with Ben-Hadad's men lying in wait outside the city walls. Inside, the people became desperate. Food and water became more and more scarce, until there was no food at all. The people were thirsty, hungry, and scared. The king of Israel tried to encourage his people, but was helpless to do anything. The king finally blamed the siege on Elisha and threatened his life.

In the presence of the city elders, Elisha answered the messenger from the king, "In twenty-four hours
15 the siege will end, and flour and barley will sell for only a shekel."

Jesus in the OT

Elijah introduced the ministry of Elisha as John the Baptist introduced the ministry of Jesus. In what other ways was Elijah like John the Baptist and Elisha like Jesus?

The next day, a miracle happened. The Arameans had completely deserted their camp outside the city walls. At first the king thought it was a trick. Yet, sure enough, all the Aramean soldiers were gone, leaving behind their tents, horses, donkeys, clothing, and food. The people in the city plundered the camp. Food was cheap, and there was plenty for everyone. Elisha's words from God, as unbelievable as they had seemed, happened just as he predicted they would.

Later, the Lord sent Elisha to Damascus, capital of Aram. While Elisha was **16**
there, Ben-Hadad, king of Aram, became ill. When Hazael, one of Ben-Hadad's officers, asked Elisha what would happen to his king, Elisha stared Hazael straight in the eyes, and prophesied, "Ben-Hadad will recover, but then he will die. You will be king of Aram and do many wicked things." A day later, the king did recover, but **17**
Hazael smothered him with a thick cloth. Hazael then became king of Aram.
18
Six different kings of Israel reigned during Elisha's lifetime. In simple ways, such as healing a village's spring water, and in dramatic ways, such as rescuing besieged Samaria, Elisha demonstrated to ordinary people and great rulers that the Lord God was King. The sovereign God reigned supreme, and nothing could stop His hand of mercy or His rod of judgment.

14 Because the Lord had delivered these Aramean soldiers into the hands of Israel's king, the Lord, whatever His reasons might be, did not want the men killed. Letting the men go was the Lord's will even though the Arameans would return to lay siege to Israel in the near future.

15 In other words, in twenty-four hours the flour that could not be found in the city, or, if found, sold for eighty shekels of silver, would be so plentiful that it would be sold for a mere shekel. This prophecy was so absurd that the king's officer laughed at the possibility.

16 The Lord sent Elisha to Damascus for a very particular mission. He was to fulfill the command that the Lord had given to Elijah years before, saying, "Go to the Desert of Damascus. When you get there, anoint Hazael king over Aram" (1 Kings 19:15). Hazael, an officer in Ben-Hadad's army, was a wicked, opportunistic man who used Elisha's prophecy as his warrant to kill Ben-Hadad, his king. As king, Hazael would bring great suffering to Israel, setting fire to its cities and murdering its young men, little children, and pregnant women (see 2 Kings 8:10-15). The Lord gave this command in the form of a prophecy to Elijah at the point of his great discouragement after his victory over the prophets of Baal on Mt. Carmel. The Lord, in essence, was saying that Israel would eventually be judged for its refusal to worship the Lord, and the judgment would come as a result of Hazael being king of Aram.

17 By God's power Elisha was able to predict that Ben-Hadad would recover but that Hazael would then kill him. Elisha also prophesied that Hazael, as king, would commit heinous crimes. The prophecy was so dire that Elisha wept. Hazael protested that he was not the wicked man that Elisha prophesied him to be, but the very next day he killed Ben-Hadad by smothering him, thus fulfilling the first portion of Elisha's prophecy.

18 In 1 Kings 19:19-21, we read about the call of Elisha, which took place during the reign of King Ahab. At this time, Elisha was an attendant of Elijah. In 2 Kings 13:10-20, Scripture records that Elisha died during the reign of Jehoash. This means that during Elisha's lifetime, the following kings reigned: Ahab, Ahaziah, Joram, Jehu, Jehoahaz, and Jehoash.

Notes:

Notes:

Review Worksheets

A. MEMORY VERSE: "[The Most High] does according to His will in the army of heaven And among the inhabitants of the earth. No one can restrain His hand Or say to Him, "What have you done?" (Daniel 4:35b)

B. KEY FACTS:

God's Sovereignty and Elisha's Life

How big is God?

Match the words with their definitions.

Sovereign — God **controls** all things.
Omnipotent — God has **all power**.
Omniscient — God **knows** all things.

How was God sovereign in these people's lives?

3 Shunammite woman	1. Made her oil fill many jars.
6 Naaman	2. Told him about Aram's war plans.
5 Hazael	3. Made her son come back to life.
1 Poor widow	4. Blinded his army's eyes.
4 Ben-Hadad	5. Predicted he would be king.
2 Elisha	6. Healed him of leprosy.

C. STORY FACTS: Fill in the blanks.

1. Elisha received a double portion of Elijah's spirit.
2. Elisha used Elijah's cloak to divide the Jordan River.
3. The siege was over after the Arameans deserted their camp.

D. WHAT DO YOU REMEMBER? Fill in blanks in the spaces beside the sentences.

S O N	Elisha raised the widow's _______ to life.
L E P R O S Y	Naaman had the disease of _______.
S E V E N	Naaman washed _______ times in the river.
F I E R Y	A _______ chariot parted Elijah and Elisha.
W H I R L W I N D	Elijah went to heaven in a _______.
M E R C Y	Elisha was the prophet of _______.
K I N G	Elisha said Hazael would be _______.
S I E G E	Ben-Hadad laid _______ to Samaria.
B L I N D N E S S	God struck the Aramean army with _____.

E. ELISHA AT DOTHAN: Elisha was not afraid of Ben-Hadad's army.

Why was Elisha not afraid? Because those who were with Elisha (God's heavenly host) were more than those who were with the enemy. God's angels were protecting the city.

Who was protecting Elisha and his servant? God, through his army of fiery chariots.

F. FIND OUT...

Elijah went to heaven without dying. The Scripture tells us about one other person who went to heaven without dying first. Read Genesis 5:22–24 and Hebrews 11:5–6.

Who was this person? Enoch

What do these verses say about this person? Enoch walked with God. He didn't experience death because God took him away. He was a man who pleased God.

Notes to Teachers and Parents:

1 When we worship an idol, we are trusting in the idol, rather than in the Lord. The nature of idolatry is that we believe that safety and security rests in our idols, and so we fiercely cling to them. The Lord wants us to reject our idols and cling to Him instead. Any time we cling to an idol, we remove ourselves from the resource of God's grace. Why? It is because God will not give us grace to trust in anything except Himself. Clinging to an idol causes us to forfeit God's freely available grace and leaves us to face the situation alone.

2 Because we are really not any different from the Israelites, the words of the prophets have great application to us today. As we study each of the prophets with their colorful language and, at times, obscure metaphors, we must remember that we are as prone to unfaithfulness as the ancient Israelites were and that we must take God's warning about sin and judgment very seriously.

Notes:

Chapter 18 Three Prophets of Judgment

LESSON SCOPE: Hosea 1–14
Amos 1–9
Jonah 1–4

READ TO ME: Hosea 11, Amos 3–4, Jonah 1–4

THEME: Through His prophets, the Lord God warns of judgment to come.

MEMORY VERSE:

1 "Those who cling to worthless idols forfeit the grace that could be theirs." (Jonah 2:8, NIV)

KEY FACTS:

What is a prophet?	
Definition:	A prophet… • is called by God. • receives messages from God. • speaks God's messages to kings and ordinary people.
Themes:	Sin, Punishment, Repentance, and Forgiveness
Message:	• Worship only the Lord. • Remember God's covenant. • Sin brings punishment. • Repentance brings God's mercy.
Test of a Prophet:	• His words must be true. • His words must agree with God's law.

THINGS TO REMEMBER:

Idol = Anything we trust in rather than God; any desire or fear that controls our behavior.

MESSAGE FROM THE KING: The King says, "Listen to the words of my prophets."

The messages of God's prophets speak to you today, telling you that sin has consequences, the Lord will always love you, and salvation is a gift you can't earn. **2**

Three Prophets of Judgment

Amos—Prophet of Justice

3 Amos was not a learned prophet, yet God called this herdsman and sycamore tree farmer from Judah to be His spokesman to Israel. From the rugged wilderness
4 Judean village of Tekoa, where cries of jackals and the bleating of sheep echoed in rocky canyons, this stern man of God traveled northward to Israel to rebuke the self-
5 righteous people of Israel for their greed, injustice, and idolatry.

The name Amos means "bearer of burdens." During the prosperous reign of Jeroboam II, the LORD sent Amos to bring the burden of judgment to God's people. The wealthy oppressed the poor, the merchants cheated their customers, and the leaders took bribes and did immoral things. The people were extravagantly religious, but they weren't devoted to the LORD. They worshipped the golden calves set up by Jeroboam I many years earlier.

Amos pronounced God's judgment on eight nations. He started with nations far away like Philistia, Phoenicia, and Aram. Judgment came closer to Israel when he spoke against Edom, Ammon, and Moab. After accusing Judah of rejecting God's law, Amos gave the longest sermon to Israel, threatening that not even the fastest or bravest warrior would escape God's judgment. These judgments had two things in common. Eight times Amos said the words "for three sins, even for four," meaning that God had been patient for a very long time. Amos used the symbol of fire to tell the people that terrible sin must bring terrible consequences. The theme verse in the book of Amos could be "let justice roll on like a river" (Amos 5:24a, NIV).

Amos warned that God would judge His people for injustice and idolatry, but that one day He would bless Israel again. Through Amos, His prophet of justice, God showed that He could speak through anyone, even a simple herdsman who was willing to serve the LORD faithfully.

Hosea—Prophet of the Broken Heart

During the years of Israel's prosperity, the people worshipped Baal and the golden calves. Hosea (whose name means "salvation") proclaimed the message of God's loving-kindness to His unfaithful people. Unlike stern Amos, Hosea spoke with ten-
6 derness and compassion. He said that Israel's love

Jesus in the OT
Hosea loved a woman who was unfaithful to him. The Lord Jesus loved you and died for you when you were unfaithful to Him.

3 At the same time that the monarchy was being established in Israel, the organized prophetic movement began. Prophets formed schools, and those in the prophetic schools were often called "the sons of the prophets" (see 1 Samuel 10:5; 1 Kings 20:35). Samuel was a significant instrument in creating these prophetic schools. In the time of the judges, before the monarchy existed, there were few prophets. After Israel had a king, God used the prophets to speak His word to the kings so that the kings would know and be able to do God's will. If the kings were godly, theocratic kings, they viewed the prophets as their counselors. (Gad and Nathan were counselors to King David, confronting him with sin and guiding him in truth.) If the kings were wicked and idolatrous, they reacted to the prophets as their enemies, and they persecuted them. Amos, however, was a prophet of a different nature. He was a simple herdsman and farmer, not a schooled prophet. God called him from a remote wilderness village in Judah. His task was to warn the sophisticated, wealthy people of Israel of their greed and idolatry.

4 Tekoa was a small village in Judah twelve miles southeast of Jerusalem. Several miles to the west of Tekoa, there was a wilderness area that was a good location for sheep herding, but it was also a place of rugged rocks, steep hills, deep canyons, and wild animals. Dry, hot winds swept up from the southern desert. This harsh land produced strong men to whom danger and hardship were part of daily life.

5 The LORD sent Amos to Israel's capital to confront the royalty, nobility, and wealthy citizens of Israel with the moral, political, and spiritual decay of their nation. Because Amos was an outsider, he had a boldness and objectivity that another prophet might not have had. Amos was the voice of God's justice and righteousness to Israel. Amos was similar to John the Baptist. He was an intelligent, stern, and bold wilderness man, proclaiming God's hard truth to stubborn ears and hardened hearts.

6 Where Amos was stern and appeared to be uncompassionate toward his listeners, Hosea was a man of strong emotion and tender feelings. In the intensity of his appeal to Israel to return to the LORD (see Hosea 6, NIV), we can almost hear his sobs and see teardrops on the pages of Scripture. His words described the persistence and depths of the LORD's love for a people "determined to turn from me" (Hosea 11:7, NIV).

Notes:

7 for the LORD was like the morning mist that quickly vanished when the sun got hot, but God, in His love, would never let go or give up.

The LORD gave Hosea a strange command. He was to marry Gomer, a woman who would not love him faithfully, and even after she betrayed him, he was to for-
8 give her and continue to be her husband. Gomer's unfaithfulness was a picture of Israel's unfaithfulness to the LORD. The names of his children, which meant "not my people" and "not loved," were to warn Israel that the God who made a
9 covenant to be Israel's God and to love the Israelites forever was righteously angry about their idolatry and sin.

Because of Gomer's unfaithfulness to him and Israel's unfaithfulness to God, Hosea was the prophet with a broken heart. He urged the people, "Come, let us return to the LORD." Because of His love, God forgives repentant people and promises to make them fruitful like a green pine tree.

Jonah—Prophet of Salvation

Although many of the prophets didn't really want to be prophets, they obeyed God and spoke His words. (Being a prophet was a difficult job, and usually meant being hated by people and suffering hardship.) Unlike the other prophets, however, Jonah refused to obey God and took a ship in the other direction from where the LORD God wanted him to go.

The LORD told Jonah to go to Nineveh, the capital of Assyria, and preach judgment upon it for its wickedness. Because Jonah hated the Ninevites, he didn't want them to repent and be forgiven, so he took a ship to Tarshish. No one, though, can run
10 away from God. The LORD sent a violent storm, and the ship going to Tarshish nearly sank in the raging waves. Realizing he was the cause of the storm, Jonah asked the sailors to throw him into the sea. They did, and God sent a great fish to swallow Jonah.

Inside the belly of the fish, Jonah repented of his stubbornness. He realized, "Salvation comes from the LORD." On the third day, the fish spit Jonah out onto the shore, and Jonah walked through the city of Nineveh, preaching a simple message to the
11 Ninevites: "In forty days Nineveh will be destroyed." The LORD had saved Jonah from the fish, and then through Jonah's message, He saved the Ninevites from judgment.

12 Nineveh's repentance angered Jonah. He sat under a vine and pouted. When the vine died, Jonah was so depressed that he wanted to die. The LORD rebuked Jonah, saying, "You have more compassion for this vine than for all the people in Nineveh
13 upon whom I had mercy."

7 In contrast to the enduring, unchangeable love of the LORD for His people, His people's love for Him is as fleeting as the morning mist. In the heat of the day, all the mist vanishes (see Hosea 6:4).

8 The LORD's request to Hosea is a strange one that we can't fully understand. Why would He require Hosea to marry a woman who He knew would be unfaithful? Yet the picture of Hosea being faithful to Gomer, who is unfaithful to him, not just once but repeatedly, is a powerful picture of our unfaithfulness to a God who has committed Himself to us. Gomer broke Hosea's heart. In the same way, over and over again, we have broken the LORD's heart by our unfaithfulness.

9 The names of Hosea's children ("not my people" and "not loved") have a covenantal meaning. In the covenant, the LORD promised to be the God of His people forever and to love His people faithfully. Hosea writes that the LORD's response to unfaithfulness is to say, "I will show my love to the one I called 'Not my loved one.' I will say to those called 'Not my people,' 'You are my people'; and they will say, 'You are my God'" (Hosea 2:23, NIV).

10 The Assyrians were a fierce, cruel people. Their acts of torture were known throughout the Middle East, and all the nations feared them. Because of his love for his fellow Israelites and his hatred of the Assyrians, Jonah didn't want the Ninevites to repent and receive God's mercy, and he certainly didn't want to be the instrument through which that repentance came. Jonah probably realized that he couldn't really run away from God; he knew that God was omnipresent and no one can flee from His presence (see Psalm 139:7). By going as quickly as he could in the opposite direction of Nineveh, Jonah was saying to the LORD, "I don't want to be the prophet to Nineveh. I am refusing the job. Get someone else." Jonah soon realized that resigning from being a prophet wasn't that simple.

11 Jonah's message was a short one, and it spoke only of judgment, not of mercy. Even so, the Ninevites heard the message and repented, and God showed them mercy for their repentance.

12 Jonah's fears had come true. The LORD had shown mercy to Jonah's enemies and granted them repentance. Instead of rejoicing in the miracle God had done, Jonah was depressed to the point of suicide. Jonah's words in Jonah 4:1-3 show us his heart and explain why he was so eager to run away from his prophetic mission.

13 The LORD showed mercy to Jonah. Even though Jonah was pouting, depressed, and angry (none of which are godly characteristics), the LORD caused a vine to grow quickly so that Jonah could have relief from the hot sun. For the first time since the people of Nineveh had repented, Jonah was happy. He was happier that he had comfort from the scorching heat than that the Ninevites had the comfort of God's forgiveness. When the vine died, Jonah selfishly became depressed and angry again. Using the vine as an object lesson, the LORD showed Jonah how self-centered, uncompassionate, and angry his heart had become.

Jonah, the prophet of salvation, learned two things. The first was that salvation is a gift from God, and no one can save himself. (Jonah could not save himself from the fish's belly). The second was that God gives salvation to those He chooses. (God gave salvation to the repentant Ninevites.) **14**

THE MESSAGES OF THE PROPHETS

(Prophets who wrote books of the Old Testament)

Prophet	Description	Audience
Isaiah	Prophet of Comfort	Judah
Jeremiah	Prophet of Tears	Judah
Ezekiel	Prophet of Visions	Jews in exile
Daniel	Prophet of God's Sovereignty	Jews in exile
Hosea	Prophet of a Broken Heart	Israel
Joel	Prophet of God's Grace	Judah
Amos	Prophet of Justice	Israel
Obadiah	Prophet of Edom's Disaster	Edom
Jonah	Prophet of Salvation	Assyria
Micah	Prophet of Hope	Judah
Nahum	Prophet of God's Wrath	Assyria
Habakkuk	Prophet of Faith	Judah
Zephaniah	Prophet of Total Destruction	Judah
Haggai	Prophet of Encouragement	Jews returned from exile
Zechariah	Prophet of Future Glory	Jews returned from exile
Malachi	Prophet of Preparation	Jews returned from exile

14 Salvation is always a gift from God. None of us can earn it or demand it from God. None of us can tell God to whom He can show mercy. God is the one who softens hardened hearts and grants repentance to the "worst of sinners" (see 1 Timothy 1:15-16, NIV).

Notes:

Notes:

Review Worksheets

A. MEMORY VERSE: "Those who cling to worthless idols forfeit the grace that could be theirs." (Jonah 2:8, NIV)

B. KEY FACTS:

What is a prophet?

A prophet must be called by God. Prophets tell people to worship only the LORD and to remember God's covenant.

They remind people that sin brings punishment, but repentance brings God's mercy.

Tests of the true prophet: His words must be true, and his words must agree with God's law.

Four themes of the prophets:

S in P unishment R epentance F orgiveness

C. STORY FACTS: Cross out the **wrong** words.

1. During the days of Amos, the Israelites were (~~humble~~/unjust).
2. Amos came from the village of Tekoa in (Judah/~~Israel~~) and went to preach to the people in (~~Judah~~/Israel).
3. The name of the woman Hosea married was (~~Jezreel~~/Gomer).
4. Hosea said Israel's love for God was like (morning mist/~~rising smoke~~).
5. Inside the great fish, Jonah (~~was angry with God~~/repented of his sin).
6. When the vine died, Jonah wanted to (die/~~preach judgment to Nineveh~~).
7. The religious Israelites to whom Hosea spoke (~~were devoted to God~~/worshipped golden calves).
8. Being a prophet meant that most people (hated/~~respected~~) you.

D. HOW WELL DO YOU KNOW THE PROPHETS?

Use the first letter of each prophet's name and match the statements to the correct prophet.

A – Amos **H – Hosea** **J – Jonah**

H	I urged Israel, "Come, let us return to the LORD for forgiveness."
J	I was angry that God granted repentance to the people I had preached to.
A	The theme of my message was "let justice roll like a river."
J	I learned that salvation comes from the LORD.
A	When I said the words, "For three sins and even for four," I meant that God had been patient.
H	I gave Israel the message of God's loving-kindness to His unfaithful people.
A	I was a herdsman and farmer. My name means "bearer of burdens."
H	I had children named "Not loved" and "Not my people."

E. WHAT WAS GOD'S MESSAGE?

Prophet of Justice: God would judge His people for injustice and idolatry, but He would one day bless Israel again.

Prophet of a Broken Heart: Because of His love, God forgives repentant people and promises to make them fruitful.

Prophet of Salvation: Salvation is a gift from God, and God gives salvation to those He chooses.

F. FIND OUT...

Salvation is a gift from God.

Read Ephesians 2:8-9. What does Paul say about your salvation?

You are saved by grace through faith, and faith is a gift from God.

Salvation is God's gift to you. Discuss with your teacher what this means to you.

Notes:

Chapter 19 Looking Backwards...Looking Ahead

LESSON SCOPE: 1 Kings 12–22
2 Kings 1–8, 2 Chronicles 10–21
Amos 1–9, Hosea 1–14, Jonah 1–4

READ TO ME: Psalms 93, 97, 99

"The Lord reigns, He is robed in majesty; and is armed with strength" (Psalm 93:1, NIV).

Sometimes it certainly didn't seem like the Lord was reigning in Israel and Judah! In the first eighty years after the kingdom split, all the kings of Israel and Judah, except Asa and Jehoshaphat, reigned as though they were the ultimate authority and the Great King didn't exist. They worshipped Baal or golden calves or they simply ignored the Lord. They killed each other for power and glory, and oppressed the people in their pursuit of wealth and fame. What was the Lord doing when this was happening?

In Unit III, you learned how the Lord is the God who reigns. He reigned even when wicked men ruled. He sent fire from heaven on Mt. Carmel and blindness upon Israel's enemies at Dothan. Through miracles, the King proved to great rulers and ordinary people that He was not absent. Through prophets' words of judgment, the King showed He was not silent.

In Unit IV, you will learn that the God who reigns is also the God who judges when His authority is disregarded and His warnings are ignored. None of Israel's kings worshipped God, and after 200 years, the Lord sent Assyria to destroy Israel. Some of Judah's kings were faithful to God's covenant, but eventually God judged Judah, too, and Babylon attacked and conquered Judah.

The Lord, the Mighty King, is also the Just Judge. The Keeper of the Kingdom protects the kingdom, even though man attempts to destroy it through wickedness and idolatry.

IMPORTANT THINGS TO KNOW:

Word	Meaning of the Word
Idol	Anything we trust in rather than God; any desire or fear that controls our behavior.
Prophet	Person called to speak for God.
Sovereign	Possesses supreme power; controls all things.
Omnipotent	Has all power.
Omniscient	Knows all things.

Review Worksheets

A. MEMORY VERSE REVIEW: Match the description to the memory verse words.

3 Truth of God	1. What an idolater forfeits
5 Worthless idols	2. What prevails
2 The Lord's purpose	3. What is exchanged for a lie
6 Army of heaven	4. Who is blessed forever
4 Creator	5. What an idolater clings to
8 Steps of a good man	6. Where God does His will
9 Creature	7. Who can restrain God's hand
1 Grace from God	8. What are ordered by the Lord
7 No one	9. Who is served instead of God

B. WHAT WAS THE THEME OF UNIT III? Cross out all the A's, B's, and C's below and write the remaining letters in the blanks.

T A B H E C A G B C O B A C D A C W A C C H A O B R E A B A I C G A N C S

T h e G o d

w h o r e i g n s

C. WHO AM I? Beside each name identify what job the person had.
Write "K" for **king**, "P" for **prophet**, or "M" for **military officer**. If the person was a king or prophet in Judah, circle the name. If the person was a king or prophet in Israel, draw a square around the name.

K Ben-Hadad	K (Rehoboam)	P [Elisha]	K [Ahab]
K (Abijah)	K (Jehoshaphat)	M Naaman	K [Omri]
P [Elijah]	K [Baasha]	P [Hosea]	P [Amos]
P (Jahaziel)	P [Jonah]	P [Micaiah]	K (Asa)

Bonus: Which prophet was born in Judah but prophesied in Israel? Amos

Notes:

D. WHAT'S THE REASON? Circle the **correct** answer.

1. The people rebelled against Rehoboam because he wouldn't _______.

   make their burdens lighter — destroy the altars of Baal

2. Jeroboam was not a godly king because he _______.

   made the people pay high taxes — didn't worship God's way

3. Elijah challenged the prophets of Baal because he wanted people to _______.

   know that Israel's God was the true God — kill all Baal's prophets

4. The king of Israel knew all about Ben-Hadad's battle plans because _______.

   Ben-Hadad had a spy in his army — God revealed them to Elisha

5. Naaman didn't want to wash in the Jordan River because he thought _______.

   it was a ridiculous idea — the river was too deep

6. Jonah ran away to Tarshish because he didn't want the Ninevites to _______.

   capture and kill him — repent and be forgiven by God

7. Hosea's marriage to Gomer was a picture of God's _______.

   love toward His unfaithful people — anger at His people's sin

8. God stopped the rain when Ahab was king of Israel because _______.

   Ahab was worshipping Baal — Ahab put Elijah in prison

E. HOW GOOD IS YOUR MATH? Find the answer to the math problem. Then draw a line from the answer to the description that matches.

1. 175 + 315 - 40 = 450 — Tribes in Israel.
2. 8 + 6 + 6 - 18 = 2 — Days Nineveh had to repent.
3. 1,642 - 1,634 = 8 — Prophets of Baal on Mt. Carmel.
4. 17 + 13 + 13 - 3 = 40 — Altars on Mt. Carmel.
5. 651 - 423 - 218 = 10 — Nations Amos warned.

F. HOW MUCH DO YOU REMEMBER?

Across:

2. The raven brought ____ to Elijah to eat every morning and evening.
4. Elisha put ____ in the water to make it pure and healthy.
5. Jeroboam built golden ____ to worship.
6. Elijah heard God's gentle whisper in a ____ at Mt. Horeb.
8. God healed Naaman of the disease of ____.
9. Elisha raised the Shunammite woman's ____.
12. At Dothan God struck the Aramean army with ____.
17. Ahab put the prophet Micaiah in ____.

Down:

1. Jehoshaphat removed the high ____ where people worshipped idols.
2. Elijah challenged the prophets of Baal on the top of ____.
3. Naaman washed in the Jordan River ____ times.
7. Two ____ were built on the top of Mt. Carmel.
10. After he washed in the river, Naaman had healthy ____.
11. Jeroboam didn't want his people to worship at the ____ in Jerusalem.
13. God said not to worship worthless ____.
14. When Jonah went to Tarshish, God sent a violent ____.
15. The widow filled all the ____ with oil.
16. The northern kingdom had ____ tribes.

Notes:

G. WHAT DID YOU LEARN ABOUT THE PROPHETS?

Three Prophets of Judgment

Amos	Hosea	Jonah
Prophet of Justice.	Prophet of a Broken Heart.	Prophet of Salvation.
Spoke to the nation of Israel.	Spoke to the nation of Israel.	Spoke to the nation of Assyria.
"Let justice flow like a river."	"Come, let us return to the LORD."	"Salvation comes from the LORD."

The message of the prophets:

1. Worship only the LORD.
2. Remember God's covenant.
3. Sin brings punishment.
4. Repentance brings God's mercy.

H. KINGDOM AND COVENANT: Unscrambled the words and fill in the blanks.

Israel: The first EIGHT (HIGET) kings of Israel worshipped IDOLS (DILOS) and FORGOT (GROOFT) the covenant. They didn't remember that the LORD was the supreme KING (GINK) in Israel. **Judah:** Two of Judah's kings did evil in God's EYES (YESE), but Asa and Jehoshaphat TURNED (UNDERT) the people back to the LORD. **Prophets:** Men who were CALLED (LACDEL) by God and warned people: "REPENT (PERTEN) and God will FORGIVE (VEFOGIR)."

UNIT IV

The Remnant Kingdom...The God Who Judges

Theme: The Keeper of the Kingdom brings judgment when people refuse to worship Him.

Why don't they learn? Oh, why don't these stubborn kings learn? As I, Tobias, the royal chronicler, write down with utmost accuracy the chronicles of the kings, I am furious! How can these kings continue to do evil in the eyes of the LORD? Don't they understand that God is holy? Don't they fear the judgment of the just Judge of all the earth?

The glorious kingdom that became the divided kingdom will now become the remnant kingdom. (Oh, by the way, the word "remnant" means, "the part left after the rest has been lost.") God who blesses His faithful people and reigns supreme is also the God who judges righteously.

Without exception, all of Israel's kings did evil in God's sight. Jeroboam, Israel's first king, made golden calves and set up his own worship centers, discouraging the people from worshipping at the LORD's temple in Jerusalem. Every king after him "did evil in the eyes of the LORD by following the sins of Jeroboam, son of Nebat." It only got worse when Ahab built a temple to Baal. In 722 BC, after 200 years of Israel's idolatry and wickedness, the LORD sent Assyria to conquer and destroy Israel. Then only the two tribes in Judah, the remnant, were left.

Several of Judah's kings followed in the footsteps of righteous Asa and Jehoshaphat, yet their devotion to the LORD was not wholehearted. They didn't destroy all idol worship from their nation, and they often strayed away from the LORD in their old age. By 586 BC, Judah's kings were lost in idolatry. The mighty kingdom of Babylon swept over Judah, destroying Jerusalem and taking God's people into captivity.

Behind the suffering and judgment, God still showed mercy. The nation would one day be restored, and the Messiah, promised by so many prophets, would someday come. God was still King, and He would not forget His covenant. There was still hope!

Notes:

PSALM 99:1–5, 8–9, NIV

1. The LORD reigns,
   let the nations tremble;
   he sits enthroned between the cherubim,
   let the earth shake.
2. Great is the LORD in Zion;
   he is exalted over all the nations.
3. Let them praise your great and awesome name—
   he is holy.
4. The King is mighty, he loves justice—
   you have established equity,
   in Jacob you have done
   what is just and right.
5. Exalt the LORD our God
   and worship at his footstool;
   he is holy.

****

8. O LORD our God,
   you answered them;
   you were to Israel a forgiving God,
   though you punished their misdeeds.
9. Exalt the LORD our God
   and worship at his holy mountain,
   for the LORD our God is holy.

Can't you just picture it? The Mighty God sits on a throne too majestic to describe with words. Winged cherubim surround Him, protecting His absolute holiness. His awesomeness is so great that the entire earth shakes in His presence as if in a massive earthquake! All nations are to praise His awesome name!

Have you ever shouted, "That's not fair!" when someone treated you unjustly? Our mighty God loves justice—He only does what is right and just. His throne sits on a solid foundation of righteousness and justice. Not one sin escapes His watchful eyes, and He judges all men fairly.

The LORD God is also a forgiving God. He doesn't hold a grudge. When you call to Him with a repentant heart, He hears you and forgives you quickly, even though sometimes He must punish you when you sin.

God is perfectly holy in everything He does. Thanking God for the just and righteous things He does is one way to fear God and worship Him.

120

Chapter 20 Israel Falls & Judah Remains

LESSON SCOPE: 2 Kings 17–19
2 Chronicles 21–28

READ TO ME: 2 Chronicles 22–26

THEME: The LORD God's patience with idolatry does not last indefinitely.

MEMORY VERSE:

"For the LORD knows the way of the righteous, But the way of the ungodly shall perish." (Psalm 1:6)

KEY FACTS: **Kings and Chronicles**

Some of the stories in the books of Kings and Chronicles are the same. How are these books different from each other?

	Kings	Chronicles
Time period	970 BC—From the reign of Solomon to the fall of Judah (stories about Israel and Judah).	1010 BC—From the reign of David to the fall of Judah (stories about Judah only).
Author	1 Unknown prophet.	Unknown priest. 2
Theme	God's blessing and judgment.	God's presence and holiness.
Content	1. History of both Israel and Judah.	1. History of Judah only.
	2. Personal stories of kings' lives.	2. No strictly personal stories.
	3. Stories of Elijah and Elisha.	3. Details about how the temple was built.
		4. Emphasis on worship.
		5. Genealogies.

MESSAGE FROM THE KING: The King says, "Remember My covenant."

"I will be your God and you will be My people"—those are the words of God's covenant. The LORD promises never to take His presence from you.

Notes to Teachers and Parents:

1 Some scholars believe that Jeremiah is the author of 1 and 2 Kings. A second belief is that a single author wrote all the books from Joshua to the Kings (excluding Ruth) sometime during the Exile. This group of books (Joshua through Kings) is called the Former Prophets in the Hebrew Bible.

2 Tradition says that Ezra wrote 1 and 2 Chronicles as well as Ezra and Nehemiah. Even though we don't know for certain if Ezra is the author, we know that the author could not have been a prophet. Most believe a priest wrote the books based on two things. First, because 1 and 2 Chronicles are part of the Writings portion of the Hebrew Bible and not the Prophets, they must have been written by someone other than a prophet, most likely a priest. Second, the emphasis in these books on the priests and Levites and on the temple building and worship indicates that the author was probably a priest.

Notes:

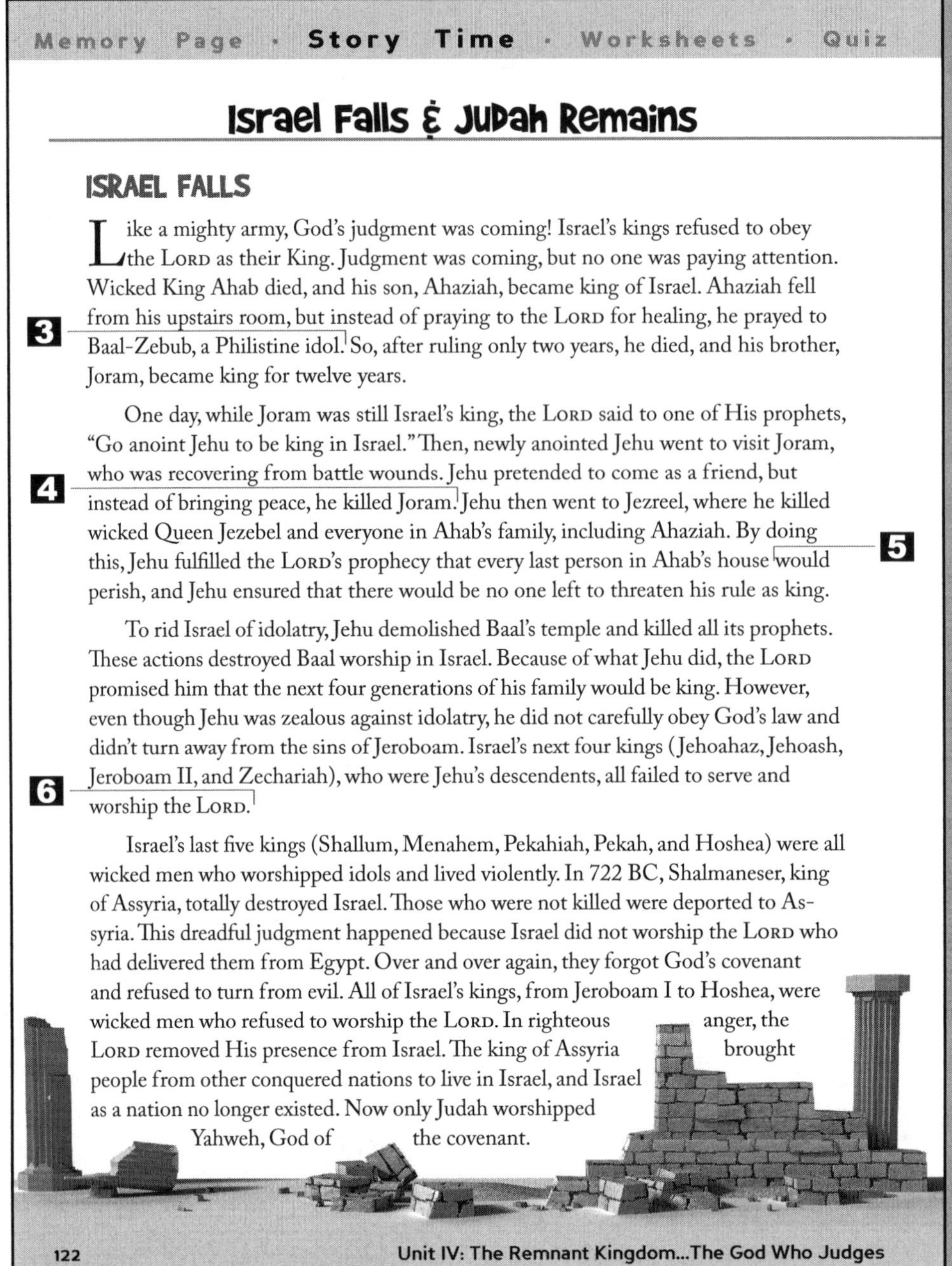
Memory Page · **Story Time** · Worksheets · Quiz

Israel Falls & Judah Remains

ISRAEL FALLS

Like a mighty army, God's judgment was coming! Israel's kings refused to obey the LORD as their King. Judgment was coming, but no one was paying attention. Wicked King Ahab died, and his son, Ahaziah, became king of Israel. Ahaziah fell from his upstairs room, but instead of praying to the LORD for healing, he prayed to
3 Baal-Zebub, a Philistine idol. So, after ruling only two years, he died, and his brother, Joram, became king for twelve years.

One day, while Joram was still Israel's king, the LORD said to one of His prophets, "Go anoint Jehu to be king in Israel." Then, newly anointed Jehu went to visit Joram, who was recovering from battle wounds. Jehu pretended to come as a friend, but
4 instead of bringing peace, he killed Joram. Jehu then went to Jezreel, where he killed wicked Queen Jezebel and everyone in Ahab's family, including Ahaziah. By doing 5
this, Jehu fulfilled the LORD's prophecy that every last person in Ahab's house would perish, and Jehu ensured that there would be no one left to threaten his rule as king.

To rid Israel of idolatry, Jehu demolished Baal's temple and killed all its prophets. These actions destroyed Baal worship in Israel. Because of what Jehu did, the LORD promised him that the next four generations of his family would be king. However, even though Jehu was zealous against idolatry, he did not carefully obey God's law and didn't turn away from the sins of Jeroboam. Israel's next four kings (Jehoahaz, Jehoash,
6 Jeroboam II, and Zechariah), who were Jehu's descendents, all failed to serve and worship the LORD.

Israel's last five kings (Shallum, Menahem, Pekahiah, Pekah, and Hoshea) were all wicked men who worshipped idols and lived violently. In 722 BC, Shalmaneser, king of Assyria, totally destroyed Israel. Those who were not killed were deported to Assyria. This dreadful judgment happened because Israel did not worship the LORD who had delivered them from Egypt. Over and over again, they forgot God's covenant and refused to turn from evil. All of Israel's kings, from Jeroboam I to Hoshea, were wicked men who refused to worship the LORD. In righteous anger, the LORD removed His presence from Israel. The king of Assyria brought people from other conquered nations to live in Israel, and Israel as a nation no longer existed. Now only Judah worshipped Yahweh, God of the covenant.

122 Unit IV: The Remnant Kingdom...The God Who Judges

3 Baal-Zebub means "lord of the flies." This is probably a distorted version of the name of the Philistine god Baal-Zabul meaning "the Lord is peace."

4 Unlike David when he was anointed king, newly anointed Jehu would not wait for God's timing to assume the throne. As soon as God's prophet anointed him king, he took the situation into his own hands. Pretending to visit the wounded king of Israel, he took the opportunity to assassinate Joram so that he could immediately become king.

5 Jehu killed "seventy sons" of Ahab (see 2 Kings 10:1-14). This probably included grandsons as well as sons. This action fulfilled the prophecy of Elijah to Ahab many years before, which foretold, "I will consume your descendents and cut off from Ahab every last male in Israel—slave or free" (1 Kings 21:21, NIV).

6 The LORD showed faithfulness to Jehu in a strange way. Jehu demolished Baal's temple and killed Baal's prophets, thus ridding Israel of Baal worship for a time. The LORD blessed his actions by promising that four generations of kings would rule in Israel after him, even though all four kings (Jehoahaz, Jehoash, Jeroboam II, and Zechariah) failed to serve the LORD. God's promise and prophecy was fulfilled after Zechariah became king. Zechariah reigned only six months and was assassinated by Shallum, who then became king. Shallum reigned only a month before Menahem assassinated him.

7 The Bible uses the names Jehoram and Joram interchangeably for these two kings of Israel and Judah. In order to alleviate confusion, this text and some Bible scholars call Israel's king Joram and Judah's king Jehoram.

8 The names of Israel and Judah's kings can become confusing because some of the kings have the same or very similar names. Israel's king, Ahaziah, who fell from the upper room, was Ahab's son. (Ahab had three children: Ahaziah, king of Israel; Joram, king of Israel; and Athaliah, queen of Judah.) Judah's king Ahaziah was the son of Jehoram and Athaliah. So Athaliah's brother, Ahaziah, was a king of Israel, and her son, Ahaziah, became a king of Judah.

9 Jehu murdered Ahaziah at the same time that he killed Joram, king of Israel. Ahaziah had gone to visit Joram, who was recovering from battle wounds. When Jehu arrived with the intention to kill Joram, Ahaziah was in the "wrong" place at the "wrong" time and was killed along with Joram. Of course, because God is sovereign, all events fulfill His holy purpose. Ahaziah's death set the stage for Athaliah to usurp Judah's throne. Athaliah's actions then led to Jehoiada rescuing baby Joash and eventually to Joash becoming king six years later. Through this series of events, Joash, Amaziah, and Uzziah brought back godly rule to Judah's throne, even though their worship of the LORD was not consistent throughout their entire reigns.

10 Isn't it amazing that God sovereignly rules despite the attempts of wicked people to secure their own fate? Athaliah believed that she had killed everyone in the royal family (all her rivals to the throne) and had safely established herself as ruler in Judah. Behind the scenes, God, the Keeper of His Kingdom, used the high priest, Jehoiada, to hide baby Joash, the only remaining son of Ahaziah (Athaliah's grandson), for six years in the temple.

Memory Page · **Story Time** · Worksheets · Quiz

JUDAH REMAINS

Jesus in the OT
The Keeper of the Kingdom protected the royal line from which Jesus, the Messiah, would come.

While Joram was king in Israel, Jehoram reigned in
7 Judah. Jehoram was evil and died after eight years as king.
8 His son, Ahaziah, succeeded him, but Israel's king, Jehu,
9 soon murdered him. After Jehu killed Ahaziah, Ahaziah's mother, Athaliah, made herself queen. To secure her position as ruler, she killed everyone in the royal family. (At least she thought she did. God was protecting His promise **10**
to David to have a descendent on Judah's throne. Remember, God is sovereign!) Secretly, Jehoiada, the high priest, captured baby Joash, son of Ahaziah (Athaliah's grandson) and hid him in the temple. For six years the child lived in the temple while Athaliah ruled. Then, with the help of loyal commanders, Jehoiada crowned Joash as king, and the people shouted, "Long live the king!" Joash was only seven years old. While the people were celebrating, the loyal commanders seized Athaliah and put her to death.

During his reign, Joash diligently repaired the temple, which was falling apart from neglect. The people renewed the covenant and promised to serve the Lord. While the high priest Jehoiada lived, Joash was faithful to the Lord, but Jehoiada grew old and died. Then Joash and the people abandoned the temple and worshipped Asherah poles and idols. When the priest, Zechariah, Jehoiada's son, warned Joash of his sin, Joash was furious and had Zechariah stoned to death. As a judgment, the Lord sent the Arameans to attack Judah. Joash was wounded and then killed
11 by his own officials, who were still angry that Joash had killed Zechariah. Joash's son, Amaziah, followed him as king.

Amaziah did right in God's eyes in some ways, but not wholeheartedly. He never destroyed all the high places. After fighting against Edom,
12 he brought back Edom's gods to Jerusalem. Conspirators chased him out
13 of Jerusalem and killed him. At sixteen, his son, Uzziah, then became king.

At first Uzziah feared God, and God gave him military success and prosperity. However, pride led to his downfall. Arrogantly, he burned incense in the temple, something only a priest could do, and the Lord gave him lepro-
14 sy. From that time, Uzziah lived alone, and his son, Jotham, ruled the nation. Jotham grew powerful, conquering the Ammonites and other enemies, and walked steadfastly in the ways of the Lord. After Jotham died, his son, Ahaz,
15 ruled Judah. Ahaz shut the temple doors and only worshipped idols. He even sacrificed his own sons. The Lord's anger against him was very great.

Good kings and bad kings—back and forth it went. At least Judah had not totally forsaken the Lord.

Chapter 20: Israel Falls & Judah Remains 123

Jehoiada used his influence as high priest to successfully overthrow Queen Athaliah when Joash was seven years old.

11 Like some of the other kings of Judah, Joash did not finish well. After Jehoiada's death, Joash turned away from the Lord. He abandoned the temple and brought back the worship of Asherah poles. The Lord sent prophets to warn Joash and the people in Judah of their idolatry, but they didn't listen. When Jehoiada's son, Zechariah, warned Joash of his sin, Joash's response was to execute him. Then the Lord sent the Arameans against Judah. God often used attacks from neighboring nations as a punishment for His people's idolatry. Joash was wounded in battle, but was ultimately killed by his own officials who were still angry about Joash's execution of Zechariah. Joash was killed in his bed as he lay dying from his wounds.

12 Amaziah's worship of God was half-hearted. Although he listened to God's prophets at times, he had not totally committed himself to the Lord. After the battle with Edom, he brought back Edom's gods and established worship of them in Jerusalem. Amaziah decided to attack Israel. Jehoash, king of Israel, tried to dissuade Amaziah from going to battle, but Amaziah would not be deterred. In the battle that followed, Jehoash wounded Amaziah and then captured him. Jehoash and his army plundered the palace and temple in Jerusalem. Despite all this, Amaziah lived for a number of years until conspirators finally killed him.

13 In 2 Kings 15:1-7, Uzziah is called Azariah. He had a long rule of fifty-two years. He was co-regent with his father, Amaziah, for the first part of his reign, and after Uzziah got leprosy, his son, Jotham, was co-regent with him.

14 In many ways, Uzziah was a good king. He reigned for a long time (fifty-two years) and diligently sought to serve the Lord. His reign was a time of prosperity. He fortified Jerusalem, secured trade routes to the sea, had military success over the Philistines, and made significant agricultural advances. His downfall came through his spiritual arrogance. He thought he could offer incense in the temple, a responsibility that God had assigned only to priests. This blatant disregard of God's standards for worship resulted in God's judgment. Uzziah contracted the deadly disease of leprosy. From that time on, he was banished from the palace and lived alone (see 2 Chronicles 26). His son, Jotham, became co-regent with him until Uzziah's death.

15 Ahaz demonstrated his great idolatry by stopping worship in the temple, setting up altars for idol worship on every street corner in Jerusalem, and building high places to worship idols in every town in Judah. His detestable idolatrous practices included offering his own son on Molech's fiery altar. This wicked king, sandwiched in between two godly kings, Jotham and Hezekiah, was one of Judah's worst kings.

Notes:

Notes:

Review Worksheets

A. MEMORY VERSE: "For the Lord knows the ___way___ of the ___righteous___, But the way of the ___ungodly___ shall ___perish___." (Psalm 1:6)

B. KEY FACTS: **Kings and Chronicles**

If the phrase describes the books of Kings, write "K" beside it. If the phrase describes the books of Chronicles, write "C" beside it.

___K___ Stories about Elijah and Elisha

___K___ History of Israel and Judah

___C___ Theme of God's presence

___K___ Begin with Solomon's reign

___C___ Details about how the temple was built

___C___ Written by a priest

___C___ Have genealogies

___K___ Written by a prophet

___K___ Theme of judgment

___K___ Personal stories of kings

C. STORY FACTS: Fill in the blanks.

1. Jehu killed ___Joram___ (king of Israel) and ___Ahaziah___ (king of Judah).
2. Two wicked queens were ___Jezebel___ (Israel) and ___Athaliah___ (Judah).
3. ___Jehu___ destroyed Baal worship in Israel by demolishing Baal's temple.
4. Joash was ___seven___ years old when he became king.
5. Joash served the Lord as long as ___Jehoiada___ lived.
6. ___Joash___ repaired the temple in Jerusalem.
7. Uzziah sinned when he ___burned___ ___incense___ in the temple because only a ___priest___ could do that task.
8. The Lord responded to Uzziah's sin by giving him ___leprosy___.
9. ___Shalmaneser___, king of ___Assyria___, conquered Israel in 722 BC.
10. ___Ahaz___ shut the doors of the temple and worshipped only idols.

D. WHO AM I? Using the following names, fill in the blank that corresponds with the person the quote bubble describes: Uzziah, Jehoiada, Amaziah, Ahaziah, Zechariah, Athaliah, Jehu

I brought the gods of Edom to Jerusalem.	Amaziah
I hid baby Joash from wicked Queen Athaliah.	Jehoiada
I was stoned because I warned Joash of his sin.	Zechariah
I destroyed Baal's temple but didn't serve the LORD myself.	Jehu
I killed all the royal family so I could be ruler in Judah.	Athaliah
I sinned by offering incense in the temple. God punished me by giving me leprosy.	Uzziah
God punished me because I prayed to Baal-Zebub for healing instead of to God.	Ahaziah

E. WHY DID IT HAPPEN? In 722 BC, Israel was destroyed by Assyria. How could such a terrible thing happen?

1. The kings of Israel refused to obey God as their King.
2. The people did not worship God as the One who had delivered them from Egypt.
3. The people forgot the covenant that God had made with them. God had said, "I will be Your God and you will be My people."

so…the LORD removed His presence from Israel.

F. FIND OUT… Read Exodus 34:10-14, NIV. How does the God of the covenant describe Himself and what He will do for Israel?

He will do wonders for Israel never done in any nation. He will do awesome work for His people. He will drive out their enemies. His name is Jealous. He is a jealous God.

Notes to Teachers and Parents:

1 What God requires of His people is simple. He wants us to be just in our actions toward others, to be loving and compassionate toward all people, and to live in humble obedience to our God, knowing that He is the sovereign LORD and is trustworthy in all circumstances. Throughout the Old Testament, the prophets warned the ungodly kings about their injustice, oppression of the poor, and idolatrous worship. The godly kings of Judah exemplified God's requirements listed in Micah 6:8 (some more than others). Though his faith wavered at times, Hezekiah did walk humbly with his God, trusting the LORD in some of the most difficult days in Judah's history.

2 The prophet Isaiah makes more Messianic prophecies and references than any other prophet. The examples given in this table are only a small sampling of the Messianic verses in the book of Isaiah.

3 The word "Messiah" is the Hebrew word that means "anointed one." The word "Christ" is the Greek word that means "anointed one." The Messiah is the one who would deliver Israel from her enemies. In the Jewish mind, the concept of the Messiah had a kingly and priestly aspect. They believed that the Messiah would be a king and would deliver Israel from the oppression of foreign nations so that once again Israel would possess her own land and be free from foreign domination. They believed that the Messiah would also have a priestly, or spiritual, function of rebuilding the temple and acting as priest to the nation. Understanding this mindset helps explain why the Jews during Jesus' days were looking for a military leader to deliver them from the Romans. Jesus did not fit their concept of what the Messiah would be like.

4 From the location of His birth to the details of His suffering and death, God gave many specific prophecies in the Old Testament about the coming Messiah. The New Testament gives example after example of Messianic prophecies, fulfilled in Jesus Christ. Through these prophecies the LORD God shows us His faithfulness because whatever He said about the Messiah was fulfilled with explicit accuracy.

Memory Page · Story Time · Worksheets · Quiz

Chapter 21 Two Prophets & a Righteous King

LESSON SCOPE: 2 Kings 18–20
2 Chronicles 27–32
Isaiah 1–66, Micah 1–7

READ TO ME: 2 Chronicles 27–32

THEME: The LORD God warns of judgment and gives hope through the promise of a Messiah.

MEMORY VERSE:

"He has shown you, O man, what is good; And what does the LORD require of you But to do justly, To love mercy, And to walk humbly with your God?" (Micah 6:8) 1

2 **KEY FACTS: Isaiah and the Messiah**

What does Isaiah say about Jesus, the coming Messiah?

Isaiah	Scripture	Meaning
7:14	"His name [is] Immanuel."	Immanuel means "God with us."
9:6	"Unto us a child is born...His name will be called Wonderful Counselor, Mighty God, Everlasting Father, Prince of Peace."	Jesus is both God and man.
1:1-11	"Root of Jesse."	Jesus was born from David's line.
29:18	"...deaf shall hear...blind shall see."	Jesus opens ears and eyes, physically and spiritually.
40:11	"He will feed His flock like a shepherd."	Jesus is the Good Shepherd.
50:6	"I gave My back to those who struck Me."	Jesus humbly submitted to men's mistreatment of Him.
53:1-12	"He was oppressed...afflicted...they made His grave with the wicked."	Jesus suffered and died as an outlaw, taking the punishment for sin.

3 **THINGS TO REMEMBER:**

Messiah = Hebrew word meaning "the Anointed One."

4 **MESSAGE FROM THE KING:** The King says, "I sent the Messiah, just as I said I would." Every prophecy about the Messiah is fulfilled in Jesus Christ. He is your hope and your salvation.

126 Unit IV: The Remnant Kingdom...The God Who Judges

Notes:

Two Prophets & a Righteous King

"Holy, holy, holy is the Lord God Almighty." The voices of the seraphim were 5
so thunderous that the doorposts of the temple shook, and smoke filled the
temple. Overwhelmed by God's holiness and majesty, Isaiah cried out, "Woe is me! I
am a sinful man!" Through this dramatic encounter, the Lord called Isaiah to be His
prophet after King Uzziah died.

Isaiah had been a prophet for more than thirty years when Hezekiah succeeded
his father Ahaz to Judah's throne. In contrast to his wicked father, Hezekiah trusted
in the Lord. He smashed the sacred stones of idols, removed the high places, and destroyed the bronze serpent that Moses had made because people were worshipping it. 6
He repaired the temple and consecrated all the temple furnishings to the Lord. Now
people could worship at the temple. Everyone was amazed how quickly all this work
was done.

However, trouble soon came to Judah. Assyria's fierce army threatened Jerusalem.
Hezekiah listened to godly counsel and refused to send tribute to Assyria. (His father
Ahaz had always secured Judah's safety by giving gold and silver to Assyria.). Hezekiah prepared Jerusalem for war, strengthening the walls of the city and constructing
a water tunnel from the Gihon spring outside the city to the center of Jerusalem. He
knew Jerusalem would need a good water supply if Assyria laid siege to the city. 7

All was well for a time, but soon Sennacherib, king of Assyria, threatened again.
He had captured all the fortified cities of Judah so that Jerusalem sat alone, an island
in Assyrian-controlled land. Once again, he demanded tribute from Hezekiah. This
time, Hezekiah panicked and paid the tribute, giving Assyria all the silver from the
temple and the gold from the temple doorposts. Hearing what Hezekiah had done, 8
Isaiah confronted him. Hezekiah repented and decided that never again would he
give in to Assyria's demands but instead would depend upon God's protection. 9

Hezekiah's tribute didn't satisfy Sennacherib.
He mocked Hezekiah's courage and sent a letter
to Jerusalem demanding surrender. "No god 10
of any nation has delivered their
people from my armies. Neither will your god protect you,"
Sennacherib boasted. "Give up
and make a bargain with me."

5 These angelic beings have six wings. With two wings they cover their faces, with two wings they cover their feet, and with two wings they fly. They surround the heavenly throne of the Holy God and constantly sing praise to Him, saying, "Holy, holy, holy is the Lord God Almighty, the whole earth is full of His glory" (see Isaiah 6:1-7, NIV). Although we know little about seraphim, this passage tells us a few important things. The seraphs can fly and can speak. They can handle hot coals without getting burned. The administering of these hot coals at God's direction represents God cleansing Isaiah's sinful lips and taking away his guilt. So the tasks of the seraphim are to declare God's holiness and majesty and, with God's permission, to participate in God's work of cleansing His people from sin.

6 The story of the bronze serpent is found in Numbers 21:4-9.

7 Hezekiah felt the pressure of the Assyrian empire expanding ever closer and closer to Jerusalem. The Assyrians used exceptionally cruel methods of torture and had the tactic of intimidating fear perfected to a twisted, yet sophisticated, art. Many nations simply caved to the Assyrians' demands and gave expensive tribute in order to protect themselves. After listening to godly counsel, Hezekiah refused to give tribute to Assyria and decided to trust in God's protection instead. At the same time, Hezekiah prepared his city for the inevitable attack by the Assyrians by strengthening the city and building a water tunnel. This tunnel would provide a sufficient water supply to Jerusalem during a siege.

8 When Assyria threatened Jerusalem's security the next time, Hezekiah relented and paid tribute. He gave Assyria the silver from the temple and stripped the gold from the doorposts of the temple. Hezekiah knew what the Assyrians had done to all the surrounding cities and panicked. Every nation that Assyria attacked was totally destroyed. Its people were either killed in unspeakably horrible ways or made slaves of Assyria. How could the city of Jerusalem defend itself against so great a foe? The situation seemed to be impossible. Hezekiah did not believe he had the resources and military might to sustain a prolonged Assyrian siege.

9 Isaiah's confrontation of Hezekiah was successful. Hezekiah realized his sin of fearing Assyria and not trusting in the Lord. He decided that no matter how impossible the situation seemed, he would trust the Lord.

10 Sennacherib's troops had surrounded Lachish, a fortified city about thirty miles southwest of Jerusalem. During the siege of Lachish, Sennacherib sent his officers to Jerusalem with a letter demanding tribute and surrender.

Notes:

11 Hezekiah took Sennacherib's letter to the temple and prayed for God's help. Hezekiah's response to Sennacherib's threats was similar to David's response to Goliath's threats. Both men were determined to defend the honor of the LORD when pagans insulted Him.

12 The irony of Sennacherib's death is that his god was not powerful enough to save him from death. Sennacherib had mocked Hezekiah's God, saying that the LORD could not deliver Judah from the might of the Assyrian army. But, the LORD annihilated Sennacherib's forces without Judah shooting an arrow or losing a man. After Sennacherib's humiliating defeat, he later was murdered in the presence of his "god."

13 After the victory over the Assyrians, Hezekiah had the respect and honor of the surrounding nations. The LORD prospered him, and he became very rich.

14 The Babylonians ostensibly visited Hezekiah to wish him good health after his serious illness. However, they actually wanted to make a treaty with Hezekiah, asking for his help in fighting the Assyrians. Hezekiah let pride rule him. He wanted to impress the Babylonians with his wealth. Hezekiah's actions distressed Isaiah, and Isaiah then predicted that Babylon would one day destroy Jerusalem, capture all the treasures that Hezekiah had amassed, and take the people as captives.

Notes:

11 Isaiah encouraged Hezekiah, saying, "Don't be afraid. The LORD will deliver Israel." Hezekiah took Sennacherib's threatening letter to the temple and spread it out before the LORD. "This king has insulted You, O LORD. Deliver us so all the nations will know that You alone are God."

Hezekiah then spoke to his people, saying, "Don't be afraid. There is a greater power with us. The LORD our God will fight our battles."

12 Without Judah shooting an arrow, the LORD gave Judah victory over the Assyrians. At night, while the people inside Jerusalem cowered in fear, the angel of the LORD moved silently amidst the Assyrian army surrounding the city. When the people awoke, they saw 185,000 dead bodies in the Assyrian camp. Defeated, Sennacherib returned to Nineveh. Years later, Sennacherib's sons murdered him while he was worshipping in the temple of his god.

13 After this great victory by God, grateful foreign nations sent rich gifts to Hezekiah, and he became a king of great wealth and honor.

Later that year, Hezekiah became very ill. Isaiah said to him, "Put your affairs in order, for you are going to die." Hezekiah begged God to let him live. God answered his prayer, restored him to health, and promised him fifteen more years to live. Hezekiah asked the LORD to give him a sign that this would happen, and the shadow outside his window miraculously went back ten steps.

14 To congratulate Hezekiah on his miraculous recovery, the king of Babylon sent envoys to Jerusalem. Hezekiah proudly showed these messengers from Babylon all the treasures of his kingdom. Upon hearing this, Isaiah was distressed. "Some day all these treasures will be taken away to Babylon, and your descendents will be their captives." Hezekiah's pride was one of several things that led to Judah's downfall.

Hezekiah repented of his pride and again became devoted to the LORD, and the LORD blessed Hezekiah. After reigning a total of twenty-nine years, Hezekiah died and his son, Manasseh, became king.

Notes:

ISAIAH—PROPHET OF COMFORT

In the year that King Uzziah died, the LORD called Isaiah to be His prophet to
the next three kings of Judah (Jotham, Ahaz, and Hezekiah). When the LORD asked **15**
16 Isaiah, "Whom should I send?" Isaiah replied, "Here I am, send me." He became the
prophet of comfort.

The book of Isaiah has two parts. In chapters 1–39, Isaiah warned the people that their sin would bring judgment. Isaiah said that Judah's two main sins were its refusal to repent and its ritualistic worship that didn't come from the heart. Again and again, Isaiah uses the words "in that day" to talk about the judgment that would come.

In the second part, Isaiah gives comfort. The first words of Isaiah 40 are these: "Comfort, comfort my people" (NIV). Because of unconfessed sin, Judah would be conquered by Babylon and taken into exile. Yet there was hope because the LORD would bring His people back from captivity and send the Messiah. More than any other prophet, Isaiah prophesied what the Messiah would be like and what He would do. Even though God's people would suffer, the Messiah would bring about the Kingdom of God, a more glorious kingdom than His people had ever known.

MICAH—PROPHET OF HOPE

Early in Hezekiah's reign, Micah, the prophet of
17 hope, prophesied that Jerusalem would be utterly destroyed. (He was the first prophet to predict Jerusalem's
destruction.) As a result of Micah's words, Hezekiah
18 began to fear God and seek His favor.

> **Jesus in the OT**
> In Matthew 2, the chief priests and teachers of the law found the answer to the wise men's question in the prophecy of Micah. The King would be born in Bethlehem.

Micah spoke out against corrupt leaders and lying prophets who rejected the LORD's authority as King and governed according to their own authority. These greedy leaders unjustly took money from the people, and proclaimed, "Peace," when there was no peace. But Micah had a message of hope! The Messiah was coming. He would be born in Bethlehem and would shepherd the people. He would bring security and peace to the land.

Micah wrote that the LORD was the light in the darkness (Micah 7:8), and the God who pardoned sin. He doesn't "stay angry forever, but delight[s] to show mercy" (Micah 7:18, NIV). Micah reminded the people that true religion is to "do justly, love mercy, and walk humbly with your God."

The book is divided into three sermons, each one beginning with the word "hear" or "listen." The LORD wants you to hear that He is the ultimate authority. He brings peace to the human heart and is the source of hope.

15 This encounter of Isaiah with the holiness of God is recorded in Isaiah 6.

16 Because of his emphasis on God's comfort to His people and his descriptions of the suffering Servant of God in Isaiah 40-66, Isaiah is known as the prophet of comfort. Although the people of Israel had been warned of the coming judgment, Isaiah brought them comfort by telling them of the promised Messiah who would one day deliver His people.

17 Micah is known as the prophet of hope because his warnings were accompanied with words of hope. Not only is the LORD the light of His people, but Micah promises that the enemies of God's people will see God's righteousness and feel shame. Enemy nations will turn in fear to the LORD God. Micah closes his book with a description of God as the one who pardons sin, does not stay angry forever, and delights in showing mercy.

18 Jeremiah told the story of Micah's prophecy and Hezekiah's subsequent conversion in Jeremiah 26:12-19.

Notes:

Review Worksheets

A. MEMORY VERSE: "He has shown you, O man, what is good: And what does the LORD require of you But to do justly, To love mercy, And to walk humbly with your God?" (Micah 6:8)

B. KEY FACTS: Isaiah and the Messiah

1. What does the word "Immanuel" mean? God with us
2. Match the words on the left with the words on the right.

Wonderful	God
Prince of	Counselor
Everlasting	Peace
Mighty	Father

(Answers: Wonderful—Counselor; Prince of—Peace; Everlasting—Father; Mighty—God)

3. In what ways does Jesus open ears and eyes? physically and spiritually
4. What do the words "Root of Jesse" mean?
Jesus was born from David's line.
5. What does the word "Messiah" mean? The Anointed One

C. STORY FACTS: Number the story boxes in the **correct** order.

5	Hezekiah prayed for God's deliverance from the Assyrian army.
1	Hezekiah repaired the temple.
6	The angel of the LORD killed the Assyrian army.
2	Hezekiah prepared for war by building a water tunnel…and fortified the city walls.
3	Assyria captured all the cities of Judah except Jerusalem.
4	Sennacherib sent Hezekiah a threatening letter and his army surrounded the city of Jerusalem.

D. WHAT'S THE REASON? Circle the **correct** answer.

1. Hezekiah destroyed the bronze serpent because ________.

   Isaiah told him to destroy it — (the people were worshipping it)

2. When the shadow moved backwards, it was a sign that God would ________.

   (make Hezekiah well) — defeat Hezekiah's enemies

3. Hezekiah wanted deliverance from Assyria so all nations would know ________.

   (the LORD was God alone) — how strong Jerusalem was

4. Hezekiah told the people not to be afraid because there was ________.

   nothing to be afraid of — (a greater power with them)

5. In the temple, Isaiah cried out, "Woe is me," because he ________.

   had never seen seraphim before — (knew he was very sinful)

6. Micah wanted people to have hope because God does not ________.

   (stay angry forever) — punish every sin

7. Hezekiah first began to fear the LORD and seek God after ________.

   (Micah prophesied) — Isaiah confronted his sin

E. TWO MESSIANIC PROPHETS: Write "I" if the words describe the book of Isaiah and "M" if the words describe the book of Micah.

M The word "hear."

M Spoke against lying prophets.

I Said, "Here I am, send me."

I Most Messianic prophecies.

M Messiah's birth in Bethlehem.

I Prophet of comfort.

I The words "in that day."

M Prophet of hope.

M Said, "Walk humbly with God."

M First to predict Jerusalem's fall.

F. FIND OUT... Read Isaiah 6:1-8. What do seraphim look like? What do they do?

They have six wings – 2 covering face, 2 covering feet, 2 to fly. They sing, "Holy..." beside God on His throne.

Notes to Teachers and Parents:

1 Josiah reigned in Judah from 640–609 BC, when he was killed in battle while fighting the Egyptians. Although there were four more kings who ruled Judah from after the death of Josiah to the eventual fall of Jerusalem, Josiah was the last king in Judah to call the people to repentance and to honor the covenant. Once again, God's people had forgotten the LORD. They had gone to great lengths to establish idol worship in the nation. God's people found it so easy to worship anything other than the LORD and so difficult to remain faithful to Him. The unfaithfulness of God's people is seen over and over again, making it that much more amazing that the LORD is so patient and longsuffering toward His people.

2 The word "jot" refers to the smallest letter of either the Greek or Hebrew alphabet. The word "tittle" refers to the smallest stroke in a Hebrew letter. In other words, this verse is saying that not even the smallest part of God's Law will pass away until it is totally fulfilled.

3 This chart summarizes the outworking of God's covenant with His people and shows how the covenant has unfolded throughout biblical history. The covenant is God's promise to be the God of His people forever and to be faithful to His people, even though His people are not faithful to Him. The covenant began in the Garden of Eden, when Adam and Eve sinned. Sin separated mankind from God, who is perfectly holy and cannot look upon sin, but God, in His mercy, promised a Savior (see Genesis 3:15). The Savior would pay the price of His people's sin and make it possible, through God's grace and man's response of repentance and faith, for reconciliation with God to occur. The covenant in Scripture is one covenant, unfolding throughout the story. From a person (Adam) to a family (Abraham) to a nation (Moses) to an everlasting kingdom (David and, finally, Christ), the covenant keeps growing larger and becoming more extensive.

Chapter 22

Two Memorable Kings—Manasseh & Josiah

LESSON SCOPE: 2 Kings 21–23
2 Chronicles 33–35

READ TO ME: 2 Chronicles 33–35

THEME: The LORD God calls His unfaithful people to remember the covenant. **1**

MEMORY VERSE: **2**

"For assuredly, I say to you, till heaven and earth pass away, one jot or one tittle will by no means pass from the law till all is fulfilled." (Matthew 5:18)

3 **KEY FACTS: Remember the Covenant**

Let's review what Scripture says about God's covenant with His people.

Person	Content	Key Verse
Adam	Promise of a Savior to come.	"...he [Christ] will crush your head, and you [Satan] will strike his heel" (Genesis 3:15b, NIV).
Noah	Promise never to destroy the earth again with a flood.	"I establish my covenant with you: Never again will...there be a flood to destroy the earth" (Genesis 9:11, NIV).
Abraham	Promise of a son, land, and the blessing of being God's people.	"I will establish my covenant as an everlasting covenant...to be your God" (Genesis 17:7, NIV).
Moses	Promise of God's presence and giving of God's Law.	"I will take you as my own people, and I will be your God" (Exodus 6:7a, NIV).
David	Promise of an everlasting kingdom.	"Your throne will be established forever" (2 Samuel 7:16b, NIV).

THINGS TO REMEMBER:

Covenant = God's promise to be the God of His people forever.
God's covenant is **one covenant** unfolding through the years.

MESSAGE FROM THE KING:

The King says, "I will be your God, and you will be My child."

Notes:

Two Memorable Kings—Manasseh & Josiah

How would you like people to remember you? What would you like your legacy to be? (A **legacy** is something you leave behind for your descendents.) Two kings of Judah—Manasseh and Josiah—left memorable, but very different, legacies behind them.

Manasseh, son of Hezekiah and the longest reigning king, left a legacy of evil. **4**
He lead God's people astray into idolatry. The people became more wicked than the fickle Canaanites who had lived in the land centuries before them. Manasseh built altars to Baal and bowed down to the stars, worshipping God's creation, not God the Creator. Instead of seeking the LORD, he asked advice from mediums and practiced witchcraft. Like Ahaz, his grandfather, he even sacrificed his own sons on fiery altars.

The LORD God sent prophets to warn the people of their sin, but the example set by Manasseh and the hardness of their hearts led the Israelites deeper into sin and farther away from the LORD.

The prophecy against Judah was frightening: "I will bring such disaster on Jerusalem that everyone's ears will tingle. I will wipe out Jerusalem as one wipes out a dish and flips it upside down. Because of My anger against their
5 sin, Judah will be plundered and looted by their foes."

After years and years of rejecting God's warnings, **6**
Manasseh was captured by Assyrian commanders and taken to Babylon. This distress caused Manasseh to call upon the LORD and repent of his sin. By His marvelous grace, the LORD accepted Manasseh's confession and, in time, brought Manasseh back to Jerusalem. When he returned, Manasseh rid Jerusalem of idols and foreign altars. He restored the altar of the LORD and urged all the people to serve the LORD. The influence of Manasseh's many years of evil, however, was too strong. The hearts of the Israelites were hardened against the LORD, and Manasseh's own son, Amon, ruled as an evil king. Despite Manasseh's heart change, the LORD determined that the **7**
prophecy regarding Jerusalem's destruction would not be changed.

Amon's son, Josiah, had a legacy of righteousness. At age sixteen, after reigning **8**
for eight years, Josiah turned to the LORD. He began a great reformation. All items of idol worship—Asherah poles, carved images, high places, and incense altars—were broken, crushed, or cut to pieces. He ordered that the temple be totally repaired, regardless of the expense.

4 Manasseh reigned for fifty-five years, and although he repented of his sin and worshipped the LORD at the end of his life, he left behind a legacy of gross idolatry and evil. He is remembered for his sin, not his repentance. In fact, the book of 2 Kings does not even record his conversion. During his reign, Manasseh instituted elements of pagan worship that had never before been practiced in Judah. The sin of Judah became greater than the sin of the Canaanites in Joshua's days. Although by God's grace Manasseh turned to the LORD at the end of his life, his conversion and the reforms that followed had little, if any, effect of turning the people away from idolatry. His legacy remained that of leading Judah astray.

5 The LORD's prophecy to Manasseh came by way of several prophets. The prophets said that Manasseh's sin was greater than the sin of the Amorites. Because he "led Judah into sin with his idols" (2 Kings 21:11, NIV), the judgment of God upon Judah and Jerusalem would be so great that "everyone who hears of it will tingle" (2 Kings 21:12-15, NIV).

6 Does this sound strange to you? An Assyrian commander captured Manasseh and carried him to *Babylon*? Recent archeological findings show that the Assyrian king Sennacherib had a son named Esarhaddon, who built a palace in Babylon and lived there. (Remember, Sennacherib was the Assyrian king who reigned while Hezekiah was reigning and whose army of 185,000 was killed by the angel of the LORD.)

7 There was a consequence of Manasseh's great sin, and that consequence was the hardening of Judah's heart toward the LORD. His example as a leader was profound, but his turnaround at the end of his life could not undo the damage that his idolatry and paganism had done during the years of his reign.

8 The transfer of godliness from father to son is not a guarantee. Each person makes his or her own choice whether or not to serve the LORD. Throughout Judah's history, there are many examples of godly fathers who had godless sons who followed them to the throne, or godless fathers who had godly sons succeed them. The son of godly Hezekiah was Manasseh, who was the most wicked of all Judah's kings. Amon, who succeeded Manasseh, was also wicked, but young Josiah, the son of Amon and the grandson of Manasseh, became the godliest king of all. Scripture records nothing bad about Josiah.

Notes:

9 Although God was honoring the faith of Josiah by not exacting judgment during Josiah's lifetime, the sin of Judah had progressed so far that not even Josiah's reformation could stop the judgment that God had decreed.

10 The people of Judah had made changes, but all the changes were outward. They had not changed in their hearts, and because their hearts still rejected God as their LORD and King, the changes they had made were empty, shallow, and temporary.

Notes:

One day, Hilkiah, the high priest, found the Book of the Law in the temple. When Josiah heard the words of the Law, he tore his robes, and lamented, "We haven't kept this law! Ask the LORD what we should do."

Hilkiah and men from the royal court went to Huldah, the prophetess, for counsel. She said, "Because the people have forsaken the LORD, all the curses of this book will come to pass. God will pour out His anger and bring disaster to Judah. But, because this king has been humble and seeks God from his heart, the disaster will not
9 happen while he lives."

Josiah assembled all the people, from the greatest to the least, at the temple, and before them all, he read through the entire Book of the Covenant. Before the LORD and all the people, he renewed the covenant and promised to follow the LORD with all his heart and soul.

Jesus in the OT

Josiah had a legacy of righteousness, but it was not a perfect righteousness. Only Jesus has a legacy of perfect righteousness.

Josiah began a crusade to purge idolatry from Judah. He smashed all the high places, including the worship center at Bethel set up by Jeroboam. He did away with priests who offered sacrifices to the sun, moon, and stars, and rid the land of mediums and those who practiced witchcraft. No longer would people sacrifice their children or act immorally in God's temple.

Josiah announced to the people, "We are going to celebrate the Passover. Consecrate yourselves and prepare for the sacrifice, just as the LORD commanded through Moses." Josiah provided 30,000 sheep and goats and 3,000 cattle for the sacrifice. There was music and rejoicing. Since the days of Samuel, none of the kings had ever celebrated such a Passover.

After reigning for thirty-one years, Josiah was killed while fighting against Egypt. No king before or after Josiah followed the LORD so wholeheartedly. Yet, the people did not change from the heart. Though outwardly they worshipped the LORD, inwardly they still walked in the sinful way of Manasseh. So, the LORD said, "I will take My Presence from Judah as I did from
10 Israel." Judgment was coming. It wouldn't be long now.

Review Worksheets

A. MEMORY VERSE: "For assuredly, I say to you, till ___heaven___ and ___earth___ pass away, one ___jot___ or one ___tittle___ will by no means pass from the ___law___ till all is ___fulfilled___." (Matthew 5:18)

B. KEY FACTS: Match the name to the covenant description.

Remember the Covenant

Adam	Promise of an everlasting kingdom
Noah	Promise of God's presence and giving of the Law
Abraham	Promise never to destroy the earth again with a flood
Moses	Promise of a Savior to come
David	Promise of a son, land, and blessing

Define covenant: God's promise to be the God of His people forever.

How many covenants did God make? ___one___

C. STORY FACTS: Circle the **correct** answer.

1. The longest reigning king of Judah was ________.

   Josiah   Hezekiah   (Manasseh)

2. After Josiah turned to the LORD, he began a reformation by ________.

   (repairing the temple)   writing songs of praise   crushing images

3. When Josiah heard the words from the Book of the Law, he ________.

   destroyed the book   read it to the people   (lamented)

4. Judgment was still coming to Judah because the people didn't ________.

   celebrate the Passover   (change from the heart)   offer sacrifices

5. The LORD said He'd take ________ from Judah because of their sin.

   (His presence)   His protection   His covenant

Notes:

D. WHAT WAS THEIR LEGACY? Fill in the spaces.

1. H I L K I A H
2. E V I L
3. C O V E N A N T
4. T I N G L E
5. S T A R S
6. B E T H E L
7. M E D I U M S
8. E G Y P T
9. P A S S O V E R
10. C U R S E S
11. A S T R A Y

Manasseh's Legacy:

2. Manasseh had an ____ legacy.
4. The prophecy made ears ____.
5. Manasseh worshipped the sun, moon, and ____.
7. Manasseh got advice from ____.
11. By worshipping idols, he led the people ____.

Josiah's Legacy:

1. ____ found the Book of the Law.
3. Josiah renewed the ____.
6. He destroyed the worship center at ____.
8. Josiah was killed in a battle with ____.
9. He celebrated the ____ for the first time since Samuel.
10. Huldah said the ____ in the Book of the Law would happen.

E. THE BOOK OF THE LAW

Hilkiah went to Huldah (LAHDUH), the prophetess, for counsel. She said, "All the curses (RESCUS) of this book will happen. Disaster (STASIRED) will come to Judah. Because the king is humble (BLUMEH), the disaster won't happen while he lives (VILES)."

F. FIND OUT... Read the verses below. In the blanks write the names of the men who renewed the covenant.

Joshua 24:16-27 Joshua

2 Chronicles 23:15-19 Jehoiada

2 Chronicles 29:1-11 Hezekiah

2 Chronicles 34:29-34 Josiah

Chapter 23

God's Voices of Judgment to the Nations

LESSON SCOPE: Habakkuk 1–3
Zephaniah 1–3, Nahum 1–3
Joel 1–3, Obadiah 1

READ TO ME: Habakkuk, Nahum

THEME: The Lord God warns the nations of the judgment to come.

MEMORY VERSE:

1 "The Lord is slow to anger and great in power; the Lord will not leave the guilty unpunished." (Nahum 1:3a, NIV)

KEY FACTS: Getting to Know the Prophets

Prophet	Meaning	Audience	Things to Remember
Obadiah Prophet of Edom's Disaster	"Worshipper"	Edom	1. Edom betrayed Judah "in the day of their disaster." 2. God judged Edom because it gloated over Judah's destruction.
Nahum Prophet of God's Wrath	"Comforter"	Assyria	1. The Lord is jealous and takes vengeance. 2. God never changes—He always punishes the unrepentant.
Joel Prophet of God's Grace	"Jehovah is God"	Judah	1. "The day of the Lord…" 2. God restores the covenant and gives grace after His people repent. 3. The plague of locusts.
Habakkuk Prophet of Faith	"Embrace"	Judah	1. The just shall live by their faith. 2. Habakkuk's two questions: a. How long before God listens? b. Why does God use the wicked to judge His people?
Zephaniah Prophet of Total Destruction	"Jehovah hides"	Judah	1. "On that day…" 2. God's terrifying wrath is upon sinners, but His mercy is upon the repentant.

MESSAGE FROM THE KING: The King says, "Listen to my warning! Repent of your sin."

Notes to Teachers and Parents:

1 This verse gives us comfort in two ways. First, we can be assured that the holy God does not impulsively react to sin. God is patient and long-suffering, pursuing His people in love and warning them of the consequences of unrepentance. Second, we can be confident that God is just and will punish the guilty. When we have been sinned against, we can leave justice in the hands of the just God (see 1 Peter 2:21-23). It is not our responsibility to personally enact justice. For every sin committed, God either gives mercy and forgiveness to the one who repents, or gives justice and punishment to the one who stubbornly refuses to acknowledge his sin. This frees us to love the sinner and protects us from the damaging effects of bitterness and revenge.

Notes:

GOD'S VOICES OF JUDGMENT TO THE NATIONS

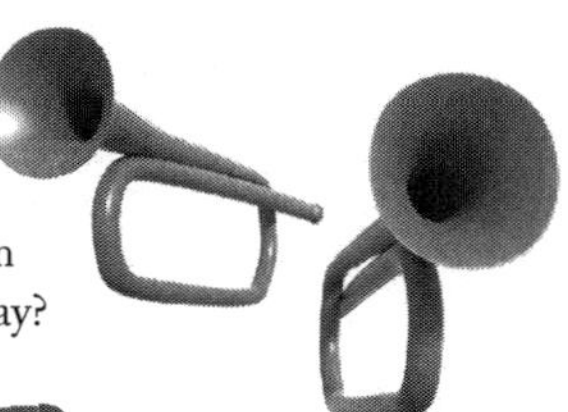

"Blow the trumpet; sound the alarm. Let everyone tremble for the day of the LORD is coming!" God sent His prophets to warn Judah, Edom, and Assyria, but none of them listened, none of them repented, and all of them felt the force of God's just wrath. What did God's prophets say?

OBADIAH—THE PROPHET OF EDOM'S DISASTER

Though no one knows exactly who Obadiah was or when he lived, his grim message for Edom is very clear. The Edomites were descendents from Esau, the brother of Jacob. Esau and Jacob were born grappling with each other, and throughout their history, the Edomites and God's people feuded and battled one another. The Edomites had watched and done nothing when Judah's enemies invaded and ransacked them. Instead of helping Judah, they cheered on the attackers and made the lives of the
2 people of Judah miserable. Obadiah's words, "in the day of their disaster," pointed out
3 Edom's betrayal of Judah.

Obadiah predicted disaster to the people of Bozrah, the capital of Edom carved out of rocky cliffs. Those who lived "in the clefts of the rocks" were full of pride and boasted, "Who can bring us down to the ground?" God's judgment on Edom would
4 be so severe that no one would survive.

Obadiah prophesied against Edom, but he wrote the book to Judah and has a message for you today. The prophet of Edom's disaster was declaring firmly and without any doubt that the LORD punishes those who harm His people, and He brings 5
comfort to His people who are suffering judgment for their sins. Because of His covenant, God restores His people and utterly destroys their enemies. Obadiah's last words, "and the kingdom shall be the LORD's," remind you that God is the supreme King of the nations.

NAHUM—THE PROPHET OF GOD'S WRATH

If a nation wants to survive, it must be built upon righteousness and truth. The LORD God could not permit Assyria, a nation of treachery and cruelty, to continue its evil legacy indefinitely. Jonah had preached repentance to Nineveh, and the city repented. Now a hundred years later, wickedness in Assyria was as horrific as it had been before Jonah's visit.

2 The attack on Jerusalem to which Obadiah refers could be one of two events: 1) the attack by the Philistines and the Arabians during the reign of Jehoram, son of Jehoshaphat (see 2 Chronicles 21:8-10, 16-17); or 2) the destruction of Jerusalem by the Babylonians. Most commentators think Obadiah is referencing the latter event.

3 Repeatedly Obadiah writes the words "in the day of their disaster...trouble...destruction" (see Obadiah 1:12-14) to emphasize Edom's betrayal of Judah. The Edomites were related to the people of Judah through the common ancestor of Jacob, the son of Isaac. Because of their common heritage, the Edomites should have aided Judah instead of gloating over Judah's misfortune and helping the enemy destroy the people of Judah. ("Do not gloat when your enemy falls; when he stumbles, do not let your heart rejoice" [Proverbs 24:17, NIV]).

4 "The Lord detests all the proud of heart. Be sure of this: They will not go unpunished" (Proverbs 16:5, NIV). A prideful person or nation is asserting independence from God, boasting in human power and strength, and claiming God's blessing as their own. Though such a person or nation may continue making its boastful claims for a time, the LORD will eventually bring them down, demonstrating the foolish and fleeting nature of their words. Obadiah said that the judgment on Edom would be so great that there would be no survivors (Obadiah 1:18). Even though the northern kingdom of Israel was conquered by Assyria, there are people alive today who can trace their ancestry back to the ten tribes of Israel. By contrast, the judgment upon Edom was so complete that no one who is alive today can legitimately claim to be an ancestor of the Edomites.

5 Obadiah spoke out against Edom's sin, but the book was actually written to the people of Judah. The LORD wanted His people to know that He does and will punish the wicked who harm His people. This knowledge should be a comfort to God's people. God punishes His own people as well, but He also promises to restore them after a time, which is in contrast to His utterly destroying the enemies of His people.

Notes:

Memory Page · **Story Time** · Worksheets · Quiz

Nahum's poetic prophecy has one theme: the downfall of Assyria. **6** Nahum's first words describe the LORD as a jealous and avenging God. But isn't God a God of love? Absolutely! But a holy, loving God must be jealous when people or nations worship idols instead of worshipping Him, and He must take vengeance upon those who dishonor Him and oppress others. The LORD is slow to anger, but when He shows His wrath, the mountains shake, the hills melt, and the rocks shatter. He can't leave the guilty unpunished!

Nahum wrote to Judah about Assyria's downfall so that God's people would be comforted. Assyria had oppressed God's people for centuries, and now unrepentant Assyria would experience God's judgment. **7** Nahum's prophecy was not a gleeful gloating over his enemy's punishment, but a righteous reaction against Assyria's disrespect of God's honor. **8** Nahum, the prophet of God's wrath, reminded God's people that God is not patient with sin forever. The unchanging God avenges His holy name and punishes evil. The strongest enemies can't overthrow God's kingdom!

ZEPHANIAH—THE PROPHET OF TOTAL DESTRUCTION

"I will sweep away everything—men, animals, birds, and fish." Zephaniah's prophecy begins with descriptive words of God's total destruction of wicked Judah. **9** His repeated words "on that day" gave grim pictures of what the great day of God's judgment would be like.

Zephaniah rebuked four groups of people: 1) officials who were like roaring lions, 2) rulers who were like devouring wolves, 3) prophets who were arrogant and deceitful, and 4) priests who profaned the temple. **10** In his lament, he made four charges against God's people: 1) they didn't obey Him, 2) they didn't accept correction, 3) they didn't trust in the LORD, and 4) they didn't want to be close to the covenant God.

Zephaniah, a descendent of King Hezekiah, lived during Josiah's reign. **11** Even though King Josiah had brought great religious reform to Judah, Zephaniah knew that the people did not serve God from their hearts. He said that God's judgment would be like a purifying fire, and from that fire a remnant would come who would trust in the name of the LORD. Zephaniah, the prophet of total destruction, ended his prophecy with the promise that the LORD would restore His people.

JOEL—THE PROPHET OF GOD'S GRACE

"A nation has invaded, powerful and unable to be numbered, with teeth like a lion." This "nation" that Joel wrote about was a swarm of locusts, millions and millions of hungry insects devouring every green plant.

Chapter 23: God's Voices of Judgment to the Nations 139

6 Nahum wrote his prophecy during the reign of Manasseh. At this time, Assyria was at the height of its power and glory. Thinking about Assyria being overthrown by any other nation was unbelievable. But God, who raises nations up and knocks them down, knew that because of Assyria's thirst for blood ("Woe to the city of blood..." [Nahum 3:1, NIV]), it could not remain. The nation that reveled in vileness and evil would itself be conquered by a nation that was destined to become the next great empire. That empire was Babylon. (Note: The Babylonian empire was often called simply "Babylon" after the name of its capital. The Babylonian empire was also called the Neo-Babylonian Empire to distinguish it from the old Babylonian Empire that existed about the time of Joseph in 1850 BC.)

7 Nahum wrote this prophecy to God's people, even though the subject of God's judgment was Assyria. Once again, through this prophecy, the LORD was telling His people that any nation that would cruelly oppress and conquer them would in turn have to face the wrath of a righteous God.

8 Although Nahum's words may sound as though he was gleefully rejoicing over the fate of an enemy, he was actually speaking out for the honor of God's name. All nations are under God's authority. Whenever any nation flaunts its wickedness, it dishonors the Creator, who made all men in His image.

9 Zephaniah describes the coming destruction as being total. It encompasses not only the death or capture of people, but the sweeping away of animals, birds, and fish. All creation would experience the impact of God's judgment because of man's sin.

10 These four groups of people were supposed to be ruling and guiding the people well. Instead, the princes were "devouring" the people they were supposed to protect; the judges were judging unfairly, thinking only of their own selfish gain; the prophets were arrogantly leading the people astray; and the priests were profaning that which God had declared to be holy and set apart for Him. None of these wicked leaders recognized their sin or experienced any shame because of it. Because the LORD is righteous and just, He had to dispense justice to His people. So, judgment was sure to come.

11 Zephaniah was the fourth generation (great-great-grandson) from King Hezekiah. In other words, Hezekiah had a son named Amariah whose son was Gedaliah whose son was Cushi whose son was Zephaniah. He prophesied during the reign of Josiah, the great-grandson of Hezekiah. As a prince, Zephaniah had intimate knowledge of the spiritual life of those associated with the royal court. Zephaniah's prophecy against Judah was severe. Even though Josiah was bringing about great religious reform, turning the nation's worship away from idolatry and back to the LORD, Zephaniah never mentions anything about the reforms. He focuses only on the nation's idolatry. This indicates that Zephaniah knew that the religious changes taking place in Judah did not come from the people's hearts, but were external changes that would quickly disappear as soon as Josiah died and another godless king reigned in his place.

Notes: ______________________

____

____

____

Most scholars think Joel's locust swarm was an actual plague of insects that the
LORD sent to Judah to bring about their repentance. Joel used the locust swarm as a
picture of invading armies bringing judgment upon Judah on the "day of the LORD." 12
Joel called the people to repentance and urged them to have broken hearts, not just
torn garments, so that the gracious God might have pity and compassion on them. 13
He promised that "everyone who calls on the name of the LORD will be saved."

Joel, the prophet of God's grace, encouraged the people with these words from
the LORD: "I will repay you for the years the locusts have eaten." God's grace is so big
14 that He gives back overwhelming blessing to His repentant people, and His people
see His wonders and praise Him.

Jesus in the OT

The prophets said, "The kingdom will be the Lord's" and spoke of "the day of the Lord." Who is the Lord? Jesus Christ!

HABAKKUK—PROPHET OF FAITH

Why? Why? The prophet Habakkuk asked the
LORD two "why" questions. In this conversation
between Habakkuk and the LORD, Habakkuk asked,
"LORD, why aren't You listening to me?" Habakkuk saw wickedness and violence ev- 15
erywhere in Judah, and it seemed that God was silent and uncaring. Then Habakkuk
asked, "LORD, if You are righteous, why are You going to use Babylon, a cruel nation, to punish Your people?" Even though Habakkuk knew how wicked Judah was,
16 it didn't seem right to him that ruthless Babylon should inflict such pain on God's
people.

Habakkuk listened to God's answer. "I judge all nations by the same laws," the
LORD answered. "Babylon will conquer Judah, but Babylon itself will one day be
17 conquered by another nation." The LORD reminded Habakkuk that He is sovereign,
absolutely righteous, and just. Habakkuk, the prophet of faith, confidently prayed, 18
"Though the fig tree does not blossom, I will rejoice in the LORD." Habakkuk realized
that "the just shall live by their faith." He learned that he could trust the LORD even
in bad circumstances because the Sovereign LORD was his strength.

12 Most scholars believe that the invasion of locusts followed by a drought and then a fire was an actual historical event that occurred in Judah. Joel used this event as a metaphor to describe the invasion of enemy armies that God would send if the nation did not respond to His call for repentance.

13 Joel challenged the people to have repentance of the heart—"rend your hearts"—not just an outward show of repentance—"not your garments" (Joel 2:13). David said the same thing in Psalm 51:17: "The sacrifices of God are a broken spirit, A broken and a contrite heart—These, O God, You will not despise."

14 This blessing is not only material blessing, but also spiritual blessing. The spiritual blessing includes the promise of a future outpouring of the Holy Spirit in ways that no one had ever seen exhibited before.

15 Habakkuk's first question was a "how long?" question. Habakkuk didn't understand how the LORD could see the wickedness in Judah and apparently do nothing. Since God is absolutely holy and righteous, it seemed to Habakkuk that He should do something about Judah's injustice and violence. Why was He silent?

16 When the LORD answered Habakkuk, the answer was shocking. The LORD replied that judgment to Judah would come through Babylon, a nation more idolatrous and wicked than Judah. If the LORD's silence was puzzling, His second answer was even more difficult to understand.

17 The LORD assured Habakkuk that even though Babylon would be the instrument of judgment upon Judah, the righteous God would then punish Babylon for its sin. God always executes justice upon nations or individuals who commit sin and never repent.

18 Habakkuk's song of praise in Habakkuk 3:17-19 is a beautiful expression of trust in the LORD's sovereign care in the midst of dire circumstances. What a comfort that we can be confident that our circumstances do not have to determine our ability to trust the LORD!

Notes:

Review Worksheets

A. MEMORY VERSE: "The LORD is slow to anger and great in power; the LORD will not leave the guilty unpunished." (Nahum 1:3a, NIV)

B. KEY FACTS: Draw a line from the title to the name of the prophet. Then draw a line from the meaning of the prophet's name to the prophet.

Getting To Know the Prophets

Title	Prophet	Meaning
Prophet of God's Wrath	Obadiah	"Embrace"
Prophet of Faith	Nahum	"Jehovah hides"
Prophet of Edom's Disaster	Joel	"Comforter"
Prophet of God's Grace	Habakkuk	"Jehovah is God"
Prophet of Total Destruction	Zephaniah	"Worshipper"

C. STORY FACTS: Fill in the blanks.

1. The Book of Obadiah is a prophecy against the nation of Edom.
2. The theme of Nahum was the downfall of Assyria.
3. God judged Edom because Edom betrayed the nation of Judah.
4. Nahum said that the LORD takes vengeance upon those who dishonor Him and oppress others.
5. Zephaniah was a descendent of King Hezekiah.
6. Zephaniah said God's judgment was like a purifying fire.
7. Zephaniah knew the people didn't serve God from their hearts.
8. The LORD sent a plague of locusts to bring repentance to Judah.
9. In Habakkuk, the LORD said Babylon would conquer Judah.
10. Habakkuk learned to trust God even in bad circumstances.

Notes:

D. WHO DID GOD SPEAK THROUGH?

In the blanks, write the initial of the prophet.

O – Obadiah N – Nahum J – Joel H – Habakkuk Z – Zephaniah

Z "I will sweep away everything."

J "I will repay you for the years the locusts have eaten."

O "And the kingdom shall be the LORD's."

J "A nation has invaded…with teeth like a lion."

H "The just will live by their faith."

N "The LORD is jealous and takes vengeance."

E. THE COVENANT AND GOD'S JUDGMENT

1. What did Nahum want to remind God's people about God?

God is not patient with sin forever.

2. What charges did Zephaniah bring against God's people?

They didn't obey God; they didn't accept correction; they didn't trust in the Lord; and they did not want to be close to the covenant God.

3. What was Zephaniah's promise to God's people? restoration

4. When Joel called God's people to repentance, what did he urge them to have?

broken hearts, not just torn garments

5. What two questions did Habakkuk ask the LORD?

1) Why aren't You listening to me?

2) Why are You using a cruel nation like Babylon to punish Your people?

6. What did Obadiah remind God's people? God is the supreme King

F. FIND OUT…

New Testament writers often quote Old Testament prophets. Which prophet is quoted in these New Testament verses?

Romans 10:13 Joel

Romans 1:17 Habakkuk

Acts 2:16-21 Joel

Galatians 3:11 Habakkuk

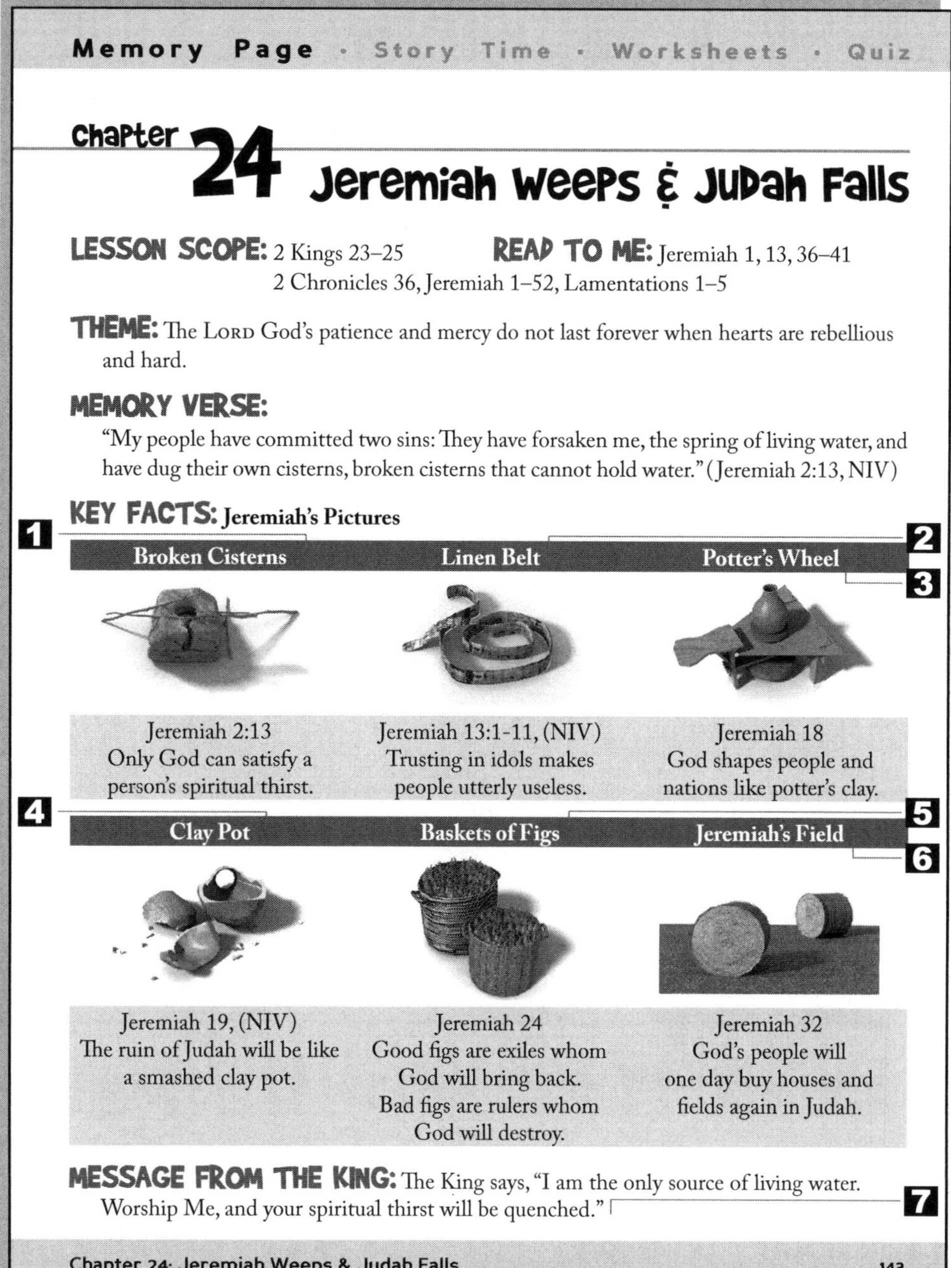
Memory Page · Story Time · Worksheets · Quiz

Chapter 24 Jeremiah Weeps & Judah Falls

LESSON SCOPE: 2 Kings 23–25 2 Chronicles 36, Jeremiah 1–52, Lamentations 1–5

READ TO ME: Jeremiah 1, 13, 36–41

THEME: The Lord God's patience and mercy do not last forever when hearts are rebellious and hard.

MEMORY VERSE:

"My people have committed two sins: They have forsaken me, the spring of living water, and have dug their own cisterns, broken cisterns that cannot hold water." (Jeremiah 2:13, NIV)

1 **KEY FACTS:** **Jeremiah's Pictures**

Broken Cisterns	Linen Belt	Potter's Wheel
Jeremiah 2:13 Only God can satisfy a person's spiritual thirst.	Jeremiah 13:1-11, (NIV) Trusting in idols makes people utterly useless.	Jeremiah 18 God shapes people and nations like potter's clay.

2 3 4 5 6

Clay Pot	Baskets of Figs	Jeremiah's Field
Jeremiah 19, (NIV) The ruin of Judah will be like a smashed clay pot.	Jeremiah 24 Good figs are exiles whom God will bring back. Bad figs are rulers whom God will destroy.	Jeremiah 32 God's people will one day buy houses and fields again in Judah.

MESSAGE FROM THE KING: The King says, "I am the only source of living water. Worship Me, and your spiritual thirst will be quenched." 7

Chapter 24: Jeremiah Weeps & Judah Falls 143

Notes to Teachers and Parents:

1 God's people had committed two sins. First, Israel had forsaken the Lord who had made a covenant to be their God and to make them His special people. At Sinai and before entering the Promised Land, the people had promised to worship and serve the Lord. However, they had broken the covenant and did not worship the Lord as the only true God and the only source of satisfaction and well-being ("living water" [John 4:10]). Second, not only did God's people forsake the Lord, but they also chose to worship other gods. Jeremiah spoke about the sinfulness and foolishness of idolatry. These idols ("broken cisterns" [Jeremiah 2:13]) couldn't hold water, and though they might temporarily or partially satisfy, the idols were empty and couldn't meet the spiritual needs of God's people.

2 The linen belt symbolized the intimate relationship between God and His people, and since priests wore linen, the linen gave a hint to the idea that God's people were a nation of priests. As a result of the linen belt being separated from its wearer and buried in the rock, the linen belt was ruined and worthless. In a like manner, when God's people are separated from God, they become soiled and ruined, no longer fit for a relationship with the holy God.

3 The Lord explained to Jeremiah that all the nations are like clay in His hands. Even though the "clay" is marred, the potter can reshape it as He wishes, and it can become a useful pot. In a like manner, even though a nation is marred by its sin, the Lord can reshape its final end if it repents. The Lord God can choose to bless, instead of judge, that nation. The repentance of a nation makes a difference in the way God responds to it. At the same time, the sovereign God is immutable in His purposes. Even the change of heart leading to repentance is part of God's plan.

4 In this picture, the Lord said that Judah was like a hard clay pot, no longer malleable under the potter's hands. Judah, hardened in its sin, was fit for nothing but being smashed beyond repair.

5 The Lord showed Jeremiah two baskets of figs, one basket of good, ripe figs ready to be eaten and enjoyed, and the other basket filled with rotten figs not fit to eat. The good figs represented the godly people who were sent away as exiles from Judah into Babylon. The Lord said He would watch over them and eventually bring them back to the land. The Lord would give them a heart to know Him, and they would be His people. The bad figs represented Zedekiah, his officials, and those who remained in Jerusalem or fled to Egypt in direct disobedience to the Lord's instructions. The Lord said He would make these people objects of ridicule and scorn. Eventually all of them would die from famine, sword, or plague because they refused to obey the Lord and acknowledge His kingship over their lives.

6 The Lord told Jeremiah to buy a field, symbolizing that the exiles would one day return to Judah, would buy land and build houses, and would live a normal life again. God made this same promise in the letter that Jeremiah sent to the surviving elders, priests, and prophets exiled in Babylon. ("I will gather you from all the nations and places where I have banished you...and will bring you back to the place from which I carried you into exile" [Jeremiah 29:14, NIV]). Jeremiah repeatedly told Zedekiah that he was to surrender the city and go with the exiles to Babylon and that if he refused, he would be killed. Zedekiah did not heed the Lord's word through Jeremiah.

Jeremiah Weeps & Judah Falls

8 "Jeremiah, listen to me. Before you were born, I set you apart to be My prophet,"
9 said the LORD. "Ah, Sovereign LORD, I don't know how to speak Your words. I'm only a child," lamented Jeremiah.

The LORD then gave Jeremiah two visions: 1) the branch of an almond tree to remind Jeremiah that the LORD's words would come true; and 2) a boiling pot
10 tilted away from the north to tell Judah that judgment would come from the north. Reluctantly, Jeremiah became the LORD's prophet. For fifty years and through the reigns of five kings, Jeremiah faithfully proclaimed God's message of coming destruction, sympathy for His rebellious people, and hope of a return from exile.

From 609 BC, when King Josiah was killed in the battle with Egypt, to 586 BC when Jerusalem was totally destroyed, Judah was controlled by either Egypt or Babylon, and these nations put godless kings on the throne. Jehoahaz, Josiah's son, ruled only three months before Egypt's Pharaoh captured him, put in him chains, and carried him off to Egypt. Jehoahaz died in Egypt.

The Egyptians then put Jehoiakim, another son of Josiah, on Judah's throne. For eleven years, Jehoiakim did only evil in God's eyes. Finally, he betrayed Egypt and gave tribute money to Babylon, doing whatever Babylon told him to do. After he died, his son, Jehoiachin, was king briefly, but the Babylonians took him to Babylon and made Zedekiah, a third son of Josiah, king. Zedekiah was the last king of Judah. During Zedekiah's reign, the promised judgment upon Jerusalem finally happened.

JEREMIAH—THE PROPHET OF TEARS

During his fifty years as a prophet in Judah, Jeremiah suffered in many ways. He lived in a time of great wickedness and proclaimed a message that no one wanted to hear. He was rejected and persecuted by the kings and the people. Sometimes he wanted to run away from people. "Oh, that I had in the desert a lodging place for travelers, so that I might leave my people and go away from them" (Jeremiah 9:2, NIV). But no matter how difficult his task or how unpopular his message, he never stopped preaching God's truth, and he always had sympathy for his countrymen.

7 Because of our sinful, rebellious hearts, we look many places other than the LORD for something or someone to satisfy our spiritual thirst, even though the LORD tells us that we are to worship only Him. In Isaiah 55:1, the LORD calls all those who are thirsty to come to Him, and when thirsty people come to the LORD, their thirst will be satisfied free of charge. In John 4, Jesus told the Samaritan woman at the well that He could give her living water and if she drank of it she would never thirst again. At first, she believed that Jesus' offer would free her from the shame of drawing water from the city well in the heat of the day, and she eagerly welcomed this gift. Later, when she realized that the living water to which Jesus referred would cleanse her from her sin and shame, she unashamedly told everyone in her village about the living water Jesus had given to her. The ways we try unsuccessfully to assuage our thirst for God and be happy—people, possessions, fame, etc.—will prove futile, because our hearts were designed to find satisfaction in our relationship with God.

8 Before Jeremiah was born, the LORD had a plan for him. God said that He formed Jeremiah in the womb. He set Jeremiah apart before he was born and appointed him as a prophet to the nations. In like manner, the LORD had a plan for each of us before we were born. Not only is He our Creator, shaping us in just the way He wants us to be without mistake or defect, but He designs a mission for us (see Ephesians 2:10).

9 Like Moses, Jeremiah thought he could not speak well enough to be a spokesman for the LORD. The LORD's response to Jeremiah was to encourage him not to be afraid of the people. He told Jeremiah what to say and assured him of His presence with him.

10 Even though Babylon was located to the east of Jerusalem, the pathway that Babylon would take to reach the city was the shape of a huge inverted U. The route moved first north, then west, and finally south through Syria and the territory that used to be Israel. The armies of Babylon would then sweep down, invading Judah from the north.

11 The LORD had told Jeremiah to prophesy to the people from the courtyard of the temple. Priests, prophets, and ordinary people heard him, and in anger they seized him. Those who had seized Jeremiah complained to the legal officials in the royal administration that Jeremiah had prophesied against the city and should be put to death. The officials disagreed, and Jeremiah was not executed. Not all the prophets escaped the wrath of the people like Jeremiah did. Urijah, another faithful prophet of the LORD, was executed by King Jehoiakim, because the king and his officials did not like Urijah predictions of Jerusalem's destruction (see Jeremiah 26:20-23).

12 Baruch, Jeremiah's scribe, helped Jeremiah compile and write down the prophecies and history that comprise the book of Jeremiah. Because Jeremiah was "restricted" from the temple (meaning that he was probably banned from the temple area because of his unpopularity with the people), Baruch went to the temple with the scroll to read the words to all the people gathered there. At this time of year, the people were having a religious fast, so many people from Jerusalem and the surrounding areas filled the temple. After Micaiah, one of the royal officials, heard the words, he reported what he had heard to the

Jeremiah spoke out harshly against Judah's kings, who thought that wealth was more important than justice and mercy. He condemned the false prophets for their lies. Though he was not as harsh toward the people, Jeremiah preached that the people would go into exile because of their sin, stay in Babylon for seventy years, and
11 then return home. No one liked what Jeremiah said. The people tried to kill him, but
God protected him.

12
Jeremiah told his scribe, Baruch, to write God's words on a scroll and read the words at the temple. King Jehoiakim burned up the scroll and tried to arrest Jeremiah and Baruch, but the Lord kept them safe. Later, when Zedekiah was king, the king's officials got
13 angry with Jeremiah and threw him into a deep cistern
with a muddy bottom. They wanted to kill him, but they changed their minds and let Jeremiah out. During much of Zedekiah's reign, Jeremiah was imprisoned in the guard's courtyard. Despite all his troubles, Jeremiah always spoke God's truth.

Jesus in the OT

Jeremiah was rejected by the people and persecuted by kings. No one wanted to hear what he had to say. Like Jeremiah, people rejected what Jesus had to say, too. Both Jeremiah and Jesus cried tears of sorrow over the hardened hearts of God's people.

Jeremiah told Zedekiah to surrender to Babylon, but he refused. Eventually the 14
Babylonian army surrounded Jerusalem and broke through the city walls. They cap-
15 tured Zedekiah, killed all his sons, and took him and almost all the people to Baby- 16
lon. Only Jeremiah and a few people remained in Jerusalem. The Babylonians put Gedaliah in charge as governor, but a group of people assassinated Gedaliah because they believed he was a traitor. After this murder, the people in Jerusalem were terrified because they had killed the governor that Nebuchadnezzar had put over them. Against Jeremiah's urgings, these people fled to Egypt, dragging Jeremiah along with them. Years later, Jeremiah died in Egypt.

Jeremiah used many different word pictures to preach his important message of judgment. But his message also had hope. This hope had three parts: 1) the exiles would return home after seventy years, 2) the Lord would make a new covenant with His people, and 3) a Messiah would come.

While in Egypt, or shortly before, Jeremiah, the prophet of tears, wrote the book of Lamentations, a poetic description of Jerusalem burning from Babylon's torches. This man of tears loved his countrymen, his beloved Jerusalem, and, most of all, his Lord.

other royal officials gathered in the secretary's office in the palace. These officials sent for Baruch and asked that he read Jeremiah's scroll to them. Upon hearing the words, the officials' response was fear, wondering how Jehoiakim, the king, would react. They confirmed with Baruch that Jeremiah had written the words, and they warned Baruch, "You and Jeremiah should leave the city and hide. Don't tell anyone where you are." Then one of the royal officials—Jehudi—read the words to Jehoiakim. Jehoiakim's response was one of contempt instead of fear. As each part of the scroll was read, the king tore that part from the scroll and tossed it into his fireplace. Eventually the entire scroll was burned up (see Jeremiah 36:23). Jehoiakim then demanded that three of his officials (one of whom was his son) immediately find Jeremiah and Baruch and arrest them. Because of His omniscience and sovereignty, the Lord knew what Jehoiakim's reaction would be to the reading of Jeremiah's prophecy. The Lord had safely hid Jeremiah and Baruch from danger. The Lord told Jeremiah to compose another scroll and send it to Jehoiakim. The Lord also said that because of Jehoiakim's contemptuous destruction of the first scroll, no son of Jehoiakim would ever sit on Judah's throne. This prophecy was fulfilled when Jehoiakim's son, Jehoiachin, was removed from power only three months after he succeeded to the throne. The intensity of Jehoiakim's reaction—burning the scroll—shows how great his rebellion against God had become.

13 Jeremiah prophesied that Babylon would capture the city and anyone who surrendered to the Babylonians would live. The king's officials thought Jeremiah was not concerned with the good of the people, and they wanted to silence him. Zedekiah reneged his authority, saying he was powerless to oppose the officials. He gave them permission to do whatever they wanted to Jeremiah. The officials' response was to put Jeremiah into an empty well with a deep, muddy bottom. One of Zedekiah's officials not involved in Jeremiah's capture was concerned that Jeremiah would starve to death in the well. He convinced the king to rescue Jeremiah from the cistern. Zedekiah agreed, and after being pulled from the well, Jeremiah was imprisoned in the guard's courtyard.

14 In Jeremiah 21, Jeremiah told Zedekiah that God was going to judge Jerusalem and allow Babylon to conquer it. Everyone who left the city and allowed himself to be taken captive would live. Anyone who remained in the city against God's command, however, would die by sword, famine, or plague. Nebuchadnezzar's army would show no mercy or compassion to the people who refused to surrender. God was laying out the way of life and the way of death. Each person had a choice.

15 Nebuchadnezzar told his officers not to harm Jeremiah: "Take him and look after him; don't harm him but do for him whatever he asks" (Jeremiah 39: 12, NIV). Several of Nebuchadnezzar's commanders released Jeremiah from his courtyard imprisonment and turned him over to Gedaliah. The intention was that Jeremiah would be a free man and therefore able to remain in Jerusalem. Somehow, Jeremiah ended up being captured and bound in chains with the other captives who were being taken to Babylon. When Nebuzaradan, commander of the imperial guard, recognized Jeremiah, he realized the mistake. He freed Jeremiah from his chains and gave him the choice to go to Babylon with the exiles or go wherever he chose to go. Nebuzaradan gave Jeremiah provisions and a present (Scripture does not identify what this present was) and let him go. Jeremiah chose to return to Jerusalem and live with those left behind (see Jeremiah 40:1-6).

16 Three times the Babylonians took captives from Jerusalem (in 605 BC, 597 BC, and 586 BC). After Josiah was killed in the battle against the Egyptians in 609 BC, Jehoahaz, Josiah's son, became king. But, Jehoahaz was king only three months when the Egyptians, having defeated Judah, removed Jehoahaz and put Jehoiakim, another son of Josiah, on the throne. The Egyptians took Jehoahaz to Egypt, where he eventually died. Though Jehoiakim sat on the throne, Judah was now under the domination of Egypt. When the Babylonians defeated the Egyptians in 605 BC, Jehoiakim switched his allegiance from Egypt to Nebuchadnezzar. Babylon invaded Judah, lay siege to Jerusalem, and took the first group of people captive. With Jehoiakim still on the throne, Judah was now under the domination of Babylon. The people in this first group of captives were primarily of the nobility and the upper classes of Jewish society. Daniel and his friends were part of this first group of captives. Eleven years later, when Jehoiakim switched his allegiance back to Egypt, Nebuchadnezzar wanted to punish Jehoiakim for his infidelity to Babylon. In 597 BC, the Babylonians attacked Jerusalem again. Jehoiakim died, and his son, Jehoiachin, became king. Jehoiachin ruled only three months before Nebuchadnezzar removed him from the throne and put Zedekiah, a third son of Josiah, in his place. At this time, the second, larger group, was taken captive. Ezekiel was part of this group. Because Daniel and Ezekiel prophesied to the exiles, both of them will be discussed in the next unit, even though they lived at the same time as Jeremiah. The third group of captives was taken in 586 BC, when Babylon attacked Jerusalem for the last time and utterly destroyed the city, leaving only the lowliest and poorest people. Jeremiah stayed in Jerusalem with these last remnants of Judah. He eventually was dragged away with them when they fled to Egypt after the assassination of the Babylonian-appointed governor, Gedaliah. Jeremiah died in Egypt.

Review Worksheets

A. MEMORY VERSE: "My people have committed two ___sins___: They have ___forsaken___ me, the spring of ___living___ ___water___, and have dug their own ___cisterns___, broken cisterns that cannot ___hold___ ___water___." (Jeremiah 2:13, NIV)

B. KEY FACTS: Match the description to the word pictures.

Jeremiah's Pictures

__4__ Broken cisterns	1. God shapes people and nations like clay.
__5__ Ruined linen belt	2. Judah will be like a smashed pot.
__1__ Potter's wheel	3. God's people will return and buy fields.
__2__ Smashed clay pot	4. Only God satisfies spiritual thirst.
__6__ Baskets of figs	5. Trusting in idols makes people useless.
__3__ Field of crops	6. God will destroy wicked rulers of Judah.

C. STORY FACTS: Fill in the blanks.

1. When the Lord called Jeremiah to be a prophet, He gave him two visions: ___almond tree branch___ and ___boiling pot tilted away from the north___.
2. Jeremiah was a prophet for ___50___ years during the reign of ___5___ kings.
3. The last king of Judah was named ___Zedekiah___.
4. When Jeremiah's scribe, ___Baruch___, gave Jehoiakim the scroll with God's words, Jehoiakim ___burned up___ the scroll.
5. Two nations, ___Egypt___ and ___Babylon___ had control over Judah in the years after Josiah died.
6. Jeremiah wrote ___Lamentations___ to describe Jerusalem's destruction.
7. The Babylonians made ___Gedaliah___ governor in Jerusalem.
8. Jeremiah said the exiles would return to Jerusalem after ___70___ years.

Notes:

D. WHAT'S WRONG WITH THIS? In the paragraph below, cross out the **wrong** words. Then write the **correct** words below, from left to right.

Before Jeremiah was ~~grown up~~ the LORD set Jeremiah apart to be His prophet. ~~Eagerly,~~ Jeremiah became His prophet. Jeremiah lived in a time of great ~~spiritual reform~~. ~~Everyone~~ wanted to hear Jeremiah's message. He was ~~accepted~~ and ~~honored~~ by kings and the people. Later, when Zedekiah was king, the king's officials threw Jeremiah into a deep ~~hole~~. Zedekiah imprisoned Jeremiah in the guard's ~~dungeon~~. After the destruction of Jerusalem, the people took Jeremiah to ~~Babylon~~ with them. Jeremiah ~~often~~ changed his message to the people. He said ~~Assyria~~ would conquer Jerusalem, but the exiles would return after ~~forty~~ years. He also said that the LORD would make a new ~~song~~ for His people and that some day in the future the ~~Romans~~ would come.

born	Reluctantly	wickedness	No one
rejected	persecuted	cistern	courtyard
Egypt	never	Babylon	seventy
covenant	Messiah		

E. PUT THE KINGS OF JUDAH IN ORDER. Put these last five kings of Judah in chronological order.

3 Jehoiakim 5 Zedekiah 2 Jehoahaz

1 Josiah 4 Jehoiachin

F. FIND OUT... What does Lamentations say...

1. About God's faithfulness (3:22-23): Great is God's faithfulness
2. About calamities and good things (3:37-38): They come from God
3. What's the same about chapters 1, 2, 4, and 5 of Lamentations? (Hint: They all have a similar number of something.)

They all have 22 verses in them.

Notes to Teachers and Parents:

1 Description of the destruction of Jerusalem is described in Jeremiah 52:12-24 and Lamentations 1:1-12, 2:1-12 and 4:1-10.

Notes:

Chapter 25 Looking Backwards...Looking Ahead

LESSON SCOPE: 2 Kings 1, 9–25, 2 Chronicles 21-36 Isaiah 1–66, Micah 1–7, Habakkuk 1–3, Zephaniah 1–3 Nahum 1–3, Joel 1–3, Obadiah 1, Jeremiah 1–52, Lamentations 1–5

READ TO ME: Psalm 68

Brilliant flames leapt high, turning the magnificent temple of the Lord into charred stone. Precious gems littered the streets, trampled under the feet of the battle-crazed Babylonian warriors. All around the city of Jerusalem, its mighty walls, built to protect God's people, lay in shambles. Not a home was left standing, and every building was being destroyed by fire. After six months under siege, the people were starving and despairing. Even being captured by the Babylonians seemed preferable to living in Jerusalem with no food, no houses, and no protection. With the temple gone, certainly God's presence must also be gone, the people believed. 1

It was sin that had brought this destruction upon Jerusalem. What was God's people's worst sin? Was it living in luxury and being greedy? Was it acting unjustly and having no mercy toward each other? Was it the lies that the false prophets told or the despicable sacrifices that the priests performed?

No, although the Lord hated all these sins, none of them was the worst. The worst sin was that the people had rejected God's covenant. The Lord had delivered them from Egypt, given them their own land, delivered them from their enemies for centuries, and blessed them in many ways. God's people had accepted all these blessings, but in return had spurned God's love by worshipping other gods and disobeying all His commands.

In Unit IV, you learned how the Lord judged first Israel and then Judah by sending vicious nations to conquer them. Many prophets tried to warn the people, but the people persisted in their rebellious ways. In Unit V, you will learn what life was like for the captives in Babylon. And, when the people returned home again after seventy years, you will also see once again that our Lord of the covenant is the God who makes promises and keeps them.

IMPORTANT THINGS TO KNOW:

Word	Meaning of the Word
Covenant	God's promise to be the God of His people forever.
Legacy	Something you leave behind for your descendants.
Messiah	Hebrew word meaning "the Anointed One."
Prophet	Person called to speak for God.
Remnant	The part left after the rest has been lost.

Review Worksheets

A. MEMORY VERSE REVIEW—WHAT DOESN'T FIT? Cross out the all the **wrong** words and write the **correct** words in the blanks. The number of blanks tells you how many words are wrong.

1. "For the LORD knows the ~~path~~ of the righteous, But the ~~life~~ of the ~~wicked~~ shall ~~end~~." (Psalm 1:6)

way ____ way ____ ungodly ____ perish ____

2. "For assuredly, I say to you, till ~~day~~ and ~~night~~ pass away, one ~~word~~ or one ~~letter~~ will by no means pass from the ~~scripture~~ till all is fulfilled." (Matthew 5:18)

heaven ____ earth ____ jot ____ tittle ____ law ____

3. "The LORD is ~~quick~~ to anger and great in ~~justice~~; the LORD will not leave the ~~wicked~~ unpunished." (Nahum 1:3a, NIV)

slow ____ power ____ guilty ____

B. MEMORY VERSE REVIEW: Answer the questions below.

1. What three things does the LORD require of you? (Micah 6:8). Do justly ____, love mercy ____, and walk humbly with your God ____.

2. What two sins did God's people commit? (Jeremiah 2:13, NIV).

They forsook the LORD, the spring of living waters ____ and dug their own broken cisterns that cannot hold water. ____

C. WHAT'S THE THEME OF UNIT IV? Starting with the second letter from the far right, circle every other letter, moving from right to left. Then, beginning with the right-most circled letter, put the letters in the blanks below, starting with the far left blank.

S E E R G E D P U T J U O R H O W A D T O L G M E R H E T O

T h e G o d w h o j u d g e s

Notes:

D. WHEN DID THE KINGS OF JUDAH REIGN? Number the kings and queens of Judah in order from 1 to 20, starting with the king who ruled after King Solomon. Then circle all the kings who were faithful to the LORD for at least part of their reign.

3 (Asa)	9 (Amaziah)	16 (Josiah)
20 Zedekiah	5 Jehoram	4 (Jehoshaphat)
1 Rehoboam	18 Jehoiakim	11 (Jotham)
2 Abijah	6 Ahaziah	8 (Joash)
13 (Hezekiah)	15 Amon	19 Jehoiachin
10 (Uzziah)	14 Manasseh	7 Athaliah
12 Ahaz	17 Jehoahaz	

E. WHAT HAPPENED NEXT? Put the story boxes in order.

3	Athaliah tried to kill baby Joash.	1	Rehoboam ruled Judah after Solomon died.	7	Manasseh ruled and left a legacy of evil.
8	Josiah read the Book of the Law to the people.	6	Hezekiah trusted God when the Assyrians attacked.	2	Godly King Asa removed idols and served God.
9	Zedekiah ruled as the last king of Judah.	4	Joash repaired the temple, and the people worshipped God.	5	Uzziah got leprosy, and his son, Jotham, became king.

F. What do you remember about the prophets?

Match the prophet with the description that tells you something about him.

	Prophet	Description
3	Joel	1. Smashed pots and baskets of figs
4	Amos	2. A large hungry fish
9	Obadiah	3. A plague of locusts
7	Habakkuk	4. Justice rolls on like a river
10	Nahum	5. An unfaithful wife
2	Jonah	6. Vision of seraphim praising God
1	Jeremiah	7. Two difficult questions
11	Micah	8. Judgment like a purifying fire
6	Isaiah	9. Judgment against Edom
5	Hosea	10. Desire to respect God's honor
8	Zephaniah	11. The Messiah born in Bethlehem

G. What is the difference between Kings and Chronicles?

Kings	Chronicles
Written by a prophet.	Written by a priest.
Theme: God's judgment and blessing.	**Theme:** God's presence and holiness.
History of Judah and Israel.	History of Judah.
Content: Stories of Elisha and Elijah.	**Content:** Lists of genealogies.

Notes:

H. WHAT'S THE REASON? Circle the **correct** answer.

1. In the temple, Isaiah cried out, "Woe is me!" because he ________.
   had never seen seraphim before | knew he was very sinful (circled)
2. Judgment came to Judah because the people didn't ________.
   change from the heart (circled) | offer enough sacrifices
3. God judged Edom because it ________ when Judah was attacked.
   cheered on Judah's attackers (circled) | sent too small an army
4. The people of Judah didn't like Jeremiah because he ________.
   spoke harsh and unkind words | preached God's truth to them (circled)
5. Joel said that God sent the swarm of locusts so that the people would ________.
   remember their slavery in Egypt | repent of their sin (circled)
6. Huldah said judgment would not come during Josiah's life because ________.
   Josiah was humble and sought God (circled) | the people celebrated Passover
7. Jehoiada, the high priest, hid baby Joash in the temple because ________.
   the Assyrians were attacking | Athaliah wanted to kill him (circled)

I. WHAT DID THE PROPHETS SAY ABOUT GOD?

God judged His people because they didn't obey Him as their **king** (NIGK), and they forgot God's **covenant** (VANECNTO). Micah reminded the people that God does not stay **angry** (GRANY) forever and delights to show **mercy** (CYREM). Nahum said God was a **jealous** (LOJEASU) God when people worshipped idols. God is not **patient** (TAPINET) with sin forever. Jeremiah said that God was the fountain of **living** (VIGLIN) water. Habakkuk learned that he could **trust** (STURT) God even in bad circumstances. Many prophets spoke about the **Messiah** (SISAMEH) who would come and bring salvation to His people.

UNIT V

The Exiled Nation...The God Who Restores

Theme: The Keeper of the Kingdom restores His people in His own time.

Oh, dear me, how sad! Judah has followed in the way of wicked Israel, and now both kingdoms have fallen into the hands of an enemy nation. Glorious Jerusalem, site of God's sacred temple and Solomon's magnificent palace, is a pile of rubble.

I, Tobias, the royal chronicler, have wept oceans of tears, and my tears have spilled, drop by drop, onto my scroll as I write with utmost accuracy the account of this tragedy. And yet, don't despair. God's story has not ended. Our God of the covenant, who makes promises and keeps them, will not forsake His people, even though they have forsaken Him.

Actually, our story in Unit V begins before the final fall of Jerusalem. Three times the Babylonians captured people from Jerusalem and carried them off to captivity in Babylon. Ezekiel and Daniel were part of the first two groups. Their mission from the LORD was to prophesy to and encourage the exiles. Daniel, captured as a young man, lived to be over 100 years old. His wisdom, leadership qualities, and ability to interpret dreams caught the attention of Nebuchadnezzar, the great Babylonian king, and Daniel's reputation and integrity earned him a position of official authority in the courts of Cyrus and Darius, Persian kings of renown.

God is so very wise. The Exile had its purpose. During those seventy long years, the LORD purged idolatry from His people and roused in them a longing for the Messiah. Although the human heart will always run after idols, the Jews as a people never again worshipped pagan idols after their return from exile. As He promised, the LORD brought the people back to their land. They had so many struggles, and their enemies made their lives very difficult, but the story of God's faithfulness is much more awesome than the story of their troubles is discouraging.

By the end of the Old Testament, God's people are once again settled in their own land. God's promises have been fulfilled, all but the most important promise: the promise of a Messiah! The Old Testament ends with hope because, someday, the King who has been keeping His kingdom safe will come in person. This King, the Messiah, is the hope for all of God's people!

Notes:

PSALM 126, NIV, A Song of Ascents

1. When the LORD brought back the captives to Zion,
   we were like men who dreamed.
2. Our mouths were filled with laughter,
   our tongues with songs of joy.
   Then it was said among the nations,
   "The LORD has done great things for them."
3. The LORD has done great things for us,
   and we are filled with joy.
4. Restore our fortunes, O LORD,
   like streams in the Negev.
5. Those who sow in tears
   will reap with songs of joy.
6. He who goes out weeping,
   carrying seed to sow,
   will return with songs of joy,
   carrying sheaves with him.

Has anything ever happened to you that was so wonderful that you thought you were dreaming? It was just too good to be true! When the exiled Jews returned to Jerusalem, it felt like a dream to them.

This joyous event was so amazing that the heathen nations around them would exclaim, "Look what great things God has done for His people!" And, God's people, too, could say, "What great thing God has done for us!" They knew it was because of God's plan, not Cyrus's decree, that they could return home.

God's people prayed that the LORD would restore such plentiful prosperity to the land that it would be like the streams in the desert at flood season. The streambeds in the Negev desert are empty for much of the year. When the winter rains come, however, the dry streambeds fill up with rushing water that nourishes the arid soil and changes barren ground to pastureland. In Psalm 126, God's people were asking the LORD to bless their work and bring good things to them.

Turning ruined Jerusalem into a pleasant place to live would require sweat, toil, and tears. But one day, when the walls were rebuilt, the fields were rich with crops, and the land was filled with people, God's children again would sing praises to their God of the covenant for His blessings.

Memory Page · Story Time · Worksheets · Quiz

Chapter 26 God's Messenger to the Exiles

LESSON SCOPE: Ezekiel 1–48 **READ TO ME:** Ezekiel 1, Psalm 137

THEME: The LORD God speaks to His people in exile.

MEMORY VERSE:

"The soul who sins is the one who will die.... 'For I take no pleasure in the death of anyone,' declares the Sovereign LORD. 'Repent and live!'" (Ezekiel 18:20a, 32, NIV) **1**

KEY FACTS: **Ezekiel's Visions and Pictures**

	Reference	Vision or Picture	Meaning
2	1:1-28	Four living creatures; wheels with eyes	God is everywhere and sees everything.
3	1:1-28	Windstorm; fiery cloud; rainbow	Judgment is coming, but God also shows grace and mercy.
4	2:9–3:9	Sweet scroll eaten by Ezekiel	Ezekiel must speak the words that God gives him.
5	4:1-17	Ezekiel lying on his side for many days	People in Jerusalem will suffer greatly when God judges their sin.
6	5:1-17	Ezekiel's hair cut into three piles; small handful of hair	Only a small number of people will survive the judgment upon Jerusalem.
7	12:1-28	Ezekiel packing his bag and pretending to go on a long journey	The exile in Babylon will be like going on a journey and not returning for a long time.
8	16:1-63	The unfaithful wife	God will punish His people for their ungratefulness and unfaithfulness.
9	37:1-14	Dry bones come back to life	God will miraculously bring His people "back to life" as a nation.
10	37:15-28	Two sticks joined together as one stick	The northern and southern kingdoms will one day be united again.

MESSAGE FROM THE KING: The King says, "I will dwell in the hearts of My people."

The LORD departed from the temple in Jerusalem, but He will never depart from the hearts of those who fear Him.

Chapter 26: God's Messenger to the Exiles 155

Notes to Teachers and Parents:

1 The LORD makes two important points in Ezekiel 18. First, He emphasizes that each person is responsible for his or her own sin. No one is to blame for the sin of his children and no one can blame his parents for his own sin. Although the home environment and the example of parents is a significant shaping influence in a child's life, being made in the image of God means that each person has a soul and a will that can decide how he or she will react in any circumstance. It is the "soul who sins" (Ezekiel 18:20) that will pay the consequence of sin if there is no repentance. (Parents do have the responsibility before God to provide a nurturing home environment and to train a child in God's ways. If a parent fails to do this and does not repent, the parent will be responsible for his sin of negligent parenting.) Second, the LORD makes it very clear that He has no pleasure in any person's death. Though unrepentant sinners will die because of their refusal to repent, God takes no joy in their deaths. The LORD desires that all men come to repentance, even though He knows not all men will repent. The ability to repent is a gift from God, and not all people receive this gift. This, however, in no way relieves anyone of his responsibility for his actions. Every person willingly and knowingly acts and reacts from his heart. Unless the heart is regenerated by God's Spirit, the heart will continue to sin without repentance. Because God is holy and good, He must punish unrepentant sin even though He takes no pleasure in doing so.

2 In his book *Explore the Book*, commentator J. Sidlow Baxter suggests that the four faces in the vision represent "strength at its greatest, service at its meekest, intelligence at its fullest, and heavenliness at its most soaring" (Baxter, 20). Through these four qualities, the living creatures epitomized everything necessary to do God's divine will. The four rapidly whirling wheels were high and vast, reaching down to earth and up to heaven. They were powered by the "spirit of the living creatures" (see Ezekiel 1:20), which is God's Spirit, and were filled with eyes that looked in every direction and saw everything. These eyes symbolize God's omniscience. The purpose of the wheels in this vision was to show that behind all the events of human history, even the judgment of God's people, was God's divine providence. In other words, the wheels connect the events of the earth with the cherubim in heaven and the cherubim connect the events to God so that we can be certain that behind all events on earth is the operation of supernatural powers in heaven.

3 The whirlwind and cloud were symbols of judgment. The fact that these came from the north indicated that the instrument of judgment was Babylon. The rainbow around the throne reminded Ezekiel of the divine covenant and God's faithfulness. The rainbow, arching over the throne, spoke of God's grace, which would accompany God's judgment.

4 The scroll contained God's words of lamentation, mourning, and woe. The LORD instructed Ezekiel to speak the words that He would give him, and even though the people would reject the words, the LORD would give Ezekiel determination and courage to preach His truth faithfully. These words of judgment would actually become sweet to Ezekiel as he preached them over and over.

5 The LORD told Ezekiel to lay down on his side—390 days on his left side to represent bearing the sin of Israel, and 40 days on his right side to represent bearing the sin of Judah. Cooking his food while lying on his side symbolized how difficult the life of the Jews would be during the Babylonian siege of Jerusalem.

6 The LORD told Ezekiel to shave off all his hair and divide the hair into three parts. He was to burn one part, cut up the second part with a sword, and throw the third part into the wind. This was to symbolize what would happen to Jerusalem's residents when judgment came. Ezekiel was to take a few strands of hair and hide them in the folds of his garment, symbolizing that a few people, a remnant, would survive the judgment and remain in Jerusalem. But then, Ezekiel was to take a portion of the saved strands and throw them into the fire to symbolize that even some of the remnant would not survive.

7 In Ezekiel 12, the LORD told Ezekiel to pack his belongings as if he were going on a long trip. A person going to exile could only carry the minimum amount of possessions (food, containers of water, a cloak, and a few personal items). This action of packing represented Jerusalem's inhabitants going to exile in Babylon. The exiles were hoping for a speedy return to Jerusalem, but this symbolic action was to emphasize that the exile would not end quickly. The final fall of Jerusalem had not happened yet, but the LORD wanted the people to know that they would have no more chances to save Jerusalem by repenting. The fall of the city of Jerusalem was certain, and optimistic hopes for going home soon were futile.

8 In Ezekiel 16, the LORD likened His unfaithful people to an unfaithful wife. The LORD told a moving allegorical story of how he loved His people from their birth. When "no one" would have pity on the "newborn" nation, the LORD had compassion. The LORD took this abandoned "child" and made her become a beautiful woman bedecked with jewels. The LORD made her to be a queen, and her fame spread abroad into the world. But this beautiful queen trusted in her beauty, not in the LORD, and she used her fame to become an immoral woman and worshipper of idols. This allegory represents the fact that God's people put their allegiance in other nations for political safety rather than in God. For all these sins, the LORD would punish His people.

God's Messenger to the Exiles

Out of the north came a mighty windstorm. It was like an immense cloud with flashing lightning ripping through it. Around the cloud was a brilliant fire, and in the fire were four strange creatures. Although these creatures looked like men, each one had four wings and four faces—the faces of a lion, an ox, a man, and an eagle. Underneath the creatures were sparkling, spinning wheels that intersected each other and were full of eyes. Over the heads of these creatures was a figure like that of a man sitting on a throne of sapphire. On top of everything was a radiant rainbow, spanning the expanse of heaven. When Ezekiel saw this vision, he fell facedown on the
11 ground. He knew he was in the presence of the LORD's glory.

In 592 BC, after Ezekiel, a priest from Jerusalem, had been in exile for five years, God called him to be His prophet to the exiles. God's message to Ezekiel in this mysterious vision of living creatures and spinning wheels was this: "I am the LORD, the God who is present everywhere, even in Babylon, and who sees everything." The sovereign God was promising to bring judgment upon wicked Jerusalem, but in the midst of God's judgment was the rainbow of God's grace and mercy.

The Babylonians took captives from Jerusalem in three stages. In 605 BC, four years after Josiah was killed in battle with the Egyptians, Nebuchadnezzar's army captured the first group. Most of these people were of wealth and nobility. Daniel was among this group. In 598 BC, Jehoiakim rebelled against Babylon, and after Babylon besieged and conquered Jerusalem, a second group of people was captured. Ezekiel was with this second group. The final conquering of Jerusalem by Babylon was in 586 BC. This time, almost everyone in Jerusalem had either died from famine, was killed by the Babylonian army, or was taken to join the others in exile. Only a small handful of people, including Jeremiah, were left in the city.

12 Compared to conditions God's people had lived in previously, life in exile was not really that bad. In Babylon, the Jews built their own houses, started businesses, and worshipped the LORD the best they could without having a temple. Some Jews even took prominent positions in government. They were content—maybe too content—with their new lives. So, God's people had two very opposite problems. One problem was that they might not want to leave Babylon when the time of the exile was over. The other problem was that some people would not settle down in this foreign land and patiently wait for God's timing. They wanted to return to Jerusalem, and they wanted to do it soon!

9 God gave Ezekiel the vision of dry bones to give hope to those who had given up hope. Through this picture of raising the dry bones again to life, God was telling His people that He would one day breathe new life into them and that He would reassemble them into a nation. At that time, God's people would know that this new life was for them personally and for the nation corporately, and that new life was accomplished by the LORD Himself.

10 The two sticks miraculously being joined together in Ezekiel's hands represent the LORD joining all the people together once again to form one nation. The picture, though, has a bigger meaning and greater promise included in it. God was promising that Christ would reign on David's throne. Christ, as Shepherd, would rule over one people—all those who believe and trust in Him as their Messiah.

11 When the Bible uses the picture of a rainbow, there is an interesting twofold meaning of judgment and grace expressed. In Genesis 9, God gave the rainbow as a sign of His covenant promise to never again to destroy the entire earth with a flood. The rainbow appeared after God's judgment upon sin and represented God's grace. In Ezekiel 1, Ezekiel saw the rainbow after he saw the windstorm and cloud that represented judgment. The radiant rainbow, a reminder of God's covenant love and grace, followed this terrifying vision of God in His magnificent glory.

God gave Ezekiel two messages. Before Jerusalem fell, Ezekiel insistently preached that Jerusalem would be destroyed. With their home city devastated, the Jews' hope of returning home quickly would not be realized. Yet, after Jerusalem fell, Ezekiel preached a message of hope. God was faithful to this promise and, after seventy years, the people would return and rebuild the land that the LORD had given them. **13**

> **Jesus in the OT**
> The rainbow of God's mercy covers the throne of God's judgment because Jesus the Savior paid the penalty for the sin of His people.

Ezekiel, the prophet of visions, saw many visions during his twenty-two years as a prophet. In another vision, Ezekiel saw pictures of crawling creatures and idols on the temple walls. In the secret chambers of the temple, the Jewish elders were doing detestable acts and offering incense to idols of animals. Beside the altar of the LORD, men were bowing down and worshipping the sun. The priests, the Jewish elders, and the ordinary people were worshipping idols and defiling the LORD's temple in many despicable ways. In a dramatic scene filled with winged cherubim and spinning wheels, the glory of the LORD departed from the
14 temple and then from the city. This vision explained that God would judge Jerusalem because He hates sin!

In symbolic pictures, Ezekiel preached to the exiles about sin and unfaithfulness to God. Ezekiel emphasized that even though the LORD doesn't take pleasure in the death of the wicked, He holds each person responsible for his own actions. Anyone who sins and does not repent will die.

In another vision, the Spirit of the LORD took Ezekiel to a valley filled with dry bones. The LORD said, "Ezekiel, prophesy to these bones!" As Ezekiel prophesied, he heard a rattling sound. One by one, the bones came together. Then the LORD breathed life into the bones, and they became a vast army, filling the whole valley. "Just as I breathed life into these bones, I will breathe life into My people and bring them back to their land. Then you will know I am the LORD," declared the Sovereign God. Ezekiel's final vision was of a gleaming temple and city of the future, where the glory of God would live forever. In this city was divine perfection, purity of worship,
15 and abundant blessing. The city's name was "The LORD is There," because God would dwell there with His people.

12 The name "Jew" came originally from the Hebrew word *yehudim* and meant a person from the tribe of Judah. In 722 BC, the ten northern tribes, called Israel, were conquered by Assyria and became assimilated into the culture to which they were transported. The only people who remained from these tribes were those who had escaped south to Judah. These people lived in Judah but continued to trace their lineage to their original tribe. After the fall of Israel, Judah was the only remaining tribe of the original twelve tribes of God's people. Then Judah was conquered by Babylon, and the people from Judah were taken into exile. From that time onward, God's people were called "Jews," or "people from the tribe of Judah." The Jews of the New Testament were primarily descendents from Judah, but the few who traced their ancestry to other tribes had descended either from those who escaped Israel and fled to Judah during the Assyrian invasion or from the tribe of Levi, which had been dispersed as priests among the other eleven tribes.

13 Ezekiel's first message was one of judgment. The people who were taken into exile in 605 and 597 BC had an unrealistic optimism. They thought that their exile would end quickly and that the promise of restoration would be fulfilled soon. Ezekiel's message to these exiles was that restoration would not happen soon. He insistently preached that Jerusalem would be totally destroyed and life as the exiles knew it in Jerusalem was over. Once the final destruction of Jerusalem occurred, Ezekiel's message changed and became one of hope for the despairing exiles. After 586 BC, the year of Jerusalem's final destruction, the exiles believed there was no future for them or their nation, but Ezekiel reminded them of God's promise that the nation would be restored and the Messiah would come.

14 The people's idolatry and desecration of the temple had become so great that the glory of the LORD departed from the temple. Idolatry was not a new problem for God's people. At Mt. Sinai, the people had built the golden calf and had participated in riotous worship during Moses's extended stay up on the mountain (see Exodus 32). Throughout the entire Old Testament, God's people repeatedly forsook the LORD and worshipped a variety of idols. In Ezekiel's vision in Ezekiel 8, the people were worshipping idols right in the middle of God's temple. Idolatry in the temple included idol worship (see Ezekiel 8:5-6), worship of animals and crawling creatures (see Ezekiel 8:7-13), worship of the god Tammuz (see Ezekiel 8:14-15), and worship of the sun (see Ezekiel 8:16). (Tammuz was the Sumerian god of vegetation. According to this pagan religion, Tammuz was betrayed by his lover, Ishtar, and as a result he died every autumn. The dying vegetation represented Tammuz's death, and every autumn when the vegetation once again died, Tammuz's worshippers mourned his death. That's why the women in Jerusalem were weeping at the entrance of the temple.) The extent of the defilement both in the seriousness of the idolatry and in the number of elders participating in the idol worship was so great that the LORD could no longer be present in the temple. In a dramatic manner, the glory of the LORD exited the temple and departed (see Ezekiel 10). In leaving the temple, the LORD was proclaiming that His presence could no longer abide with the people in Jerusalem. The absence of the LORD from Jerusalem made judgment and destruction a certainty.

15 Ezekiel's final vision of a new temple and a new Jerusalem, found in Ezekiel 40–48, is long and detailed. Most scholars believe that the vision is not to be understood literally.

Instead, they feel that the vision, which describes a temple with no holy place, no high priest, and no ark of the covenant, is a symbolic picture of the truth that the LORD is always in the midst of those who are truly His people. Even though Jerusalem and the temple would be destroyed, there was still the promise that God would dwell in the hearts of His people forever. The promises of the Old Testament are fulfilled through Jesus Christ, the Messiah and great High Priest. The temple of God is now in the hearts of His people.

Notes:

Review Worksheets

A. MEMORY VERSE: "The soul who sins is the one who will die.... 'For I take no pleasure in the death of anyone,' declares the Sovereign LORD. 'Repent and live!'" (Ezekiel 18:20a, 32, NIV)

B. KEY FACTS: Match the word picture to its meaning.

Two sticks	Dry bones	Piles of hair	Unfaithful wife	Scroll eaten
A packed bag and a journey	Living creatures and spinning wheels	Windstorm and rainbow	Lying on his side	

Ezekiel's Visions and Pictures

1. God will bring His people back to life as a nation. Dry bones
2. God will unite the two kingdoms. Two sticks
3. God will punish His unfaithful people. Unfaithful wife
4. Ezekiel must speak God's words to the people. Scroll eaten
5. God is everywhere and sees everything. Creatures/wheels
6. The exile would last a long time. Bag and journey
7. The people in Jerusalem will suffer when judged. Lying on his side
8. God judges and shows mercy and grace. Windstorm and rainbow
9. Few people will survive the attack on Jerusalem. Piles of hair

C. STORY FACTS: Circle "T" if true and "F" if false.

1. Ezekiel was a priest before he became a prophet. (T) F
2. Exiles in Babylon were treated very badly by the Babylonians. T (F)
3. God's glory left the temple because of the people's great idolatry. (T) F
4. God holds each person responsible for his own sin. (T) F
5. The name of the city in Ezekiel's last vision was "The LORD lives." T (F)
6. When Ezekiel prophesied to the dry bones, they became alive. (T) F

D. THE STAGES OF CAPTIVITY: Fill in the blanks.

First	Second	Third
Year: 605 BC.	Year: 598 BC.	Year: 586 BC.
Key people captured: Daniel and his friends.	Key people captured: Ezekiel.	Key people captured: Most of the people left in Jerusalem.
Event: Four years after the Egyptians killed Josiah and defeated Judah.	Event: After King Jehoiakim rebelled against Babylon.	Event: After the final destruction of Jerusalem.

E. LIFE AS AN EXILE IN BABYLON: Answer the questions.

1. God's people in exile had two opposite problems. What were they?

   Some people were too content in Babylon and might not want to leave.

   Some people were discontent and wanted to return home right away.

2. God gave Ezekiel two messages for His people. What were they?

   Before Jerusalem's fall: Jerusalem will be destroyed.

   After Jerusalem's fall: God is faithful and the exiles would return one day.

F. FIND OUT... Read Ezekiel 1. Draw a picture below of what you think his vision looked like. Include as many details as you can.

Answers will vary, but students should include some major aspects of the vision, such as four creatures with four wings and faces, and four wheels that are wheels within wheels and with rims full of eyes.

Notes to Teachers and Parents:

1 God cares for His people who fear Him, but that doesn't mean His people always escape hard situations. The sovereign God governs all life circumstances and is present with His people no matter what happens to them. Indeed, through all their experiences in pagan Babylon, the LORD was with Daniel and his friends. For instance, when Shadrach, Meshach, and Abednego were thrown into the fiery furnace, they were confident that God would care for them, even if God didn't rescue them from the flames of the furnace. They held fast to their faith and trusted the LORD.

2 Most of the miracles in Scripture occurred during four main periods of biblical history: 1) the Exodus and wilderness wanderings; 2) the time of Elijah and Elisha; 3) the life of Daniel; and 4) the life of Jesus and the early church. In each of these periods God used these clusters of miracles for a particular purpose in furthering His kingdom. In the first and fourth periods, God used miracles to establish a new phase of His kingdom. During the time in the wilderness, God was creating His nation with His covenant, through which He would bring redemption to mankind. By these miracles, God was showing the Israelites who He was and what it meant for them to be His people by entering into a covenant with Him. In the New Testament, God was establishing a new form of His kingdom—a spiritual kingdom in which Jesus the Messiah ruled the entire earth and the gospel went throughout the world to Jew and Gentile alike. In the second and third periods, God used miracles to protect His people from Satan's onslaughts. In the days of Elijah and Elisha, Baal worship was particularly strong in Israel, and King Ahab's idolatry threatened to snuff out the worship of Yahweh. God used mighty miracles, performed by Elijah and Elisha, to preserve the covenant during those dark days of intense idolatry. The paganism of Babylon was a similar threat to God's people, but the dramatic demonstrations of Yahweh's power and protection, found in the book of Daniel, kept faith alive in the remnant of God's people during the years of exile.

Chapter 27 Daniel & His Friends

LESSON SCOPE: Daniel 1–3 **READ TO ME:** Daniel 1–3

THEME: The LORD God cares for His people who fear Him and obey His commandments. **1**

MEMORY VERSE:

"But the mercy of the LORD is from everlasting to everlasting On those who fear Him,… To such as keep His covenant, And to those who remember His commandments to do them." (Psalm 103:17a, 18)

2 **KEY FACTS: The God of Miracles**

God did most of His miracles during four periods in biblical history. Each time there was a reason why so many miracles happened.

Bible Books	Historical Period	Reason for Miracles
Exodus & Numbers	Days of Moses and the wilderness journey	God was establishing His nation, with which He had made a covenant.
1 & 2 Kings	Days of Elijah and Elisha	God was protecting His people from Baal worship.
Daniel	Years of exile in Babylon	God was protecting His people from the pagan influence of Babylon.
The Gospels & Acts	Days of Jesus and the early church	God was establishing His spiritual kingdom.

By miracles, God established His people and His kingdom.
By miracles, God protected His people from idolatry and pagan influences.

Miracles show God's **omnipotence** (all power) and **omniscience** (all knowledge).

MESSAGE FROM THE KING: The King says, "Fear me and be wise."

True wisdom begins with understanding what it means to fear the LORD. The LORD honors and exalts the one who shows honor to Him.

Notes:

Daniel & His Friends

From outward appearances, the four young men—handsome, strong, and intelligent—looked like all the other youths in King Nebuchadnezzar's court. But one thing made these Jewish men different from all the others: They worshipped Yahweh, the God who kept His covenant with Judah.

3 In 605 BC, Nebuchadnezzar's army captured Daniel and his three friends
(Hananiah, Mishael, and Azariah). Life in pagan Babylon brought many changes
into their lives. First, they were given new names. Daniel became Belteshazzar, named
4 after a Babylonian god, and his friends' names were changed to Shadrach, Meshach,
and Abednego. They lived in royal luxury and were taught the Babylonian language
and literature by the wisest teachers in the Babylonian empire. They were being
trained to enter the service of the great Babylonian king, Nebuchadnezzar.

These four men determined that, even though they lived in a pagan land, they
would not dishonor the Lord, the God of their ancestors. They refused to defile 5
themselves with the royal food and wine given to them. Daniel pleaded with the court
guard, "Please give us only vegetables and water for ten days. You will see that we will
be as strong and healthy as the men who eat the king's fancy food." Reluctantly, the
guard agreed to do this. At the end of ten days, the guard was surprised. Daniel and
his friends looked stronger and healthier than the men who had eaten the king's food. 6

For three years, the four men studied, and God gave them wisdom and knowledge of all kinds of literature and learning. When they appeared before Nebuchadnezzar for their final test, they were ten times more knowledgeable in every subject than all the magicians and enchanters in the kingdom. Nebuchadnezzar gave them prominent positions in his government.

One night, Nebuchadnezzar had a disturbing dream.
He called together all his wise men and astrologers, and demanded, "Tell me what I dreamed and what it means." Appalled, they said, "How
can we interpret the dream unless you tell us first what the dream was? There is not a
man on earth who can do this!" But the king didn't change his mind. If no one inter- 7
preted his dream, he intended to kill all of them, including Daniel and his friends.

God had given Daniel the ability to interpret dreams. Daniel urged his friends to pray that God would give him the answer to the king's demand. Then, after a night of seeking the Lord, Daniel received from God both the dream and the interpretation

3 Nebuchadnezzar's army took the first group of captives from Jerusalem in 605 BC during the reign of Jehoiakim. These men were of the wealthy class and were most likely part of the nobility. Nebuchadnezzar's intent was to take the brightest and most capable of Jerusalem's youth and train them in the ways and culture of the Babylonians. The challenge for Daniel and his three friends was to maintain their religious distinctiveness and faith in Yahweh in a totally pagan environment.

4 A person's name is part of his identity. Daniel and his friends each had Hebrew names that incorporated God's name. However, when they were taken captive by the Babylonians, they were forced to change their names. Daniel was given the name Belteshazzar, one of the possible meanings of which is "Bel will protect his life." Bel is another name for Marduk, the chief Babylonian god. Similarly, all three of the Babylonian names given to Daniel's friends have a connection to one of the Babylonian gods. Mishael, which means "who is what God is," was changed to Meshach, which means "who is what Aku is." Hananiah, which means "Yahweh is gracious," was changed to Shadrach, which means "circuit of the sun." Azariah, which means "Yahweh is strong," was changed to Abednego, which means "servant of the shining one." How difficult it must have been for these four godly young men to have their Jewish names, which represented some attribute of the Lord, changed to a Babylonian name designed to give them an identity linked to a pagan Babylonian god!

5 How the Babylonian food would defile the men is uncertain. Maybe the food had been offered to Babylonian gods. Maybe the food itself or the method in which it was prepared was forbidden in Scripture. Whatever the reason, the men believed that eating this food was an act of disobedience to the Lord. Standing up for what they believed to be right was both bold—they could have suffered severe consequences for their action—and self-disciplined—the king's food included the choicest delicacies that Babylon had to offer.

6 The Lord blessed Daniel and his friends for their courage to stand up for what they believed to be right in God's eyes. In every way, they excelled far above their fellow students, and even Nebuchadnezzar himself recognized that they were ten times better in knowledge, understanding, and physical health than all the other young men trained by the Babylonian wise men.

7 Nebuchadnezzar knew that his dream had some particular meaning regarding his kingdom's future, and the dream concerned him. Not only did he not know what the dream meant, but he couldn't even remember the details of the dream. The Babylonians believed that if a dream could not be remembered, then the gods were angry with the person who had the dream. Knowing that the dream had a meaning for his kingdom and believing the gods to be angry with him because he couldn't remember the dream was terrifying to Nebuchadnezzar. He formulated a test—telling him the content of the dream and then interpreting it—for his wise men, enchanters, and astrologers to see who was really wise and trustworthy. The wise men of Babylon realized how unreasonable and impossible the king's demand was and were unable to do anything about it. Only Daniel, to whom God had given the ability to understand and interpret dreams and visions, was able to help Nebuchadnezzar. That help was possible only because the Lord gave Daniel both the content and the meaning of the dream.

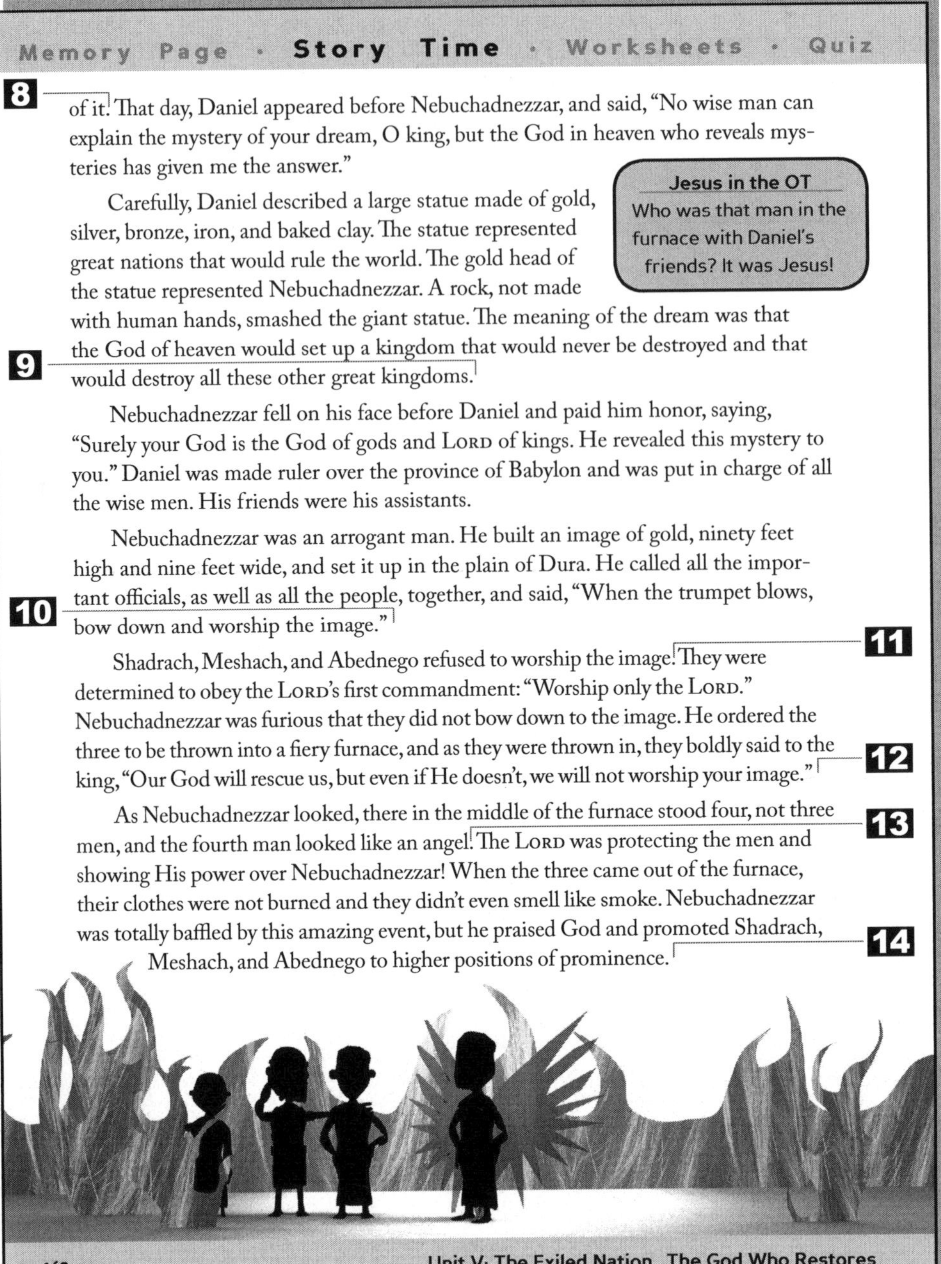
Memory Page • **Story Time** • Worksheets • Quiz

8 of it. That day, Daniel appeared before Nebuchadnezzar, and said, "No wise man can explain the mystery of your dream, O king, but the God in heaven who reveals mysteries has given me the answer."

Carefully, Daniel described a large statue made of gold, silver, bronze, iron, and baked clay. The statue represented great nations that would rule the world. The gold head of the statue represented Nebuchadnezzar. A rock, not made with human hands, smashed the giant statue. The meaning of the dream was that
9 the God of heaven would set up a kingdom that would never be destroyed and that would destroy all these other great kingdoms.

Jesus in the OT
Who was that man in the furnace with Daniel's friends? It was Jesus!

Nebuchadnezzar fell on his face before Daniel and paid him honor, saying, "Surely your God is the God of gods and Lord of kings. He revealed this mystery to you." Daniel was made ruler over the province of Babylon and was put in charge of all the wise men. His friends were his assistants.

Nebuchadnezzar was an arrogant man. He built an image of gold, ninety feet high and nine feet wide, and set it up in the plain of Dura. He called all the important officials, as well as all the people, together, and said, "When the trumpet blows,
10 bow down and worship the image."

Shadrach, Meshach, and Abednego refused to worship the image. 11
They were determined to obey the Lord's first commandment: "Worship only the Lord." Nebuchadnezzar was furious that they did not bow down to the image. He ordered the three to be thrown into a fiery furnace, and as they were thrown in, they boldly said to the
king, "Our God will rescue us, but even if He doesn't, we will not worship your image." 12

As Nebuchadnezzar looked, there in the middle of the furnace stood four, not three 13
men, and the fourth man looked like an angel. The Lord was protecting the men and showing His power over Nebuchadnezzar! When the three came out of the furnace, their clothes were not burned and they didn't even smell like smoke. Nebuchadnezzar was totally baffled by this amazing event, but he praised God and promoted Shadrach, 14
Meshach, and Abednego to higher positions of prominence.

162 Unit V: The Exiled Nation...The God Who Restores

8 Daniel realized how helpless he was to interpret the dream without the help of the Lord. He pleaded with his friends to pray with and for him, and all of them took this request to the Lord. The request was not simply for an interpretation of a dream, but for God's preservation of their lives. If Daniel did not satisfy the king with his explanation and interpretation, he and his friends would be killed along with all the wise men of Babylon. It was during the night, after much prayer, that the mystery of the dream was revealed to Daniel, and he responded to God's answer to his prayer by praising the Lord.

9 The statue in Nebuchadnezzar's dream represented future great kingdoms of the world. The golden head represented Nebuchadnezzar. Each succeeding kingdom was represented by a different metal or substance (silver, bronze, iron, baked clay) that, except for the feet of clay, decreased in the value of the substance but increased in the strength of the material. (For example, gold is more valuable than silver, but not as strong.) The rock not made with human hands represented a kingdom formed by God Himself that would be so great that it would destroy all the other great kingdoms, turning them into dust and blowing them away. God's spiritual kingdom would then become so strong that it would fill up and control the entire world.

10 It is interesting how easily sinful man can forget that God alone is to be worshipped. After Daniel interpreted his dream, Nebuchadnezzar fell down on his face before Daniel and acknowledged Daniel's God as "God of gods and Lord of kings and a revealer of mysteries" (Daniel 2:47, NIV). Yet in his arrogance, Nebuchadnezzar later created a great image and commanded that all men bow down before it. Scholars are uncertain as to whether this image was a representation of Nebuchadnezzar himself or of one of Babylon's gods. Most likely, the image was of Bel, the chief Babylonian god, or of Nabu, Nebuchadnezzar's personal deity. Either way, bowing down to this statue meant that a person was giving submission to Nebuchadnezzar in a way that was over and above what was acceptable recognition of human governmental authority.

11 Scripture does not tell us where Daniel was when this event happened. Daniel was either not present or was exempt from following this command because of his high position in Nebuchadnezzar's court.

12 These three men definitely understood that bowing down to the statue was a form of worship that was violating the first commandment. They refused to give their worship to another god in this way, even if it meant dying a painful death in a fiery furnace. The men stood firm in their faith and in their belief of who God was. They had faith that God could rescue them but knew that God was not obligated to do so. God would still be good, faithful, and just if they died in the fire. They had decided to obey God rather than Nebuchadnezzar, not knowing if the result would be a dramatic rescue or a horrible death. In the same way, God does not always deliver us from painful suffering or even, at times, death. He does, however, promise to be with us through every trial, including death, and to provide all the faith, grace, and strength we need to be obedient in our suffering.

13 Most scholars believe that the fourth man was the preincarnated Christ. Whether it was indeed Jesus Christ or an angel from God, it is obvious that the Lord was sending

Memory Page • Story Time • **Worksheets** • Quiz

Review Worksheets

A. MEMORY VERSE: "But the mercy of the LORD is from everlasting to everlasting On those who fear Him,…To such as keep His covenant, And to those who remember His commandments to do them." (Psalm 103:17a,18)

B. KEY FACTS: The God of Miracles

1. Name the four historical periods in which God did many miracles:
time of Moses and wilderness journey; time of Elijah and Elisha; time of Daniel and exile; time of Jesus and early church
2. God used miracles to protect His people from idolatry (Baal) worship and pagan influence of Babylon.
3. In the days of Moses, God used miracles to establish His covenant nation.
In the New Testament God used miracles to establish His spiritual Kingdom.
4. Miracles show God's omnipotence (all power) and God's omniscience (all knowledge).

C. STORY FACTS: Circle the **correct** answer.

1. Daniel and his friends were different from the other men because they ___________.
had a better education — **(worshipped the LORD)**
2. Daniel didn't want to eat the royal food because he didn't ___________.
(want to defile himself) — think the food was healthy
3. Before Daniel interpreted Nebuchadnezzar's dreams, he ___________.
(asked his friends to pray) — studied books about dreams
4. Nebuchadnezzar's dream meant that the LORD's kingdom would ___________.
be made of gold and silver — **(destroy other great kingdoms)**

Chapter 27: Daniel & His Friends 163

a message to the three men and all those watching the event that He was God and was present with His people.

14 God's protection of Shadrach, Meshach, and Abednego was so perfect that there were no burns on their bodies, their clothes were not scorched in any way, and there was no smell of smoke on them. Nebuchadnezzar's response to this miracle was to give praise to the LORD for His deliverance of His people from this fiery furnace. His praise was not, however, an acknowledgement that God alone was God, but only that He was the most powerful "god" because no other god could save a person in this way.

Notes:

Notes:

D. WHO SAID THIS? Draw a line from the quote to who said it.

Daniel Nebuchadnezzar Daniel's Friends Babylon's wise men

There is not a man on earth who can do what Nebuchadnezzar asks.

Even if God does not rescue us, we will not worship the image.

When the trumpet sounds, bow down to the image.

Please give us only vegetables and water to eat.

Surely your God is the God of gods. He has revealed this mystery to you.

The God in heaven who reveals mysteries has given me the answer.

E. NEBUCHADNEZZAR'S DREAM: Unscramble the words and write them in the blanks.

Nebuchadnezzar dreamed of a statue (USTEAT) made of gold, silver, bronze (NEBROZ), and baked (KADBE) clay (YCLA). The statue represented four nations (TANNIOS). The gold (DLOG) head (ADEH) represented Nebuchadnezzar. A rock not made with human hands (SHAND) smashed the statue. The meaning of the dream was that the God of heaven (VAHEEN) would set up a kingdom that would never (RENEV) be destroyed but would destroy other great (REGAT) kingdoms.

F. FIND OUT... Read Genesis 41. Both Daniel and Joseph interpreted dreams for foreign kings. How are Daniel and Joseph alike? (Hint: See verses 15-16 and 39-40).

1. Both said that the interpretation of dreams comes from God and only God can give the answer.

2. Both Pharaoh and Nebuchadnezzar recognized God gave the dream's interpretation and then they made Joseph/Daniel authority in their kingdom. Only the king was greater.

Memory Page · Story Time · Worksheets · Quiz

Chapter 28 Daniel's Faith

LESSON SCOPE: Daniel 4–12 **READ TO ME:** Daniel 4–6

THEME: The LORD God answers His people when they pray to Him in faith.

MEMORY VERSE:
"But without faith it is impossible to please Him [God]." (Hebrews 11:6a)

KEY FACTS: What Faith Does

Scripture	Event	Faith means…	
Daniel 1	Daniel not eating the king's food	Having courage to stand up for what's right when everyone else is doing what's wrong.	1
Daniel 2	Daniel interpreting Nebuchadnezzar's dream of the large statue	Praying for God's help and believing that God will answer according to His will.	2
Daniel 4-5	Nebuchadnezzar's dream of the large tree; the handwriting on the wall	Speaking the truth even when doing so may bring unpleasant consequences.	3
Daniel 6	Daniel in the lions' den	Obeying God's commands instead of man's rules.	4

What is faith?

5 **Faith** is believing that what God says is true and acting on this truth even before you see the results with your own eyes.

6 **Remember**…faith is a gift from God!

MESSAGE FROM THE KING: The King says, "Do
7 you know who I am? If you're not sure who I am, how can you have faith in Me?"

Chapter 28: Daniel's Faith 165

Notes to Teachers and Parents:

1 Not eating the king's food was a conscience issue, and a faith issue, for Daniel and his friends. They believed that eating that food would in some way defile them, and they would be disobeying God if they partook of it. It took boldness and courage to stand up for what they believed to be right. There was no guarantee that the guards in the king's court would respect their conviction, and severe consequences, possibly even death, were a real possibility. Also, their conviction made them different from the rest of the young men at the court in a very visible way. Even if no serious consequences occurred, Daniel and his friends risked ridicule and rejection from the other young men for standing up for their beliefs.

2 Daniel believed that God answered prayer, and in faith he and his friends prayed for God's interpretation of Nebuchadnezzar's dream. Nebuchadnezzar was a mighty king, and life and death were in his hands, yet Daniel knew that life was ultimately in God's hands. Daniel sought God's help because he believed God could give him the correct interpretation of the dream and thus save Daniel's life and all the lives of the Babylonian wise men.

3 In both these situations, Daniel had to confront a pagan king with God's words of judgment, and both times Daniel spoke the truth confidently and boldly because he knew that he did not have to be afraid of any man. His life was in God's hands.

4 Daniel's regular habit was to pray three times a day facing toward Jerusalem. He refused to be intimidated by Darius's decree not to pray to any god or man for thirty days. He understood that his first responsibility was to obey God's laws and to respect and obey man's laws only if they did not conflict with what God had commanded. Once again, it took faith to trust God. Daniel had trust in the character of God, even though he couldn't know what would happen in the future or what the outcome of the circumstances would be.

5 Faith in the LORD involves two things: 1) having an intellectual knowledge of the facts about who God is and what He does; and 2) making a conscious choice to trust Him based upon that knowledge. Our faith is a faith with content, not a faith that proclaims "I believe" without knowing what we believe in.

6 This truth is explicitly expressed in Ephesians 2:8.

7 The only way to know who God is, to understand His character, is to read about who He is in Scripture. People have all kinds of ideas about who they think God is. People even make statements like "My God would never…" or "My God is always…." What matters is not what we *think* about who God is but what God says in His Word about who He is. In order to withstand the trials and temptations of life, we need a faith that is based upon a biblical understanding of God's character and nature.

Notes:

8 The magnificent tree was a picture of mighty Nebuchadnezzar. Because of his pride, the Lord would "cut him down," but the judgment would be just for a time. The remaining stump indicates that after seven years, Nebuchadnezzar would be restored to his throne. The birds and animals scattered away from the tree indicates that Nebuchadnezzar would be like a beast rejected by the people and driven away from the city into the wilderness.

9 Even though Nebuchadnezzar proclaimed God's sovereignty over all nations and dominions, he did not acknowledge that God was the only true God, the supreme Creator of the universe. He merely understood the Lord to be the mightiest of all pagan gods.

10 Belshazzar was blatantly defying the Lord of the Israelites. He took the sacred goblets from Solomon's temple, vessels created for the purpose of worshipping the Lord, and used them to praise the gods of gold and silver while he indulged himself in drunken revelry. This action showed such contempt for the Lord that the Lord brought immediate judgment upon Belshazzar. That night, Darius, king of the Medes, invaded the city, killed Belshazzar, and took over Belshazzar's kingdom (see Daniel 5:30).

11 Daniel 5:26-28 gives the meaning of these words written on the palace walls. In summary, God was saying that He had numbered Belshazzar's days as king. Belshazzar's defiance and his defilement of God's holy vessels of worship had made him unacceptable to God. God was sending the Medes and Persians to conquer his land and bring his magnificent kingdom to an end.

Notes:

Daniel's Faith

What is faith? Faith is believing certain facts to be true and then acting on those facts, even before you see the results with your own eyes. Daniel's faith in God was like this. He believed that God was sovereign and should be obeyed no matter what happened. He also knew that the Lord was good and that He would take care of His people when they trusted Him.

Daniel became an old man in exile. He served four mighty kings from three powerful nations, yet he always remained true to the Lord, because he knew that God was the supreme King of all empires.

Later in his life, King Nebuchadnezzar had another mysterious dream. This dream was about a magnificent tree with plump ripe fruit and branches that reached high into the sky. Birds made nests in its branches, and many animals found shelter under its leafy shade. Suddenly, a heavenly messenger cut down the tree, all except the stump, and scattered all the birds and animals
8 away from the tree. The dream troubled the king, and he called on Daniel to interpret it.

At first, Daniel was puzzled by the dream, and then he was terrified. The dream was a picture of God's judgment upon Nebuchadnezzar for his pride. What would happen if Daniel told the king the true meaning of the dream? But Daniel acted in faith, and said, "You are the tree, O king. You are strong, and your greatness reaches to faraway places. But, a holy messenger will cut you down, just like this tree, and you will live like the wild animals. But the stump of the tree remains. You will get your kingdom back, but only after you acknowledge that God rules the world."

It happened just as Daniel said. A year later, Nebuchadnezzar was boasting about how great he was and God made the dream come true. Nebuchadnezzar became like an animal, eating grass and living as a wild beast in the fields. After seven years, God gave him back his sanity, and Nebuchadnezzar acknowledged that God was the ex-
9 alted King of heaven.

Many years later, Belshazzar became king in Babylon. One day, he held a great
banquet, and he and his guests drank wine from sacred goblets from Solomon's temple. 10
Then, the fingers of a human hand appeared from nowhere and wrote in bold letters the
words "MENE, MENE, TEKEL, UPHARSIN" on the walls of the palace. The king 11
was so terrified that his knees knocked together, and he collapsed onto the floor.

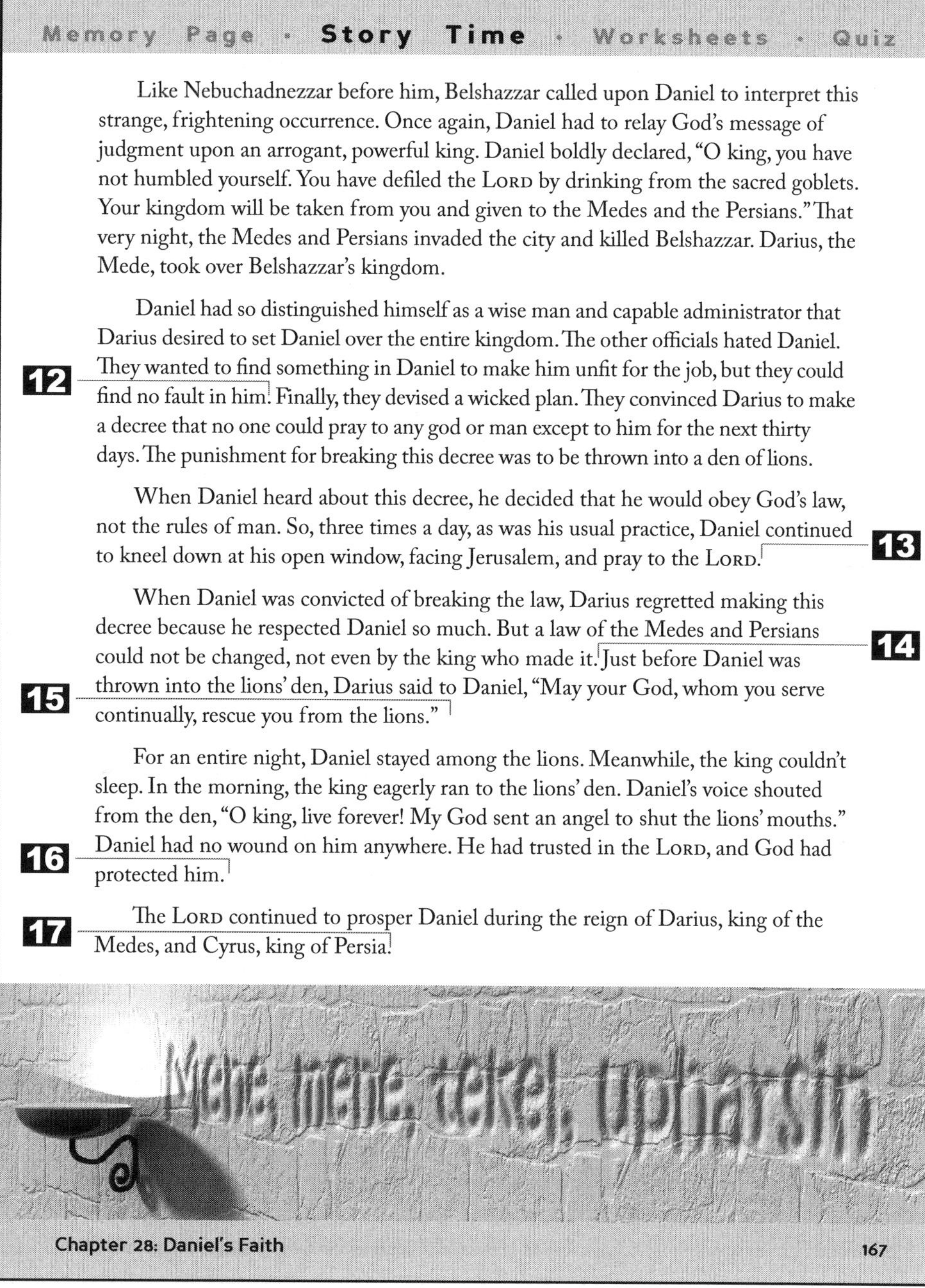

Like Nebuchadnezzar before him, Belshazzar called upon Daniel to interpret this strange, frightening occurrence. Once again, Daniel had to relay God's message of judgment upon an arrogant, powerful king. Daniel boldly declared, "O king, you have not humbled yourself. You have defiled the Lord by drinking from the sacred goblets. Your kingdom will be taken from you and given to the Medes and the Persians." That very night, the Medes and Persians invaded the city and killed Belshazzar. Darius, the Mede, took over Belshazzar's kingdom.

Daniel had so distinguished himself as a wise man and capable administrator that
Darius desired to set Daniel over the entire kingdom. The other officials hated Daniel.
They wanted to find something in Daniel to make him unfit for the job, but they could
12 find no fault in him. Finally, they devised a wicked plan. They convinced Darius to make
a decree that no one could pray to any god or man except to him for the next thirty
days. The punishment for breaking this decree was to be thrown into a den of lions.

When Daniel heard about this decree, he decided that he would obey God's law,
not the rules of man. So, three times a day, as was his usual practice, Daniel continued 13
to kneel down at his open window, facing Jerusalem, and pray to the Lord.

When Daniel was convicted of breaking the law, Darius regretted making this
decree because he respected Daniel so much. But a law of the Medes and Persians 14
could not be changed, not even by the king who made it. Just before Daniel was
15 thrown into the lions' den, Darius said to Daniel, "May your God, whom you serve
continually, rescue you from the lions."

For an entire night, Daniel stayed among the lions. Meanwhile, the king couldn't
sleep. In the morning, the king eagerly ran to the lions' den. Daniel's voice shouted
from the den, "O king, live forever! My God sent an angel to shut the lions' mouths."
16 Daniel had no wound on him anywhere. He had trusted in the Lord, and God had
protected him.

17 The Lord continued to prosper Daniel during the reign of Darius, king of the
Medes, and Cyrus, king of Persia.

Mene, mene, tekel, upharsin

12 Daniel had exhibited such exceptional qualities that Darius wanted to set him up as ruler over the entire kingdom. The lesser administrators were jealous of Daniel, but try as hard as they might, they could find absolutely no fault in him by which they could discredit him to Darius. Being unable to displace Daniel for any just cause, the men devised a wicked plan. Daniel's consistent prayer life was so well-known that they were confident that their plan would accomplish their purpose.

13 Nothing about Daniel's behavior changed as a result of this decree. He continued his practice of praying by an open window three times a day. Daniel did not succumb to the pressure to stop praying, nor did he begin to pray in secret. Daniel was resolute in his conviction and remained faithful to His God, no matter what the outcome would be.

14 The irrevocableness of Persian law is written about in secular writings as well as in the story of Esther (see Esther 1:19 and 8:8). Once a law was made, no one, not even the king, could reverse it. The administrators conspiring against Daniel knew this, and they forced Daniel to choose between obeying God's law or man's law. Daniel knew that when in conflict with each other, God's law always had authority over human law.

15 King Darius knew that even he could not revoke a Persian law, and he deeply regretted having made the decree. All day long, Darius tried everything he could to rescue Daniel from being thrown into the lions' den. The administrators reminded Darius that no order of the king could be changed, and Darius was trapped by his own decree. Helpless to do anything, Darius knew that the only one who could rescue Daniel was his God, and Darius desperately hoped Daniel's God was big enough to save Daniel.

16 The king spent a sleepless night worrying about the fate of Daniel in the den of lions. When he saw that Daniel was alive, he was filled with joy. Daniel explained, "The lions did not hurt me because God sent an angel to shut their mouths. God knew I was innocent before Him and before you, O king" (see Daniel 6:21-22). The king's response was to throw the conniving administrators and their families into the den of lions.

17 Daniel had an influential position in the governments of four great kings: Nebuchadnezzar, Belshazzar, Darius, and Cyrus. God prospered everything Daniel did because Daniel did everything in faith for the glory of God.

Notes:

Notes:

Review Worksheets

A. MEMORY VERSE: "But without ___faith___ it is ___impossible___ to ___please___ Him [God]." (Hebrews 11:6a)

B. KEY FACTS: What does faith mean?

1. Faith stands up for what's ___right___ when everyone else is doing what's ___wrong___.
2. Faith prays and believes that ___God___ ___will___ ___answer___ according to His will.
3. Faith speaks truth when speaking truth brings ___unpleasant___ ___consequences___.
4. Faith obeys ___God's___ ___commands___ instead of ___man's___ ___rules___.

Faith is believing that ___what God says is true___.

Faith is acting on ___God's truth___.

C. STORY FACTS: Unscramble the words on the right and use them to fill in the blanks.

1. What troubled Nebuchadnezzar? ___DREAMS___
2. What Nebuchadnezzar boasted that he was: ___GREAT___
3. Number of years Nebuchadnezzar acted like an animal: ___SEVEN___
4. Number of days no one could pray: ___THIRTY___
5. Who shut the lions' mouths? ___ANGEL___
6. What Darius made that couldn't be changed: ___DECREE___
7. What was left of the tree in the dream: ___STUMP___
8. What wrote on the palace walls? ___FINGERS___
9. What officials could not find in Daniel: ___FAULT___

VESNE
LATFU
RITTHY
SMEDRA
GIFRENS
GENLA
TEGAR
PUMST
CEDERE

D. DANIEL AND THE KINGS: Fill in the blanks.

Nebuchadnezzar	Belshazzar	Darius
King of Babylon.	King of Babylon.	King of Medes.
God judged him because he boasted about how great he was.	God judged him because he defiled the LORD by drinking from sacred goblets.	He made a decree that no one could pray to any man or god but Darius.
When God gave him back his sanity, he acknowledged God was the exalted King of heaven.	The very night that the handwriting appeared on the wall, the Medes and Persians invaded and killed Belshazzar.	He regretted his decree and said to Daniel, "May your God rescue you from the lions".

E. GOD'S PERFECT CARE: Cross out the **wrong** words.

1. God sent an angel to (~~kill the lions~~/shut the lions' mouths).
2. Darius wanted God to (rescue Daniel from the lions/~~judge him for his disobedience~~).
3. In the morning, Daniel had (no wound/~~only a scratch~~) from the lions.
4. The lions didn't hurt Daniel because he (~~was stronger than the lions~~/ had faith and God protected him).

F. FIND OUT... Read Daniel 5:25-28. What is the meaning of the writing on the wall?

Mene: God has numbered the days of your reign and brought it to an end.

Tekel: You have been weighed on the balances and found wanting.

Peres: Your kingdom is divided between the Medes and Persians.

Notes to Teachers and Parents:

1 Here at the end of Zechariah's prophecy are the words of the covenant: "I will be your God, and you will be My people." These are the same words that the LORD gave to Abraham centuries before. Zechariah gave them as a promise to the returning exiles as a reminder that God does not change, and He will never forsake His people.

2 Just as there were three times that God's people were taken into exile (605 BC, 597 BC, and 586 BC), so there were three significant historical "returns" to Jerusalem. Zerubbabel and Jeshua led the first group of returning Jews immediately after Cyrus made his decree in 538 BC. Eighty years later, in 458 BC, Ezra went to Jerusalem with a large group of Jews, and Nehemiah followed a little over a decade later in 445 BC. The first six chapters of Ezra relate the adventures of Zerubbabel and Jeshua as the people rebuilt the temple. The second part of Ezra and the book of Nehemiah tell the story of Ezra and Nehemiah in Jerusalem and of the obstacles that the people faced in constructing the city walls.

3 It's impossible to earn God's blessings because all of God's blessings come to us from His bountiful grace. At the same time, the LORD tells us that the natural result of obeying Him is His blessing (see Jeremiah 17:5-10). When we do what's right, we avoid the hardships that come with disobedience, and we gain the peace of God's blessing given to those who are faithful to Him. (Of course, we must remember that our ability to be faithful comes only as a result of God's grace to us.) Even though God's blessing comes through our faithfulness, the perceived absence of God's blessing doesn't mean that we are being punished for sin. Two principles are important to remember. First, although God's blessing to us may include prosperity and good health, it is greater than these temporal things. Second, God tells us in Scripture (see Psalm 73, 1 Peter 4:12-19) that people who obey God will still experience suffering. The presence of trials or the lack of temporal blessing do not in themselves indicate that a person is unrepentant of sin.

Memory Page · Story Time · Worksheets · Quiz

Chapter 29 The People Return—The Temple Is Rebuilt

LESSON SCOPE: Ezra 1–6, Haggai 1–2, Zechariah 1–14 **READ TO ME:** Ezra 3–4, 6

THEME: The LORD God keeps His promise and restores His people to their land.

MEMORY VERSE:

"They will call on My name, And I will answer them. I will say, 'This is My people'; And each one will say, 'The LORD is my God.'" (Zechariah 13:9b) **1**

2 **KEY FACTS: The People Return**

Date	Event	Key People
605 BC	First group of people taken captive	Daniel
597 BC	Second group of people taken captive	Ezekiel
586 BC	Jerusalem falls to Babylon	Jeremiah
539 BC	Persia conquers Babylon	King Cyrus
538 BC	Cyrus's decree	King Cyrus
538-535 BC	First exiles return to Jerusalem	Zerubbabel, Jeshua
520-516 BC	Temple rebuilt	Haggai, Zechariah
487-465 BC	Esther saves her people	King Xerxes, Esther, Mordecai, Haman
458 BC	Ezra returns to Jerusalem	Ezra
445 BC	Nehemiah returns to Jerusalem	Nehemiah

MESSAGE FROM THE KING:

The King says, "If you love Me, be obedient, and I will bless you."

You cannot earn God's blessing by doing the right thing. But, the LORD is pleased when you obey Him, and He will bless you when you are faithful. **3**

170 Unit V: The Exiled Nation...The God Who Restores

Notes:

The People Return—The Temple Is Rebuilt

4 It was better than anyone could imagine! How wonderful it was! After seventy years in exile, the LORD moved the heart of Cyrus, king of Persia, to let God's people return home to Jerusalem. Cyrus decreed, "Any Jew may return to Judah. People living in the land should provide the Jews with gold, silver, livestock, and offerings."

Many Jews stayed in exile. It had become comfortable there, and they were content. But in 538 BC, under the leadership of Zerubbabel, their governor, and Jeshua, 5 the priest, more than 40,000 Jews packed up their things and started home to Jerusalem. What a glorious thing! Who could imagine that this day would finally come? They
6 longed to return to the land of their ancestors and to worship God as Moses's Law commanded. Along the journey, they praised the LORD who had kept His promises.

But, it was also worse than they had imagined. Jerusalem was a pile of rubble. The few people who had remained there lived in poverty, and enemies surrounded them. How sad it was!

Zerubbabel and Jeshua wouldn't let the people despair or be afraid. They urged them, "Let's rebuild the altar and offer sacrifices to our God." In the blackened ruins of the temple, they built an altar. Morning and evening they made sacrifices and celebrated their religious feasts. They began the difficult task of rebuilding the temple, and after the foundation was laid, they sang, "The LORD is good; His love endures forever." But rebuilding the temple was also sad. The older people remembered the splendor of Solomon's temple, and they knew this temple could never be that magnificent.

7 Three years after the Jews returned to Jerusalem, the Samaritans, enemies of the Jews, sent a letter to Artaxerxes, the new king of Persia, falsely accusing the Jews of being troublemakers. These enemies wanted the rebuilding of the temple to stop. King Artaxerxes believed the Samaritans' lies, and demanded that no more work on the temple be done. Afraid, the people stopped their work.

4 Jeremiah had predicted that the exile would last seventy years (see Jeremiah 25:11-12). The LORD, the God of history, moved Cyrus, the Persian king, to make his decree. Cyrus's decree applied not only to the Jews, but also to other captured peoples. Cyrus's motive was not to fulfill the prophecies of the God of the Jews. Instead, his motive was to allow all these captured peoples to resume worship of their gods, and maybe these gods would show favor to him as a result. Regardless of Cyrus's motivation, the sovereign God used Cyrus's action to move His redemptive purposes forward.

5 Some versions of the Bible write this man's name as "Jeshua" and some write it as "Joshua." These are two ways to spell the same name.

6 Most of the people who remained in exile had assimilated themselves into their new culture and were content with their lives. Their contentment did not include worship of the LORD. They didn't want to return home because they didn't want to leave the comfort of their new life to endure hardship in Jerusalem. (Some of the exiled remnant, like Mordecai and Esther, continued to worship the LORD.) The returnees were those who loved the God of the covenant more than the pleasure of a comfortable life. They were willing to endure hardship in ruined Jerusalem and work hard to rebuild the temple. Worshipping the LORD in the way set forth in the Law was important to them. The 40,000 people who left Babylon were few compared to the number of people who remained in exile, but the faithfulness of the few was rewarded. They formed the nucleus of the reestablished nation from whom the Messiah would be born.

7 The Samaritans were a group of people from various conquered nations who had been transplanted by the Assyrians to Samaria, the land that the ten tribes of Israel had inhabited before they were conquered by Assyria. Many of the transplanted people had intermarried with the few remaining Israelites, so there was a bloodline link between the Samaritans and the remnant in Jerusalem. However, the Jews in Jerusalem did not consider the Samaritans to be related to them, and thus refused to accept the Samaritans' assistance in rebuilding the temple. The religion of the Samaritans was not a pure worship of Yahweh, and the prudence of not trusting them to be allies became evident when the Samaritans wrote the letter to Artaxerxes. This initial animosity between the Samaritans and the Jews continued through the centuries, and evidence of the ongoing enmity is seen in the gospels (see John 4:9).

Notes:

8 Haggai was not as poetic in his discourse as Nahum and did not use word pictures like Amos ("let justice roll like a river" [Amos 5:24, NIV]). Haggai did not have an exciting big fish adventure like Jonah or a tragic life experience like Hosea. Yet, in plain words, using probing questions, Haggai communicated God's message to His people. This message was "rebuild God's temple right now." Haggai made his point, because the people aroused themselves from their fear, lethargy, and comfortableness to build the temple on the new foundation that had been laid fifteen years earlier. Within four years, the temple was completed.

9 For every excuse and every complaint, Haggai had a word of encouragement that took the people's focus off themselves and turned it toward the LORD.

10 These four lessons from Haggai are a paraphrase from Homer Hailey's book, *A Commentary on the Minor Prophets*, p. 301.

11 Over twenty-five times Haggai used the words "declares the LORD," "the word of the LORD," or something similar. Through these phrases, Haggai emphasized that the words he spoke were not his message to the people, but God's message.

Notes:

Fifteen years passed. People forgot about the temple. They built their houses, worked hard to survive, and tried to forget about the ugly temple ruins. Then two prophets—Haggai and Zechariah—spoke up, "How do you expect God to bless you when you refuse to rebuild the temple?"

The rebuilding began again. But, in 520 BC, enemies wrote another accusing letter, this time to the new Persian king, Darius, asking, "Did Cyrus really decree that this temple should be built in Jerusalem?" When King Darius received the letter, he researched the situation. Sure enough, deep in the archives of Babylon's treasury, Darius found Cyrus's original decree. He responded firmly, "I decree that the temple is to be built. Give the Jewish elders what expenses they need to accomplish the task. Let no man change this decree or he will be executed. Let this be done with diligence."

With great joy, the people rebuilt the temple and dedicated it to the LORD. Then they celebrated the Passover, remembering the LORD who had delivered them from Egypt and had kept all His promises.

HAGGAI—PROPHET OF ENCOURAGEMENT

Haggai was chosen by God to give one important message to God's people: "It's time to rebuild the temple." He aroused the people to action, saying, "How can God bless you when you build fancy houses for yourselves, but leave His house in ruins?" **8**

Haggai, the prophet of encouragement, had a word of encouragement for every situation. When the people said, "It's not time," he said, "Start building right away, and the LORD will be with you." When the people complained, "This temple is not good enough," Haggai promised that the glory of this new temple would be greater than the last one. (This was because one day Jesus Christ would stand within its walls.) When the people despaired because of their poverty, Haggai declared that the LORD would bless them abundantly because of their faithfulness in building Him a house. **9**

Haggai taught four important lessons: 1) there's a connection between being faithful to the LORD and receiving His blessings; 2) being discouraged is not a good enough reason to neglect doing what God tells you to do; 3) when a task must be done, you should do it right away; and 4) all words of encouragement or rebuke
10 should be based upon what the LORD says. Over and over again, Haggai said the **11**
words, "This is what the LORD the Almighty says."

Haggai encouraged the people, and in four years the temple was built.

ZECHARIAH—THE PROPHET OF FUTURE GLORY

More than any other prophet, except possibly Isaiah, Zechariah prophesied about the Messiah and the glory that God has in store for His people. The book of Zechariah is the longest of the twelve minor prophets and the most difficult to understand because of the dramatic visions in the first six chapters and the three mysterious messages in the second part of the book.

> **Jesus in the OT**
> What is the future glory? It is a glorious day when Jesus will come and establish His Kingdom.

Zechariah had visions about horns, dirty and clean clothes, chariots, a flying scroll, a woman in a basket, a man with a measuring line, a golden lampstand, and a man on a red horse. The visions were different pictures of how the
12 LORD reacts when people repent of their sin.

In this book, the LORD promised to destroy His people's enemies, take away their sin, and reign over the whole earth as King. He repeated His covenant promise to be the God of His people. The words of Zechariah, the prophet of future glory, have meaning for all of God's people—Jews and Gentiles—because they prophesy about the Messiah. He said that this Messiah, the LORD Jesus Christ, would set up His glorious kingdom and would dwell with His people forever. Zechariah spoke about two temples—the temple being rebuilt in Jerusalem and the temple in the hearts of God's people.

12 Zechariah described the visions, but does not provide the reader with their meanings. Therefore, it is difficult to discern their interpretations. However, we do know that the underlying theme of the visions is repentance—the need for repentance, what repentance looks like, what happens when a person is truly repentant, etc.

Notes:

Notes:

Review Worksheets

A. MEMORY VERSE: "They will call on My ___name___, And I will ___answer___ them. I will say, 'This is My ___people___'; And each one will say, 'The ___LORD___ is my ___God___.'" (Zechariah 13:9b)

B. KEY FACTS: Write the name of the person that the statement describes.

The People Return

Statement	Person
I decreed that God's people could return to Jerusalem.	Cyrus
I was taken into exile to Babylon in 605 BC.	Daniel
I told the people to start building the temple right away.	Haggai
I was appointed governor over the people who returned to Jerusalem.	Zerubbabel
Zerubbabel and I led the first group of exiles back to Jerusalem.	Jeshua
I prophesied about the future glory of the temple.	Zechariah

C. STORY FACTS: Fill in the blanks.

1. God moved the heart of ___Cyrus___ to let His people return home.
2. God's people were in exile for ___70___ years.
3. ___Jeshua___ and ___Zerubbabel___ led the first group back to Jerusalem.
4. The prophets ___Haggai___ and ___Zechariah___ encouraged the people to rebuild the temple even when it was hard to do so.
5. For ___15___ years the people forgot about the temple and did nothing.
6. The older people were sad because they remembered the splendor of ___Solomon's___ ___temple___.
7. Zechariah's visions were about God's reaction when people ___repent___.
8. Haggai taught that there is a connection between being ___faithful___ and receiving God's ___blessing___.

D. TWO LETTERS FROM THE ENEMIES OF GOD'S PEOPLE:

First Letter (535 BC)	Second Letter (520 BC)
To: Artaxerxes The people in Jerusalem are troublemakers. Make them stop building the temple.	To: Darius Please answer our question: Did Cyrus really decree that the temple should be built in Jerusalem?
The king's response: He believed the accusation and stopped the work.	The king's response: He researched the situation and decreed the temple building continue.

E. HAGGAI OR ZECHARIAH:

Put "H" if the sentence describes Haggai and "Z" if it describes Zechariah.

Z The longest of the minor prophets.

H Connected the people's faithfulness to God's blessing.

H Said the words, "This is what the LORD says" over and over again.

Z Saw visions of a flying scroll, a man on a red horse, and other strange things.

Z Prophesied about the Messiah and future glory for God's people.

F. FIND OUT...

Read Psalm 126. How did the people feel when they returned to Jerusalem from exile?

They were like men who were dreaming. They laughed and were filled with joy. Nations were saying that the LORD had done great things for them.

Notes to Teachers and Parents:

1 The Scriptures give us assurance that absolutely nothing can happen to us unless the Lord has decreed it. This does not mean that God does evil, but it means that the Almighty God controls all circumstances, good and bad. Even calamities that we don't expect and we believe to be harmful to us can occur only if decreed by the Lord.

2 This definition of God's providence is a shortened paraphrase of Question 11 from the Westminster Shorter Catechism. God's governing of His universe is all-inclusive and characterized by the qualities of holiness, wisdom, and power. These qualities of God, which are revealed to us by Him, help us to understand the essence of who God is.

3 In Chapter 29, we discussed the connection between God's blessing and our faithfulness. Our obedience makes a difference in the way God chooses to prosper us. (Don't forget, the connection between obedience and blessing is not absolute, and hardship often happens to obedient Christians.) Although God promises to bless and prosper us in accordance with our faithfulness to Him, His love and protection of us are independent of our response of faithfulness or unfaithfulness. God is faithful to us because He has made a covenant with us and has promised to keep that covenant. Because of our sinful hearts, we are not always faithful to Him and, in fact, can only be faithful when we depend upon His grace to help us. God, on the other hand, is always faithful, regardless of how we respond to Him.

Notes:

Chapter 30 The Story of Esther

LESSON SCOPE: Esther 1–10 **READ TO ME:** Esther 1–10

THEME: The Lord God protects His people from the schemes of wicked men.

MEMORY VERSE:

1 "Who can speak and have it happen if the Lord has not decreed it? Is it not from the mouth of the Most High that both calamities and good things come?" (Lamentations 3:37-38, NIV)

KEY FACTS: **Drama in Exile**

When wicked men schemed to kill God's people, God protected them with an amazing plan.

Characters:	King Xerxes: King of Persia Esther: Jewish woman who became queen Haman: Persian official who tried to kill the Jews Mordecai: Esther's cousin
The Scene:	Palace of King Xerxes in the city of Susa in Persia
The Plot:	Haman plotted the destruction of the Jews, and the Lord saved His people through a strange set of events.
Esther's Role:	Esther risked her life to save her people, trusting that whether she lived or died, the Lord would honor her faithfulness.
God's Message:	God saved His people from destruction, according to the covenant He made with them, even though many of them were not faithful to Him.

THINGS TO REMEMBER:

2 Providence of God = God's holy, wise, and powerful preserving and governing of everything in His creation.

3 **MESSAGE FROM THE KING:** The King says, "My faithfulness to you does not depend upon your faithfulness to Me."

The Story of Esther

Danger and suspense, a plot with unexpected twists and turns, a surprise ending—these are what make Esther's story exciting. And, even though God is not mentioned by name in the story, it is obvious that He directed every scene of this intriguing drama.

The story begins at a lavish banquet in the grand palace of King Xerxes, the mighty king of Persia. (Persia had conquered Babylon, and the Jewish exiles were now living under Xerxes's rule.) For seven days, the king partied with his guests, eating, drinking, and acting rowdy. On the seventh day, when he was drunk, King Xerxes demanded that his wife, Queen Vashti, come and show her beauty to his guests.

Queen Vashti appropriately refused the king's request, and the king was furi-
4 ous. He was also embarrassed that his wife would not obey him. At the advice of his
wise men, the king decreed that Vashti would no longer be queen. Afterwards, King 5
Xerxes regretted his rash decision, but he couldn't change it. He
began a search for a new queen. Women came from all over the
kingdom, but no one pleased the king enough to be the queen.

Living in the king's fortified palace was a Jewish man
named Mordecai. With him was his cousin named Hadassah
(her Persian name was Esther) whom he had raised from a
child. She was young and beautiful, and everyone who knew
her loved her. Esther caught the eye of one of the king's officials,
6 and after a time of preparation, Esther was taken before the king.
Immediately, the king was attracted to her, more than to any other
7 woman, and Esther, a Jewish girl, became the queen of Persia.

One day, while busy at his official business at the palace, Mordecai heard about a plot to kill the king. Quickly, he told Queen Esther
about the conspiracy, and the two conspiring officials were caught and
8 hanged.

After this, King Xerxes honored one of his royal officials, Haman,
making him the highest of all the king's nobles. After that, Haman, an
arrogant man, required that everyone kneel down and pay honor to him.
All palace officials—except Mordecai—did as Haman asked. As a faithful
9 worshipper of Yahweh, Mordecai refused to kneel down to any man.

4 Although Scripture is not clear what King Xerxes expected of Queen Vashti, it never criticizes her refusal to obey the king. Some have suggested that the king expected her to appear naked or that his intention was in some way immoral or was degrading to his queen. The fact that he was drunk when he made the request, and that he later regretted his decision to depose her, gives some indication of the inappropriateness of his request. His rash decision had more to do with his pride and embarrassment than it did with anything Queen Vashti did wrong.

5 A decree made by a Persian king could not be revoked by anyone, including the king who decreed it. In his drunken state, Xerxes had made a decree that he regretted once he was sober, but he could not change it. Isn't it comforting to know that our King, the LORD Almighty, never makes a rash, unwise decree?

6 The process of preparing a young woman to appear before the king was extravagant and excessive. Esther had seven maids to attend to her and was given body treatments and special foods for twelve months before she was presented to the king.

7 Esther did not reveal her nationality to the king. He chose her to be his queen, not knowing that she was Jewish. Isn't it amazing how God orchestrates events using the free-will choices of men to accomplish His divine purposes?

8 This is another point in the story where we can see God working sovereignly behind the scenes. By uncovering this plot, Mordecai saved the king's life, but the king was unaware of what Mordecai had done. It was much later when Xerxes was reading accounts in the kingdom record books that he learned about how Mordecai had saved his life (see Esther 6). God uses all the pieces of this complex drama and fits them neatly into place to bring about His divine purposes.

9 Although many of the exiled Jews had assimilated so completely into the Persian culture that they had forgotten about the LORD, there was still a faithful remnant. Mordecai was one of those faithful few, and he had nurtured Esther in the faith of Yahweh as well. Mordecai's decision not to honor Haman in ways that he thought were idolatrous took courage similar to the courage of Daniel and his friends while under Babylonian rule.

Notes:

10 Mordecai recognized the providence of God in Xerxes's choice of Esther as queen. He was quick to encourage Esther to have faith and to trust that God had placed her in a prominent place for a divine purpose. Being an official in the palace, Mordecai was aware of the risks involved in Esther's appearing unannounced before the king. Though he loved her as a daughter, he was willing to ask her to risk her life for her people because he believed that God had a special purpose for her.

11 Historically, King Xerxes was known to be capricious and rash. Someone who was in his favor one moment could almost instantly gain his disfavor and be immediately executed. Esther's assessment of her situation was accurate, and her decision to approach the king was evidence of her faith.

12 The second decree did not cancel out the first decree, but it made it possible for the Jews to gather together and defend themselves. In fact, not only were the Jews able to defend themselves, but they were able to take the offensive. This event became a large victory for the Jews instead of an occasion of destruction. The result was that the various people groups who lived around the Jews gained a new respect for them, and the Jews were able to live in an environment of greater peace and security.

13 The name "Purim" came from the Hebrew word *pur*, which means "lot." The day of destruction was chosen by the casting of lots, and this feast memorialized the victory of God's people over their enemies and God's sovereign protection. God is the sovereign God who is over the lots that men choose.

14 This story ended very differently than Haman had planned. At the end, Esther remained queen over Persia, Mordecai was promoted to Haman's position of power and authority, and God's people had earned the respect of the people among whom they lived. God's name is not mentioned once in the book of Esther, but this book, as much as any other book in Scripture, tells God's story clearly.

Haman was so angry with Mordecai that he told the king that all Jews were dangerous people. The king believed this lie, and decreed that on a certain day all Jews, young and old, should be killed. When Mordecai heard of the decree, he persuaded
10 Esther to help. He said to Esther, "Who knows whether you have become queen for such a time as this?"

Esther's task was risky. If she approached the king and he didn't hold out his scepter to her, she would be killed. She said, "I will go to the king, and if I perish, I perish." **11** Bravely, she put on her royal robes and entered the king's inner chamber. Amazingly, he put out his scepter and welcomed her. Then she made a strange request, "Please, I want you and Haman to come to dinner with me." The king agreed.

Meanwhile, two other events happened. First, Haman built a gallows seventy-five feet high upon which to hang Mordecai. At the same time, the king learned that Mordecai had saved his life from the conspirators and decided to honor him. The next day, King Xerxes asked Haman, "What should be done to honor a man that the king delights in?" Haman, thinking the king wanted to honor him, described an elaborate celebration. "Good," said the king. "Go at once and do as you described for Mordecai."

What a surprise for Haman! He had to lead Mordecai through the city, proclaiming, "This is the man the king delights to honor!" But the situation got even worse for Haman. Esther had two special dinners for King Xerxes and Haman. At the second dinner, she told the king that she was Jewish and that Haman, the Jews' enemy, had plotted her people's destruction. In a rage, the king shouted, "Hang Haman on the gallows built for Mordecai!"

Haman was killed, but what about the decree? No decree written by a Persian king and sealed with his ring could ever be changed, even by the king. So, the king made a second decree: "Jews in every city can protect themselves and kill those who try to kill them." Just like the first decree, this decree went
12 throughout all the land by couriers riding on royal horses.

God protected His people, even though many had not been faithful to Him. On the appointed day, the Jews defended themselves from all those who tried to kill them.
13 Esther and Mordecai told the people to have a great feast, and from that time onward, this feast, called Purim, was
14 celebrated every year to remember God's deliverance of the Jews from their enemies.

Notes:

Review Worksheets

A. MEMORY VERSE: "Who can speak and have it happen if the Lord has not decreed it? Is it not from the mouth of the Most High that both calamities and good things come?" (Lamentations 3:37-38, NIV)

B. KEY FACTS: Put the story boxes in order.

Drama in Exile

5	Haman was hanged on the gallows he made for Mordecai.	4	At a special dinner, Esther told King Xerxes about Haman's plot.	3	Haman persuaded King Xerxes to decree that the Jews should be killed.
1	King Xerxes chose Esther to be his new queen.	2	Mordecai saved the king's life by uncovering a conspiracy against him.	6	King Xerxes's second decree allowed the Jews to defend themselves.

C. STORY FACTS: Circle the **correct** answer.

1. King Xerxes wanted to honor Mordecai because he ________.

   (had saved the king's life) was a competent official

2. Haman wanted to kill Mordecai because he wouldn't ________.

   (kneel down to him) conspire against the king

3. The king made a second decree so that the Jews could ________.

   hang Haman on the gallows (defend themselves)

4. Even though His people weren't faithful, God ____.

   (saved them from destruction) gave them many blessings

Notes:

D. WHAT DO YOU REMEMBER?

Across

4. The king made a _____ to kill the Jews.
5. Queen _____ was King Xerxes's first wife.
7. The king held out his ____ to Esther.
11. Haman wanted everyone to kneel down to him and pay _____ to him.

Down

1. The _____ decree of King Xerxes said the Jews could defend themselves.
2. _____ was a feast to celebrate God's deliverance.
3. The king's banquet lasted _____ days.
4. Esther invited the king to two _____.
6. _____ wanted to kill Mordecai.
8. The king regretted his decision but couldn't _____ it.
9. King Xerxes was king of _____.
10. _____ was a Jewish girl who became queen of Persia.

Across: 4 DECREE, 5 VASHTI, 7 SCEPTER, 11 HONOR
Down: 1 SECOND, 2 PURIM, 3 SEVEN, 4 DINNER, 6 HAMAN, 8 CHANGE, 9 PERSIA, 10 ESTHER

E. ESTHER'S RISKY JOB: Going to the king was risky. What did Esther say before she visited the king? Starting with the first letter on the left, cross out every other letter and then put the remaining letters on the spaces below to find out.

F I S F R I M P I E T R U I L S A H T I H P C E V R W I F S O H

I f I p e r i s h, I p e r i s h.

F. FIND OUT... Read Psalm 135:6, Psalm 145:17, and Proverbs 15:3. What do these verses say about God's providence (his care and governing of all the earth)?

Psalm 135:6 He does as He pleases in heaven, on earth, in the seas.

Psalm 145:17, NIV He is loving toward all He has made.

Proverbs 15:3 God's eyes keep watch on the evil and the good.

Memory Page · Story Time · Worksheets · Quiz

Chapter 31 The Story of Ezra & Nehemiah

LESSON SCOPE: Ezra 7–10, Nehemiah 1–13, Malachi 1–4

READ TO ME: Ezra 7–8, Nehemiah 1–2, 4–6, 8–9

THEME: The Lord God helps His people, who trust in Him.

MEMORY VERSE:

"You have kept your promise because you are righteous." (Nehemiah 9:8b, NIV) [1]

KEY FACTS: **Messages to God's People**

Scripture	Event	God's Message
Ezra 1–6	God's people rebuilt the temple in Jerusalem.	God's desire: "I want My people to meet together and worship me." [2]
Esther 1–10	God saved His people from being destroyed by Cyrus's decree.	God's promise: "I am the supreme King, and I will protect My people." [3]
Ezra 7–10	God's people repented of marrying foreign wives and of being unfaithful to the Lord.	God's warning: "My people must be separate from everything that might make them unfaithful to Me." [4]
Nehemiah 1–6	Nehemiah rebuilt Jerusalem's walls in spite of obstacles and troubles.	God's encouragement: "When My people trust Me, I help them do difficult things." [5]
Nehemiah 7–13	Ezra read God's Word to the people, and they confessed their sins and renewed the covenant.	God's command: "Listen to My Word and confess your sin because I am your God." [6]
Malachi 1–4	Malachi's task was to prepare God's people for the coming Messiah.	God's conclusion: "Because you are My people, and I love you, I am sending the Messiah. Be watchful and wait for His coming."

MESSAGE FROM THE KING: The King says, "I am your God and you are My people. I will always keep My promises to you."

Chapter 31: The Story of Ezra & Nehemiah 181

Notes to Teachers and Parents:

1 What an appropriate way to end the story of the Old Testament! The Lord God, who made a covenant promise in Genesis 3, has kept His promise. Throughout the entire story, He has faithfully loved, forgiven, guided, protected, and restored His unfaithful people. At the end of the Old Testament story, God's people have returned from exile, have rebuilt the temple and the city walls, and have renewed the covenant with the Lord. In this prayer at the end of the book of Nehemiah, the Levites praised the Lord for His faithfulness to the covenant through the centuries. They realized that God's faithful keeping of His promise was linked to His righteousness, just as their unfaithfulness to the Lord was the result of their sin.

2 Building the temple was an important part of restoring proper worship of the Lord. It was not enough to return to the land and worship Yahweh in whatever way the people chose. The Lord had given instructions about the way He wanted His people to worship Him. He not only desired the worship of His people, but He desired that they worship together at a certain place and in a certain way. That's why Haggai was so insistent that the work of rebuilding the temple begin again after fifteen years of being idle. "How can God bless us if we leave His temple in ruins?" Haggai asked the people (see Haggai 1). Haggai emphasized the direct connection between God's blessing and proper, corporate worship of Him.

3 The story of Esther shows how no one, not even a mighty king such as Xerxes, or a scheming man like Haman, can destroy God's people. The sovereign God orchestrated all of history to put the right people in the right places and to bring about the right events at the right time to preserve His covenant with His people. To this day, God continues to preserve His people.

4 Ezra's concern with intermarriage was not a racial concern, but a spiritual concern. How could God's people remain faithful to Him when their spouses worshipped pagan gods and performed ungodly religious practices? Preserving the integrity of covenant worship was absolutely necessary if the nation was to survive and the Jews were to be the people from whom the Messiah would come. Ezra needed to do something drastic to impress upon the people the importance of worshipping only Yahweh. This drastic action included totally separating themselves from the source of temptation—pagan spouses. In a similar way, the Apostle Paul warns of being "unequally yoked together with unbelievers" (2 Corinthians 6:14-15).

5 Nehemiah was a man of both faith and action. Before he spoke or made a decision, he prayed about it, even if his prayer was a brief, on-the-spot prayer. He believed that the Lord would hear and answer him. At the same time, he did not allow trouble or obstacles to get in the way of doing the Lord's work. First he prayed; then he acted: "But we prayed to our God and posted a guard day and night to meet this threat" (Nehemiah 4:9, NIV). One amusing instance of Nehemiah's penchant for action is his bold words to Sanballat in Nehemiah 6:3 (NIV): "I am carrying on a great project and cannot go down. Why should the work stop while I leave it and go down to you?" The Lord blessed Nehemiah's work and the seemingly impossible task of rebuilding the city walls was finally completed. Nehemiah's life is an excellent example of what it means to trust the Lord: 1) believing that God's words are true; and 2) acting upon that truth no matter how impossible the task may seem because we are confident that the Lord will provide all the resources we need to finish the task well.

6 When the people heard God's Word, they had sorrow for their sin, showing that there is a direct connection between hearing Scripture and repenting of sin. God's Word convicted the people of their unfaithfulness. Then the Lord reminded them that He was their God and they were His people. He showed mercy to them and renewed the covenant with them.

7 Ezra was confident enough of God's providential protection that he was ashamed to ask for a military escort on this long, dangerous journey from Babylon to Jerusalem. The Lord rewarded his faith, and the entire company arrived safely. On the other hand, Nehemiah requested that King Artaxerxes give him letters to ensure safe passage from the countries through which he would travel. The king granted his request. Scripture does not specifically say that Nehemiah's request indicated any deficiency in Nehemiah's faith and never rebuked Nehemiah for this action.

8 When Nehemiah prayed, he called upon the Lord as the God of the covenant. Nehemiah understood that God was a God who made promises and kept them. God had promised that His people would return to their land after an exile of seventy years. Nehemiah had a passion to be part of the restoration of his nation and, more particularly, the reconstruction of the city of Jerusalem. In making his request to God, Nehemiah approached God as the covenant-making, promise-keeping God. In our prayers, we, too, should approach God as the covenant-keeping God, while being careful not to be demanding or presumptuous in our requests.

9 Nehemiah had a great desire to go to Jerusalem to help the Jews rebuild the city walls. He had earnestly prayed that the Lord would give him favor from the king so that the king would release him from his court responsibilities and allow him to go to Jerusalem. When the king asked, "What do you want?" Nehemiah was prayerfully prepared. He shot a quick arrow prayer to the Lord and immediately made his request of the king. Nehemiah knew what it meant to "pray without ceasing" (1 Thessalonians 5:17).

10 In addition to being a man of faith and action, Nehemiah was a man of prayer. His natural response to situations was to turn to the Lord in prayer.

11 The people had a legitimate complaint. Building the city wall took time away from their ordinary working lives. They had less time to harvest crops, manage their livestock, and earn money to provide for their daily needs. Since working on the wall was not an income-producing activity, some of the workers had to mortgage their properties in order to have money to buy food for their families. The workers had mortgaged their homes and fields to other members of the Jewish community in Jerusalem, and some of the lenders were taking advantage of their neighbors by charging excessive prices. In addition, the landowners were having trouble paying taxes to the Persian king. Building the wall was a huge project that was having a financial impact on many people in Jerusalem. Nehemiah real-

Memory Page • **Story Time** • Worksheets • Quiz

The Story of Ezra & Nehemiah

As Erza looked at the people camped beside the canal, he realized something was wrong. That's it! There were no Levites in the assembly. How could God's people go to Jerusalem and worship the Lord if no Levites went with them? God spoke to Sherebiah, a capable Levite, and he, his sons, and his brothers as well as a number of other men agreed to go with the Jews from Babylon to Jerusalem.

It was a long and dangerous journey. "I am ashamed to ask the king for soldiers and horsemen to protect us," Ezra said to himself, "because I told the king that God's gracious hand was with us." So they traveled the whole way without military protection. The Lord was with them, and everyone arrived safely in Jerusalem. **7**

Once in Jerusalem, Ezra became distressed. The remnant in Jerusalem had married sons and daughters of the pagan people around them. Even the leaders had been unfaithful to the Lord in their marriages. Ezra prayed, "O my God, I am so ashamed. Your people are all guilty and cannot stand in Your presence. The guilt of our sin has reached to the heavens. We have filled the land with impurity. But You, O Lord, are righteous and gracious." The people heard Ezra's prayer, and, with great sorrow and weeping, they confessed their sin. They separated themselves from the foreigners and made an oath to serve the Lord.

Meanwhile, Nehemiah, a cupbearer in King Artaxerxes's court, heard about Jerusalem's broken walls and burned gates, and he wept. He prayed, "O God who keeps
8 the covenant, listen to my prayer and give me success by giving me the favor of the
9 king." Nehemiah wanted permission from King Artaxerxes to go to Jerusalem and help rebuild Jerusalem's walls.

10 The king saw Nehemiah's sad face, and asked, "What do you want?" Quickly, Nehemiah prayed, then said, "If it pleases you, let me go to Jerusalem so I can rebuild the walls." The king agreed, and Nehemiah left.

Immediately upon his arrival in Jerusalem, Nehemiah set about repairing the city walls. It wasn't easy! There were so many troubles and obstacles. Three men (Sanballat, Tobiah, and Geshem) shouted out, "What are you feeble men doing? Your wall is so weak that if a fox walked on it, it would fall down!" In spite of constant ridicule, the people labored with all their strength. The task was so great that they often got discouraged, but eventually, the wall was halfway built.

182 Unit V: The Exiled Nation...The God Who Restores

However, the trouble wasn't over yet. Enemies threatened the Jews. Nehemiah prayed to the Lord, then posted guards around the city. The builders had to hold a sword in one hand and carry stones in the other. But God frustrated the scheming plots of the enemies, and the work on the wall continued.

Then the people complained, "We need to stop building the wall so we can harvest our crops. We must earn money to protect our fields and houses." Some Jewish landowners were burdening the people with unjust mortgages. Angry, Nehemiah reproached these unjust men. "What you are doing is not just! This must stop! You must fear the Lord and be fair." Amazingly, these landowners stopped
charging the people unfair mortgages and gave back what they had taken unjustly. **11**

Now the building project was going well, but Sanballat and his friends were not done causing trouble. Once again, they tried to frighten Nehemiah, saying, "Come down and talk with us." Nehemiah stubbornly replied, "I am doing a great work. I can't stop what I'm doing to talk with you." After Nehemiah refused four times, Sanballat sent a letter to him, accusing him of trying to be king in Jerusalem and
12 conspiring against the Persian king. Nehemiah's response was to pray, saying, "Lord, strengthen my hands." The Lord answered Nehemiah's prayer. No obstacle was too big and no enemy too frightening to prevent Nehemiah and his workers from completing the repair of the city walls.

Finally the project was done. Strong walls surrounded the city and protected the Jews from their enemies. It was time to renew the covenant. Ezra, the priest, stood before the people and read the Book of the Law. When the people heard God's Word, they wept, because they were aware of their sin. Nehemiah encouraged the
13 people, "Do not weep. Do not grieve, for the joy of the Lord is your strength." The people confessed their sin and worshipped the Lord.

In front of all the people, the Levites prayed, "Blessed be Your glorious name, O Lord. You alone are the Lord. You made the heavens and gave life to everything. You made promises to Abraham, and You have kept Your promises because You are righteous."

Chapter 31: The Story of Ezra & Nehemiah 183

ized that the people had legitimate concerns and acted quickly and decisively to remedy the problem. He rebuked the unjust lenders and urged them to treat their neighbors justly. The Lord honored Nehemiah's efforts, and the unjust lenders not only stopped their excessive charges, but also gave back the overcharged money.

12 Nehemiah was singleminded regarding the wall-building project. His response to distractions or intimidation was to pray that God would give him strength.

13 Nehemiah encouraged the people to have joy, not to weep or mourn. Even though weeping for sin is an appropriate response, Nehemiah wanted the people to rejoice because they were celebrating the Feast of Tabernacles, which was to be a time of joy.

Notes:

14 Instead of giving the LORD the best of their flocks—animals without blemishes or disease—the priests were bringing sacrifices that were not fit and perfect. Not only were the priests unfaithful in worship, but they were teaching error to the people, causing many to stumble. The people were unfaithful in their marriages and easily resorted to divorce. Many men were marrying women who worshipped idols. In addition to these sins, the people had become neglectful in giving tithes and offerings to God. All these sins indicated the sad state of the people's hearts. The LORD wanted to remind the people that His blessings were linked to His people's obedience. If His people repented and prepared their hearts for worship, God's blessing would rush forth like an overflowing river.

15 The LORD's last written words to His people in the Old Testament ended with the promise of the coming Messiah. God promised that His messenger, whom He called the prophet Elijah, would come to announce the day of the Messiah's coming. Jesus would later identify John the Baptist as this messenger (see Matthew 11:7-19). The Old Testament ends with words of hope—the Messiah is coming!

Notes:

MALACHI—PROPHET OF PREPARATION

By the time Malachi wrote his short book, the LORD had spoken many times to His people. He had made promises and kept them. He had warned of judgment and reassured His people of His everlasting love. Over and over again, He had repeated the covenant promise: "I will be your God, and you will be My people." What was left to say?

Malachi's task was to prepare God's people for the coming Messiah. His message of preparation had three parts. First, the LORD reminded His people that He loved them ("I have loved Jacob, but Esau I have hated"). Both the Jews (the descendents of Jacob) and the Edomites (the descendents of Esau) had been defeated by enemies. After seventy years in exile, the LORD showed His love to the Jews by allowing them to return to their land and become a nation again. By contrast, after its fall, Edom was never again a nation.

Jesus in the OT
The LORD said, "Look for My messenger. He will announce the Messiah."

Second, God reminded His people that He is always holy and hates sin. Because God does not change, preparing for the Messiah meant repentance. God's people were sinning in their worship by bringing crippled or diseased animals for the sacrifices and by robbing God of tithes and offerings. They were also sinning by being unfaithful in their marriages and divorcing each other. The LORD does not bless His people when they stubbornly sin against Him and each other. But when His people obey Him, His blessings pour forth like a flooding river. 14

Third, the LORD told His people to look for His messenger, the prophet Elijah, who would precede the Messiah and announce the wonderful day of the LORD's
15 coming.

The words of Malachi, the prophet of preparation, did not change everyone who heard them, only those who feared the LORD. What did the LORD Almighty say about those who fear Him? The covenant LORD promised, "They will be mine, on the day when I make up my treasured possession."

Review Worksheets

A. MEMORY VERSE: "You have kept your promise because you are righteous." (Nehemiah 9:8b, NIV)

B. KEY FACTS:

God's Messages to His People

Draw a line from the message God gave His people to the book in which the message is found.

Message	Book	Message
"I am the supreme King, and I protect My people."	Ezra	"Listen to My Word and confess your sin because I am your God."
"When My people trust Me, I help them do difficult things."	Esther	
"I want My people to meet together and worship Me."	Nehemiah	"My people must be separate from everything that might make them unfaithful to Me."

C. STORY FACTS: Circle the **correct** answer.

1. Levites went with Ezra to Jerusalem so that the people could _____.

   worship God — have skilled workers

2. The Jews had a safe journey to Jerusalem because ______.

   they had military protection — the LORD was with them

3. The first thing Nehemiah did when the king saw his sad face was ____.

   ask to go to Jerusalem — pray to the LORD

4. When the people repented of their sin, Nehemiah told them ______.

   to weep and grieve — that God's joy was their strength

Notes:

D. NEHEMIAH'S TROUBLES: While building the city wall, Nehemiah had many troubles. Put the events in order.

4 The people wanted to stop building the wall to harvest their crops.

1 Sanballat and his friends ridiculed Nehemiah and the workers.

5 Four times Sanballat asked Nehemiah to stop working and talk with him, and each time Nehemiah refused.

3 Nehemiah gave the workers swords to hold while they worked.

6 Sanballat accused Nehemiah of conspiring against the Persian king.

2 Enemies threatened to attack the Jews working on the wall.

7 The people completed the wall and renewed the covenant.

E. MALACHI'S MESSAGE OF PREPARATION: Fill in the blanks.

Message of Love

God showed His love to Judah because after seventy years the Jews could

1. Return to their land.
2. Become a nation again.

Message of Repentance

God's people sinned in their worship and in their marriages. God never changes. He is always holy and hates sin.

Message of the Messiah

God said, "Look for My messenger." The messenger will announce the wonderful day of the Lord's coming.

F. FIND OUT... Nehemiah was a man of prayer and action. Read the verses below to find out what his prayer request was or what action he took after he prayed.

Nehemiah 2:4-5 (Action) He prayed and then answered the king.

Nehemiah 4:7-9 (Action) He prayed and then posted a guard for protection.

Nehemiah 6:8-9 (Request) "Strengthen my hands."

Chapter 32 Looking Backwards...Looking Ahead

LESSON SCOPE: Ezekiel 1–48, Daniel 1–12
Ezra 1–10, Nehemiah 1–13, Esther 1–10
Haggai 1–2, Zechariah 1–14, Malachi 1–4

READ TO ME: Isaiah 40

The Old Testament is over, and it's not exactly a happily-ever-after ending. There's no glorious kingdom with a rich and famous king. There's no mighty army or magnificent palace with a gold and ivory throne. There's not even a vast company of people who worship God with all their hearts.

Arising from the ruins of conquered Jerusalem is a poverty-stricken city populated by a remnant of God's people—people who are supposed to fear God but who continue to sin against Him. What happened to the LORD's promise to make a great nation from the descendents of Abraham? How can this sorry bunch of refugees bring blessing to the whole world?

The failures of God's people in the Old Testament show one thing—there has to be a new and better way. God has not failed. He is still the covenant LORD who says to His people, "I am your God, and you are My people." He is still the supreme King who keeps His kingdom secure. He is still the God who makes promises and keeps them. But something needs to change. For the next 400 years, the prophets will be silenced. Then the LORD will make a new covenant. A baby will be born in Bethlehem—a baby who is a King and Savior.

The story is not over. The LORD has gathered together the exiles in Jerusalem, but there are still others who must be gathered into His kingdom. So be patient. Be alert because the King Himself is coming!

"The Sovereign LORD declares—he who gathers the exiles of Israel: 'I will gather still others to them besides those already gathered.' "(Isaiah 56:8, NIV)

IMPORTANT THINGS TO KNOW:

Word	Meaning of the Word
Faith	Believing that what God says is true and acting on this truth even before you see the results with your own eyes; a gift from God.
Providence of God	God's holy, wise, and powerful preserving and governing of everything in His creation.

Notes:

Review Worksheets

A. MEMORY VERSE REVIEW—UNSCRAMBLE THE VERSES: Put the words in the boxes in the **correct** order for these memory verse phrases.

Ezekiel 18:20a, NIV: The soul who sins is the one who will die.

soul die one The who the will is sins who

Nehemiah 9:8b, NIV: You have kept your promise because you are righteous.

your righteous have are kept promise you You because

Hebrews 11:6a: But without faith it is impossible to please Him.

without please faith to But impossible is Him it

B. MEMORY VERSE REVIEW—FILL IN THE BLANKS: Answer these questions.

1. What two things come from God's mouth? calamities and good things (Lamentations 3:37-38, NIV)

2. Upon whom does God show His everlasting mercy? To "those who fear Him,...[and] To such as keep His covenant, And... remember His commandments to do them." (Psalm 103:17a, 18)

3. What will God say to those who call on Him? (Zechariah 13:9b)
"This is My people."

C. WHAT IS THE THEME OF UNIT V? Decode the message to find out. (Clue: Write down the letter that occurs in the alphabet after each letter written. For example, if the letter in the message is "S," write the letter "T" in the blank.)

S G D F N C V G N Q D R S N Q D R

T h e G o d w h o r e s t o r e s

D. WHO WERE THE PROPHETS OF THE EXILE?

Identify which prophet the words describe by using the prophet's first initial.

E – Ezekiel D – Daniel H – Haggai Z – Zechariah M – Malachi

M Declared Elijah as God's messenger

H "It's time to rebuild the temple"

D Handwriting on the wall

M Prophet of preparation

M "I, the LORD, do not change"

H Prophet of encouragement

Z Dramatic visions about repentance

D Prophet of God's sovereignty

Z Prophet of future glory

M Last prophet

E Vision of dry bones

E Prophet to exiles

Z Two temples

D Interpreted king's dream

D Eating vegetables

M "Don't rob God"

E Prophet of visions

D Lion's den

E. WHAT DO YOU REMEMBER ABOUT THESE KINGS?

Unscramble the king's name and then draw a line from the king's name to the words that describe the king.

SADIUR	Darius	His army was defeated by Egypt
HOSIJA	Josiah	Married the Jewish girl named Esther
REXXES	Xerxes	Threw Daniel into a lions' den
SUCRY	Cyrus	Decreed that the exiles could go home

Notes:

F. WHAT HAPPENED NEXT? Starting at the star, draw a line connecting the events in chronological order, ending at the X.

★

Daniel is taken into exile.

Cyrus makes a decree and the first exiles return to Jerusalem.

Jeshua and Zerubbabel return to Jerusalem with the people.

The people finish the walls of Jerusalem.

Ezekiel is taken into exile.

Jerusalem is conquered by Babylon.

Haggai said, "It's time to build the temple."

Malachi prophesies that the Messiah will come.

The people finish rebuilding the temple.

Esther saves her people from Xerxes's decree of death.

Ezra and Nehemiah return to Jerusalem.

✖

G. WHAT IS FAITH? What is God's providence?

1. Faith has two parts: believing that what God says is true

acting on God's truth

How did these people show their faith in the LORD?

2	Daniel	1. Didn't bow down to the image
3	Esther	2. Continued to pray to God every day
4	Nehemiah	3. Invited King Xerxes to dinner
1	Daniel's friends	4. Built the wall in spite of many troubles

2. God's providence is God's holy, wise, and powerful preserving and governing of everything in His creation.

H. WHAT'S THE REASON? Circle the **correct** answer.

1. Daniel and his friends didn't eat the king's food because they didn't _________.
   (want to defile themselves) — like the taste of foreign food
2. Daniel asked his friends to pray that God would give him _________.
   (the dream's interpretation) — power over all the wise men
3. Many Jews stayed in exile in Babylon because they were _________.
   afraid to make the long journey — (too content to leave Babylon)
4. Haman wanted to kill Mordecai because Mordecai _________.
   had saved the king's life — (wouldn't bow down to him)
5. Ezra was ashamed of the people in Jerusalem because they were _________.
   (unfaithful in their marriages) — complaining all the time
6. Nehemiah had a sad face when he went before the king because _________.
   (Jerusalem had broken walls) — the exiles had gone home

I. WHAT HAS HAPPENED AND WHAT IS TO COME?

What Has Happened	What Is To Come
God made a **covenant**, saying, "I will be your God, and you will be My people." God was always **faithful** to keep His covenant, but His people were **unfaithful**. Even when His people sinned, God was the Keeper of His **Kingdom**.	Through the prophets, God promised that a **Messiah** would come. God would send His **messenger**, Elijah, to announce the wonderful day of the **LORD**'s coming. God would make a **new covenant**. Be alert because the **King** Himself is coming!

Notes:

Appendix A

Memory Verse Summary

Unit 1: The Early Kingdom...The God Who Anoints

PSALM 23, A Psalm of David

1. The LORD is my shepherd;
   I shall not want.
2. He makes me to lie down in green pastures;
   He leads me beside the still waters.
3. He restores my soul;
   He leads me in the paths of righteousness
   For His name's sake.
4. Yea, though I walk through the valley of the shadow of death,
   I will fear no evil;
   For You are with me;
   Your rod and Your staff, they comfort me.
5. You prepare a table before me in the presence of my enemies;
   You anoint my head with oil;
   My cup runs over.
6. Surely goodness and mercy shall follow me
   All the days of my life;
   And I will dwell in the house of the LORD
   Forever.

Chapter 1: The Call of Samuel

"In those days there was no king in Israel; everyone did what was right in his own eyes." (Judges 21:25)

Chapter 2: Samuel—The Last Judge

"Remember the former things of old, For I am God, and there is no other; I am God, and there is none like Me." (Isaiah 46:9)

Chapter 3: Saul—The First King

"Behold, to obey is better than sacrifice, And to heed than the fat of rams." (1 Samuel 15:22b)

Chapter 4: David Anointed as King

"For the LORD does not see as man sees; for man looks at the outward appearance, but the LORD looks at the heart." (1 Samuel 16:7b)

Chapter 5: David in Saul's Court

"In God I trust; I will not be afraid. What can mortal man do to me?" (Psalm 56:4b, NIV)

Chapter 6: David—The Fugitive

"For the word of the LORD is right, And all His work is done in truth. He loves righteousness and justice; The earth is full of the goodness of the LORD." (Psalm 33:4-5)

Unit II: The Glorious Kingdom...The God Who Blesses

PSALM 51:1-6, A Psalm of David

1. Have mercy upon me, O God,
According to Your lovingkindness;
According to the multitude of Your tender mercies,
Blot out my transgressions.
2. Wash me thoroughly from my iniquity,
And cleanse me from my sin.
3. For I acknowledge my transgressions,
And my sin is always before me.
4. Against You, You only, have I sinned,
And done this evil in Your sight—
That You may be found just when You speak,
And blameless when You judge.
5. Behold, I was brought forth in iniquity,
And in sin my mother conceived me.
6. Behold, You desire truth in the inward parts,
And in the hidden part You will make me to know wisdom.

Chapter 8: The Covenant with David

"I have made a covenant with My chosen, I have sworn to My servant David: 'Your seed I will establish forever, And build up your throne to all generations.'" (Psalm 89:3-4)

Chapter 9: David's Kindness & David's Sin

"Blessed is he whose transgression is forgiven, Whose sin is covered." (Psalm 32:1)

Notes:

Chapter 10: Troubles in the Kingdom

"But you, O Lord, are a shield for me, My glory and the One who lifts up my head… I lay down and slept; I awoke, for the Lord sustained me." (Psalm 3:3, 5)

Chapter 11: The Wisdom of Solomon

"The fear of the Lord is the beginning of wisdom, And the knowledge of the Holy One is understanding." (Proverbs 9:10)

Chapter 12: The Reign of Solomon

"Praise be to the Lord who has given rest to his people Israel just as he promised. Not one word has failed of all the good promises he gave through his servant Moses." (1 Kings 8:56, NIV)

Unit III: The Divided Kingdom…The God Who Reigns

PSALM 121, A Song of Ascents

1. I will lift up my eyes to the hills—
   From whence comes my help?
2. My help comes from the Lord,
   Who made heaven and earth.
3. He will not allow your foot to be moved;
   He who keeps you will not slumber.
4. Behold, He who keeps Israel
   Shall neither slumber nor sleep.
5. The Lord is your keeper;
   The Lord is your shade at your right hand.
6. The sun shall not strike you by day,
   Nor the moon by night.
7. The Lord shall preserve you from all evil;
   He shall preserve your soul.
8. The Lord shall preserve your going out and your coming in
   From this time forth, and even forevermore.

Chapter 14: A Nation Divided

"[They] exchanged the truth of God for the lie, and worshiped and served the creature rather than the Creator, who is blessed forever. Amen." (Romans 1:25)

194 Appendix A: Memory Verse Summary

Chapter 15: Elijah—God's Voice of Judgment to a Wicked King

"The steps of a good man are ordered by the LORD, And He delights in his way. Though he fall, he shall not be utterly cast down; For the LORD upholds him with His hand." (Psalm 37:23-24)

Chapter 16: Ahab & Jehoshaphat—Two Very Different Kings

"Many are the plans in a man's heart, but it is the LORD's purpose that prevails." (Proverbs 19:21, NIV)

Chapter 17: Elisha—God's Voice to Rulers & Ordinary People

"[The Most High] does according to His will in the army of heaven And among the inhabitants of the earth. No one can restrain His hand Or say to Him, 'What have you done?'" (Daniel 4:35b)

Chapter 18: Three Prophets of Judgment

"Those who cling to worthless idols forfeit the grace that could be theirs." (Jonah 2:8, NIV)

Unit IV: The Remnant Kingdom...The God Who Judges

PSALM 99:1-5, 8-9, NIV

1. The LORD reigns,
   let the nations tremble;
   he sits enthroned between the cherubim,
   let the earth shake.
2. Great is the LORD in Zion;
   he is exalted over all the nations.
3. Let them praise your great and awesome name—
   he is holy.
4. The King is mighty, he loves justice—
   you have established equity,
   in Jacob you have done
   what is just and right.
5. Exalt the LORD our God
   and worship at his footstool;
   he is holy.

*****

Notes:

8. O LORD our God,
you answered them;
you were to Israel a forgiving God,
though you punished their misdeeds.

9. Exalt the LORD our God
and worship at his holy mountain,
for the LORD our God is holy.

Chapter 20: Israel Falls & Judah Remains

"For the LORD knows the way of the righteous, But the way of the ungodly shall perish." (Psalm 1:6)

Chapter 21: Two Prophets & a Righteous King

"He has shown you, O man, what is good; And what does the LORD require of you But to do justly, To love mercy, And to walk humbly with your God?" (Micah 6:8)

Chapter 22: Two Memorable Kings—Manasseh & Josiah

"For assuredly, I say to you, till heaven and earth pass away, one jot or one tittle will by no means pass from the law till all is fulfilled." (Matthew 5:18)

Chapter 23: God's Voices of Judgment to the Nations

"The LORD is slow to anger and great in power; the LORD will not leave the guilty unpunished." (Nahum 1:3a, NIV)

Chapter 24: Jeremiah Weeps & Judah Falls

"My people have committed two sins: They have forsaken me, the spring of living water, and have dug their own cisterns, broken cisterns that cannot hold water." (Jeremiah 2:13, NIV)

Unit V: The Exiled Nation...The God Who Restores

PSALM 126, NIV, A Song of Ascents

1. When the LORD brought back the captives to Zion,
we were like men who dreamed.

2. Our mouths were filled with laughter,
our tongues with songs of joy.
Then it was said among the nations,
"The LORD has done great things for them."

3. The LORD has done great things for us,
and we are filled with joy.

4. Restore our fortunes, O LORD,
like streams in the Negev.

5. Those who sow in tears
will reap with songs of joy.

6. He who goes out weeping,
carrying seed to sow,
will return with songs of joy,
carrying sheaves with him.

Chapter 26: God's Messenger to the Exiles

"The soul who sins is the one who will die.... 'For I take no pleasure in the death of anyone,' declares the Sovereign LORD. 'Repent and live!'" (Ezekiel 18:20a, 32, NIV)

Chapter 27: Daniel & His Friends

"But the mercy of the LORD is from everlasting to everlasting On those who fear Him, ...to such as keep His covenant, And to those who remember His commandments to do them." (Psalm 103:17a, 18)

Chapter 28: Daniel's Faith

"But without faith it is impossible to please Him [God]." (Hebrews 11:6a)

Chapter 29: The People Return—The Temple Is Rebuilt

"They will call on My name, And I will answer them. I will say, 'This is My people'; And each one will say, 'The LORD is my God.'" (Zechariah 13:9b)

Chapter 30: The Story of Esther

"Who can speak and have it happen if the Lord has not decreed it? Is it not from the mouth of the Most High that both calamities and good things come?" (Lamentations 3:37-38, NIV)

Chapter 31: The Story of Ezra & Nehemiah

"You have kept your promise because you are righteous." (Nehemiah 9:8b, NIV)

Notes:

Appendix B Pictures of Jesus Christ in the Old Testament

Jesus Christ is not mentioned by name in the Old Testament. Yet, in many ways—sometimes in comparison and sometimes by contrast—you can see glimpses of Jesus in the Old Testament biblical story. In the Old Testament, you read about prophets, priests, and kings. Sometimes a person was both a prophet and a priest, such as Samuel. Sometimes a person was a king who tried to act like a priest. Saul did this when he offered a sacrifice instead of waiting for Samuel to come and make the sacrifice to the LORD. The LORD judged Saul severely for his rash action.

Some prophets, priests, and kings were godly and worshipped the LORD. Many, however, were not godly and angered the LORD by speaking lies, sacrificing to other gods, and ruling as though they were the supreme king instead of acknowledging that God is the King.

Jesus Christ is unique because He is the only Person who holds (or ever has held) all three roles of prophet, priest, and king. As you read stories of the Old Testament prophets, priests, and kings, you will see pictures of Jesus, the perfect Prophet, Priest, and King who fulfilled all His roles perfectly and without sin.

In this book, you will see text "bubbles" that give you biblical truths about who Jesus is and what He has done for you as your Savior and King. Be alert. Maybe you can find even more pictures of Jesus than are mentioned in this text.

Chapter 1: The Call of Samuel

A prophet is a person called to speak God's words. How is Samuel, the prophet, like Jesus Christ, the Prophet?

A prophet is a person chosen by God and equipped by God's Spirit to speak truth to God's people. Often, speaking God's truth involves pointing out sin and calling God's people to repentance. As a child, Samuel had the difficult and unpleasant task of giving God's message of judgment to Eli. Jesus Christ is the divine Prophet. In the Gospels, Jesus spoke God's truth to people, pointing out their sin and calling them to repentance.

Chapter 2: Samuel—The Last Judge

What does a priest do? A priest makes sacrifices for sin. Samuel, as priest, offered a sacrifice for the people's sin, and the LORD forgave them. What does Jesus' sacrifice on the cross do for you?

As priest, Samuel assembled the people at Mizpah so they could confess their sins and make a sacrifice to the LORD. The LORD knew that the people had repentant hearts, so He accepted Samuel's offering. The LORD not only forgave their sin, but He protected them from their enemies. (The Philistines had tried to take advantage of this great gathering and attacked Israel during the sacrificial ceremony.) Jesus is the great High Priest. He not only prays for you when you sin, but He is the sacrifice for sin as well. When you confess your sin, Jesus' sacrifice on the cross gives you forgiveness and deliverance from your greatest enemy—sin!

Chapter 3: Saul—The First King

Saul thought that because he was king he could do whatever he wanted. He forgot that God is the great King above all kings. In the New Testament, we learn that Jesus is the King of kings.

Saul usurped God's authority as supreme King when he disobeyed God and did as he pleased. By punishing Saul for his disobedience, the LORD was telling Saul and all the people that He was and always will be the supreme King. Jesus Christ is the King of kings and LORD of lords. All kings and peoples from every nation must obey Him, and if they choose to disobey, they will have to give account of their actions when they stand before the LORD.

Chapter 4: David Anointed as King

How is David, the shepherd, like the Lord Jesus? How is Jesus, the Good Shepherd, greater than David?

In Psalm 23, David used his experiences as a shepherd to write a beautiful picture of the Lord Jesus. As the Great Shepherd, Jesus tenderly guides and cares for His people. John 10 describes Jesus as the Good Shepherd who protects His sheep even to the point of dying for them. What else can you learn from Psalm 23 and John 10 about how much Jesus loves you?

David was anointed king, but it wasn't time for him to rule yet. How is this like the Lord Jesus' life?

God had anointed David as king, but before he took over the throne, David had to suffer many hard things and learn what it meant to trust the LORD His God. Jesus has always been the King of all kings, but He laid aside His kingly glory to wander on the earth, suffer, and die. He was obedient to God the Father, even when obedience meant dying on the cross. Jesus was humiliated before He was exalted.

Chapter 6: David—The Fugitive

Rejected, homeless, hated by authorities—there are so many ways in which David's life as a fugitive was like Jesus' life.

Notes:

Both David and Jesus were rejected by the people that God had anointed them to rule over. They were wanderers, having no permanent place to live. (Jesus said, "Foxes have holes and birds of the air have nests, but the Son of Man has no place to lay His head" [Matthew 8:20, NIV]). Both David and Jesus were hated by wicked kings and those in authority. In many ways, the life of David gives you pictures of the life of Jesus.

Chapter 8: The Covenant With David

Jesus Christ is the fulfillment of God's covenant promises to David. He is the Son of David who rules forever and whose kingdom will never fail.

The covenant promises that the LORD made to David have been fulfilled in two ways. In the short-term of history, Solomon was David's son who ruled after him and built a temple for the LORD. But the greater fulfillment of the covenant is through Jesus Christ. Jesus is the Messiah born from David's line—a king who reigns forever in heaven on the throne at God's right hand. Jesus is building a temple much greater than Solomon's temple. Jesus' temple is a spiritual temple being built of "living stones," who are people from every nation who trust Jesus as Savior and Lord (see 1 Peter 2:4-5).

Chapter 9: David's Kindness & David's Sin

What did Mephibosheth do to merit kindness from King David? Absolutely nothing. What do you do to merit salvation from Jesus? Absolutely nothing. It's all by grace.

Mephibosheth did nothing to deserve David's kindness. It was by grace that he enjoyed the blessings of David's household. In the same way, you do nothing to deserve God's kindness and forgiveness. Although what you do can please or displease God, nothing you do can ever earn His favor, even if you live in a God-pleasing way. This is because our obedience to God is always imperfect, due to our sinful nature. Even our best behavior cannot be worthy of God, whose love for us is perfect, constant, and eternal, which is why we must always approach Him in humility and gratitude. You are forgiven of your sin and become a child in God's family because of Jesus' gift of grace. That's what grace is all about—unmerited, unearned favor and blessing from a gracious God!

Chapter 10: Troubles in the Kingdom

David was a good king, but his son, Absalom, plotted against him and the people turned against David. Jesus Christ is the perfect King, yet people refused to allow Him to rule over them.

David was not a perfect king. He sinned in many ways. Yet he was a good king and a man who had a heart to follow the LORD. Many times during David's reign, people rejected him.

From the short reign of Ishbosheth to the rebellions of Absalom and Sheba, David felt the sting of his people turning against him. In a like manner, the people that the LORD has created continue to reject His rule in their lives. Even Christians often refuse to acknowledge the rightful Lordship of Jesus Christ in their lives.

Chapter 11: The Wisdom of Solomon

Was Solomon really the wisest man of all? In Colossians 2:2-3, the Apostle Paul said that all the treasures of wisdom and knowledge are found in Jesus Christ.

Solomon was the wisest man living during the days of his life. His wisdom was a gift from God, and wise men from all over the world came to learn from him. In Colossians 2:2-3, the Apostle Paul said that all wisdom and knowledge are in Jesus Christ. No person who has ever lived or will ever be born has greater wisdom than Jesus, because Jesus is God Himself.

Chapter 12: The Reign of Solomon

"I will establish your throne forever." These were God's words to Solomon. Who would be on Solomon's throne forever? Jesus Christ!

The LORD renewed the covenant with Solomon, and promised, "I will establish your royal throne...forever" (1 Kings 9:5, NIV). How could Solomon's throne last forever? That's a long time! Solomon's throne could be eternal because Jesus Christ, the Son of David, would reign forever as King of kings and Lord of lords.

Chapter 14: A Nation Divided

Rehoboam promised to put heavy burdens on the people. In contrast, King Jesus' "burdens" are not hard to carry. In fact, Jesus said, "My yoke is easy, and My burden is light."

Jesus rules as a wise king who looks after the well-being of His people. He is a strong, powerful ruler, but He never uses His power to oppress His subjects. In Matthew 11:28-29, Jesus says that he will not impose heavy burdens upon people. He says, "My yoke is easy and My burden is light" (Matthew 11:30). How different King Jesus is from King Rehoboam, who vowed to make the burdens of his people even heavier than his father, Solomon, had!

The king was the representative of the covenant between God and the people. Isn't it sad that most of the kings forgot the covenant and led their people far from the Lord? Jesus, the King, is the representative of the covenant with you. Following Him brings you closer to your heavenly Father.

The LORD used Israel's monarchy to fulfill His covenant promises. As political head of the nation, the king represented his people in a special way. His obedience led to blessing for the

Notes:

nation, and his sin brought judgment. He was responsible to obey and enforce the law of God, and his obedience or disobedience set the pattern for how the entire nation would go. The role of king did not eliminate the need for prophets and priests, because the prophets spoke God's counsel and rebuke to the king, and the priests offered sacrifices for the sins of the king and his people. In contrast to the wicked kings of Israel and Judah, Jesus is the perfect king. He represents His people before Almighty God, and He is the mediator who takes the prayers of His people before God's throne (see 1 Timothy 2:5-6). When you follow Jesus, God blesses you.

Chapter 15: Elijah—God's Voice of Judgment to a Wicked King

Even when Elijah was discouraged and ready to die, the LORD was with him, speaking in a gentle, encouraging voice. Jesus, your Lord, is always with you. He promises, "I will never leave you nor forsake you."

In Hebrews 13:5, God promises, "Never will I leave you; never will I forsake you" (NIV). God's presence is always with His people because He promises to be with them. God's presence was with Elijah at the most discouraging moment in his life. Elijah was all alone, hiding for his life, feeling worthless and afraid. The LORD was gently and lovingly giving Elijah encouragement, telling him that he was not alone and that God still had work for him to do. The LORD's words gave Elijah strength, just like Jesus' words can give you strength when you are discouraged.

Chapter 16: Ahab & Jehoshaphat—Two Very Different Kings

When Ahab refused to kill Ben-Hadad, he was not a faithful king. He wasn't defending the honor of the LORD and wasn't protecting his people from enemies who wanted to destroy them. Jesus, as King, always honors God the Father and protects His people from those who would destroy them.

The kings of Israel and Judah were supposed to rule in such a way that they would point God's people to Jesus, the supreme King. However, all the kings of Israel were ungodly, so their reigns were a stark contrast to the way Jesus rules as King. As leader of Israel, Ahab's job was to protect the people from their enemies and to defend the honor of the LORD before pagan rulers. When Ahab refused to kill Ben-Hadad, he failed to do both these things. By contrast, King Jesus always brings honor to God the Father, and always protects and defends His people from whatever forces threaten to destroy them.

Chapter 17: Elisha—God's Voice to Rulers & Ordinary People

Elijah introduced the ministry of Elisha as John the Baptist introduced the ministry of Jesus. In what other ways was Elijah like John the Baptist and Elisha like Jesus?

Elijah was a voice of judgment in the land of Israel. He wandered throughout the land dressed in a garment of animal hair (see 2 Kings 1:8), and in a direct, often confrontational manner, he called the people of Israel, particularly King Ahab, to repentance. The prophet Malachi prophesied about God's coming messenger, the one who would announce the Messiah (see Malachi 3:1). Malachi's prophecy was fulfilled by John the Baptist. As God's messenger, John the Baptist wore clothing made from camel's hair and preached in the same forthright style as Elijah. He spoke about the need for repentance and declared judgment on those who refused to repent, saying, "Repent, for the kingdom of heaven is near" (Matthew 3:2, NIV). On the other hand, Elisha's ministry was similar to Jesus' ministry. Both Elisha and Jesus performed many miracles of mercy and compassion. Also, they both wandered throughout the land, getting involved in people's lives and turning hearts back to the LORD.

Chapter 18: Three Prophets of Judgment

Hosea loved a woman who was unfaithful to him. The Lord Jesus loved you and died for you when you were unfaithful to Him.

The LORD told Hosea to marry a woman who would be unfaithful to Him. This was a strange command, but the LORD wanted Hosea's sad marriage to be a vivid picture of the LORD's love for His people through His faithfulness to His covenant with them. Just like Gomer was unfaithful to Hosea, not once but several times, so God's people were repeatedly unfaithful to Him. God's love for His people did not depend upon their faithfulness, but upon His faithfulness. And, just as Hosea had a broken heart when Gomer was unfaithful to him, so the Lord Jesus has a broken heart when we worship idols. Even though our love for God may at times be as wispy as the morning mist, God never stops loving us.

Chapter 20: Israel Falls & Judah Remains

The Keeper of the Kingdom protected the royal line from which Jesus, the Messiah, would come.

Wicked Queen Athaliah was tricky. She thought she had successfully secured her kingdom by killing everyone in the royal family. But she had forgotten that Judah was not her kingdom. It was God's kingdom! Through the secretive actions of Jehoiada, the LORD preserved Joash's life, the only person left from the royal line of David. The LORD had promised that David's kingly line would last forever, and Joash was the one through whom Jesus the Messiah would come.

Chapter 21: Two Prophets & a Righteous King

In Matthew 2, the chief priests and teachers of the law found the answer to the wise men's question in the prophecy of Micah. The King would be born in Bethlehem.

Notes:

Micah 5:2 is one of the best-known fulfilled prophecies of the Old Testament. When the wise men led by the brilliant star came to Jerusalem looking for the new king, the learned Jewish scholars found the answer to the wise men's question in the book of Micah. The prophecy said that the King of the Jews would be born in Bethlehem. The books of Micah and Isaiah give many prophecies about the Messiah, and every one of them came true exactly as it was written.

Chapter 22: Two Memorable Kings—Manasseh & Josiah

Josiah had a legacy of righteousness, but it was not a perfect righteousness. Only Jesus has a legacy of perfect righteousness.

Josiah was a godly king and left behind him a legacy of righteousness. His heart for God delayed the judgment that would eventually come upon Judah. Jesus, also, left behind a legacy of righteousness, but his legacy was different from Josiah's in two ways. First, Jesus' righteousness is perfect. He never sinned either in His actions or in His heart. Second, He gives His righteousness to every person who turns away from his sin and toward Him in sincere repentance. When you repent, God takes away your sin and gives you Jesus' righteousness.

Chapter 23: God's Voices of Judgment to the Nations

The prophets said, "The kingdom will be the Lord's," and spoke of "the day of the Lord." Who is the Lord? Jesus Christ!

See Obadiah 1:15, 21; Joel 2:1, 11, 31; 3:14; and Zephaniah 1:14. When the prophets said, "The kingdom will be the Lord's," they were speaking about Jesus, the King who would come to earth some day. When the prophets warned about the "day of the Lord," they were reminding people that the Messiah who saves would also be the judge who judges all men justly according to their deeds. Those who trust Him can rest secure under His sovereign rule, but those who harden their hearts against Him should fear Him as a God of righteous anger.

Chapter 24: Jeremiah Weeps & Judah Falls

Jeremiah was rejected by the people and persecuted by kings. No one wanted to hear what he had to say. Like Jeremiah, people rejected what Jesus had to say, too. Both Jeremiah and Jesus cried tears of sorrow over the hardened hearts of God's people.

God's message of repentance has never been a message that people want to hear. Jeremiah said hard words to the people in Jerusalem, and then they did terrible things to him because they did not want to hear about their sin. But Jeremiah's tears were not just because the people treated him badly. Jeremiah cried because he had compassion on God's people. Likewise, Jesus' words were not accepted, and the stubbornness of people's hearts made Jesus weep over Jerusalem's sins (Luke 19:41-44).

204 Appendix B: Pictures of Jesus Christ in the Old Testament

Chapter 26: God's Messenger to the Exiles

The rainbow of God's mercy covers the throne of God's judgment because Jesus the Savior paid the penalty for the sin of His people.

The rainbow around God's throne reminded Ezekiel that God would show mercy to His sinful people by providing a Savior. Without the death of Jesus Christ, there could be no permanent sacrifice for sin, but through Jesus' death, God could make a way for forgiveness and grace.

Chapter 27: Daniel & His Friends

Who was that man in the furnace with Daniel's friends? It was Jesus!

The Lord protected Shadrach, Meshach, and Abednego in an amazing way! When Nebuchadnezzar looked into the furnace, he saw four, not three, men. The fourth man was Jesus Himself. This is called a "theophany." (A theophany is an appearance of Jesus during Old Testament times, before He was born in Bethlehem.) There are several occasions when Jesus appeared to people in the Old Testament (for example, He appeared to Abraham [Genesis 18] and Joshua [Joshua 5:13-15]).

Chapter 29: The People Return—The Temple Is Rebuilt

What is the future glory? It is a glorious day when Jesus will come and establish His Kingdom.

Zechariah's visions spoke of two "days of the Lord" and two temples. The first day of the Lord was when Jesus came to earth to live and die as a man and as your God and Savior. The second day of the Lord will happen when Jesus comes again to judge and rule the earth as King of kings and Lord of lords. The first temple was the temple in Jerusalem built by the returning exiles. The second temple is found in the bodies of believers. The Holy Spirit dwells within all God's people, who are part of the spiritual temple God is building for His eternal Kingdom.

Chapter 31: The Story of Ezra & Nehemiah

The Lord said, "Look for My messenger. He will announce the Messiah."

The Lord ends the Old Testament story by saying, "Look for My messenger. He will announce the Messiah." God has kept His Kingdom safe. He has protected the remnant through the trials of judgment and exile. He will continue to guard His people while, at the same time, He prepares the world for the coming of the King. Jesus Christ is coming! Watch for Him!

Appendix B: Pictures of Jesus Christ in the Old Testament 205

Notes:

Appendix C

How to Use the Psalms

Through centuries of recorded history, has God ever changed? Absolutely not! God never changes. ("I the LORD do not change" [Malachi 3:6, NIV]).

Through the ages of time, has mankind changed? Yes. In a short span of time, the languages, geographical boundaries, religions, and political systems of mankind have changed, and nations and cultures have disappeared forever. Yet at the same time, the hard things that happen to people (sickness, death, poverty, broken friendships, etc.) and the way people think and feel about these circumstances don't change. The LORD gave you the book of Psalms, God's "Book of Praises," written 3,000 years ago, so that you can find songs to sing in every situation.

When you read the psalms, ask yourself several questions. These questions will help you understand each psalm better and will help you find encouragement from its words.

Question #1: Who sang this psalm at the time it was written?

Some psalms were written for God's people to sing together in the temple while they worshipped or on their pilgrimages as they walked. Other psalms were written as personal songs of prayer or praise. Knowing who sang the psalm helps you to understand the reason why the psalmist wrote the psalm and how it can encourage you.

Question #2: What is the purpose of this psalm?

Men wrote psalms for many reasons, including praising God, confessing sin, giving thanks, remembering God's faithfulness, and crying out for God's help. For every life situation, the LORD has provided a divinely written song to help you praise Him and feel His comfort. (Chapter 4 describes the different types of psalms.)

Question #3: What does this psalm teach you about yourself?

Just like David, you get angry when friends betray you (see Psalm 55:12-14). Just like Asaph, you're confused when everything goes well for wicked people but goes wrong for you (see Psalm 73). Sometimes it seems that you pray and pray, and God doesn't hear you (see Psalm 13). The psalmists have put into words what you are often thinking and feeling, but can't find the words to say, and then they point you to the LORD, who shows you the world from His point of view.

Question #4: What does this psalm teach you about God?

The Lord is the Shepherd who tenderly cares for His people (see Psalm 23), yet He sends a storm of fiery coals upon violent men who hurt others (see Psalm 11:6). The Lord hears and answers prayer (see Psalm 34:4), but sometimes it seems as though He is silent (see Psalm 88:13-14). Each psalm lets you see another part of what God is like, and putting all the pieces together gives you a big picture of all the traits that make God who He is.

The book of Psalms is a hymnbook, giving you beautiful songs of worship. Today, some churches sing only songs from the book of Psalms in their worship services. Through the years, some psalms, like Psalm 23, have been put to music using many different tunes. Maybe you can make up your own musical tune for a favorite psalm.

The book of Psalms is a prayer book. Praying the words of the psalms as though they are your own thoughts and words can be a powerful way to talk to the Lord when you just don't know what to say.

Through the book of Psalms you can ask the Lord the questions that bother you. "Why, O Lord,...do you hide yourself in times of trouble?" (Psalm 10:1, NIV). "Has the Lord's love vanished forever? Has God forgotten to be merciful?" (see Psalm 77:7-9). The psalmist asked these questions, just as the Lord wants us to ask questions when we are doubting or afraid.

Most important, you must remember that the book of Psalms is poetry that expresses the deepest thoughts and emotions of the human soul. Isn't it amazing that the Lord included in His Holy Scriptures these precious poems to remind you how much our God of the covenant loves you?

Notes:

Appendix D How to Understand the Proverbs

"Trust in the LORD with all your heart, And lean not on your own understanding" (Proverbs 3:5).

It's not education and it's not experience that makes a person wise. It's only when knowledge and experience are linked with fearing God that a person becomes truly wise.

The book of Proverbs is a collection of wise sayings written for the purpose of attaining wisdom, developing discipline and self-control, and doing what is morally right and just (Proverbs 1:1-6).

The first nine chapters of Proverbs describe in poetic pictures the conflict between Lady Wisdom and Woman Folly. Woman Folly is "loud;...undisciplined and without knowledge" (Proverbs 9:13, NIV), while Lady Wisdom "dwell[s] together with prudence" and "possess[es] knowledge and discretion" (Proverbs 8:12, NIV). Following in the footsteps of Lady Wisdom brings life and happiness, while the path of Woman Folly only leads to destruction, unhappiness, and eventually death.

The book of Proverbs has something to say about anger, friendship, wealth, poverty, the wise use of words, justice, hard work, and many other topics. All through the book, you read about the contrast between wisdom and folly, good and evil, and self-control and bad judgment. Though the proverbs are generally simple, "tell it like it is" life truths wrapped in picturesque language, they are not always easy to understand. Several important principles must be remembered when trying to understand the book of Proverbs.

Principle #1: The sayings in Proverbs are principles, not promises. In other words, Proverbs tells you that, generally speaking, certain actions bring specific results. For example, Proverbs 10:27 says that a person who fears God will live a long time. ("The fear of the LORD adds length to life, but the years of the wicked are cut short," NIV.) But some godly people die young and some wicked people seem to live forever. So, God is not promising that every godly person will live a long time or that every wicked person will die young. God is, however, making a strong connection between being obedient to God and living a long, complete life.

Principle #2: All proverbs can be misunderstood, so you must read them carefully. Because of our sinful hearts, we can make a proverb mean just about whatever we want it to mean, often distorting its real meaning. One biblical proverb can't contradict another one, however, so all Scripture must be understood in the context of all other Scripture.

Principle #3: The sayings in the book of Proverbs can sound as though the writer is saying two opposite things at the same time. Because all Scripture is inspired by God, all Scripture is true. Therefore, when trying to understand the meaning of contradictory proverbs, you must assume both proverbs are true and then try to understand what each proverb means in its own context. (Proverbs 26:4-5 is an example of two proverbs that appear to contradict each other.)

Principle #4: The book of Proverbs teaches you that consequences follow actions. When you do the right thing, generally speaking, good things happen. When you do the wrong thing, generally speaking, misfortune and bad consequences follow. Most of the time, bad consequences are the result of poor decisions or disobedience, not the deliberate punishment from an "angry" God.

Principle #5: The book of Proverbs makes comparisons between two disagreeable things. ("Better to live in a desert than with a quarrelsome and ill-tempered wife" [Proverbs 21:19, NIV]). These "better" proverbs have an uncomfortable feel, taking something that most reasonable people would think is unpleasant and comparing it with an even more disagreeable thing so that the first thing actually becomes something you would choose. These strange comparisons give little windows into the mind of God, whose thoughts are so very different from our thoughts.

So, a wise person fears God, makes good choices, and acts rightly. Do you want to be wise? Try this. Since Proverbs has thirty-one chapters, you can read one chapter on each day of the month. Without even trying too hard, you will remember these sayings, and then, by practicing them, you can become a wise person.

Notes:

Appendix E

Kings & Prophets

JUDAH			ISRAEL	
Kings	Prophets	Date	Prophets	Kings
Rehoboam		930 BC	Ahijah	Jeroboam
Abijah		913 BC		
ASA	Azariah	910 BC		
	Hanani	909 BC		Nadab
		908 BC	Jehu	Baasha
		885 BC		Elah, Zimri, Tibni
		880 BC		Omri
		874 BC	Elijah	Ahab
JEHOSHAPHAT		869 BC	Micaiah	
		853 BC	Elisha	Ahaziah
	Jahaziel	852 BC		Joram (a.k.a. Jehoram)
Jehoram	Obadiah (Edom)	848 BC		
Ahaziah Queen Athaliah		841 BC		Jehu
JOASH (a.k.a Jehoash)	Joel*	835 BC		
		814 BC		Jehoahaz
AMAZIAH		798 BC		Jehoash
		782 BC		Jeroboam II
UZZIAH (a.k.a. Azariah)		767 BC		
		760 BC	Amos Hosea (760–725)	
		753 BC		Zechariah
		752 BC	Jonah (Assyria)	Shallum Menahem
		742 BC		Pekahiah

JUDAH			ISRAEL	
Kings	**Prophets**	**Date**	**Prophets**	**Kings**
JOTHAM	Isaiah (740–687)	740 BC		Pekah
Ahaz		731 BC		Hoshea
HEZEKIAH		727 BC		
		722 BC		**Israel's Fall**
	Micah	701 BC		
Manasseh		687 BC		
Amon	Nahum (Assyria)	642 BC		
JOSIAH	Zephaniah (630–620)	640 BC		
	Jeremiah (627–586)	627 BC		
Jehoahaz Jehoiakim	Habakkuk (610–600) Daniel (605–536)	609 BC		
Jehoiachin		598 BC		
Zedekiah		597 BC		
Judah's Fall	Ezekiel (593–571)	**586 BC**		
Post-Exilic Prophets	Haggai Zechariah	520 BC		
	Malachi	433 BC		

NOTE: The kings whose names are in capitalized italics were kings who served the Lord for at least part of their reign. None of Israel's kings did right.

NOTE: All dates are approximate. Different dating timelines are used by various biblical scholars. Dates for this timeline are taken from *Old Testament Survey* by Paul R. House.

*Biblical scholars are uncertain as to exactly when Joel was prophesying. Some sources cite the 800s BC and others the 300s BC.

Notes:

Appendix F Reigns of the Kings of Israel & Judah

KINGS OF ISRAEL

King	Father	Years Reigned	Death
Jeroboam	Nebat	22	Natural death
Nadab	Jeroboam	2	Killed by Baasha
Baasha	Ahijah	24	Natural death
Elah	Baasha	2	Killed by Zimri
Zimri	unknown	7 days	Died at Tirzah
Tibni	Ginath	1	Unknown
Omri	unknown	12	Natural death
Ahab	Omri	22	Killed in battle
Ahaziah	Ahab	2	Accident; died from injuries
Joram	Ahab	12	Killed by Jehu
Jehu	Jehoshaphat (son of Nimshi)	28	Natural death
Jehoahaz	Jehu	17	Natural death
Jehoash	Jehoahaz	16	Natural death
Jeroboam II	Jehoash	41	Natural death
Zechariah	Jeroboam II	6 months	Killed by Shallum
Shallum	Jabesh	1 month	Killed by Menahem
Menahem	Gadi	10	Natural death
Pekahiah	Menahem	2	Killed by Pekah
Pekah	Remaliah	20	Killed by Hoshea
Hoshea	Elah	9	Captured by Assyria

KINGS OF JUDAH

King	Father	Years Reigned / Age When Reign Began	Death
Rehoboam	Solomon	17 yrs/age 41	Natural death
Abijah	Rehoboam	3 yrs	Natural death
ASA	Abijah	41 yrs	Natural death
JEHOSHAPHAT	Asa	25 yrs	Natural death
Jehoram	Jehoshaphat	8 yrs/age 32	Natural death
Ahaziah	Jehoram	1 yr/age 22	Killed by Jehu
Athaliah	Omri (grandfather)*	6 yrs	Killed by Jehoiada's action
JOASH	Ahaziah	40 yrs/age 7	Murdered by his officials
AMAZIAH	Joash	29 yrs/age 25	Killed by conspirators
UZZIAH	Amaziah	52 yrs/age 16	Died of leprosy
JOTHAM	Uzziah	16 yrs	Natural death
Ahaz	Jotham	16 yrs/age 20	Natural death
HEZEKIAH	Ahaz	29 yrs/age 25	Natural death
Manasseh	Hezekiah	55 yrs/age 12	Natural death
Amon	Manasseh	2 yrs/age 22	Assassinated by his officials
JOSIAH	Amon	31 yrs/age 8	Killed in battle against Egypt
Jehoahaz	Josiah	3 mths/age 23	Captured and died in Egypt
Jehoiakim	Josiah	11 yrs/age 25	Natural death
Jehoiachin	Jehoiakim	3 mths/age 18	Taken to Babylon
Zedekiah	Josiah	11 yrs/age 21	Taken captive to Babylon and died

NOTE: The kings whose names are in capitalized italics were kings who served the LORD for at least part of their reign. Many of these kings began their rule well, but turned away from the LORD before they died.

*It is unclear as to who Athaliah's father was. Some sources suggest that it was Ahab, but Scripture is unclear on this point.

Notes:

Appendix G

Intertestamental History

And then, God was silent. No booming voices of judgment from wild-eyed Elijahs or soulful pleadings from Jeremiahs. No dramatic displays of fire from heaven or unexplainable healings. The Jews, having returned from exile, lived in Palestine for 400 years as one empire after another rose to power and then collapsed. Yet, while God was silent, He was not sleeping. God was changing and maneuvering governments, religious practices, languages, and literature so that at just the right time, when the King Himself would come to earth, the earth would be ready for Him!

History

In the years from Malachi to Matthew, five different empires ruled Palestine. The Persians, whose rule began under Cyrus in 536 BC, governed the Jews for 200 years. Persian rule was tolerant, and the Jews were able to practice their religion. During this time, the Samaritans erected a separate temple in Samaria. (The Samaritans were an interracial mixture of remnant Israelites and people from conquered Assyrian cities.) Building this temple brought about a total separation between the Jews of Judea and the Samaritans of Samaria, and explains why they hated each other so much. (John 4 tells you about this ongoing hatred between the Jews and the Samaritans.)

In 332 BC, Alexander the Great marched southward to Jerusalem, and Judea became part of the Greek empire. Though Alexander treated the Jews well, another danger threatened God's people. The Greeks were determined to unite the world with one language and culture, a process called "Hellenization." This process had damaging effects on Jewish worship, but it set into place certain things that prepared the world for the King's coming.

When Alexander died at a young age, chaos erupted in the empire. With no strong leader to guide the empire, it split into four parts under four generals. After fierce fighting, Judea came under the control of Ptolemy, who ruled his part of the empire from Egypt. (The Ptolemies were a dynasty of Greeks, each named Ptolemy, who ruled Egypt and the surrounding territories.) Under the first three Ptolemies, the Jews had kind treatment, and they prospered, growing in population and wealth. Later Ptolomies didn't treat the Jews well. Then Palestine became a battleground between the Ptolemies of Egypt and the Seleucid empire of Syria. In 204 BC, all of Palestine, including Judea, Samaria, and Galilee came under Syrian rule.

The Syrian rulers were harsh toward the Jews, but the most infamous of all the Syrians was Antiochus Epiphanes. This tyrant used the Jews' rebellious attitude toward Syria as a reason to plunder Jerusalem and defile the temple. In 170 BC, after massacring thousands of people and selling women and children as slaves, he desecrated the temple by offering a pig on the altar as a sacrifice. He also erected a statue of the Greek god Zeus in the middle of the temple. His intention was to destroy the Jewish religion.

An old priest named Mattathias, a father of five sons, began the next "empire" in Judea, called the Maccabean Period. After killing a messenger of Antiochus Epiphanes, Mattathias led a revolt against the Syrian oppressors. His rebel army grew in number and fought against traitorous Jews and hated Syrians. His passion was to restore true religion to the Jews. After his death, his son, Judas Maccabeus, the best known of the Maccabean leaders, became military commander. He was a fierce fighter who employed guerilla army tactics to fight the Syrians.

Judas Maccabeus was killed in battle, but his brothers, first Jonathan and then Simon, continued the revolt, a twenty-four year struggle that resulted in independence for the Jews that lasted until the Romans conquered Palestine in 63 BC. Between the time of Simon's death and the Roman conquest, several Maccabean descendents ruled Judea, beginning with Simon's son, John Hyrcanus. These rulers are called the Hasmonean dynasty.

The Hasmonean rule started well, with prosperity and peace in the land, but with John Hyrcanus's death, strife and civil war erupted. The rulers adopted Hellenistic ways of thinking, and Mattathias's passion for pure religion was rejected for a mixture of Greek thought and Jewish religion.

In 63 BC, Pompey conquered Jerusalem after a three-month siege. Because this Roman general massacred the priests and raided the Most Holy Place of the temple, the Jews hated the Romans. This hatred remained unchanged and was the basis for the hatred between the Jews and the Romans during the time of Jesus' life.

Language, Literature, and Religion

The religious and cultural impact that these 400 years had upon the world made it possible for Jesus Christ to be born "when the fullness of the time had come" (Galatians 4:4).

The conquering of the known world by the Greeks changed history permanently. The Greek language soon became the one language that united people. In Alexandria, during the reign of the Ptolemies, a group of scholars gathered together, and in a short time they translated the Jewish Scripture into Greek. This book is called the Septuagint, meaning "seventy." (Legend says that seventy-two men completed the entire translation in seventy-two days.)

Notes:

This meant that as the Jews became Hellenized and could no longer speak Hebrew, and as the gospel later spread to Gentiles in the Roman world, God's Word was still accessible to many people.

During this time, the books of the Apocrypha were written. This collection of fifteen books provides historical and cultural information about life during the silent years. Though some Bibles today include these books, the Church does not consider them to be divinely inspired Scripture.

God used the Romans to prepare the world for Christ's coming. The Romans united the known world in a more complete way than even the Greeks had. They built a system of roads, some of which can still be walked on today. Once Rome conquered the nations, the Pax Romana (meaning "the peace of Rome") settled over the empire. This one-government system, and the ability to travel between distant parts of the empire, made it possible to spread the gospel message to many countries during the first century AD.

A very significant change happened in the Jewish nation after the Exile. From the time of their wilderness journey to the destruction of Jerusalem, God's people repeatedly turned from the Lord and worshipped the gods of other nations. However, after returning from Babylon, the Jews never again worshipped Baal, Asherah, Molech or other pagan gods. Though they were not always faithful to the Lord, and did not always worship Him appropriately, they always claimed that Yahweh was their God.

In the Jewish community, two major religious institutions came about during this time. The synagogue that didn't exist before the Exile and was an established part of Jewish society in the New Testament had its origins in Babylon. Separated from the temple and surrounded by pagan idolatry, the Jews in Babylon didn't want to forget the religion of their ancestors. They met in groups to study the Torah (the five books of Moses). By the time they went back to Jerusalem, they regularly studied and discussed the Scriptures and made this habit part of their new life. They called these meeting places "synagogues." During the time of Jesus' life, synagogues were found in cities throughout Judea and Galilee.

Another religious institution that began in the silent years of the Exile was the formation of new religious and social groups (scribes, Pharisees, and Sadducees) that, along with the chief priests, controlled Jewish life. The scribes were a group of professionals who were experts in interpreting and applying the Old Testament Law. Arising out of the synagogue movement, their function was different from that of the priests who offered sacrifices in the temple. The passion of the scribes was instilling the idea of the Law's holiness into the people's minds and protecting Judaism from outside influences or internal heresy that would defile God's Law and lead His people astray.

The Pharisees and Sadducees were different from the scribes and priests because they were distinguished by their religious views, not their religious function. A man could be a scribe or a priest or actually do both jobs. As a scribe or priest a man could have the religious views either of a Pharisee or Sadducee (although there is no known record that any scribe was a Sadducee) or be independent from either religious viewpoint.

The Pharisees and Sadducees had different religious views and opposed each other on everything. The word "Pharisees" means "Separatists." They believed in strict obedience to the written law given by the LORD and to the oral law and traditions that they created to help them to keep God's Law "perfectly." They concentrated on behaving correctly, but didn't always keep the Law in their hearts. Sadducees for the most part belonged to wealthy priestly families and were more of a social group than a religious one. They were more interested in political power than in the hope of a coming Messiah or in keeping God's Law. They were religious skeptics and didn't believe in the universal resurrection.

Four hundred years of preparation—a Greek-speaking world, the Pax Romana throughout the known world, and an established Jewish religious system were all part of God's way of getting the world ready because the King Himself was coming!

Notes:

Glossary

– A –

Abednego (n.): Babylonian name of Azariah, who was with Daniel in exile in Babylon

Abiathar (n.): Son of Ahimelech, a priest at Nob; the only priest who escaped slaughter at Nob; banished after he supported Adonijah's attempt to be king

Abijah (n.): Wicked king of Judah; son of Rehoboam

Abishai (n.): One of David's men; went with David to cave and stole Saul's spear and water jug

Abinadab (n.): Man at whose house the ark of the covenant stayed for twenty years

Abner (n.): Commander of Saul's army; made Ishbosheth king in Israel after Saul died; killed Asahel, Joab's brother

Absalom (n.): Son of David; led a conspiracy against David; killed Amnon; killed by Joab

Adonijah (n.): Son of David who tried to become the king who succeeded David

Agag (n.): King of the Amalekites whose life Saul spared

Agur (n.): One of the writers of Proverbs

Ahab (n.): Wicked king of Israel; son of King Omri; husband of Queen Jezebel; enemy of Elijah

Ahaz (n.): Son of Jotham and father of Hezekiah who became king of Judah; known for his great idolatry

Ahaziah (n.): Ahab's son who became king of Israel after Ahab died; brother of Queen Athaliah; worshipped Baal-Zebub instead of the LORD

Ahaziah (n.): Jehoram's son who became king of Judah after Jehoram died; son of Queen Athaliah

Ahijah (n.): Prophet who prophesied that Jeroboam would be king of ten tribes of Israel

Ahimelech (n.): Priest at Nob who gave David and his men consecrated bread to eat

Ahio (n.): Son of Abinadab who guided the ark from Abinadab's house; brother of Uzzah

Amalekites (n.): Descendents of Amalek, the grandson of Esau; enemy of Israel

Amasa (n.): Commander of Absalom's army; killed by Joab

Amaziah (n.): Son of Joash who became king of Judah; brought Edom's gods to Jerusalem

Amnon (n.): Son of David who sinned against his half sister Tamar and was killed by Absalom

Ammonites (n.): Descendents of Ben-Ammi, son of Lot and his second daughter; enemy of Israel

Amos (n.): Herdsman and tree farmer from Tekoa in Judah called to be a prophet of God to Israel; prophet of justice; name means "bearer of burdens"

Anoint (v.): Chosen by God and equipped by God's Spirit to serve the LORD in a particular job (priest, prophet, king, etc.)

Ark of the Covenant (n.): Box that contained the Ten Commandments and reminded Israel that God was with them; located in the Holy of Holies in the tabernacle

Aram (n.): Nation north of Israel that often fought against Israel; Ben-Hadad was a king of Aram (Syria)

Artaxerxes (n.): King of Persia during the days of Zerubbabel and Jeshua

Asa (n.): Godly king in Judah; son of wicked king Abijah

Asahel (n.): Brother of Joab who was killed by Abner

Asaph (n.): Writer of some of the book of Psalms

Ashdod (n.): City in Philistia where Dagon's temple was located; God sent a plague of tumors and rats to this city

Asherah (n.): Name of a Canaanite goddess

Ashtoreth (n.): Name of a goddess of the Sidonians in Phoenicia

Athaliah (n.): Queen who killed the royal family and then ruled in Judah; sister of Ahaziah (king of Israel) and mother of Ahaziah (king of Judah)

Azariah (n.): Prophet of God in Judah to King Asa

Azariah (n.): Son of Amaziah who became king of Judah; commonly called Uzziah

Azariah (n.): Hebrew name of one of Daniel's three friends who was with Daniel in exile in Babylon

– B –

Baal (n.): Canaanite god

Baal-Zebub (n.): Philistine idol to which Ahaziah (Israel) prayed; means "lord of the flies"

Baasha (n.): Wicked king in Israel; killed Nadab, Jeroboam's son, and all Jeroboam's family

Babylon (n.): Nation that conquered Judah in 586 BC and took God's people as captives

Baruch (n.): Jeremiah's scribe who wrote the scroll sent to Jehoiakim

Bathsheba (n.): Wife of Uriah; woman whom David loved as only a husband should love

Belteshazzar (n.): The Babylonian name of Daniel, who was taken into exile in Babylon

Belshazzar (n.): King of Babylon during Daniel's life; king who saw the handwriting on the palace walls and was then killed by Darius, king of the Medes

Ben-Hadad I (n.): King of Aram in Damascus who made a treaty with King Asa in Judah

Ben-Hadad II (n.): King of Aram who attacked Israel during the time of Elisha

Notes:

Benjaminite (n.): Person from the tribe of Benjamin

Bethel (n.): One of two cities where Jeroboam set up a worship center with a golden calf

Bethlehem (n.): City where David was born; city in which the Messiah was to be born

Blessed (adj.): Contented because God is pleased with you

Boaz (n.): Name of northern pillar of Solomon's temple; means "in Him is strength"

Bozrah (n.): Capital of Edom carved out of rocky cliffs

– C –

Chemosh (n.): Name of the chief god of the Moabites

Continuing (adj.): Type of Hebrew poetry in which the second line adds meaning to or continues the thought of the first line

Contrasted (adj.): Type of Hebrew poetry in which the second line has an opposite meaning to the first line

Covenant (n.): God's promise to be the God of His people forever

Cyrus (n.): King of Persia who was king when Daniel lived in exile; king who decreed that Jews could go back to their land

– D –

Dagon (n.): One of the primary gods of the Philistines; his temple was located at Ashdod

Dan (n.): One of two cities where Jeroboam set up a worship center with a golden calf

Daniel (n.): One of God's people who was captured and taken to Babylon, where he became prominent in the courts of Nebuchadnezzar, Cyrus, and Darius; prophet of God's sovereignty

Darius (n.): King of the Medes who killed Belshazzar and took over his kingdom; king who made the decree that resulted in Daniel being thrown into the lions' den

Darius (n.): One of the kings of Persia during the days in which the Jews had returned to Jerusalem

David (n.): Israel's second king; writer of many of the Psalms; the Lord called David, "a man after [My] own heart"

Desert of Ziph (n.): Desert where David and his men hid in caves

Doeg (n.): The Edomite who killed the eighty-five priests at Nob

Dothan (n.): City where the Aramean army was struck with blindness by Elisha

Dura (n.): Plain where Nebuchadnezzar set up the large image that he commanded to be worshipped

– E –

Ebenezer (n.): Memorial stone set up by Samuel after Israel's victory over the Philistines; means "thus far has the Lord helped us"

Ecclesiastes (n.): Book in the Old Testament written by The Preacher that teaches how to find purpose in the fear of God, not earthly pleasures

Edomites (n.): Descendents of Esau; enemy of Israel

Ekron (n.): City in Philistia where God sent a plague of tumors and rats because the Philistines had captured the ark of the covenant

Elah (n.): Wicked king in Israel

Eleazar (n.): Man who guarded the ark of the covenant while it stayed in his father Abinadab's house

Eliab (n.): Oldest son of Jesse; the brother of King David

Elijah (n.): Prophet of God who spoke judgment to Ahab and challenged the prophets of Baal

Elisha (n.): Prophet of God who succeeded Elijah

Elkanah (n.): The husband of Hannah and the father of Samuel

Eli (n.): Priest in Israel with whom Samuel lived

Elohim (n.): Hebrew name for God that means might, strength, and majesty; the name that reminds us that God is the creator of all things

Endor (n.): Town where medium who called up Samuel for Saul lived

Esther (n.): Jewish woman who became the wife of King Xerxes, king of Persia, and who saved her people from destruction

Ezekiel (n.): Prophet of visions; prophet of God to the exiles in Babylon

Ezra (n.): Jewish priest who led the people from exile in Babylon back to Jerusalem

– F –

Faith (n.): Believing what God says is true and acting on this truth even before you see the results with your own eyes; a gift from God

Fear God (v. + n.): Be in awe of God so that you respect and obey Him

– G –

Gath (n.): City in Philistia where God sent a plague of tumors and rats because the Philistines had captured the ark of the covenant

Gedaliah (n.): Man appointed governor over Jerusalem by Babylon after the destruction of the city

Geshur (n.): Country that Absalom fled to after killing Amnon

Geshem (n.): One of the three men who gave Nehemiah problems as he was rebuilding the walls of Jerusalem

Gibeon (n.): City where the tabernacle was located during the reigns of David and Solomon until the temple was built

Goliath (n.): Giant whom David killed

Gomer (n.): Unfaithful wife of the prophet Hosea

– H –

Habakkuk (n.): Prophet to Judah who asked the Lord two questions; prophet of faith

Haggai (n.): Prophet who encouraged the returned exiles in Jerusalem to rebuild the temple; prophet of encouragement

Notes:

Hallelujah Psalm (n.): Psalm that gives praise to God (Psalms 146–150)

Haman (n.): Official in King Xerxes's court who plotted to have all the Jews killed

Hannah (n.): The mother of Samuel; dedicated Samuel to the Lord after He answered her prayer for a child

Hanani (n.): Seer who rebuked Asa for making a treaty with Ben-Hadad

Hananiah (n.): Hebrew name of one of Daniel's friends who was with Daniel in exile in Babylon

Hazael (n.): King of Aram anointed by Elijah; killed Ben-Hadad II

Hebron (n.): City in Judah where David was anointed king after Saul died

Hilkiah (n.): High priest during Josiah's reign; found the Book of the Law in the temple

Hiram (n.): King of Tyre who gave Solomon cedar wood for the temple

Historical Psalm (n.): Psalm that reminds Israel of who God is and what He has done (Psalms 105–106)

Holy (adj.): Means "set apart by God" or "living in a way that pleases God"

Hophni (n.): One of Eli's wicked sons

Hosea (n.): Prophet of God to the nation of Israel; prophet of the broken heart; name means "salvation"; married Gomer, an unfaithful woman because God told him to marry her; his marriage was a picture of Israel's unfaithfulness to the LORD

Hoshea (n.): Son of Elah who was the last king of Israel before Assyria conquered Israel

Huldah (n.): Prophetess during the reign of Josiah; she said Judah would suffer all the curses in the Book of the Law

Huram (n.): Skilled craftsman from Tyre hired by Solomon to make the two bronze pillars for the temple

– I –

Ichabod (n.): Name of Phinehas's wife's son; means "the glory [of the LORD] has departed from Israel"

Idol (n.): Anything we trust in rather than God; any desire or fear that controls our behavior

Immanuel (n.): Name of Jesus Christ, the Messiah; means "God with us"

Ishbosheth (n.): King over eleven tribes in Israel after Saul died

Isaiah (n.): Prophet of comfort; prophesied to kings of Judah (Jotham, Ahaz, and Hezekiah)

Israel (n.): Name for God's people, with whom He made a covenant; also, name for the northern kingdom after the nation of Israel split in two (ten tribes)

– J –

Jabesh Gilead (n.): Israelite city besieged by the Ammonites

Jachin (n.): Southern pillar of Solomon's temple; means "He establishes"

Jahaziel (n.): Prophet of Israel who told Jehoshaphat that God would deliver Israel from the Moabites and Ammonites

Jehoahaz (n.): Son of Jehu who became king of Israel

Jehoahaz (n.): Son of Josiah who became king of Judah for three months

Jehoash (n.): Son of Jehoahaz who became king of Israel

Jehoiachin (n.): Son of Jehoiakim who became king of Judah for three months

Jehoiada (n.): High priest who hid baby Joash from wicked Athaliah

Jehoiakim (n.): Son of Josiah who became king of Judah

Jehoram (n.): King of Judah who became king after his father Jehoshaphat; also called Joram

Jehoshaphat (n.): Godly king of Judah who ruled when Ahab was king of Israel

Jehovah (n.): The name of God as used in the covenant; written as "LORD" in the English Bible; same as the word "Yahweh"

Jehu (n.): Prophet of God who warned Baasha, king of Israel, of his wickedness and blessed Jehoshaphat, king of Judah

Jehu (n.): Man who became king of Israel after killing Joram (Israel) and Ahaziah (Judah); also killed Jezebel and all Ahab's family

Jeremiah (n.): Prophet to Judah during the last five kings; prophet of tears

Jeroboam (n.): First king of Israel after the kingdom split in two

Jeroboam II (n.): Son of Jehoash who became king in Israel

Jerusalem (n.): Jebusite city captured by David and made the capital of Israel; capital of the southern kingdom of Judah after the nation of Israel split in two

Jeshua (n.): Priest who led the first group of exiles back home to Jerusalem (some versions of the Bible call him Joshua)

Jesse (n.): Son of Obed and father of King David (Obed was the son of Ruth)

Jezebel (n.): Wicked queen in Israel; wife of King Ahab; enemy of Elijah

Joab (n.): Commander of David's army; killed Abner (commander king of Saul's army), Absalom, and Amasa

Joash (n.): Son of Ahaziah (Judah) who became king of Judah at age seven; hid by the high priest Jehoiada to protect him from wicked Athaliah

Joel (n.): Prophet to Judah; spoke about the plague of locusts; prophet of God's grace

Jonah (n.): Prophet of God to the city of Nineveh; prophet of salvation

Jonathan (n.): King Saul's son, who made a covenant of friendship with David

Joram (n.): Son of Ahab who became king of Israel after his brother Ahaziah died (also called Jehoram)

Joshua (n.): Man chosen by God to lead the Israelites into the Promised Land and conquer it

Notes:

Josiah (n.): King of Judah who read the Book of the Law at the temple and began great religious reform; considered the godliest of Judah's kings

Jotham (n.): Son of Uzziah who became king of Judah after Uzziah got leprosy

Judah (n.): Name of the southern kingdom after the nation of Israel split in two (two tribes)

Judge (n.): Person chosen by God to be a deliverer, peacemaker, and civil leader in Israel

Judgment Psalm (n.): Psalm that asks God to judge the wicked (Psalms 35, 52, 55, 109)

– K –

Keilah (n.): Town David saved from the Philistines; Keilah's inhabitants were not friendly toward David

Kerith Ravine (n.): Place where the ravens fed Elijah

– L –

Lamentations (n.): Book written by Jeremiah describing the destruction of Jerusalem

Legacy (n.): Something you leave behind for your descendents

Lemuel (n.): One of the writers of Proverbs

Levites (n.): Tribe of Israel responsible for transporting the ark and fulfilling the priestly functions in worship

Lyre (n.): Small stringed musical instrument that David played

– M –

Malachi (n.): The prophet who wrote the last book of the Old Testament; prophet of preparation

Manasseh (n.): Son of Hezekiah who was the longest reigning king of Judah; considered one of Judah's most wicked kings

Medium (n.): Person who talks to the spirits of people who have died

Menahem (n.): Wicked king of Israel who reigned after Shallum

Meshach (n.): Babylonian name of Mishael, who was with Daniel in exile in Babylon

Mephibosheth (n.): Son of Jonathan and grandson of Saul that David showed kindness

Messiah (n.): Hebrew word meaning "the Anointed One"; the prophets spoke of the Messiah as the one who was to come to deliver God's people; He was to have a kingly and a priestly role; Jesus Christ fulfilled all the prophecies of the Messiah

Messianic Psalm (n.): Psalm that talks about the Messiah who will come (Psalms 2, 22, 45, 72)

Micaiah (n.): Prophet in Israel during the reign of King Ahab

Micah (n.): Prophet of hope; prophesied in Judah during the reign of Hezekiah

Michal (n.): Daughter of King Saul and first wife of David

Mishael (n.): Hebrew name of one of Daniel's friends who was with Daniel in exile in Babylon

Mizpah (n.): City where Samuel called the people to repentance; location of the Ebenezer stone; city where Saul was anointed as king

Moabites (n.): Descendents of Moab, son of Lot and his first daughter; enemy of Israel

Molech (n.): Name of the chief god of the Ammonites

Mordecai (n.): Jewish man living in court of King Xerxes; cousin of Esther

Moses (n.): Man chosen by God to lead the Israelites out of Egypt and to the Promised Land

Mt. Carmel (n.): Mountain where Elijah challenged the prophets of Baal

Mt. Horeb (n.): Mountain where the LORD spoke to Elijah in a gentle whisper; also called the "mountain of God"

– N –

Naaman (n.): Commander of Ben-Hadad's army; Elisha healed him from leprosy

Naboth (n.): Man whose vineyard King Ahab coveted and then stole; Jezebel falsely accused him of blasphemy, and he was therefore stoned to death

Nadab (n.): Wicked king in Israel; Jeroboam's son

Nahum (n.): Prophet who prophesied destruction to Assyria; prophet of God's wrath

Nathan (n.): Prophet who spoke God's words to David

Nazirite (n.): Person set apart for God; he could not drink wine, cut his hair, or touch a dead body

Nebuchadnezzar (n.): King of Babylon who conquered Judah

Nehemiah (n.): Jewish man who was cupbearer to King Artaxerxes and went to Jerusalem to rebuild the city walls

Nineveh (n.): Capital of Assyria; city that repented after Jonah warned it of God's judgment

Nob (n.): Town where the tabernacle was located during Saul's reign; town where Doeg the Edomite killed eighty-five priests

– O –

Obadiah (n.): Prophet who prophesied disaster to Edom; prophet of Edom's disaster

Obed-Edom (n.): Man in whose house David kept the ark after Uzzah died

Omnipotence (n.): Having all power

Omniscience (n.): Having all knowledge

Omri (n.): Wicked king in Israel; father of King Ahab

– P –

Passover Psalm (n.): Psalm sung during the Passover meal (Psalms 113–118)

Pekah (n.): Wicked king of Israel who followed Pekahiah

Pekahiah (n.): Wicked king of Israel who reigned after Menahem

Peninnah (n.): Elkanah's second wife, who teased Hannah about her barrenness

Notes:

Persia (n.): Nation who conquered Babylon

Phinehas (n.): One of Eli's wicked sons

Philistines (n.): People from the Aegean Sea and Captor (Crete) who settled in Canaan; enemy of Israel

Pilgrim Psalm (n.): Psalm sung by the Israelites on their journeys to Jerusalem to worship (Psalms 120–134)

Priest (n.): Man in charge of offering sacrifices and offerings in the tabernacle

Prophet (n.): Person called to speak for God

Proverbs (n.): Book in the Old Testament that contains wise sayings and teaches wisdom through the fear of the LORD and godly choices

Providence of God (n.): God's holy, wise, and powerful preserving and governing of everything in His creation

Psalms (n.): Book in the Old Testament that contains Hebrew poetry for the worship and praise of God; also called the "Book of Praises"

Purim (n.): Feast celebrated by the Jews to remember their deliverance from the decree of King Xerxes to kill them

– Q –

Queen of Sheba (n.): Queen who heard of Solomon's wisdom and wealth and therefore came to visit him

– R –

Rehoboam (n.): Solomon's son who became the first king in the southern kingdom of Judah

Remnant (n.): The part left after the rest has been lost

Repeated (adj.): Type of Hebrew poetry in which the second line has a similar meaning to the first line

Repentance Psalm (n.): Psalm expressing sorrow for sin and asking for God's forgiveness (Psalms 6, 32, 51, 130)

– S –

Samaria (n.): Capital of the northern kingdom (Israel); city where Ahab built the temple to Baal

Samaritans (n.): People who lived in Samaria, the land that once belonged to Israel's ten tribes; they were enemies of the Jews who returned from exile

Samuel (n.): The last of the judges and the first of the great Old Testament prophets; means "heard of God"

Sanballat (n.): One of the three men who caused Nehemiah problems when Nehemiah was rebuilding the walls of Jerusalem

Saul (n.): Israel's first king; he was eventually rejected by God because of his disobedience

Sennacherib (n.): King of Assyria who captured Samaria and threatened Judah during the reign of Hezekiah

Shadrach (n.): Babylonian name of Hananiah, who was with Daniel in exile in Babylon

Sherebiah (n.): The Levite who went to Jerusalem with Ezra

Shalmaneser (n.): King of Assyria who conquered Israel in 722 BC

Shallum (n.): Wicked king of Israel who reigned one month

Shechem (n.): First capital of the northern kingdom of Israel

Sheba (n.): Man who led a revolt against David when he was king

Shiloh (n.): The place where the tabernacle was located during the days of Eli and Samuel

Shunammite woman (n.): Woman whose son was raised from the dead by Elisha

Solomon (n.): Second son of David and Bathsheba; king of Israel after David; means "peace"

Song of Songs (n.): Book in the Old Testament written by Solomon that celebrates the gift of God's love

Sons of Korah (n.): Writers of some of the book of Psalms

Sovereign (adj.): Possesses supreme power; controls all things

– T –

Tamar (n.): Sister of Absalom who was sinned against by her half brother Amnon

Tarshish (n.): City to which Jonah tried to flee when he was running away from God

Tekoa (n.): Hometown village of the prophet Amos

Thanksgiving Psalm (n.): Psalm thanking God for His mercy and answers to prayer (Psalms 18, 66, 107, 138)

Theophany (n.): An appearance of Jesus during Old Testament times, before He was born in Bethlehem

Tibni (n.): Wicked king of Israel who vied with Omri for the throne and lost

Tobiah (n.): One of the three men who caused problems for Nehemiah when he was rebuilding the walls of Jerusalem

Transgression (n.): The breaking of one of God's laws

– U –

Uriah (n.): Husband of Bathsheba killed in the battle with the Ammonites

Uzzah (n.): Son of Abinadab who guided the move of the ark from Abinadab's house; killed when he touched the ark to steady it

Uzziah (n.): Son of Amaziah who became king of Judah; also called Azariah; got leprosy after he offered incense in the temple

– V –

Valley of Elah (n.): Valley where David killed Goliath

Vashti (n.): Queen of the Persian king Xerxes

Notes:

– W –

Wisdom Psalm (n.): Psalm giving wise counsel to the godly and warning the ungodly (Psalms 1, 37, 49)

– X –

Xerxes (n.): Persian king who married the Jewish woman Esther

– Y –

Yahweh (n.): Hebrew word for the God who established a covenant with His people, Israel; same meaning as the word "Jehovah"

– Z –

Zadok (n.): Priest during the reign of David and Solomon; anointed Solomon to be king

Zarephath (n.): City where the widow lived who cared for Elijah

Zechariah (n.): Son of Jeroboam II; became king of Israel

Zechariah (n.): Son of the high priest Jehoiada; killed by Joash when he warned Joash of his sin

Zechariah (n.): Prophet who prophesied to the people in Jerusalem who had returned from exile; prophet of future glory

Zedekiah (n.): Son of Josiah who became king after Jehoiachin was removed by the Babylonians

Zephaniah (n.): Prophet to Judah during reign of Josiah; prophet of total destruction

Zerubbabel (n.): Governor and leader of the first group of Jews who returned to Jerusalem after the exile

Ziba (n.): Servant in Saul's household who told David about Mephibosheth

Zimri (n.): Wicked king in Israel who reigned for seven days; killed King Elah of Israel

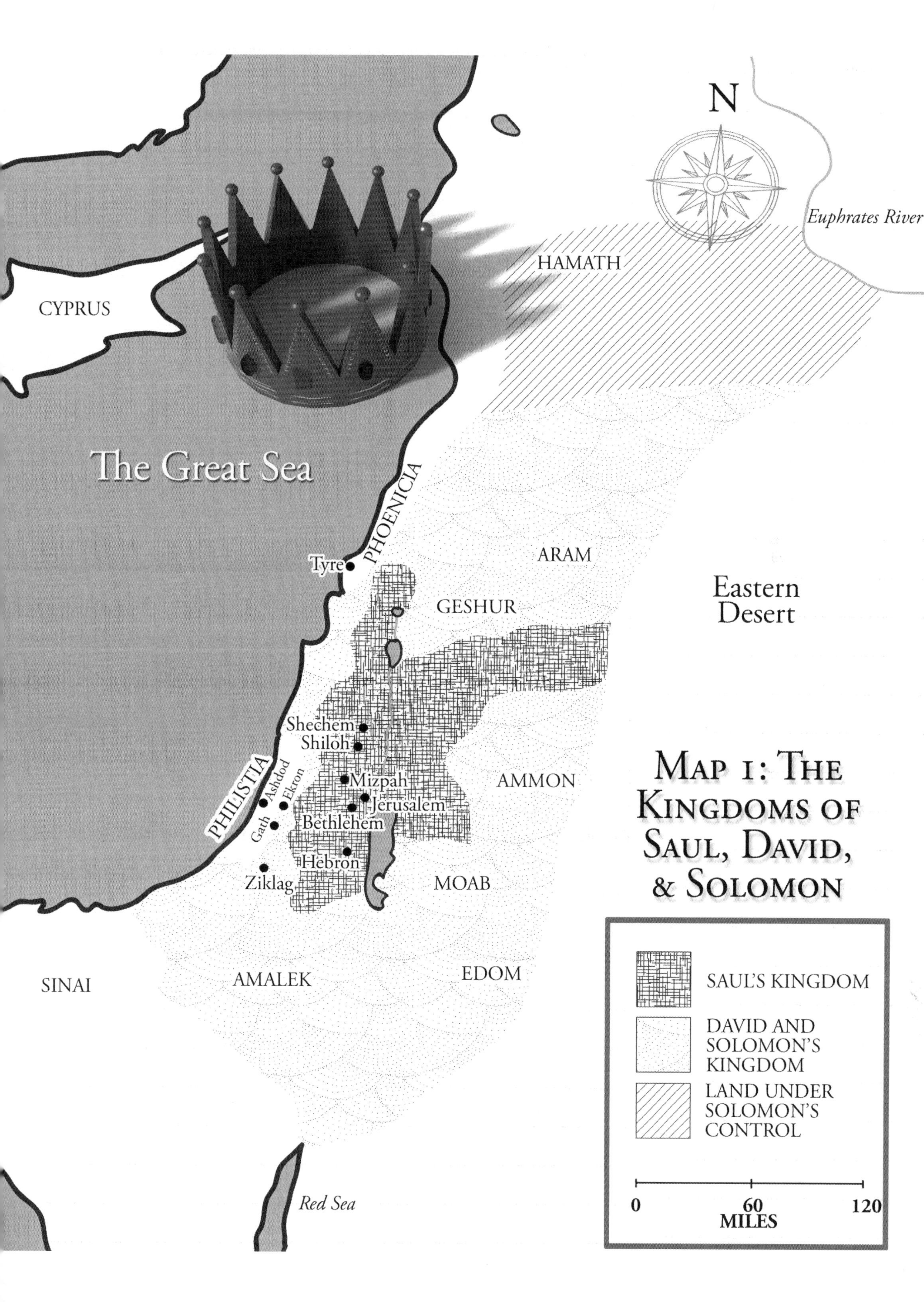
N
Euphrates River
HAMATH
CYPRUS
The Great Sea
PHOENICIA
Tyre
ARAM
GESHUR
Eastern
Desert
Shechem
Shiloh
PHILISTIA
Ashdod
Ekron
Mizpah
Jerusalem
Gath
Bethlehem
Hebron
Ziklag
AMMON
MOAB
MAP 1: THE KINGDOMS OF SAUL, DAVID, & SOLOMON
SINAI
AMALEK
EDOM
SAUL'S KINGDOM
DAVID AND SOLOMON'S KINGDOM
LAND UNDER SOLOMON'S CONTROL
0
60
120
MILES
Red Sea

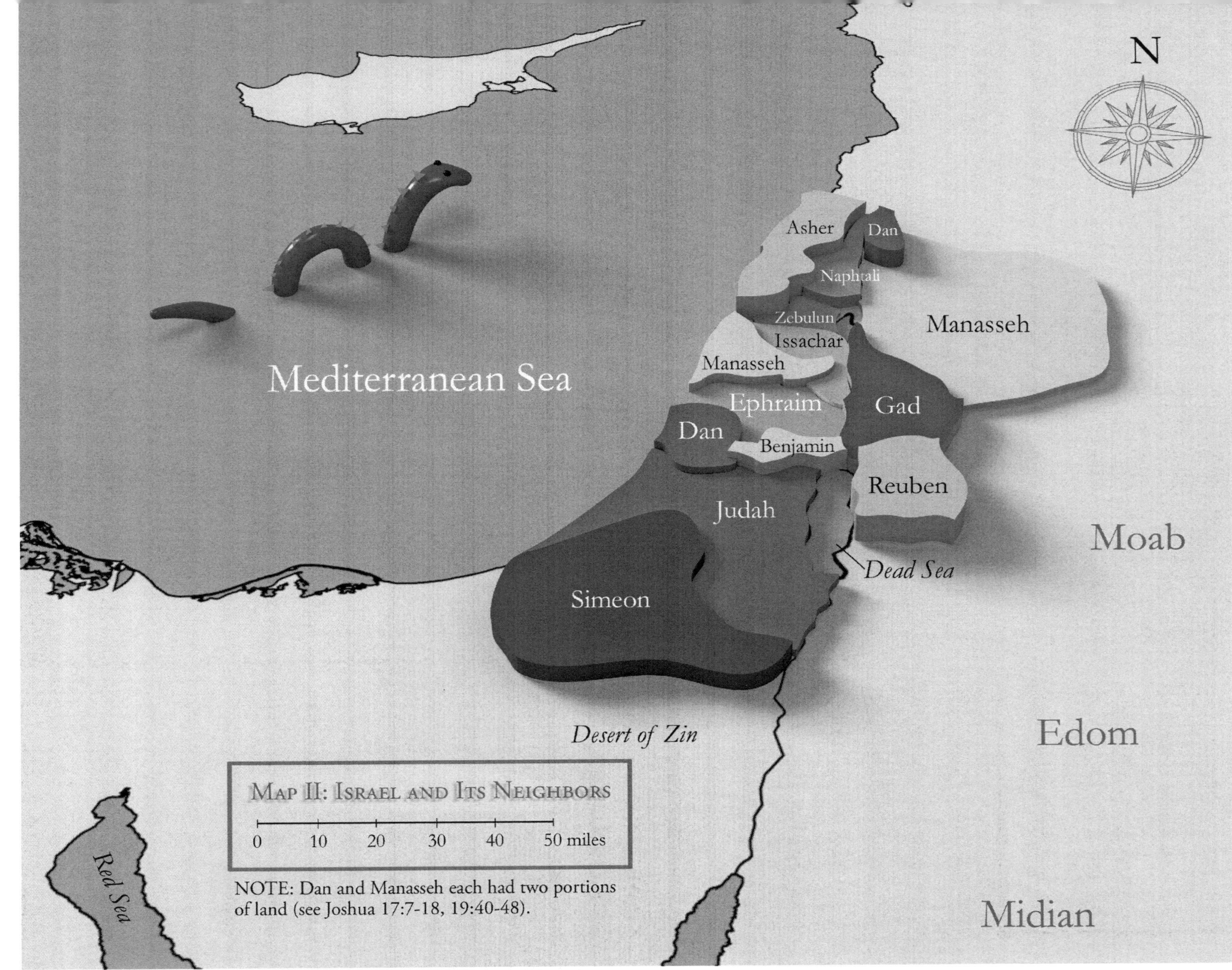
N
Mediterranean Sea
Asher
Dan
Naphtali
Zebulun
Issachar
Manasseh
Manasseh
Ephraim
Gad
Dan
Benjamin
Reuben
Judah
Moab
Dead Sea
Simeon
Desert of Zin
Edom
Red Sea
Midian
MAP II: ISRAEL AND ITS NEIGHBORS
0
10
20
30
40
50 miles
NOTE: Dan and Manasseh each had two portions of land (see Joshua 17:7-18, 19:40-48).

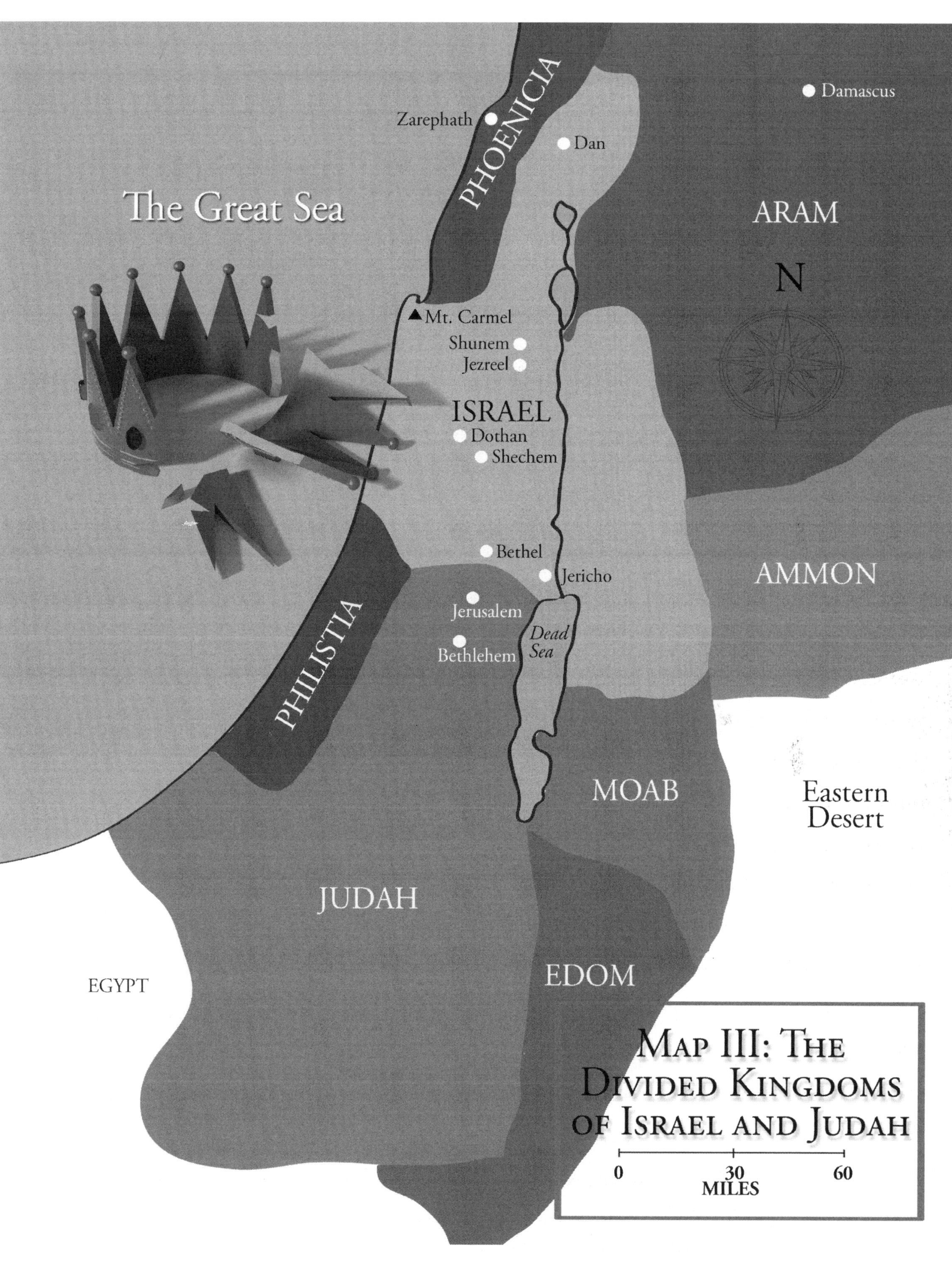

Map III: The Divided Kingdoms of Israel and Judah

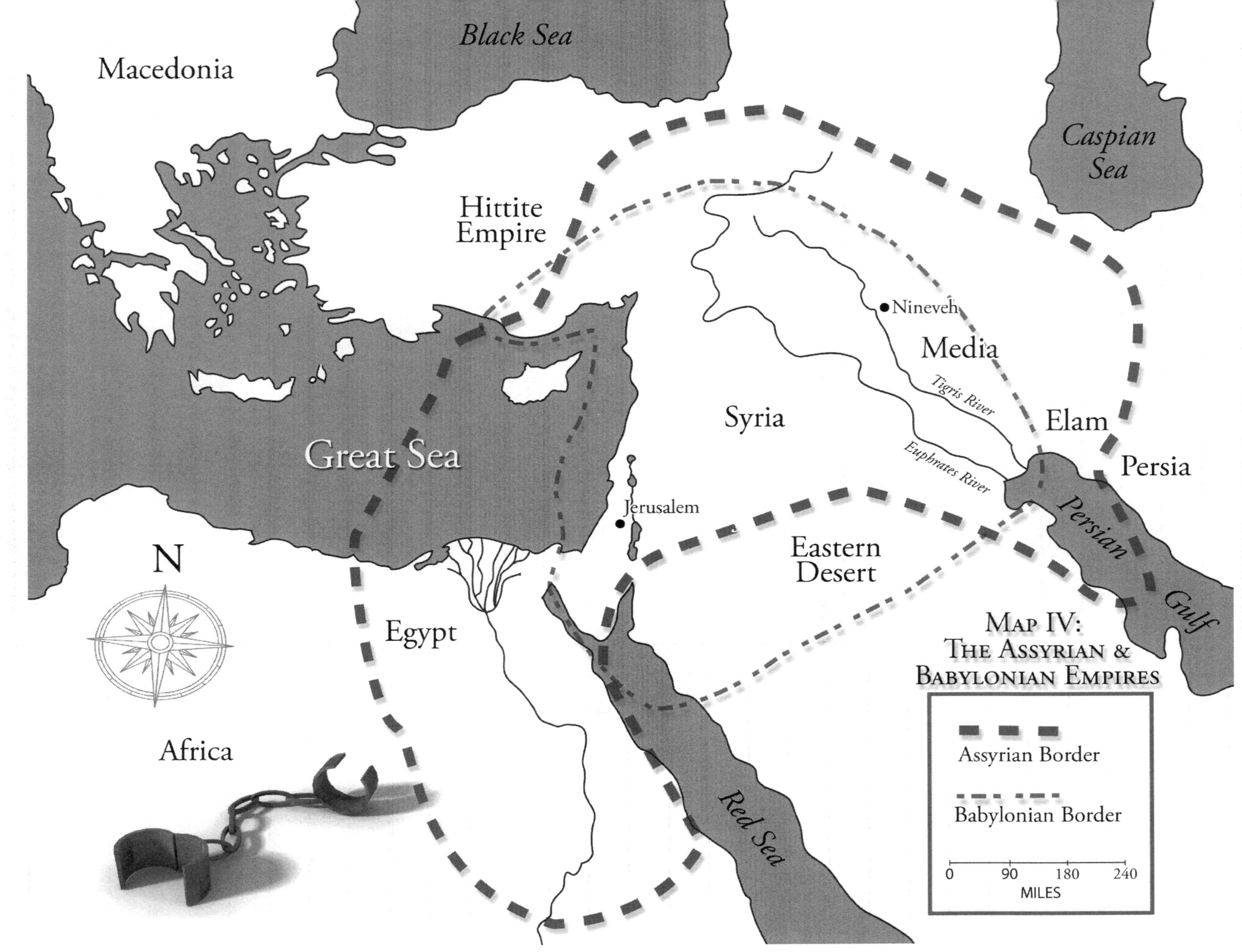
Black Sea
Macedonia
Caspian Sea
Hittite Empire
Nineveh
Media
Tigris River
Syria
Elam
Great Sea
Euphrates River
Persia
Jerusalem
Persian Gulf
N
Eastern Desert
Egypt
Map IV: The Assyrian & Babylonian Empires
Assyrian Border
Babylonian Border
Africa
Red Sea
0 90 180 240
MILES

Chapter 1 Quiz

A. MEMORY VERSE:

"In those days there was no ___king___ in Israel; everyone did what was ___right___ in his own ___eyes___." (Judges 21:25)

B. KEY FACTS: Circle "T" if the sentence is true and "F" if the sentence is false.

1. Samuel was a judge all the days of his life. (T) F
2. In his job as judge, Samuel offered sacrifices in the tabernacle. T (F)
3. Samuel judged Israel for only a few years. T (F)
4. Samuel was set apart to be a Nazirite before he was born. (T) F
5. Everyone in Israel knew that Samuel was called to be a prophet. (T) F

C. STORY FACTS: Cross out the word(s) that is/are not correct.

1. God's promise to be the God of His people is His (covenant/~~blessing~~).
2. The tabernacle was located in the city of (~~Shechem~~/Shiloh).
3. The LORD's message to Eli was a message of (~~blessing~~/judgment).
4. The word "anoint" means (chosen to serve/~~make sacrifices to~~) God.

D. WHO AM I? Use the names below to fill in the blanks.

Hannah Eli Samuel Phinehas The LORD

1. I was the priest at the tabernacle in Shiloh. ___Eli___
2. I called Samuel four times in one night. ___The LORD___
3. I prayed that the LORD would give me a son. ___Hannah___
4. Before I was born, I was set apart to serve the LORD. ___Samuel___
5. I was a wicked priest who sinned against God. ___Phinehas___

233

Notes:

Notes:

Across

3. A person called to speak for God is a ________________.
5. Eli ____________ God's judgement on his family.
8. Who called Samuel one night when he was in bed?
9. A person set apart to serve God is a _______.
10. Hannah prayed that God would give her a _______.

Down

1. A man who offered sacrifices is a __________.
2. God's promise to be the God of His people forever is His ____________.
4. A deliverer, peacemaker, and civil leader is a ________.
6. Judges 21:25 says that "everyone did what was right in his own ____________."
7. Elkanah's family worshipped at the tabernacle at ________.

Chapter 2 Quiz

A. MEMORY VERSE: "Remember the former things of old, For I am God, and there is no other; I am God, and there is none like Me." (Isaiah 46:9)

B. KEY FACTS: Number these events from 1 to 5 in the correct order.

The Ark of the Covenant's Journey

5 The ark was at Abinadab's house for 20 years.

2 The priests took the ark to the battlefield.

1 The ark sat in the tabernacle at Shiloh.

3 God sent rats and tumors to the people at Ekron and Gath.

4 The LORD destroyed the idol Dagon at Ashdod.

C. STORY FACTS: Fill in the blanks.

1. Eli fell backwards and died when he heard that the ark had been captured by the Philistines.
2. Phinehas' wife named her son Ichabod, meaning "the glory [of the LORD] has departed."
3. The LORD wanted Israel to know that He blessed those who obeyed Him and brought judgment to those who disobeyed Him.
4. The LORD sent a plague of rats and tumors to the Philistines in Ashdad, Gath, and Ekron.
5. Samuel called the memorial stone Ebenezer.
6. Dagon was the chief god of the Philistines.
7. When Samuel assembled the Israelites at Mizpah, they did two things:
   a. Confessed their sin.
   b. Sacrificed to the LORD.
8. The Philistines sent Israel a guilt offering of gold tumors.

Notes:

	1 M	I	Z	2 P	A	H													
				H															
				I		3 I													
				L		C													
				I		H				4 J	U	D	G	5 E					
				S		A								B					
6 G	U	I	L	T		B			7 B	8 A	T	T	L	E	F	I	E	L	D
				I		O				S				N					
	9 A	B	I	N	A	D	A	B	S	H	O	U	S	E					
				E						D				Z					
				S					10 N	O	N	E		E					
										D				R					

Across

1. Samuel assembled the people at _______.
4. Samuel ruled over Israel as a _______.
6. The Philistines sent a ________ offering of five gold tumors and five gold rats.
7. Where did the Israelites take the ark to give them good fortune?
9. Where did the ark stay for twenty years?
10. In Isaiah 46:9 God says "I am God, and there is __________ like me."

Down

2. The Israelites moved the ark from Shiloh to the battlefield because they thought it would protect them from the ____________?
3. What name means "the glory of the Lord has departed"?
5. What name means "thus far has the Lord helped us"?
8. Where was Dagon's temple located?

Chapter 3 Quiz

A. MEMORY VERSE: "Behold, to ___obey___ is better than sacrifice,

And to ___heed___ than the fat of rams." (1 Samuel 15:22b)

B. KEY FACTS: Draw a line from the nation to the phrase that describes it.

Israel's Neighbors

Amalek	Ehud defeated King Eglon from this nation.
Ammon	This nation captured the ark.
Edom	Agag was this nation's king.
Moab	Esau was the founder of this nation.
Philistia	Defeating them led to accepting Saul as king

C. STORY FACTS: Cross out the **wrong** answer.

1. The Lord said that the people were rejecting (~~Samuel~~/the Lord).
2. Saul was looking for his father's (donkeys/~~sheep~~).
3. Samuel's sons were (wicked/~~righteous~~) men.
4. Samuel was (~~pleased~~/sad) that the Israelites wanted a king.
5. Saul was (~~eager~~/reluctant) to become Israel's first king.
6. After the battle with the Ammonites, the people had (~~doubts~~/no doubts) that Saul should be king.
7. Saul could not make a sacrifice because he was not a (priest/~~prophet~~).
8. Because Saul disobeyed, God said He would take away Saul's (~~army~~/kingdom).
9. Samuel said that (obedience/~~sacrifice~~) was the better way to please God.
10. The Lord was (~~pleased~~/grieved) that He had made Saul king in Israel.

Notes:

															1 P
		2 E	G	L	3 O	N				4 A	G	A	G		R
		D			B					M					I
		O			E					M					E
		M			D				5 D	O	N	K	E	Y	S
				6 K	I	N	G			N					T
					E					I					
7 C	O	M	M	A	N	D	M	E	N	T	S				
					C					E					
		8 T	H	R	E	E				S					

Across

2. Who was the king of Moab?
4. Who was the king of the Amalekites?
5. What was Saul looking for when Samuel anointed him?
6. The Israelites demanded to have a ________.
7. In John 14:15 Jesus says "If you love Me, you will keep My __________."
8. Saul was anointed ________ times.

Down

1. Saul was not allowed to make sacrifices because he was not a ________.
2. Esau was the founder of ________.
3. What does the LORD say is better than sacrifice?
4. What was the nation that Jephthah fought and defeated?

Chapter 4 Quiz

A. MEMORY VERSE: "For the Lord does not see as ___man___ sees; for man looks at the ___outward___ ___appearance___, but the Lord looks at the ___heart___." (1 Samuel 16:7b)

B. KEY FACTS: Draw a line from the type of psalm to the words that best describe its purpose.

Types of Psalms

Repentance Psalm	Gives good advice
Hallelujah Psalm	Sung on a journey
Pilgrim Psalm	Confesses sin
Judgment Psalm	Praises God
Wisdom Psalm	Requests justice

C. STORY FACTS: Circle "T" for true or "F" for false.

1. Samuel was happy that the Lord rejected Saul as king. T (F)
2. David's family lived in the city of Jerusalem. T (F)
3. Psalm 119 is the longest psalm in the Bible. (T) F
4. The Lord chose David even though he was Jesse's youngest son. (T) F
5. While watching the sheep, David killed a lion and a wolf. T (F)

D. WHAT DO YOU REMEMBER? Circle the **correct** answer.

1. God's plan ________________.
   (is always good) depends upon our choices
2. A distressing spirit came upon Saul because __________.
   he worried too much (the Lord had left him)
3. In God's time, David would one day rule over Israel because ___________.
   he was handsome and strong (he had a godly heart)
4. David would be a good king for Israel because _______________.
   (he served God as his King) he was a brave man

Notes:

1 B																				
O																				
O																				
K																				
O																2 H				
F																I				
3 P	I	L	G	4 R	I	M						5 J		6 W	I	S	D	O	M	
R				E						7 P		U				T				
A				P						A		D				O				
I				E						S		G				R				
S				N						S		8 M	E	S	S	I	A	N	I	C
E				T						O		E				C				
S		9 T	H	A	N	K	S	G	I	V	I	N	G			A				
				N						E		T				L				
				C						R										
10 H	A	L	L	E	L	U	J	A	H											

Across

3. What type of psalm is sung on journeys to Jerusalem?
6. What type of psalm gives wise counsel
8. What type of psalm talks about the Messiah?
9. What type of psalm thanks God for His mercy?
10. What type of psalm gives praise to God?

Down

1. What is the Hebrew title for Psalms?
2. What type of psalm reminds Israel of what God did?
4. What type of psalm expresses sorrow over sin?
5. What type of psalm asks God to judge the wicked?
7. What type of psalm is sung during the Passover meal?

Chapter 5 Quiz

A. MEMORY VERSE: "In God I ___trust___; I will not be ___afraid___. What can mortal ___man___ do to me?" (Psalm 56:4b, NIV)

B. KEY FACTS: Put an "X" in front of the sentences that are true.

__X__ David trusted the LORD by faith.

_____ When facing Goliath, David put his confidence in his slingshot skills.

__X__ David was successful because the LORD gave him success.

_____ Saul sent David to battle so people would sing David's praises.

__X__ Saul threw spears at David because he was jealous of David.

__X__ David played music for Saul even after Saul tried to kill him.

__X__ When David went to battle, God gave him victory over his enemies.

_____ Jonathan refused to help David escape from Saul's anger.

C. STORY FACTS: Circle the **correct** answer.

1. David wanted to accept Goliath's challenge because Goliath _________.
   had insulted King Saul — (had defied Israel's God)
2. David was confident when he faced Goliath one-on-one because _______.
   (the LORD was with him) — he had good slingshot skills
3. Saul was jealous of David because _______________.
   (all the people praised David) — David played the lyre well
4. Saul was afraid of David because ___________________.
   the people praised David — (the LORD was with David)
5. The message of Jonathan's three arrows was ___________________.
   Saul didn't want to kill David — (Saul did want to kill David)

Notes:

				1 J									
	2 G			E						3 K			
4 M	O	R	T	A	L		5 M			I		6 T	
	L			L			7 I	D	O	L		H	
	I		8 S	O	N		C			9 L	O	R	D
	A			U			H					E	
	T			10 S	P	E	A	R				E	
	H						L						

Across

4. Psalm 56:4b says "What can ______ man do to me?"
7. What did David's wife put in the bed to trick Saul's soldiers?
8. Jonathan was Saul's ________.
9. David put his trust in the ___________.
10. What did Saul throw at David?

Down

1. The women's praise of David made Saul _________.
2. Who did David kill with one stone?
3. Saul's intention was to ______ David.
5. Who was David's wife?
6. How many arrows did Jonathan shoot to warn David?

Chapter 6 Quiz

A. MEMORY VERSES: "For the word of the LORD is ___right___, And all His work is done in ___truth___. He loves ___righteousness___ and ___justice___; The earth is full of the ___goodness___ of the LORD." (Psalm 33:4-5)

B. KEY FACTS: Match the word on the left with its meaning on the right.

__4__ Fortress	1. God gives you strength.
__5__ King	2. God cares for you perfectly.
__7__ Light	3. God never changes.
__3__ Rock	4. God is a strong, safe place to hide.
__2__ Shepherd	5. God is in charge of the whole world.
__6__ Shield	6. God defends you from your enemies.
__1__ Strength	7. God shows you the right thing to do.

C. STORY FACTS: Cross out the **wrong** word and put the **correct** word in the blank at the end of the sentence.

1. ~~Abiathar~~ killed the eighty-five priests at Nob. ___Doeg___
2. At Gath the Philistines thought David was ~~silly~~. ___insane___
3. David secretly took Saul's spear and ~~shield~~. ___water jug___
4. When David was in hiding, the tabernacle was located at ~~Shiloh~~. ___Nob___
5. Ahimelech gave David consecrated ~~meat~~ to eat. ___bread___
6. Ahimelech also gave David Goliath's ~~helmet~~. ___sword___
7. Saul went to a ~~prophet~~ to get advice before the battle. ___medium___

D. WHAT'S THE POINT? Complete these sentences.

David knew that the LORD's plan was ___right___ and ___good___.

He had to ___wait___ patiently for the LORD's will to happen.

Notes:

			1 M		2 L	I	3 G	H	T												
			E				O														
			D				O														
4 A	N	O	I	N	T	E	D														
			U				N					5 R								6 S	
			M				E					I								H	
							7 S	T	R	E	N	G	T	H						I	
							S					H						8 G		E	
												9 T	A	B	E	R	N	A	C	L	E
																		T		D	
															10 Z	I	P	H			

Across

2. David depicts God as __________ because He shows His people the right thing to do.
4. David did not kill Saul because Saul was God's ________________.
7. When you feel weak and helpless, God is your _____________.
9. Ahimelech gave David consecrated bread from the ________________.
10. In what hills did David and his men hide?

Down

1. Saul visited a ______________ to get advice.
3. Psalm 33:5 says "The earth is full of the __________ of the LORD."
5. Psalm 33:4 says "For the word of the Lord is ______."
6. God is like a ______________ because He protects His people from their enemies.
8. Where did David pretend to be insane?

244

Chapter 7 Quiz

A. MEMORY VERSE: Cross out the **wrong** word.

1. "To obey is better than (~~worship~~/sacrifice)." (1 Samuel 15:22b)
2. "The earth is full of the (goodness/~~lovingkindness~~) of the LORD." (Psalm 33:5)
3. "In those days there was no (king/~~judge~~) in Israel." (Judges 21:25)
4. "In God I (trust/~~hope~~); I will not be (~~sad~~/afraid)." (Psalm 56:4b, NIV)
5. "The LORD looks at the (heart/~~outward appearance~~)." (1 Samuel 16:7b)

B. STORY FACTS: Circle "T" for true and "F" for false.

1. The LORD was faithful to David because he never sinned. T (F)
2. Israel wanted a king so it could be like other nations. (T) F
3. The covenant is God's promise to be the God of His people. (T) F
4. A judgment psalm asks God for forgiveness of sin. T (F)
5. Pilgrim psalms were sung at the Passover meal. T (F)
6. The LORD rejected Saul because Saul didn't obey God as King. (T) F
7. David killed Goliath with Saul's sword. T (F)
8. David refused to kill Saul because he was God's anointed king. (T) F

C. WHICH OF THESE GO TOGETHER? Match the things on the right with the correct description on the left.

5 Samuel	1. A Philistine god
7 Saul	2. Means "thus far has the LORD helped us"
4 Jonathan	3. Priest at the tabernacle in Shiloh
2 Ebenezer	4. David's loyal friend
6 Ichabod	5. Last judge of Israel
3 Eli	6. Means "the glory [of the LORD] has departed from Israel"
1 Dagon	7. First king of Israel

Notes:

				R																	
S	A	M	U	E	L																
				P														C			
				E		J	O	N	A	T	H	A	N				N	O	B		
		H		A					G									V			
		O	U	T	W	A	R	D	A	P	P	E	A	R	A	N	C	E			
		L		E					G									N	I	N	E
		Y		D														A			
									R	I	G	H	T	E	O	U	S	N	E	S	S
																		T			

Across

2. Who was the last judge in Israel?
4. Who was a loyal friend of David?
6. In what town were eighty-five priests killed?
8. 1 Samuel 16:7b says that "Man looks at the ____________ ____________, but the LORD looks at the heart."
9. How many feet tall was the giant Goliath?
10. According to Psalm 33:4-5, the LORD loves ________________ and justice.

Down

1. If the second line in a Hebrew poem has a similar meaning to the first line, then it is part of what category?
3. God's promise to be the God of His people forever is His ________________.
5. Who was the king that Saul didn't kill?
7. If something is "set apart by God" then it is _________.

Chapter 8 Quiz

A. MEMORY VERSE: "I have made a covenant with My chosen, I have sworn to My servant David: 'Your seed I will establish forever, And build up your throne to all generations.'" (Psalm 89:3-4)

B. KEY FACTS: Fill in the blanks below.

1. What four things about the covenant with David were like the covenant with Abraham?

   son land name blessing

2. God promised David that his son would build the temple.
3. The Messiah would be born from David's line.
4. God said that David's kingdom would endure forever.
5. The everlasting kingdom is the kingdom of Jesus Christ.

C. STORY FACTS: Circle the **correct** answer.

1. David was anointed king of Judah in the city of ________.

   Jerusalem (Hebron) Shiloh

2. Joab killed Abner because Abner killed ________.

   (Asahel) Ishbosheth Uzzah

3. The Lord told Nathan that ________ would build the temple.

   David (David's son) Obed-Edom

4. Uzzah was killed when the ark was moved because ________.

   people were dancing Uzzah laughed (Uzzah touched it)

D. WHAT'S THE POINT? Complete these sentences.

The covenant with David promised David a great name, and a kingdom that would last forever. God also promised that the Messiah would come from David's line.

Notes:

Across

3. The Lord promised that David's son would build God a __________.
6. The everlasting kingdom is the kingdom of ______________.
8. Who was the prophet that told David not to build a temple?
9. Who touched the ark and died?
10. What city did David make his capital?

Down

1. In what city was David first crowned king?
2. In Psalm 89:4 the Lord says to David that He will "build up your throne to all __________________."
4. The Lord promised that the __________________ would be born from David's line.
5. David eventually became king of _______.
7. Who was Saul's commander?

Chapter 9 Quiz

A. MEMORY VERSE: "Blessed is he whose __transgression__ is forgiven, Whose __sin__ is covered." (Psalm 32:1)

B. KEY FACTS: Fill in the blanks.

When David sinned…

1. He stayed home while his army went to __war__.
2. He loved another man's __wife__.
3. He __killed__ Uriah and then __married__ Bathsheba.

When God showed His grace to David…

1. God sent __Nathan__ to confront David.
2. David __repented__, and God __forgave__ him.
3. Even though he was forgiven, David had to bear consequences from his __sin__.

C. STORY FACTS: Match the word on the left with its description on the right.

_5_ Mephibosheth		1. Husband of Bathsheba killed in battle
_4_ Ziba		2. Prophet who confronted David
_6_ Joab		3. Woman whom David loved too much
_2_ Nathan		4. Servant of Saul's household
_3_ Bathsheba		5. Son of Jonathan
_1_ Uriah		6. Commander of David's army

D. WHAT'S TRUE AND WHAT'S NOT? Circle "T" for true, and "F" for false.

1. David showed kindness instead of revenge to Mephibosheth. (T) F
2. By his own words, David condemned himself for his sin. (T) F
3. The Lord opened David's eyes to his sin. (T) F

249

Notes:

1 A					2 R				3 M	E	P	H	I	B	O	4 S	H	E	T	H
M					E											T				
M					P											5 U	R	I	A	H
O					E								6 J	O	A	B				
7 N	A	T	8 H	A	N											B				
I			E		9 T	R	A	N	S	G	R	E	S	S	I	O	N			
T			A		E											R				
E			R		D			10 C	O	N	S	E	Q	U	E	N	C	E	S	
S			T																	

Across

3. David showed kindness to __________________ because of his friendship with Jonathan.
5. When __________ refused to go home to be with his wife, David plotted to have him killed.
6. Who was David's chief commander?
7. God sent ____________ to confront David with his sin.
9. Psalm 31:1 says "Blessed is he whose ______________ is forgiven"
10. David had to bear the _____________ of his sin, and his son died.

Down

1. In the spring, David should have led his army against the ________________.
2. David ______________ after he heard Nathan's story about the rich man.
4. David had a ___________ heart and refused to repent for a long time.
8. David was a man after God's __________.

250

Chapter 10 Quiz

A. MEMORY VERSE: "But You, O LORD, are a shield for me,
My glory and the One who lifts up my head.... I
lay down and slept; I awoke,
for the LORD sustained me." (Psalm 3:3, 5)

B. KEY FACTS: Number (1-7) the events in the **correct** order.

2 Absalom killed Amnon when Amnon was not punished for his sin.

5 Sheba revolted against David, and eleven tribes rejected David.

3 Absalom plotted to take the kingdom from his father, David.

7 David ordered a census to count the number of fighting men.

6 Joab killed Amasa and then pursued Sheba to kill him.

4 Joab killed Absalom in battle.

1 Amnon sinned against his half sister Tamar.

C. STORY FACTS: Circle the **correct** answer.

1. David had troubles in his family and in his kingdom because _________.
   God was angry with him — (his sin had consequences)
2. When Amnon sinned against Tamar, David _______________.
   (did nothing) — punished him severely
3. David made Amasa commander of his army because __________.
   Joab was not loyal to him — (he wanted to win back Israel)
4. When David took a census of fighting men, he was trusting in ________.
   the LORD's strength — (the strength of his army)
5. David was a king who pleased the LORD because he ____________.
   showed kindness to people — (remembered God was King)

Notes:

						1 S	H	I	E	L	D				
						I									
						C						2 E			
		3 A		4 A		5 K	I	N	G			6 L	O	R	D
7 S	O	L	O	M	O	N						E			
		T		A		E				8 J		V			
		A		S		S				O		E			
		R		A		9 S	U	S	T	A	I	N	E	D	
										B					

Across

1. "But You, O Lord, are a ____________ for me..." (Psalm 3:3)
5. David pleased God because he remembered that the LORD was the real _______ of Israel.
6. When David took a census, he was trusting in the strength of his army instead of in the ____________.
7. Who was the son of David and Bathsheba?
9. "I lay down and slept; I awoke for the LORD ______________ me." (Psalm 3:5)

Down

1. After David sinned and ordered the census, he chose three days of ____________ as a consequence.
2. How many tribes followed Sheba?
3. David worshipped God by building an _______.
4. Who was the commander that replaced Joab?
8. Who killed Absalom?

Chapter 11 Quiz

A. MEMORY VERSE: "The ___fear___ of the LORD is the beginning of ___wisdom___, And the knowledge of the ___Holy___ ___One___ is ___understanding___." (Proverbs 9:10)

B. KEY FACTS: Cross out the **wrong** word(s) in each sentence and write the **correct** word(s) in the blank beside it.

1. ~~Psalms~~ is the book that teaches us how to be wise. ___Proverbs___
2. The Preacher tells us to find purpose in ~~fame and possessions~~. ___the fear of God___
3. Most of the book of ~~Proverbs~~ was written by David. ___Psalms___
4. Song of Songs tells you to celebrate God's gift of ~~wisdom~~. ___love___
5. Job teaches you how to trust God in times of ~~happiness~~. ___suffering___

C. STORY FACTS: Circle "T" if the sentence is true and "F" is the sentence is false.

1. Nathan and Zadok anointed Solomon as king. (T) F
2. To fear God means God's children should be terrified of God. T (F)
3. Job never asked God why he was suffering. T (F)
4. The woman willing to give up the child was the real mother. (T) F
5. When God came to Solomon in a dream, Solomon asked for joy. T (F)
6. The Old Testament has five books of poetry. (T) F
7. Solomon was wiser than the greatest wise men of Egypt. (T) F

D. WHO AM I? Match the person with the description.

__2__ Solomon	1. Solomon's mother
__4__ Adonijah	2. David's son who became king
__5__ Agur	3. Priest who anointed Solomon
__3__ Zadok	4. David's son who schemed to be king
__1__ Bathsheba	5. Man who wrote a few Proverbs

Notes:

								1 C														
								U														
								R														
								S														
								E		2 P						3 S						
						4 U	N	D	E	R	S	T	5 A	N	D	I	N	G				
					6 W					O			S			N						
					I					V			A			7 F	E	A	R	I	N	G
8 E	C	C	L	E	S	I	A	S	T	E	S		P			U						
					D					R			H			L						
9 V	I	R	T	U	O	U	S			B												
					M					10 S	O	L	O	M	O	N						

Across

4. "And the knowledge of the Holy One is ____________." (Psalm 9:10)
7. Wisdom begins with ____________ God.
8. What Old Testament book is about finding purpose in the fear of God?
9. Proverbs 31 descibes the ______________ woman.
10. Who wrote Song of Songs?

Down

1. Job never __________ God.
2. What Old Testament book is about being wise and making good choices?
3. Job's friends said he was suffering because he was ________________.
5. David, the Sons of Korah, and _____________ wrote Psalms.
6. "The fear of the LORD is the beginning of ____________." (Psalm 9:10)

Chapter 12 Quiz

A. MEMORY VERSE: "Praise be to the LORD, who has given rest to his people Israel just as he promised. Not one word has failed of all the good promises he gave through his servant Moses." (1 Kings 8:56, NIV)

B. KEY FACTS: Circle the **correct** answer.

1. God wanted Solomon to have an ______ heart before Him.
   (upright) honest fearful
2. God said he would establish Solomon's ____ forever if he obeyed God.
   wisdom temple (throne)
3. If Solomon worshipped idols, then the LORD would reject ______.
   Solomon's family (the consecrated temple) the Israelites
4. If Solomon turned from the LORD, then other nations would ____ Israel.
   (laugh at) give gifts to attack

C. STORY FACTS: Fill in the blanks.

1. David couldn't build the temple because he had been a warrior.
2. Hiram, king of Tyre, gave Solomon cedars for the temple.
3. Building the temple took seven years.
4. The queen of Sheba heard of Solomon's fame and visited him.
5. Ahijah told Jeroboam that someday he would rule ten tribes.

D. HOW DID SOLOMON SIN? Write a sentence about one way that Solomon sinned against the LORD.

Solomon married many wives of foreign nations. He built altars on the high places to worship idols.

Notes:

```
      P I L L A R S
      R           E
      O           V
      M     F     E
   U  I   C O V E N A N T
 S P  S     R       H
T H I R T E E N     R       I
 E I  D     I       J
 B G        G       A
 A H        N       H
   T Y R E
```

Across

1. The names of the two temple __________ were Boaz and Jachin.
5. The LORD was angry with Solomon because he forgot the ________________.
8. How many years did it take to build the palace?
9. Hiram of ________ gave Solomon cedars of Lebanon for the temple.

Down

1. "Praise be to the LORD, who has given rest to his people Israel just as he ________________." (1 Kings 8:56)
2. How many years did it take to build the temple?
3. One way Solomon sinned against the LORD was by marrying ________ wives.
4. God's covenant with Solomon required Solomon to have an ______________ heart and obey God.
6. The prophet _______ told Jeroboam he would rule ten tribes.
7. The Queen of _________ heard of Solomon's fame and visited him.

Chapter 13 Quiz

A. MEMORY VERSE: Use the words in the box to answer the questions below. Use the words only once.

Holy One | My chosen | The LORD | His people | Servant David

1. To whom did the LORD swear, "I will establish your seed." Servant David
2. The knowledge of whom gives understanding? Holy One
3. To whom did the LORD make a covenant? My chosen
4. To whom did the LORD give rest? His people
5. Who is the One that sustains me when I lay down and sleep? The LORD

B. STORY FACTS: Fill in the blanks with the correct answers.

1. Because David was a warrior, he couldn't build the temple.
2. Uzzah was killed when he touched the ark because the ark was holy.
3. Blessed means being contented because God is pleased with you.
4. Fearing God means respecting and being in awe of God.
5. When God appeared to Solomon in a dream, Solomon asked for wisdom.
6. Satan wanted Job to curse God, but Job never did.
7. Solomon loved his many wives and began to worship idols.

C. WHICH OF THESE GO TOGETHER? Match these things.

4 Joab	1. Prophet who spoke to David
3 Ishbosheth	2. Author of Ecclesiastes
5 Absalom	3. Saul's son who was king briefly
6 Molech	4. Commander of David's army
1 Nathan	5. David's rebellious son
2 The Preacher	6. God of the Ammonites

Notes:

		1 S				2 B							
		O				R							
	3 B	L	E	S	S	E	D			4 G			
		O				A		5 L	Y	R	E		
6 N	A	M	E			K				E			
		O				I		7 F		A			8 W
		N		9 L		N		I		T			I
			10 F	O	R	G	I	V	E	N	E	S	S
				V				E		E			D
				E						S			O
										S			M

Across

3. What word means “contented because God is pleased with you”?
5. What instrument did David play?
6. God promised to make David’s _______ great.
10. God blesses us by giving ____________ for sins.

Down

1. Who built the temple?
2. Transgression is the ___________ of one of God’s laws.
4. After God asked Job question upon question, Job was overwhelmed by God’s ____________.
7. How many books of poetry are in the Old Testament?
8. Solomon was the wisest of all men because he asked God for ___________.
9. Song of Songs celebrates God’s gift of ________.

258

Chapter 14 Quiz

A. MEMORY VERSE: "[They] exchanged the ___truth___ of God for the ___lie___, and ___worshipped___ and ___served___ the creature rather than the ___Creator___, who is blessed ___forever___. Amen." (Romans 1:25)

B. KEY FACTS: Match the words with their descriptions.

__2__ King Rehoboam	1. Prophet in Israel
__1__ Ahijah	2. Solomon's son who became king
__5__ Bethel	3. First capital of Israel
__7__ King Asa	4. King who made golden calves
__4__ King Jeroboam	5. A worship center in Israel
__3__ Shechem	6. Capital of Judah
__6__ Jerusalem	7. A godly king of Judah

C. STORY FACTS: Circle "T" for true and "F" for false.

1. After Rehoboam became king, the people's lives were easier. T (F)
2 Jeroboam wanted his people to worship in Jerusalem. T (F)
3. Ahijah had prophesied that Jeroboam would be king in Israel. (T) F
4. Asa's heart was committed to worshipping the LORD. (T) F
5. Israel's neighbors thought Omri was an impressive king. (T) F
6. Rehoboam listened to the advice of the older, wise men. T (F)
7. Jeroboam was more evil than all who had lived before him. (T) F

D. WHY WAS ASA A GODLY KING?

Write one thing that Asa did that pleased the LORD:

He smashed the foreign altars and removed the detestable idols.

Notes:

						1 W	I	2 F	E							
								O								
	3 Y		4 I		5 H			R								
6 W	O	R	S	H	I	P	P	E	D							
	U		R		G			I								
	N		A		H			G			7 B					
	G		E		T			8 N	A	D	A	B			9 J	
			L		A						A				U	
					X						S				D	
					E				10 R	E	H	O	B	O	A	M
					S						A				H	

Across

1. Jeroboam sent his ________ to Ahijah to ask for his son's healing.
6. "They exchanged the truth of God for the lie, and ________ and served the creature rather than the Creator..." (Romans 1:25)
8. What was the name of Jeroboam's son who ruled after him?
10. Who was Solomon's son?

Down

2. Because Asa was committed to them Lord, he smashed _________ altars and removed idols.
3. Rehoboam took the advice of the ________ men.
4. Ahab was a king of ______________.
5. When Rehoboam became king, the people got upset about the ______ ______ and harsh labor.
7. Who plotted against and killed Jeroboam's family?
9. Jehoshaphat was a king of ______________.

Chapter 15 Quiz

A. MEMORY VERSE: "The steps of a good man are ordered by the LORD, And He delights in his way. Though he fall, he shall not be utterly cast down; For the LORD upholds him with His hand." (Psalm 37:23-24)

B. KEY FACTS: Answer the questions below.

1. What did God stop in Israel for several years? rain and dew
2. Who did Elijah bring back to life? widow's son
3. What did God provide for the widow to eat? flour and oil
4. What was the name of Ahab's wicked wife? Jezebel
5. How did the LORD speak to encourage Elijah? in a gentle whisper

C. STORY FACTS: Match the words/numbers with their description.

8 Rain	1. What fell down on Elijah's sacrifice
11 Flour and oil	2. Person Elijah brought back to life
7 450	3. Times water was poured on sacrifice
9 Mt. Carmel	4. Where the LORD encouraged Elijah
3 Three	5. What the ravens brought Elijah to eat
4 Mt. Horeb	6. Person who wanted to kill Elijah
6 Jezebel	7. Number of prophets of Baal
2 Widow's son	8. What didn't fall in Israel for several years
10 Widow from Zarephath	9. Where Elijah challenged Baal's prophets
5 Bread and meat	10. Person who provided food for Elijah
1 Fire	11. What God provided for the widow

D. WHY WAS AHAB A WICKED KING?

Write one way that Ahab sinned against the LORD.

He married Jezebel, a worshipper of Baal, and built a temple to Baal.

Notes:

									1 W	A	T	E	R				
									H								
									I			2 B					
							3 S		S		4 R	A	V	E	N	S	
							L		P			A					
						5 J	E	Z	E	B	E	L					
							E		R								
					6 F		P										
	7 R				L		I										
8 C	A	S	T	D	O	W	N										
	I				U		9 G	O	O	D							
	N				R												

Across

1. What did Elijah have poured on his sacrifice three times?
4. The LORD sent ________ to bring food to Elijah.
5. Who was the wife of Ahab?
8. "Though he fall, he shall not be utterly __________ __________..." (Psalm 37:24)
9. "The steps of a ________ man are ordered by the LORD..." (Psalm 37:23)

Down

1. God spoke to Elijah in a _______________.
2. Abah was more wicked than Jeroboam because he built a temple for _______.
3. Elijah said, "Shout louder. Maybe your god is ______________."
6. Elijah promised the widow would always have _______ and oil to make bread.
7. When Elijah spoke the words from God, the ______ and dew stopped for several years.

Chapter 16 Quiz

A. MEMORY VERSE: "Many are the plans in a man's heart, but it is the LORD's purpose that prevails." (Proverbs 19:21, NIV)

B. KEY FACTS: Circle "T" for true and "F" for false.

1. Jehoshaphat turned his people back to the LORD. (T) F
2. Ahab put the prophet Jehu in prison. T (F)
3. Ahab followed in the ways of King Jeroboam. (T) F
4. Jehoshaphat was always in battle with neighboring nations. T (F)
5. The nation of Aram attacked Judah several times. T (F)
6. Jehoshaphat prayed before he went to battle with his enemies. (T) F
7. Ahab built a temple to worship the Canaanite god, Baal. (T) F

C. STORY FACTS: Circle the **correct** answer.

1. The prophet said that Ahab would die because he _______.
   (refused to kill Ben-Hadad) — took Naboth's vineyard
2. When he wanted to go to war with Aram, Ahab listened to _______.
   (400 prophets) — the prophet Micaiah
3. Jezebel's false witnesses accused Naboth of _______.
   stealing from the king — (blaspheming God)
4. Ahab was killed on the battlefield by _______.
   the king of Aram's sword — (a random arrow)
5. Before the battle, the prophet Jahaziel told Jehoshaphat that _______.
   (God would deliver Judah) — he would die in battle

D. WHAT'S THE POINT? From the battle of Jehoshaphat and Ahab against the king of Aram, what do you learn about God?

God's plan always happens just as God says it will. God's purpose prevails.

Notes:

							1 N	A	2 B	O	T	H									
									E												
						3 P	L	A	N	S											
									H												
				4 C	O	V	E	N	A	N	T										
									D												
							5 W		6 A	F	R	A	I	7 D							
						8 L	O	R	D					E							
							R						9 C	A	R	E	F	U	L	L	Y
10 A	P	P	O	I	N	T	S							D							
							H														
							I														
							P														

Across

1. Who owned the vineyard that Ahab wanted?
3. "Many are the _________ in a man's heart, but it is the LORD's purpose that prevails." (Proverbs 19:21)
4. When Ahab worshipped Baal, he was rejecting God's __________.
6. The prophet Jahaziel told Jehoshaphat not to be _________.
8. King Jehoshaphat served the _________ and walked in the ways of David.
9. Jehoshaphat told his judges to fear the LORD and judge _____________.
10. A person becomes a prophet when the LORD sends, _________, and speaks to them (see Jeremiah 14:14, NIV).

Down

2. Ahab disobeyed God when he refused to kill ________________.
5. If a prophet says to ____________ idols, he is not from God.
7. When Judah arrived at the battlefield, they saw only _____________ bodies.

Chapter 17 Quiz

A. MEMORY VERSE: "[The Most High] does according to His will in the army of heaven And among the inhabitants of the earth. No one can restrain His head Or say to Him, 'What have you done?'" (Daniel 4:35b)

B. KEY FACTS: God is sovereign over everything. Draw a line from the category on the left to the event on the right.

Category	Event
God is sovereign over…	**By God's power Elisha was able to…**
Nature	Fill jars with oil
Ordinary People	Bring the dead to life
Life and Death	Divide the Jordan River
Disease	Know when the siege would end
Enemies and Nations	Prophesy who will be king
Disaster/Good Fortune	Heal from leprosy
Rulers	Know enemy battle plans

C. STORY FACTS: Cross out the **wrong** answer.

1. Elijah went to heaven in a (~~chariot~~/whirlwind).
2. Elisha received a double portion of Elijah's (spirit/~~boldness~~).
3. Elisha put (~~oil~~/salt) in the bad spring water to make it healthy.
4. Elisha was not afraid because (God's heavenly host/~~Israel's army~~) was protecting the city of Dothan.
5. God's sovereignty means that God (~~knows~~/controls) everything.

D. WHAT'S THE POINT OF ELISHA'S MINISTRY?

God is sovereign.

Notes:

												1 S	O	N			
2 A		3 E	N	O	4 C	H						O					
N					L				5 S			V					
G					6 O	M	N	I	P	O	T	E	N	T			
7 E	L	I	S	H	A				I			R					
L					K				R			E					
S						8 O	M	N	I	S	C	I	E	N	T		
									T			G					
												9 N	A	A	M	A	N

Across

1. God made the Shunammite woman's ________ come back to life.
3. Elijah and ___________ both went to heaven without dying first.
6. God has all power. That means he is _______________.
7. God told _________ about Aram's war plans.
8. God knows all things. That means he is ______________.
9. God healed _________ of leprosy

Down

1. God controls all things. That means he is ______________.
2. Elisha was not afraid because God's __________ were protecting the city.
4. What item did Elisha use to divide the Jordan River?
5. Elisha received a double portion of Elijah's _________.

Chapter 18 Quiz

A. MEMORY VERSE: "Those who cling to worthless idols forfeit the grace that could be theirs." (Jonah 2:8, NIV)

B. KEY FACTS: Circle "T" for true and "F" for false.

1. A true prophet is always called by God. (T) F
2. One test of a prophet is that his words must come true. (T) F
3. All the prophets wrote books in the Old Testament. T (F)
4. A prophet doesn't talk about sin, only about God's love. T (F)
5. A prophet reminds people that repentance brings mercy. (T) F
6. A true prophet spoke only to people in Israel and Judah. T (F)

C. STORY FACTS: In the blanks, write the name of the prophet who fits the description (Amos, Hosea, Jonah).

1. I was a herdsman and farmer in a wilderness village. Amos
2. I didn't want to be God's prophet and ran away. Jonah
3. I spoke about fire to remind people that sin was terrible. Amos
4. I had a broken heart over Israel's unfaithfulness. Hosea
5. I learned that God gives salvation to whom He chooses. Jonah
6. I had children named "not loved" and "not my people." Hosea
7. My name means "bearer of burdens." Amos
8. I urged Israel to return to the LORD because He loved them. Hosea
9. I said the words, "Let justice roll like a river." Amos
10. I was angry when the people I talked to repented. Jonah

D. WHAT'S THE REASON? What is the meaning of Amos's words "for three sins and even for four sins?"

God had been patient with Israel's sin for a long time.

Notes:

Across

4. Inside the great fish, Jonah __________ of his sin.
5. When Amos said, "For three sins, and even for four," he meant that God had been __________.
6. A prophet must be __________ by God.
9. The religious Israelites to whom Hosea spoke worshipped golden ____________.
10. Four themes of prophets are: sin, punishment, repentance, and _________________.

Down

1. Who did Hosea marry?
2. The test of the true prophet is that his words must be true and _______ with God's law.
3. "Those who cling to ________ idols forfeit the grace that could be theirs." (Jonah 2:8)
7. Being a prophet meant that most people _________ you.
8. Who came from the village of Tekoa in Judah and went to preach to the people in Israel?

268

Chapter 19 Quiz

A. MEMORY VERSES: Cross out the **wrong** word and write the **correct** word in the blank.

1. "[They] exchanged the ~~purposes~~ of God for the lie." truth
2. "The ~~ways~~ of a good man are ordered by the LORD." steps
3. "Many are the plans in a man's ~~mind~~." heart
4. "No one can restrain His ~~power~~." hand
5. "Those who cling to worthless idols forfeit the ~~mercy~~ that could be theirs." grace

B. STORY FACTS: Cross out the **wrong** word.

1. God spoke to Elijah through (~~an earthquake~~/a gentle whisper).
2. The kingdom split in two when (Rehoboam/~~Jeroboam~~) became king.
3. Hosea's marriage to Gomer was a picture of God's (love/~~power~~).
4. Jonah didn't want the Ninevites to (~~kill him~~/repent of their sin).
5. All of the first eight kings of Israel worshipped (idols/~~the LORD~~).
6. The (~~kings~~/prophets) were called by God to speak God's words.
7. (~~Elijah~~/Elisha) told Naaman to wash in the river to be healed.
8. The prophets told the people that repentance brings (mercy/~~judgment~~).

C. WHICH OF THESE GO TOGETHER? Match these things.

3 Jonah	1. King of Aram who fought against Israel
1 Ben-Hadad	2. King of Israel who made golden calves
4 Ahab	3. Prophet of salvation
6 Elijah	4. King who disguised himself in battle
7 Amos	5. Prophet who loved an unfaithful woman
8 Jehoshaphat	6. Prophet who challenged prophets of Baal
5 Hosea	7. Prophet of justice
2 Jeroboam	8. King of Judah who turned people back to God

Notes:

		1 K	I	N	2 G					3 A	4 M	O	S		
					R						I			5 J	
		6 U	N	F	A	I	T	H	F	U	L			O	
	7 T				C						I			R	
8 P	R	O	P	H	E	T					T			D	
	U										A			A	
	9 E	L	I	S	H	A			10 B	U	R	D	E	N	S
											Y				

Across

1. Abijah was a _________.
3. Which prophet was born in Judah but prophesied in Israel?
6. Hosea's marriage to Gomer was a picture of God's love toward His __________ people.
8. Micaiah was a __________.
9. The king of Israel know all about Ben-Hadad's battle plans because God revealed them to _______________.
10. The people rebelled against Rehoboam because he wouldn't make their ______ lighter.

Down

2. An idolater forfeits ____________ from God.
4. Naaman was a _______________ officer.
5. Naaman didn't want to wash in the _____________ River because he thought it was a ridiculous idea.
7. Elijah challenged the prophets of Baal because he wanted people to know that Israel's God was the _________ God.

Chapter 20 Quiz

A. MEMORY VERSE: "For the Lord knows the ___way___ of the ___righteous___, But the way of the ___ungodly___ shall ___perish___." (Psalm 1:6)

B. KEY FACTS: Draw a line from the phrase to the proper box.

History of both Israel and Judah — KINGS
Written by a priest — CHRONICLES
Stories of Elijah and Elisha — KINGS
Have genealogies — CHRONICLES
Theme of judgment — KINGS
Written by a priest — CHRONICLES
Theme of God's presence — CHRONICLES

C. STORY FACTS: Circle the **correct** answer.

1. _________ hid baby Joash from wicked Queen Athaliah.
   Jeroboam (Jehoiada) Jehu
2. _________ of the kings of Israel were wicked kings.
   Most Some (All)
3. Uzziah sinned against the Lord when he _________ in the temple.
   (offered incense) destroyed the altar killed priests
4. _________ was stoned when he warned Joash of his sin.
   Jehoiada (Zechariah) Amaziah
5. In 722 BC, Israel was conquered by the nation of _________.
   (Assyria) Babylon Egypt

D. WHAT'S THE REASON?

Israel was destroyed because the kings didn't obey God as their ___King___ and the people forgot God's ___covenant___.

Notes:

	1 R															
2 K	I	N	G	S												
	G						3 J							4 S		
	H						O			5 A	M	A	Z	I	A	H
	T				6 P		R			S				N		
7 Z	E	C	H	A	R	I	A	H		8 S	E	V	E	N		
	O				I		M			Y				E		
	U				E					R				D		
	S				S					I						
				9 A	T	H	A	L	I	A	H					

Across

2. The stories about Elijah and Elisha are in the books of ____________.
5. Who brought the gods of Edom to Jerusalem?
7. Who was stoned because he warned Joash of his sin?
8. How old was Joash when he became king?
9. Two wicked queens were Jezebel and __________.

Down

1. "For the LORD knows the way of the ______________, But the way of the ungodly shall perish." (Psalm 1:6)
3. Jehu killed __________, king of Israel, and Ahaziah, king of Judah.
4. Uzziah __________ when he burned incense in the temple because only a priest could do that.
5. Shalmaneser, king of _________, conquered Israel in 722 BC.
6. The books of Chronicles was written by a _________.

Chapter 21 Quiz

A. MEMORY VERSE: "He has shown you, O man, what is ____good____; And what does the LORD require of you But to do ____justly____, To love ____mercy____, And to walk ____humbly____ with your God?" (Micah 6:8)

B. KEY FACTS: Cross out the **wrong** word.

1. The word "Messiah" means the (Anointed One/~~redeemer~~).
2. The Messiah will be called (Mighty God/~~Everlasting Savior~~).
3. Micah says that the Messiah would be born in (~~Jerusalem~~/Bethlehem).
4. The "Root of Jesse" means Jesus would be born of (~~Abraham~~/David).
5. The name Immanuel means ("God with us"/~~"loved of God"~~).
6. Isaiah said the Messiah would open (eyes and ears/~~mouths and hearts~~).

C. STORY FACTS: Number the events from 1-7 in chronological order.

__7__ Envoys from Babylon visited King Hezekiah.

__1__ Hezekiah removed the high places and repaired the temple.

__5__ The angel of the LORD killed 185,000 Assyrian soldiers.

__2__ Hezekiah fortified Jerusalem and constructed a water tunnel.

__3__ Assyria conquered all Judah's cities but Jerusalem.

__6__ Hezekiah became ill, but the LORD healed him.

__4__ The Assyrian army surrounded the city of Jerusalem.

D. WHO ARE THE PROPHETS?

Isaiah – Prophet of ____comfort____: When God asked, "Who should I send?" Isaiah said, "____Here____ ____I____ ____am____, ____Send____ ____me____."

Micah – Prophet of ____hope____: Micah knew that God does not stay ____angry____ forever and delights to show ____mercy____."

Notes:

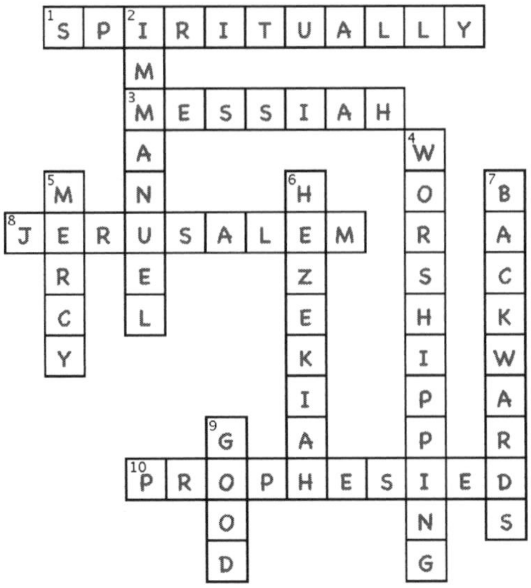

1 S	P	2 I	R	I	T	U	A	L	L	Y

Crossword grid (filled): 1 Across SPIRITUALLY; 3 Across MESSIAH; 8 Across JERUSALEM; 10 Across PROPHESIED; 2 Down IMMANUEL; 4 Down WORSHIPPING; 5 Down MERCY; 6 Down HEZEKIAH; 7 Down BACKWARDS; 9 Down GOOD

Across

1. Jesus opens ears and eyes both physically and ___________.
3. The word ________ means "The Anointed One."
8. Assyria captured all the cities of Judah except ______________.
10. Hezekiah first began to fear the Lord and seek God after Micah ______________.

Down

2. The word __________ means "God with us."
4. Hezekiah destroyed the bronze serpent because the people were ____________ it.
5. "And what does the Lord require of you But to do justly, To love __________, And to walk humbly with your God?" (Micah 6:8)
6. _____________ prayed for God's deliverance from the Assyrian army.
7. When the shadow moved ___________, it was a sign that God would make Hezekiah well.
9. "He has shown you, O man, what is _________..." (Micah 6:8)

Chapter 22 Quiz

A. MEMORY VERSE: "For assuredly, I say to you, till __heaven__ and __earth__ pass away, one __jot__ or one __tittle__ will by no means pass from the __law__ till all is __fulfilled__." (Matthew 5:18)

B. KEY FACTS: Match the name with the description.

_3_ **Adam**	1. Promise of God's presence/giving of the Law
_4_ **Noah**	2. Promise of an everlasting kingdom
_5_ **Abraham**	3. Promise of a coming Savior
_1_ **Moses**	4. Promise never to flood the earth again
_2_ **David**	5. Promise of a son, land, and blessing

"Covenant" means, God's __promise__ to be the God of His people __forever__.

C. STORY FACTS: Circle "T" if true and "F" if false.

1. Manasseh had the longest reign of all Judah's kings. (T) F
2. Manasseh served the LORD wholeheartedly all his life. T (F)
3. When Manasseh returned from Babylon, he served the LORD. (T) F
4. When Hilkiah found the Book of the Law, Josiah lamented. (T) F
5. Because Josiah served the LORD, God decided not to judge Judah. T (F)
6. Josiah read the Book of the Covenant to all the people. (T) F
7. Josiah smashed the worship center at Bethel that Jeroboam built. (T) F
8. Josiah celebrated the first Passover since the days of Joshua. T (F)

D. WHAT'S THE POINT?

Even though Josiah served the LORD wholeheartedly, __judgment__ was still coming to Judah because the people didn't change from the __heart__. The LORD said He would take His __presence__ from Judah just as He had from Israel.

Notes:

Across

7. Who was the longest reigning king of Judah?
8. God made a covenant with _________, and promised a Savior would come.
9. The Lord said He'd take His _____________ from Judah because of their sin.
10. God made a covenant with ___________, and promised never to destroy the earth again with a flood.

Down

1. With whom did God make a covenant promising His presence and giving the Law?
2. To whom did God promise a son, land, and blessing?
3. "For assuredly, I say to you, till ____________ and earth pass away, one jot or one tittle will by no means pass from the law till all is fulfilled." (Matthew 5:18)
4. Josiah celebrated the Passover for the first time since ______________.
5. To whom did God promise an everlasting kingdom?
6. After Josiah turned to the Lord, he began a reformation by repairing the _________.

Chapter 23 Quiz

A. MEMORY VERSE: "The LORD is slow to ___anger___ and great in ___power___; the LORD will not leave the ___guilty___ unpunished." (Nahum 1:3a, NIV)

B. KEY FACTS: Write the initial of the prophet in the blanks.

O – Obadiah N – Nahum J – Joel H – Habakkuk Z – Zephaniah

___J___ Prophet of God's grace

___H___ Asked God two questions

___N___ Spoke about God's vengeance

___Z___ Descendent of King Hezekiah

___N___ Prophet of God's wrath

___O___ Means "worshipper"

___O___ Prophesied about Edom

___N___ Name means "comforter"

___J___ Spoke about a locust plague

___N___ Prophesied against Assyria

___H___ Prophet of faith

___O___ Spoke about betrayal of Judah

C. STORY FACTS: Circle the **correct** answer.

1. Obadiah reminded God's people that God was ___________.

   jealous (supreme King) good

2. Zephaniah said God's judgment was like a ___________.

   plague of locusts strong tornado (purifying fire)

3. Nahum prophesied against Assyria, but wrote the words to ___________.

   (Judah) Babylon Edom

4. Joel called people to repentance and told them to have ___________.

   torn garments pleasing sacrifices (broken hearts)

5. Nahum's prophecy against Assyria was a ___________.

   gleeful gloating (righteous reaction) angry revenge

D. WHAT'S THE POINT?

Habakkuk learned that he could trust God even in ___bad___ circumstances.

Notes:

Across

2. Zephaniah was a descendent of King ____________.
4. Joel was a prophet of God's __________.
6. "The Lord will not leave the guilty _______________." (Nahum 1:3a)
8. The theme of Nahum was the downfall of ________.
9. The name "Zephaniah" means "Jehovah _________."
10. The Book of Obadiah is a prophey against the nation of __________.

Down

1. The name "Obadiah" means ____________.
3. "The Lord is slow to ___________ and great in power..." (Nahum 1:3a)
5. Who was a prophet of faith?
7. What prophet's name means "comforter"?

Chapter 24 Quiz

A. MEMORY VERSE: "My people have committed two ___sins___: They have ___forsaken___ me, the spring of ___living___ ___water___, and have dug their own ___cisterns___, broken cisterns that cannot ___hold___ ___water___." (Jeremiah 2:13, NIV)

B. KEY FACTS: Circle "T" if true and "F" if false.

1. The broken cistern is a picture of the destruction of Jerusalem. T (F)
2. God shapes nations and people like clay on a potter's wheel. (T) F
3. The ruined linen belt described the wicked rulers. T (F)
4. God used a picture of a field to show that the exiles would return. (T) F
5. The smashed pot was a picture of a person's spiritual thirst. T (F)
6. The good figs are a picture of faithful prophets. T (F)

C. STORY FACTS: Match the things on the left with the description on the right.

8	Gedaliah	1. King who burned up Jeremiah's scroll
7	50 years	2. Nation where Jeremiah died
5	Baruch	3. Vision God gave to Jeremiah
3	Almond tree branch	4. Years exiles would be in Babylon
9	Zedekiah	5. Jeremiah's scribe
4	70 years	6. Picture used to describe the exiles
10	Babylon	7. Years Jeremiah was a prophet to Judah
1	Jehoiakim	8. Jerusalem's last governor
2	Egypt	9. Judah's last king
6	Baskets of figs	10. Nation who destroyed Jerusalem

D. JEREMIAH'S MESSAGE: Even though Jeremiah prophesied about Jerusalem's destruction, his message gave God's people hope. Write down one hopeful thing Jeremiah said.

The exiles would return; the Messiah would come; and God would make a new covenant.

Notes:

1 FORSAKEN
2 BURNED
3 BARUCH
4 CROP
5 FIFTY
6 BABYLON
7 YEARS
8 BROKEN
9 DESTRUCTION
10 ZEDEKIAH

Across

3. Who was Jeremiah's scribe?
6. Egypt and ____________ had control of Judah in the years after Josiah died.
9. Jeremiah wrote Lamentations to describe Jerusalem's ________________.
10. The last king of Judah was named ______________.

Down

1. "My people have committed two sins: They have __________ me, the spring of living water..." (Jeremiah 2:13)
2. King Jehoiakim ____________ up the scroll with God's words.
4. Jeremiah's image of a field of ________ indicated that God's people would return and buy fields.
5. Jeremiah was a prophet for ________ years during the reign of five kings.
7. Jeremiah said the exiles would return to Jerusalem after seventy ___________.
8. "...and have dug their own cisterns, ____________ cisterns that cannot hold water." (Jeremiah 2:13)

Chapter 25 Quiz

A. MEMORY VERSES: Connect the parts of these verses.

Beginning:	Ending:
The LORD knows…	…the spring of living water
One jot or one tittle…	…to walk humbly with your God
They have forsaken…	…will not leave the guilty unpunished
The LORD is slow to anger…	…the way of the righteous
What does the LORD require…	…till all is fulfilled

B. STORY FACTS: Circle "T" if true and "F" if false.

1. In 1 and 2 Chronicles you can read stories about Elisha. T (F)
2. Manasseh reigned longer than any other king in Judah. (T) F
3. Jehoiada hid baby Joash to protect him against the Assyrians. T (F)
4. Rehoboam, the first king of Judah, ruled over two tribes. (T) F
5. People didn't like Jeremiah because he preached God's truth. (T) F
6. The LORD promised that the people would return in forty years. T (F)
7. Judah's worst sin was forgetting God's covenant. (T) F

C. WHO AM I? Write the **correct** name in the blank.

Obadiah Joel Habakkuk Isaiah Zephaniah Micah Jeremiah

1. I said the Messiah would be born in Bethlehem. Micah
2. I asked the LORD two difficult questions. Habakkuk
3. I talked about a swarm of locusts. Joel
4. I said judgment was like a purifying fire. Zephaniah
5. I saw a vision of seraphim singing, "Holy." Isaiah
6. I prophesied against the nation of Edom. Obadiah
7. I saw pictures of baskets of figs and smashed pots. Jeremiah

Notes:

	1 J				2 R				3 F					
4 G	O	D		5 J	E	R	E	M	I	A	H			
	T		6 I		H				R					
	H		S		O		7 P	R	E	S	E	N	C	E
	8 A	S	A		B									
	M		I		O									
			A		A									
			9 H	U	M	B	10 L	Y						
							A							
							W							

Across

4. Hezekiah trusted __________ when the Assyrians attacked.
5. Which prophet smashed pots and baskets of figs?
7. The theme of the book of Chronicles is God's ___________ and holiness.
8. Who was the third king to rule after King Solomon?
9. The LORD requires you to "walk _________ with your God." (Micah 6:8)

Down

1. Uzziah got leprosy, and his son, __________, became king.
2. Who was the first king to rule after King Solomon?
3. Zephaniah proclaimed judgement like a purifying ________.
6. Which prophet had a vision of seraphim praising God?
10. Josiah read the Book of the ______ to the people.

282

Chapter 26 Quiz

A. MEMORY VERSE: "The soul who ___sins___ is the one who will ___die___.... 'For I take no ___pleasure___ in the ___death___ of anyone,' declares the Sovereign LORD. '___Repent___ and ___live___!'" (Ezekiel 18:20a, 32, NIV)

B. KEY FACTS: Match the description with its meaning.

_2_ Two sticks	1. Ezekiel must speak God's words.
_4_ Packed bag and journey	2. The nation will one day be united.
_7_ Dry bones	3. People will suffer when judged.
_6_ Living creatures and wheels	4. The exile will last a long time.
_3_ Lying on his side	5. God judges and God gives grace.
_1_ Scroll eaten	6. God is everywhere and sees all.
_5_ Windstorm and rainbow	7. God breathes life into His people.

C. STORY FACTS: Cross out the **wrong** answer.

1. Ezekiel was a (priest/~~prophet~~) before he was exiled.
2. Ezekiel was exiled to Babylon with the (~~first~~/second) group of people.
3. Life in exile was (not too bad/~~worse than living in besieged Jerusalem~~).
4. Before the fall of Jerusalem, Ezekiel's message was that (Jerusalem would be destroyed/ ~~the people would be going home soon~~).
5. Anyone who sins and does not repent will (~~receive mercy~~/die).
6. The city of the future is named ("the LORD is there"/~~"the LORD lives"~~).
7. In Ezekiel's vision, the people in the temple were (worshipping the sun/ ~~offering sacrifices to the LORD~~).

D. WHO WAS EZEKIEL? Fill in the blanks.

Ezekiel, the Prophet of ___visions___, preached to the people in ___exile___.

Notes:

												¹E	X	I	L	E	
						²B						G					
					³I	D	O	L	A	T	R	Y					
	⁴D						N					⁵P	R	I	E	S	T
⁶J	E	R	U	⁷S	A	L	E	M				T					
	A			I			S		⁸W			I					
	T			N					O			A					
	H			S					R			N					
					⁹K	I	N	G	D	O	M	S					
									S								

Across

1. Ezekiel's image of a bag and a journey indicated that the _____ would last a long time.
3. God's glory left the temple because of the people's great ____________.
5. Ezekiel was a _________ before he became a prophet.
6. The final destruction of ______________ happened in 586 BC.
9. Ezekiel's image of two sticks indicated that God would unite the two ___________.

Down

1. Daniel and his friends were captured four years after the ______________ killed Josiah and defeated Judah.
2. When Ezekiel prophesied to the dry _________, they became alive.
4. " 'For I take no pleasure in the ___________ of anyone,' declares the Soverign LORD. 'Repent and live!' " (Ezekiel 18:32)
7. "The soul who _______ is the one who will die..."(Ezekiel 18:20a)
8. When Ezekiel ate the scroll, he was showing that he must speak God's __________ to the people.

284

Chapter 27 Quiz

A. MEMORY VERSE: "But the mercy of the LORD is from everlasting to everlasting On those who fear Him,... To such as keep His covenant, And to those who remember His commandments to do them." (Psalm 103:17a, 18)

B. KEY FACTS: Draw a line from the **historical period** to the **reason** that matches it.

The God of Miracles

God did miracles in four historical times for four reasons.

Historical Period	Reason
Exodus/wilderness journey	Protection from idolatry
Elijah and Elisha	Establishment of the spiritual kingdom
Babylonian exile	God's establishment of His nation
Jesus and the early church	Protection from pagan influence

C. STORY FACTS: Circle the **correct** answer.

1. Daniel and his friends were different from the other men because they _____.
   worshipped the LORD (circled) liked to eat vegetables
2. Before interpreting the king's dream, Daniel asked his friends to _____.
   give him advice pray for him (circled)
3. The statue in Nebuchadnezzar's dream represented four _____.
   great nations (circled) plagues from God
4. Nebuchadnezzar's dream meant that God's kingdom would _____.
   last four hundred years destroy other great kingdoms (circled)
5. Daniel's three friends were thrown into the fiery furnace because they _____.
   refused to worship the image (circled) wouldn't eat the king's food

Notes:

												1 W					
												O					
												R					
												S					
												H					
									2 H			I					
3 M							4 D		U			5 P	R	A	Y		
6 E	L	I	S	H	A		E		M			P					
R							7 S	T	A	T	U	E					
8 C	O	V	E	N	A	N	T		N			9 D	E	F	I	L	E
Y							R										
			10 N	A	T	I	O	N	S								
							Y										

Across

5. Before Daniel interpreted Nebuchadnezzar's dreams, he asked his friends to ________.
6. During the time of Elijah and _________ God did many miracles.
7. Nebuchadnezzar dreamed of a __________ make of gold, silver, bronze, and clay.
8. "To such as keep His ____________, And to those who remember His commandments to do them." (Psalm 103:18)
9. Daniel didn't want to eat the royal food because he didn't want to __________ himself.
10. The statue in Nebuchadnezzar's dream represented four ___________.

Down

1. Daniel and his friends were different from the other men because they ____________ the Lord.
2. A rock not made with ________ hands smashed the statue in Nebuchadnezzar's dream.
3. "But the ________ of the Lord is from everlasting to everlasting On those who fear Him" (Psalm 103:17a)
4. Nebuchadnezzar's dream meant that the Lord's kingdom would ______________ other great kingdoms.

Chapter 28 Quiz

A. MEMORY VERSE: "But without faith it is impossible to please Him [God]." (Hebrews 11:6a)

B. KEY FACTS: Fill in the blanks.

1. When Daniel refused to eat the king's food, he was standing up for what God said was right.
2. When Daniel prayed for the interpretation of the dream, he believed that God would answer him.
3. Daniel spoke the truth even if it meant bad things would happen.
4. Daniel obeyed God's commands, not man's rules.

C. STORY FACTS: Circle "T" if true and "F" if false.

1. When Nebuchadnezzar got his sanity back, he acknowledged God as King of heaven. (T) F
2. Belshazzar laughed when he saw the handwriting on the wall. T (F)
3. Officials in Darius's court could find no fault in Daniel. (T) F
4. Daniel obeyed the king's decree and didn't pray to the LORD. T (F)
5. King Darius regretted the decree he made about prayer. (T) F
6. A law of the Medes and Persians could never be changed. (T) F
7. God sent an angel to shut the lions' mouths. (T) F

D. FOUR MIGHTY KINGS: Match the nations with the kings. Use one answer twice.

Babylon The Medes Persia

Darius The Medes
Belshazzar Babylon
Cyrus Persia
Nebuchadnezzar Babylon

Notes:

						1 S	T	U	2 M	P				3 F		
									E					A		
		4 D							5 D	R	I	N	K	I	N	G
		E							E					T		
		6 C	O	M	M	7 A	N	D	S					H		
		R				N										
8 G	R	E	A	T		9 S	E	V	E	N						
		E				W										
			10 A	N	G	E	L									
						R										

Across

1. What was left of the tree in the dream?
5. God judged Belshazzar because he defiled the LORD by _______ from sacred goblets.
6. Faith obeys God's __________ instead of man's rules.
8. God judged Nebuchadnezzar because he boasted about how _______ he was.
9. How many years did Nebuchadnezzar act like an animal?
10. Who shut the lions' mouths?

Down

2. Darius was king of what country?
3. "But without __________ it is impossible to please Him [God]." (Hebrews 11:6a)
4. Darius made a __________ that couldn't be changed.
7. Faith prays and believes that God will __________ according to His will.

Chapter 29 Quiz

A. MEMORY VERSE: "They will call on My ___name___, And I will ___answer___ them. I will say, 'This is My ___people___'; And each one will say, 'The ___LORD___ is my ___God___.'" (Zechariah 13:9b).

B. KEY FACTS: Number the events in the **correct** order.

_3_ Cyrus decrees that God's people can return to Jerusalem.

_1_ Daniel is taken captive and goes to Babylon.

_6_ The rebuilding of the temple is completed.

_4_ Zerubbabel and Jeshua return to Jerusalem.

_7_ Ezra and Nehemiah return to Jerusalem.

_2_ Ezekiel is taken captive and goes to Babylon.

_5_ Haggai and Zechariah prophesy about rebuilding the temple.

C. STORY FACTS: Circle **all** the **correct** answers.

1. The men who led the first group of people back to Jerusalem were _____.
   Cyrus — (Zerubbabel) — (Jeshua)
2. God's people were in exile for _________ years.
   15 — 40 — (70)
3. Artaxerxes believed the letter accusing the Jews and told them to _____.
   keep building — (stop building) — get permission to build
4. Haggai made a connection between being faithful to God and ________.
   God's grace — (God's blessing) — God's power
5. Zechariah had visions about __________.
   (a flying scroll) — spinning wheels — (chariots)
6. Zechariah's visions relate to us today because he talks about ______.
   (the Messiah) — God's presence with us — God's wrath

Notes:

		1 F		2 C							3 R				4 Z
		I		Y						5 P	E	O	P	L	E
		F		R			6 H				P				R
		T		U			7 A	N	S	W	E	R			U
8 B	L	E	S	S	I	N	G				N				B
		E					G				T				B
		N					A								A
			9 M	E	S	S	I	A	H						B
															E
										10 D	A	N	I	E	L

Across

5. "...I will say, 'This is My _________'; And each one will say, 'The Lord is my God.'" (Zechariah 13:9b)
7. "They will call on My name, And I will _______ them..." (Zechariah 13:9b)
8. One prophet taught that there is a connection between being faithful and receiving God's ______________.
9. Zechariah prophesied about the ___________ and future glory for God's people.
10. Who was taken into exile to Babylon in 605 BC.?

Down

1. For ________ years the people forgot about the temple and did nothing.
2. God moved the heart of __________ to let His people return home.
3. Zechariah's visions were about God's reaction when people ___________.
4. Jeshua and __________________ led the first group back to Jerusalem.
6. The prophets __________ and Zechariah encouraged the people to rebuild the temple even when it was hard to do.

290

Chapter 30 Quiz

A. MEMORY VERSE: "Who can __speak__ and have it __happen__ if the Lord has not __decreed__ it? Is it not from the mouth of the Most High that both __calamities__ and __good__ __things__ come?" (Lamentations 3:37-38, NIV)

B. KEY FACTS: Circle "T" if true and "F" if false.

1. It was wrong for Queen Vashti to refuse the king's request. T (F)
2. Haman required that everyone kneel down and honor him. (T) F
3. Mordecai refused to kneel before Haman because he hated him. T (F)
4. The king held out his scepter and welcomed Esther. (T) F
5. The king believed the lie that all Jews were dangerous. (T) F
6. The king delighted in Mordecai and wanted to honor him. (T) F
7. The second decree said that Jews could defend themselves. (T) F

C. STORY FACTS: Draw a line from the word to its description.

Esther	Feast to celebrate God's protection
Mordecai	A mighty king
Purim	An unchangeable command
Decree	Jewish girl who became queen
Providence	Cousin of Queen Esther
Haman	Land where Jews were exiled
Persia	An enemy of the Jews
Xerxes	God's wise governing of everything

D. WHAT'S THE POINT? God's message to His people in the book of Esther was that even though His people were not __faithful__ to Him, He would still __protect__ them from __destruction__.

Notes:

	1 G	O	O	2 D				3 D			4 C				5 K
				6 E	S	T	H	E	R		7 H	A	M	A	N
				C				F			A				E
				R			8 S	E	V	E	N				E
	9 L	I	F	E				N			G				L
				E				D			E				
10 S	A	V	E	D											

Across

1. "Is it not from the mouth of the Most High that both calamities and ________ things come?" (Lamentations 3:38)
6. King Xerxes chose __________ to be his new queen.
7. Who was hanged on the gallows he made for Mordecai?
8. How many days did the king's banquet last?
9. Mordecai saved the king's ________ by uncovering a conspiracy against him.
10. Even though His people weren't faithful, God __________ them from destruction.

Down

2. "Who can speak and have it happen if the Lord has not __________ it?" (Lamentations 3:37)
3. The king's second decree said that Jews could _________ themselves.
4. Once the king had made a decree, he could not ___________ it.
5. What would Mordecai not do?

Chapter 31 Quiz

A. MEMORY VERSE: "You have kept your ___promise___ because you are ___righteous___." (Nehemiah 9:8b, NIV)

B. KEY FACTS: Put these events in the **correct** order from 1-6.

__2__ God's people rebuilt the temple.

__6__ Ezra read God's Word to the people, and they renewed the covenant.

__3__ Ezra led the second group of Jews to Jerusalem.

__4__ God's people in Jerusalem repented of marrying foreign wives.

__5__ Nehemiah finished building the walls despite many obstacles.

__1__ Jeshua and Zerubbabel led the first group of Jews to Jerusalem.

C. STORY FACTS: Cross out the **wrong** word.

1. Ezra took (~~Jews~~/Levites) with him so the people could worship God.
2. On the journey, the people were protected by the (~~king's army~~/LORD).
3. Sanballat ridiculed the people, saying the wall was (weak/~~crooked~~).
4. When enemies threatened, Nehemiah (~~stopped working~~/posted guards).
5. Nehemiah got Sanballat's letter and then (~~talked to him~~/prayed to God).
6. When the people repented, Nehemiah told them to (~~weep and grieve~~/ have joy in the LORD).

D. MALACHI, PROPHET OF PREPARATION—HIS MESSAGES:

1. The LORD God ___loved___ His people.
2. God does not ___change___, so ___repent___ of your sin.
3. Look for God's ___messenger___. The day of the ___LORD___ is coming.

Notes:

Across

3. Levites went with Ezra to ____________ so that the people could worship God.
4. In the book of Ezra God said, "I want My people to meet together and ________ Me."
6. In what book was the message that God promised, "I am the supreme King, and I protect My people?"
7. The people wanted to stop building the wall to harvest their __________.
9. Who ridiculed Nehemiah and the workers?

Down

1. The first thing Nehemiah did when the king saw his sad face was _____ to the LORD."
2. "You have kept your __________ because you are righteous." (Nehemiah 9:8b)
4. In the book Nehemiah God said, "Listen to my __________ and confess your sin because I am your God."
5. When the people repented of the sin, Nehemiah told them that God's joy was their ____________.
8. Nehemiah gave the workers _________ to hold while they worked.

294

Chapter 32 Quiz

A. MEMORY VERSES: Match the parts of these verses.

Beginning:	Ending:
But without faith..	..I will answer them
The soul who sins..	..because you are righteous
They will call on My name..	..it is impossible to please Him
But the mercy of the LORD..	..is the one who will die
You have kept your promise..	..is from everlasting to everlasting

B. STORY FACTS: Cross out the **wrong** answer.

1. (Ezekiel/~~Zechariah~~) saw a vision of dry bones that came back to life.
2. Daniel said his ability to interpret dreams came from (~~wise men~~/God).
3. Belshazzar was frightened by (handwriting on the wall/~~visions of spinning wheels~~).
4. Judah was conquered by the nation of (~~Assyria~~/Babylon).
5. Haggai told the people it was time to rebuild (~~the city walls~~/the temple).
6. Haman wanted Mordecai to (bow down to him/~~plot against the king~~).
7. Daniel was thrown into the lions' den because he (~~ate vegetables~~/prayed).

C. WHO AM I? Match the name with the description.

5 Malachi	1. Decreed that exiles could return home
6 Ezekiel	2. Saw a vision of two temples
2 Zechariah	3. Interpreted a dream about a large statue
7 Haggai	4. Married the Jewish girl Esther
1 Cyrus	5. Wrote the last Old Testament book
4 Xerxes	6. Left Jerusalem in second group of exiles
3 Daniel	7. Encouraged people to build the temple

Notes:

																	1 D
																	A
											2 H		3 M				N
										4 M	A	L	A	C	H		I
											G		R				E
		5 C			6 J		7 E				G		R				L
		Y			O		8 Z	E	C	H	A	R	I	A	H		
9 X	E	R	X	E	S		E				I		A				
		U			I		K						G				
		S		10 D	A	R	I	U	S				E				
					H		E						S				
							L										

Across

4. Who declared Elijah as God's messenger?
8. Who was the prophet of future glory?
9. What king married Esther?
10. Who decreed that the exiles could go home?

Down

1. Who was the prophet of God's sovereignty?
2. Who was the prophet of encouragement?
3. Ezra was ashamed of the people in Jerusalem because they were unfaithful in their ____________.
5. Who threw Daniel into a lions' den?
6. Whose army was defeated by Egypt?
7. Who had visions of dry bones?

Five-Day Lesson Plan Suggestion

Suggested Lesson Time Per Day: Approximately 20 minutes

Day 1: Read MEMORY PAGE.
- Discuss theme.
- Discuss memory verse and practice saying it.
- Discuss KEY FACTS and THINGS TO REMEMBER.
- Read the STORY TIME pages, either independent reading or read aloud.

Day 2: Read all or part of the READ TO ME Scripture passage.
- Discuss the story.
- Discuss how the KEY FACTS table relates to the story.
- Review Memory Verse.

Day 3: Complete WORKSHEETS.
- Review KEY FACTS and memory verse.

Day 4: Review WORKSHEETS.
- Discuss the MESSAGE FROM THE KING and the JESUS IN THE OT
- Make the information personal and practical to the children's lives.
- Review Memory Verse and KEY FACTS table

Day 5: Take QUIZ.

Welcome, Detective.

Classical Subjects
Creatively Taught
A–Ω
GREEK
ALPHABET
CODE CRACKER
Dr. Christopher Perrin
YOUR MISSION:
Learn the Greek Alphabet from A to Ω as you
solve the "Great Grecian Urn Caper."

Are you looking for an engaging first step to learning Greek? In *The Greek Alphabet Code Cracker*, understanding the Greek alphabet is the key to decoding clues and recovering the stolen Urn of Achilles!

Learn all of the Greek letters from Alpha to Omega, and their phonetic pronunciation. Practice writing the letters, gather the clues from witnesses, and trace the path of the thief! You will first learn to sound out simple English words with the Greek alphabet, and then will go on to learn Greek words as well! This workbook text is an excellent introduction to Greek for students of all ages.

- Full color workbook text
- 8 chapters, to be completed approximately one chapter per week, considering the age of the student
- Learn all of the consonant and vowels sounds, as well as consonant blends, and diphthongs (vowel blends or combinations) by systematic, phonetic lessons
- An excellent preparation for *Song School Greek* or *Greek for Children*